The Bristol FSF

by Steve Chislett

Foreword
by Dr. Mike Walker

As a bus enthusiast growing up in Bristol I was lucky enough to have started my interest in buses at the time that the first forward entrance 70 seat "Bristol" FLF double deckers were entering service. I was even more fortunate to be able to ride on them to and from school when they were only a few months old. With the keen interest I had developed I thought that I knew all there was to know about these new buses and so you can imagine my surprise when a fellow enthusiast pointed out to me that some of these new double deckers were not actually the 70 seat FLF model but the 60 seat FSF version. My misconception was compounded by the fact that, initially, Bristol Omnibus Company numbered both the 60 seaters and 70 seaters in the same series!

The short FSF soon lost favour with Bristol Omnibus Company who decided to standardise on the longer 70 seat model, a trend that was repeated within many of the Tilling Group companies. The result was that production numbers of the FSF chassis were very low compared with its longer brother. My own memories of the FSF, both as a passenger and a conductor, centre around the seemingly claustrophobic nature of the platform, conductor's area and luggage pen which took up a larger proportion of the downstairs passenger area than on the longer FLF model, giving the impression of a dark and uninviting space.

By the time that I became a bus depot manager the FSF was in its last years in the Bristol fleet. When allocating buses it seemed something of a crime to allocate such a small bus when the extra ten seats of its larger variant were really what was wanted. There is no doubt, however, that although they may have been one of the less successful versions of the "Bristol Lodekka" the FSFs lost nothing of the rugged reliability for which the "Bristol" products were famous. Many went on to lead active lives for many years after their normal service lives had ended, both at home and abroad. Indeed, it is highly appropriate that one of these buses, former Bath Services 6041, which, at one time, was owned by the author was found to be "alive", well and still working in Croatia in June 2011 when nigh on 50 years old whilst Steve was writing this book!

From the enthusiasts' point of view, the Bristol FSF has been overlooked within the "Lodekka" family and we should be grateful to Steve Chislett for taking the time and effort to produce this fine volume dedicated solely to this Cinderella of the "Bristol" marque.

Dr. Mike Walker
Dinder, Somerset

First published in the United Kingdom, 2017,
by Stenlake Publishing Ltd.
Telephone: 01290 551122
www.stenlake.co.uk
ISBN 9781840336795

Printed by:
Berforts, 17 Burgess Road, Hastings, TN35 4NR

Publisher's Note

The author passed away before being able to check the proofs of this book. His family wished publication to go ahead posthumously. We have had the book reviewed by a fellow bus enthusiast but apologise for any errors that may have slipped through due to the circumstances.

Acknowledgements

My initial sincerest thanks must go to my wife Deirdre and daughter Anna who have put up with book "clutter" for a considerable time. Numerous people have been of great help in supplying photographs and information for inclusion that makes this book far more readable than I could have achieved on my own. Each individual photographer is acknowledged and every attempt has been made to identify these accurately. Particular thanks must go to Tony Robbins who agreed to post his entire collection of FSF photographs to give me complete access to these; Dr. Mike Walker; Allan Macfarlane; Denis Clark who, unfortunately, died before this book was printed; Geoff Gould; Dave Mant; Dave Withers who has a great involvement with Bristol Vintage Bus Group; Rob Sly; Steve Kelly; Alistair Douglas and Donald Hudson who have all either provided me with copies of their high quality personal photographs or given immense help by spending many hours "proof reading" numerous drafts of the book and advised of corrections.

Every effort has been made to acknowledge copyright of all photographs accurately and if this has not been achieved I apologise to those affected by these unintentional errors. This book is not intended to be a technical or accurate detailed history of Bristol FSF buses. It is more of a photographic record and reflection of the areas in which these buses operated before, during and after the National Bus Company. My aim is for you to relax and enjoy leafing through the pages.

Technical Details

FSF stands for **F**lat floor **S**hort wheelbase with **F**ront entrance.

Built with either Bristol or Gardner engines, all examples were bodied by Eastern Coach Works with seating for 34 passengers on the upper deck and 26 passengers on the lower deck. Four buses for Bristol Joint Services C6014–C6017 (713–716 JHY) had the standard seating reduced to 58 to accommodate additional luggage space especially for Service 17 from Bristol Temple Meads–Clifton (Bristol Zoo). Bodies were 27 feet 7 inches long (8.2 metres) and 8 feet wide (2.4 metres) with the standard Lodekka height of 13 feet 6 inches (4.1 metres).

Destination layout was according to operator's requirements, for example Bristol City buses carried the standard four track "T" type display at the front with only a four track numeral box on the rear; Bath Services, Cheltenham District, Bristol Country and Gloucester buses carried "T" type displays front and rear. Brighton Hove & District were similar but with three track blinds with an additional three track number display over the front canopy. Crosville and the sole West Yorkshire examples were equipped with two or three aperture displays for service number, final destination and via points blinds. Scottish Motor Traction buses featured their unusually shaped standard destination display being used on the front only. There were also window ventilator and body trim variations arranged as specified by the operating companies. Certain vehicles were supplied with an offside illuminated advertisement panel when this style of advertising was "in vogue" and expected to increase advertising revenues. The "Cave-Browne-Cave" heating system was optional and vehicles so fitted were easily identified by radiator grilles either side of the front destination.

Introduction

Just 218 Bristol FSFs were built by Bristol Commercial Vehicles at their factory in Brislington, Bristol between 1960 and 1963 when the vast majority of buses in use throughout Britain were "rear loaders". Sales of Bristol vehicles were, at that time, restricted to nationalised companies and after completion of the chassis at Brislington were driven to Lowestoft in Suffolk where all bodies for these buses were built by Eastern Coach Works. Many survived in active passenger service into the late 1970s and early 1980s. Quality of manufacture and reliability must have been a major factor in this great achievement.

As a young boy I well remember laughing heartily to see one of these new vehicles allocated to Bath depot being operated on Bath City Service 3A at Elmhurst Estate, where I lived. Watching passengers instinctively going to the rear of the bus to board where the entrance should be it was very amusing to witness the completely confused look on their faces searching for the door to board the vehicle! No doubt the conductors shouting instructions to them to come to the front also laughed to themselves.

The first Bristol FSF was delivered in May 1960 to West Yorkshire Road Car Co. Ltd. as Fleet No. DX82 (YWW 77) and was their only example of a front entrance Bristol Lodekka ever owned. It was an FSF6B equipped with a driver-controlled sliding door that was later altered to the standard electrically operated four-leaf folding door and subsequently exchanged in 1967 with a standard rear entrance FS6B of similar age at United Automobile. All further deliveries to West Yorkshire reverted to the rear entrance Bristol FS version. The last Bristol FSF, delivered in September 1963, was an FSF6G for Central Scottish as fleet number B170 (FGM 170).

My interest in buses and trains started at an early age and it is difficult to now remember what started this passion for transport that eventually saw me complete 24 years in the bus industry and ending up working on the railways for South West Trains at Salisbury. A varied career in both industries saw me start as a driver and conductor allocation clerk at Bath Bus Station in 1974 that led to a Bristol Omnibus Company management training course for two years in 1978. There I experienced working in all departments and at various depots and offices throughout the company's area. After completion of the training course I returned to Bath as area traffic assistant which involved producing timetables, fare charts, crew rotas and schedules, bus running cards and an involvement in negotiating changes with the trades unions. Market analysis projects were carried out by the National Bus Company in the 1980s and the results often produced some interesting results and proposals. Conductor operated services outside London were greatly reduced in the early 1980s, eliminating the need for crew type vehicles including the Bristol FSF and its larger variant the Bristol FLF and all other half cab crew operated buses. Cost savings of one person operated rear engine double deckers together with the grants offered by the Government to transport companies ordering these was an added attraction.

When privatisation of the NBC was introduced under the 1985 Transport Act many of the larger companies were split into smaller units and sold to the highest bidder by secret tender. Bristol FSFs had been withdrawn and the larger capacity Bristol FLF was by then quite a rare sight. The first company privatised was National Holidays on 15th July 1986 closely followed by Devon General on 19th August 1986, Badgerline the former country bus division of Bristol Omnibus on 23rd September 1986, Southern Vectis on 8th October 1986, Cheltenham & Gloucester the former northern division of Bristol Omnibus on 1st November 1986 with all NBC subsidiaries being sold by the end of 1987. One of the main intentions of the Conservatives in the 1985 Transport Act was to introduce competition on bus routes and to remove monopolies and, they had hoped, encourage lower fares. Many companies saw the minibus as the answer to stem the falling patronage. Variations based on the Ford Transit were introduced on urban and rural services and were often referred to as "bread vans" because of the restricted room offered by these vehicles. Some companies, however, attempted to combat competition by re-introducing crew working with conductors often using ex London Transport Routemasters.

When Western National were selling their FSF examples the opportunity arose in August 1978 for Euel Lane, a bus driver at the Bath depot of Bristol Omnibus, and I to purchase ex Bath Electric Tramways 6041 (806 MHW) a 1961 Bristol FSF6G equipped with an offside illuminated advertisement panel. The bus was collected from the company's Dartmouth depot in November 1978 by Dave Bennett, a mechanic at Bath depot. Geoff Gay, a tyre fitter at the same site and Chris Carr the service licensing manager at Bristol Omnibus Company's head office at Lawrence Hill, Bristol. The bus, after filling the depot at Dartmouth full of smoky diesel fumes, performed well on the long journey to Bath via Weston-super-Mare to drop off Chris Carr. Before the bus could be repainted there were days of sanding down panels, fitting the seats with replacement moquette seat squabs and backs on both decks and inserting a rear "T" style 4 track number box and minor engine repairs. A sponsorship advertisement for Pearl Assurance was fitted into the illuminated panel, with one for Midland Bank on the nearside and one for The Kingsmead Motor Company, a Ford dealer, below the rear destination display box and general 1960s bus company paper adverts on other sites. The final finishing touch was the application of very impressive gold leaf "BATH SERVICES" fleet names.

Upon my move to Salisbury in 1990 there was nowhere for me to keep the bus so I sold my share in the vehicle to Ken Horler who at that time was the depot engineer at Bath for Badgerline. The bus was subsequently sold and exported to Croatia. Since starting this book the vehicle has been located in Varazdin. It is still working and appears to be performing well and mechanically sound.

Steve Chislett, Salisbury.

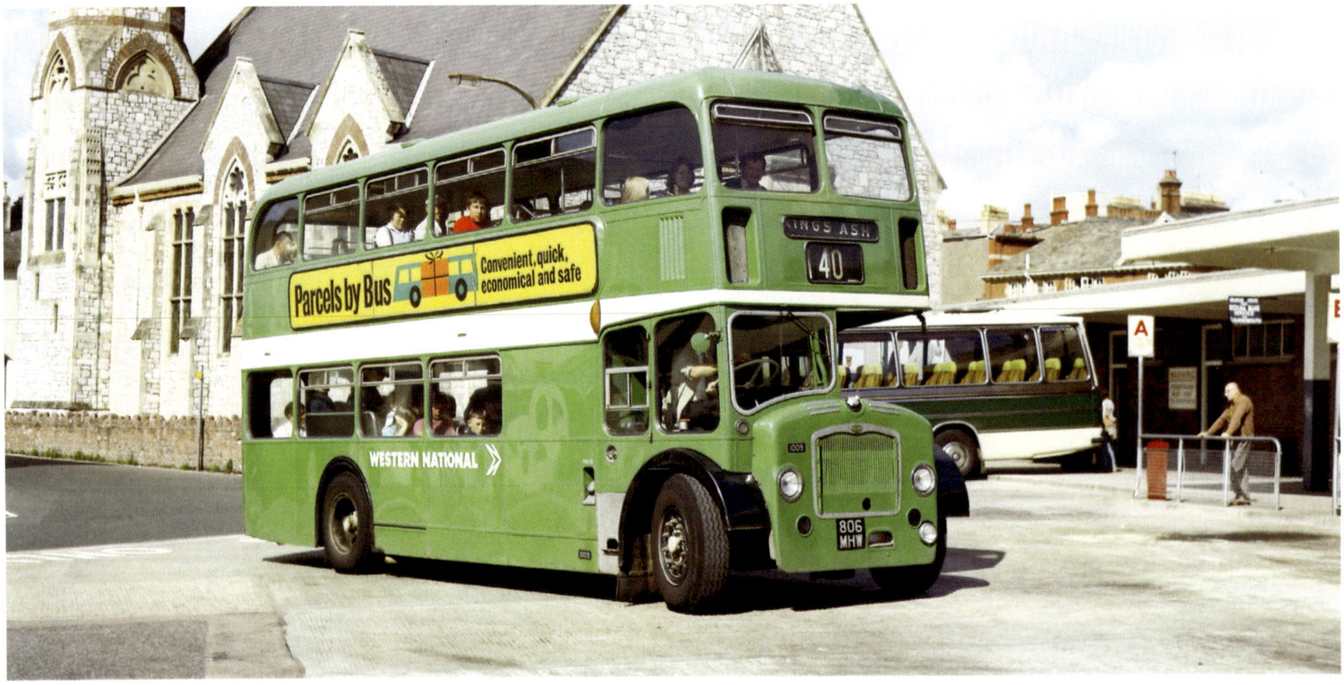

Western National 1009 (806 MHW) was the last FSF received by the Bristol Omnibus group of companies in October 1961. It was purchased by Western National in August 1967 and is seen arriving in Paignton Bus Station 17th August 1974. (Steve Thoroughgood)

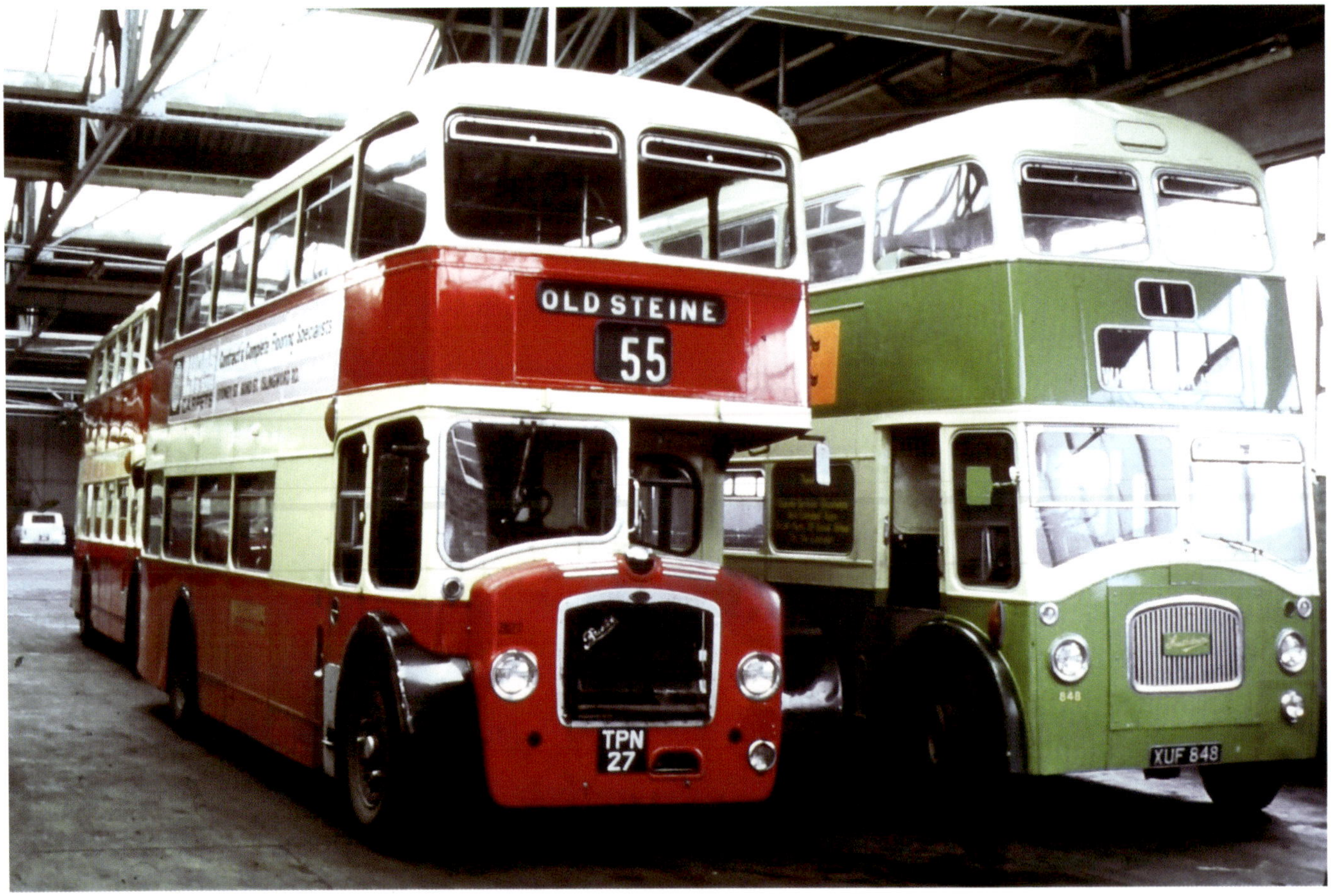

Still in traditional Brighton Hove & District colours and fleet name but with its new Southdown fleet number, 2027 (TPN 27) was one of fifteen Bristol FSF6Bs new to BH&D. Purchased in January 1961 it is pictured alongside Southdown 848 (XUF 848) a 1959 Leyland PD3 with fully fronted Northern Counties FH 39+30F bodywork around the time of the transfer date of 1st January 1969 when the National Bus Company was formed. (Chris Riley collection)

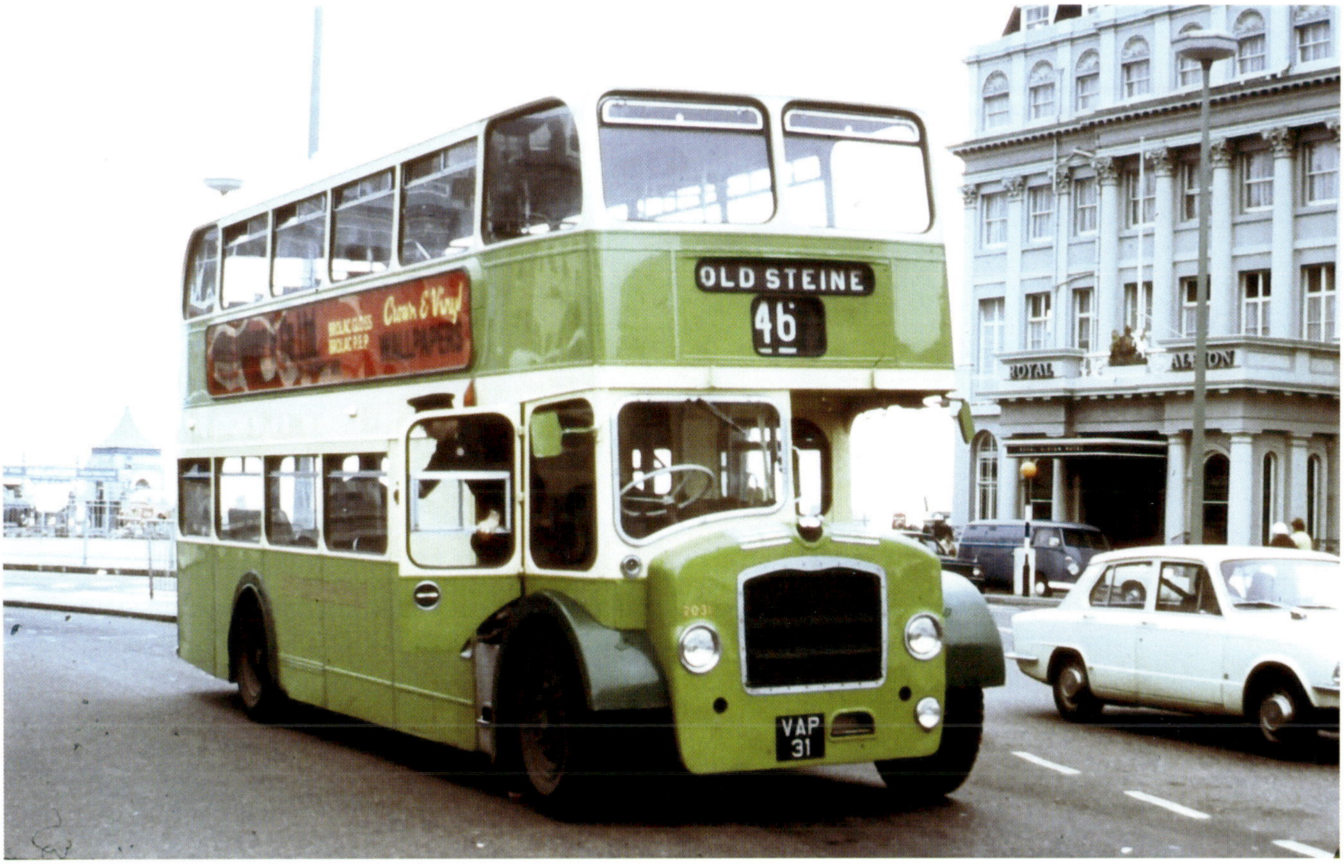

The driver of Southdown–BH&D 2031 (VAP 31) eases himself out of the cab at Old Steine in Brighton opposite the Royal Albion Hotel after arrival from Hollingbury on Service 46. (Chris Riley collection)

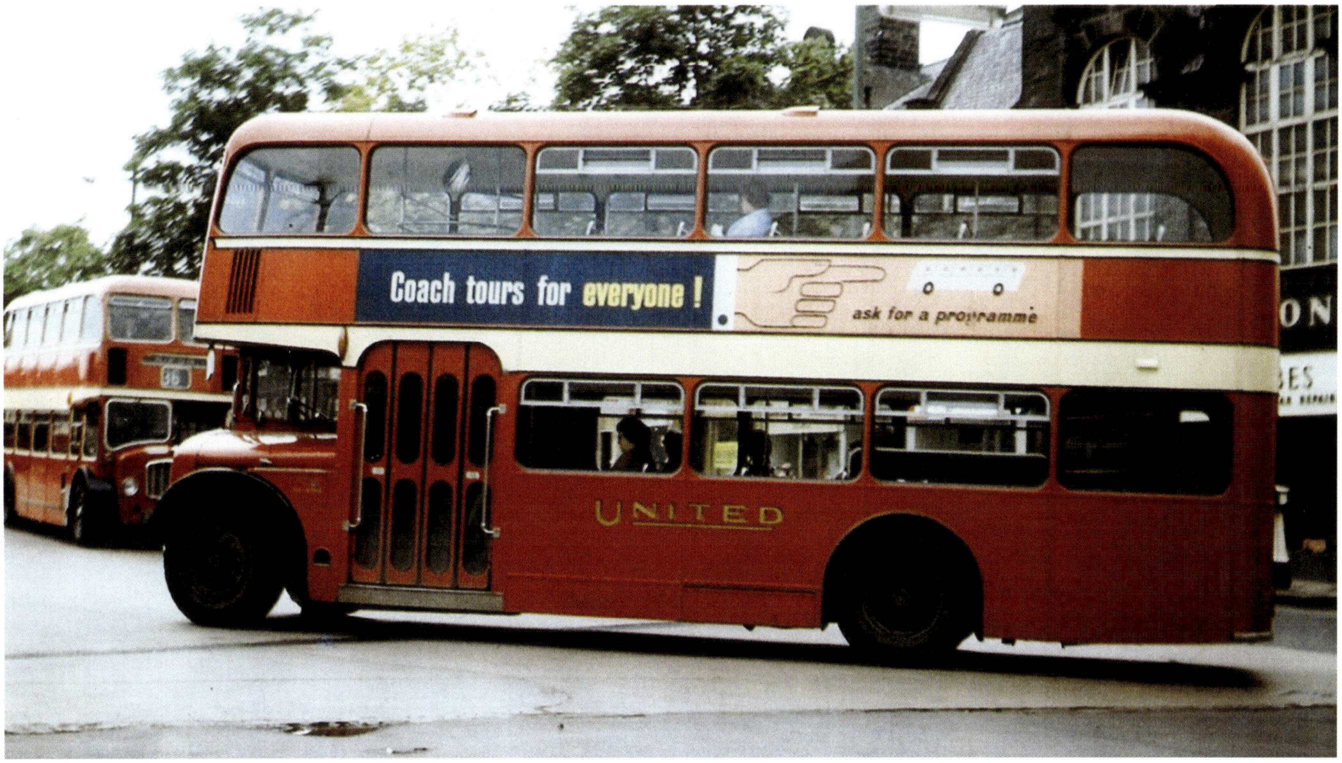

A full broadside view of one of the 28 FSF6Bs new to United Automobile emphasises the pleasant proportions of the Eastern Coach Works body at Harrogate. (Neil Halliday collection)

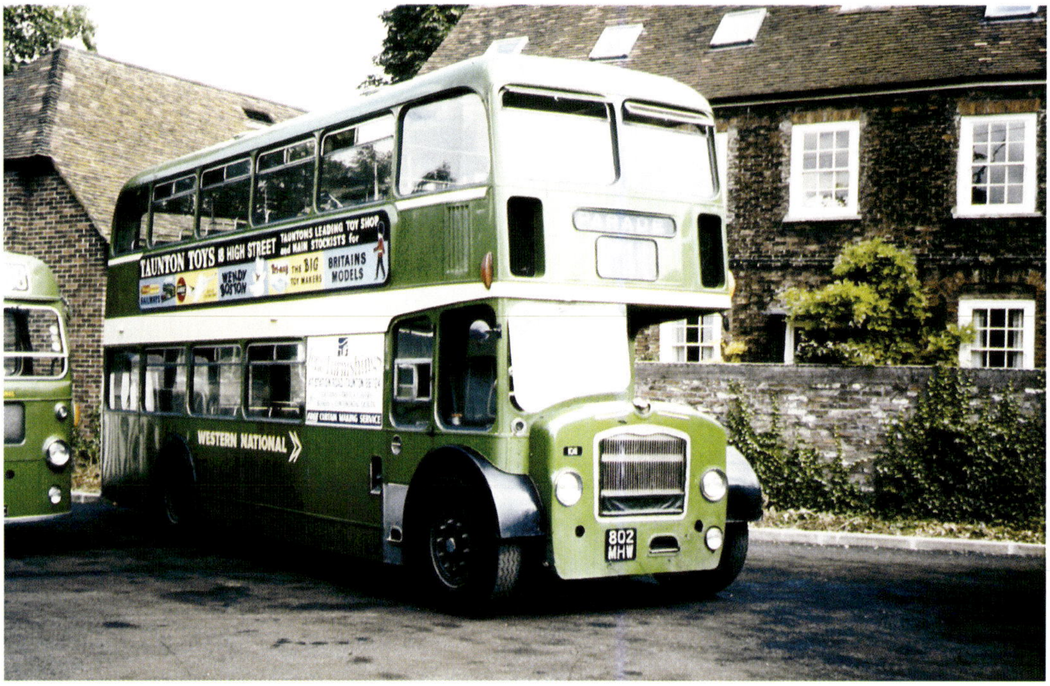

Originally with Cheltenham District Traction Company as 6037 (802 MHW) in the Bristol Omnibus Company fleets in October 1961 this FSF6G was sold to Western National and given fleet number 1011 in June 1967 after delivery to Cheltenham of the first Bristol RELL vehicles seating 53 passengers to the BOC group of companies. Photographed on 11th August 1973 at Taunton it is standing spare between duties. When withdrawn in 1978 the vehicle was still based at Taunton. It is now preserved at Wythall Transport Museum, Birmingham. (Author's collection)

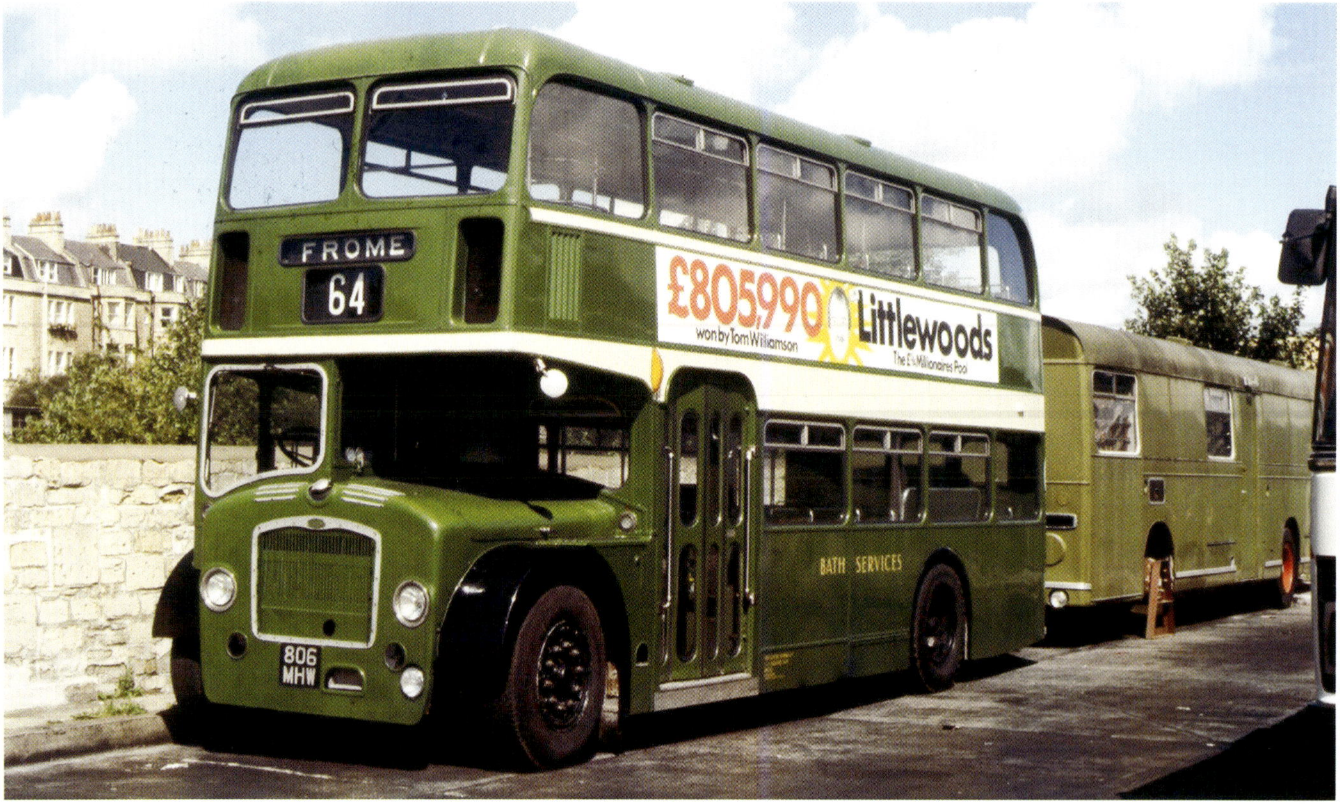

Purchased by the author and Bath driver Euel Lane in November 1978 from Western National for preservation 6041 (806 MHW) is pictured at Kensington Depot in Bath around 1987. Behind it is the "battle bus" converted from a Bristol RELL for use as an office at Salisbury during the post National Bus Company privatisation bus wars against Wilts & Dorset in both Poole and Salisbury. (Cliff Essex)

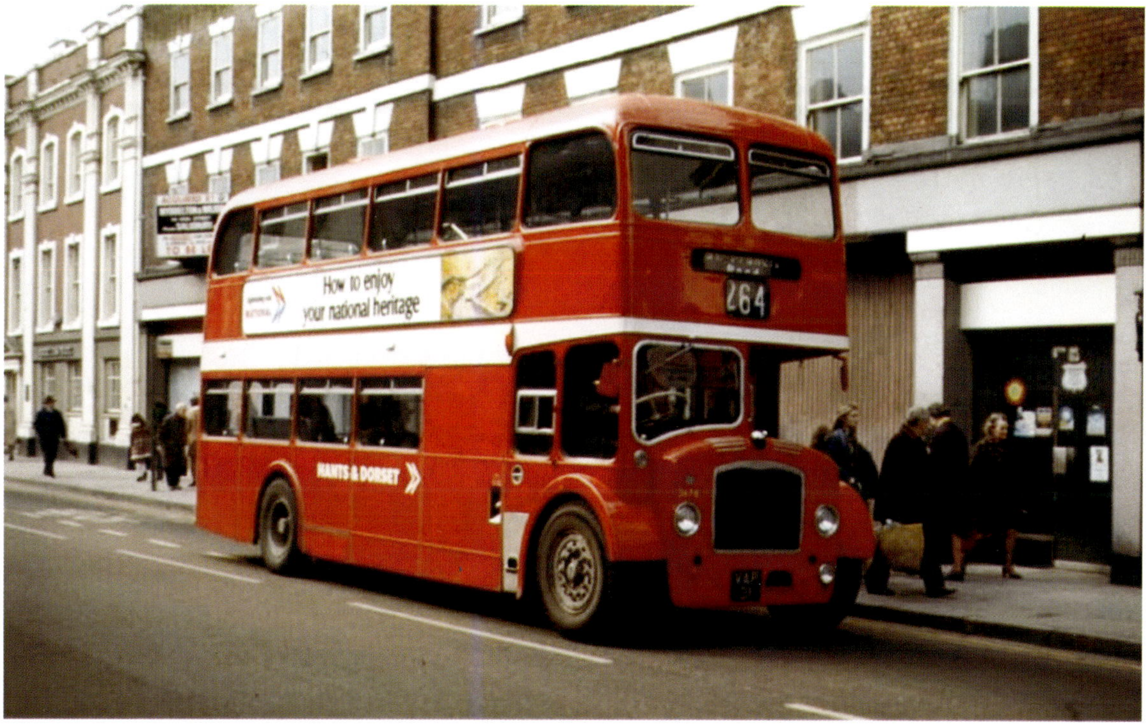

All FSFs operated in Salisbury, except one operated by Salisbury Health District, were fitted with Bristol engines including 3476 (VAP 31) a 1961 former Southdown Motor Services vehicle that was new to Brighton Hove & District. Retaining its distinctive Beetenson "Rapide Type W" ventilators and louvers it is seen at New Canal in Salisbury on 15th March 1975 working a journey to St Francis Road on Salisbury City Service 264. (Dave Mant)

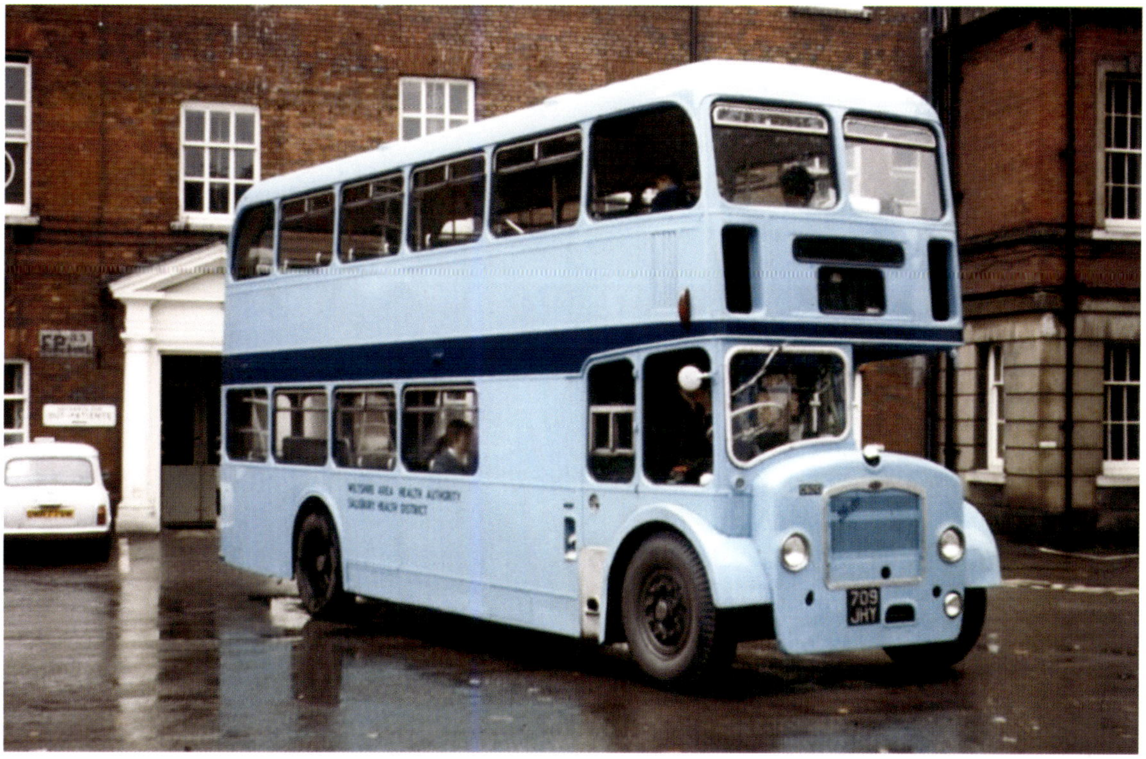

In a smart blue livery Salisbury Health District 709 JHY, a 1960 FSF6B, still carries its former Bristol Omnibus fleet number C6010 as it stands in the rain on the forecourt of Salisbury Infirmary on 2nd October 1976. Free transport for staff and patients had been provided between the Infirmary in Fisherton Street, now converted to housing, and the newer Odstock Hospital, on the southern outskirts of the city, where all National Health facilities are now located. Previously these journeys that ran every day of the year including over Christmas were operated by ex Southampton Corporation Guy Arab double deck vehicles. (Dave Mant)

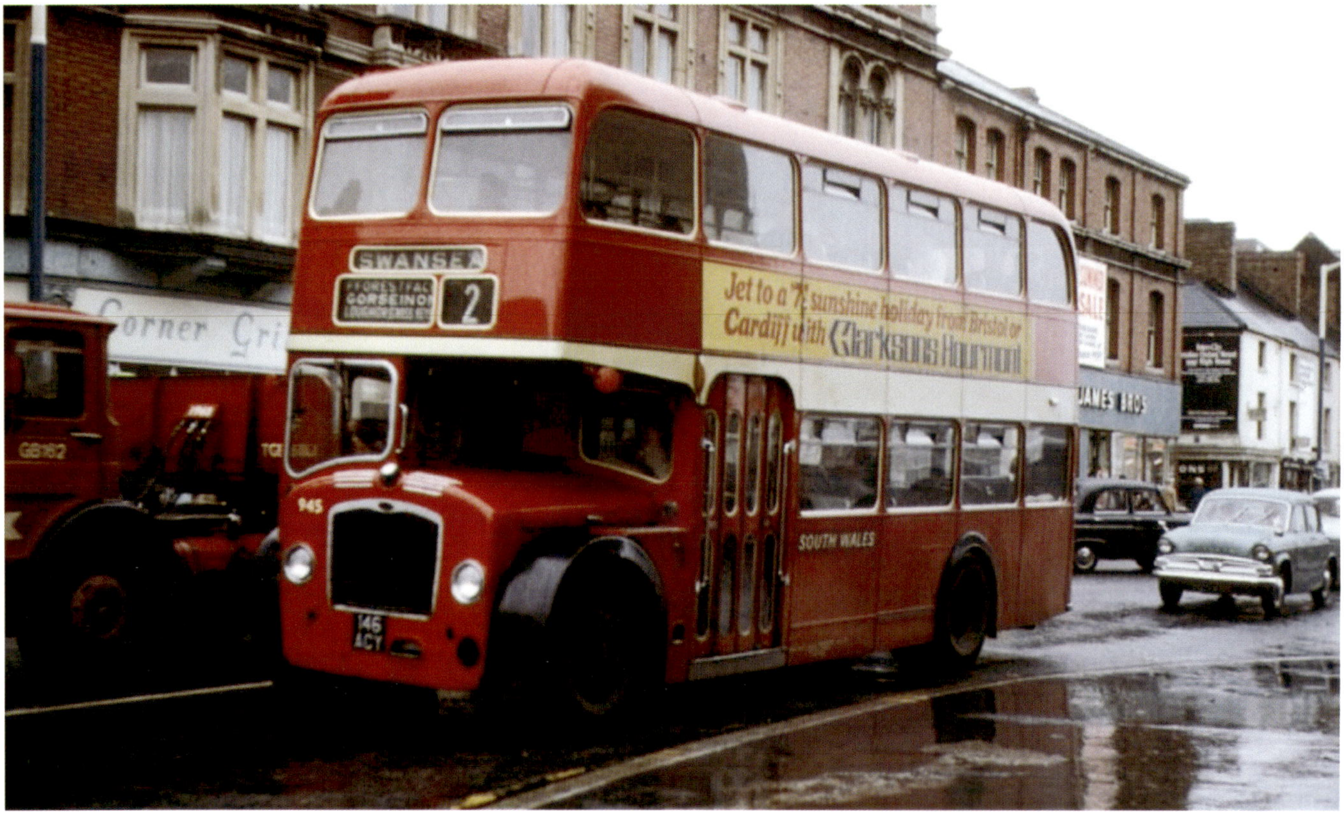

Splashing its way into Swansea on 13th August 1971 South Wales Transport 945 (146 ACY), a 1961 former United Welsh FSF6G, looks to be in remarkably good condition. (Dave Mant)

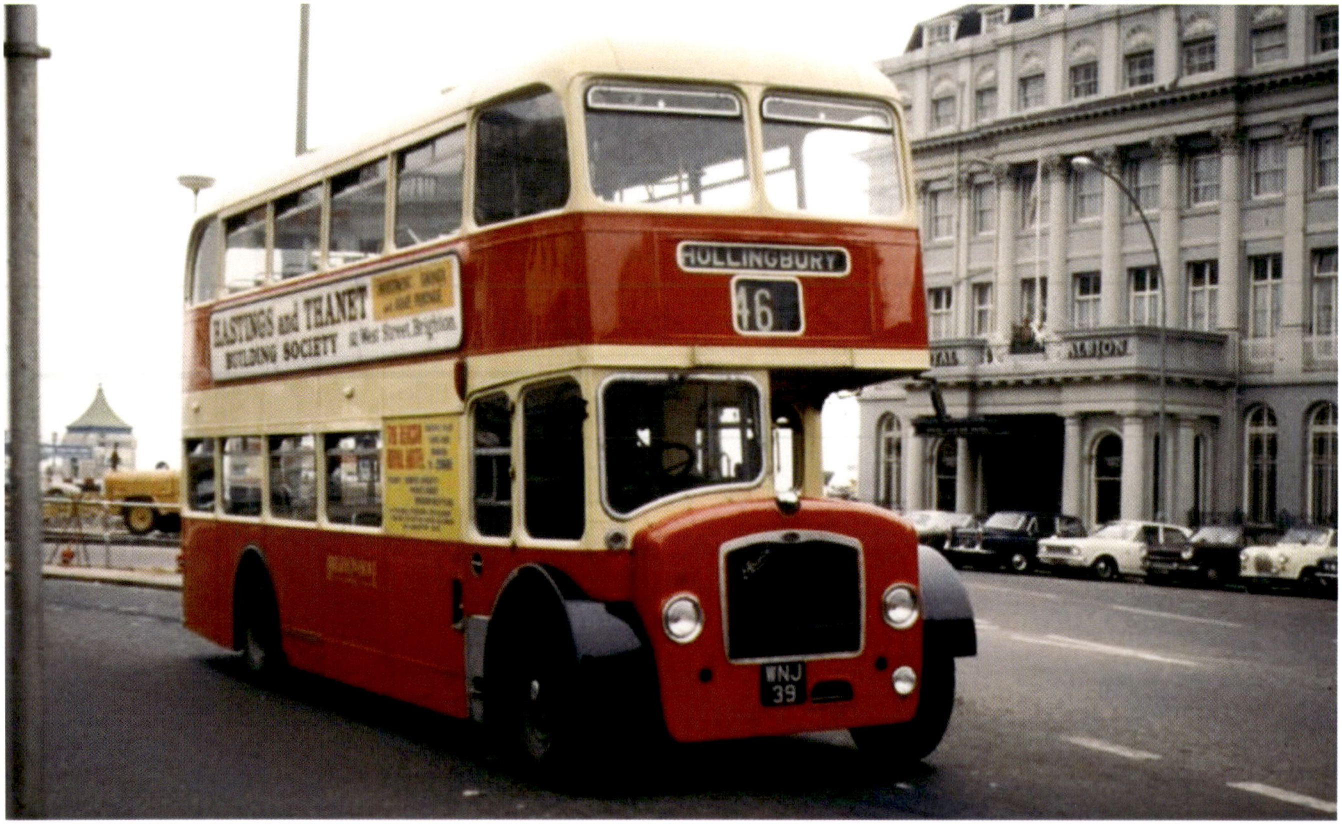

Waiting for passengers at Old Steine in Brighton for stops to Hollingbury on Service 46 on 9th May 1969 is 39 (WNJ 39), one of the last three FSFs for the Brighton Hove & District fleet delivered in April 1962. (Dave Mant)

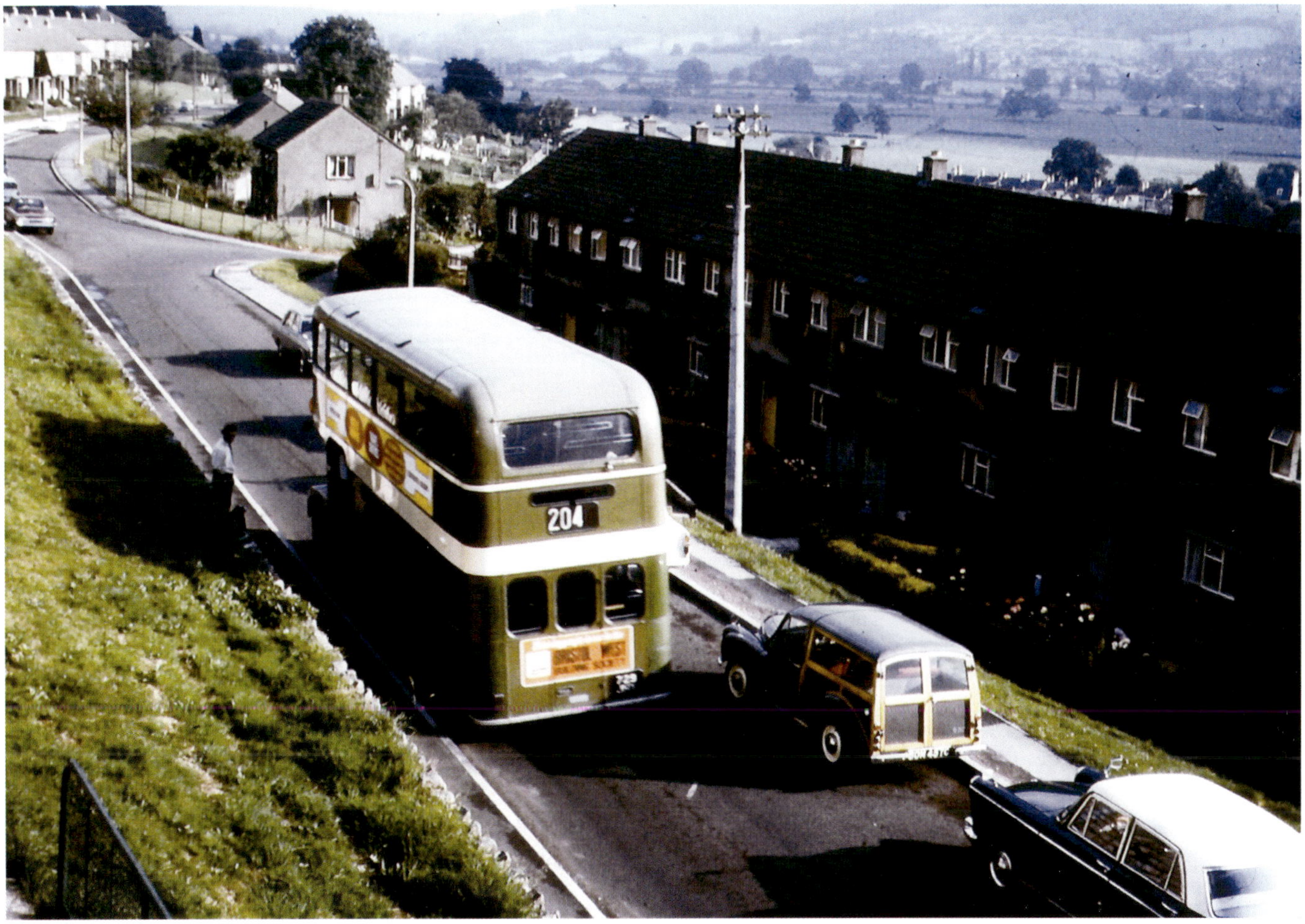

With very few cars evident, unlike these days, Bath based 6032 (729 JHY) departs Elmhurst Estate in the early 1970s displaying the incorrect service number on the rear. The conductor should have changed the blinds to either 203 for Combe Down, Ralph Allen School or Claverton Down, or 213 for a journey to Foxhill Estate. (Author's collection)

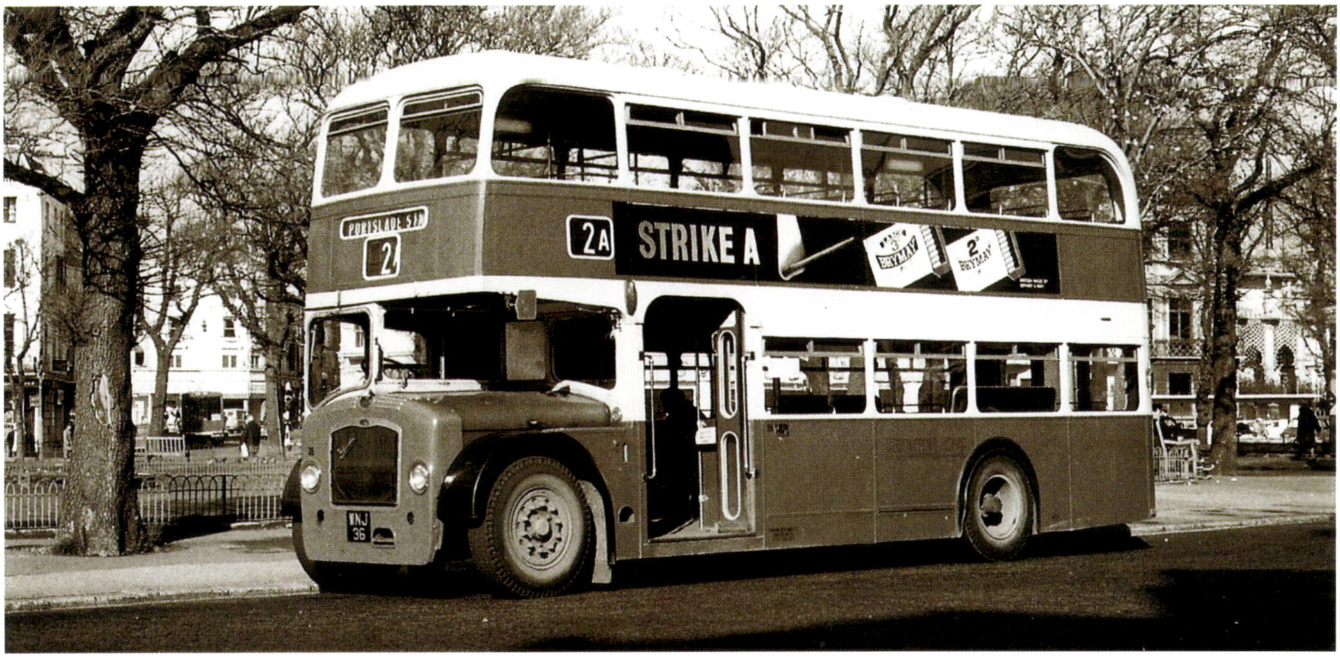

The platform doors are open and the destination and canopy service number boxes are set on Brighton Hove & District 36 (WNJ 36) to work a journey to Portslade Station on Service 2A. (Peter Hirst)

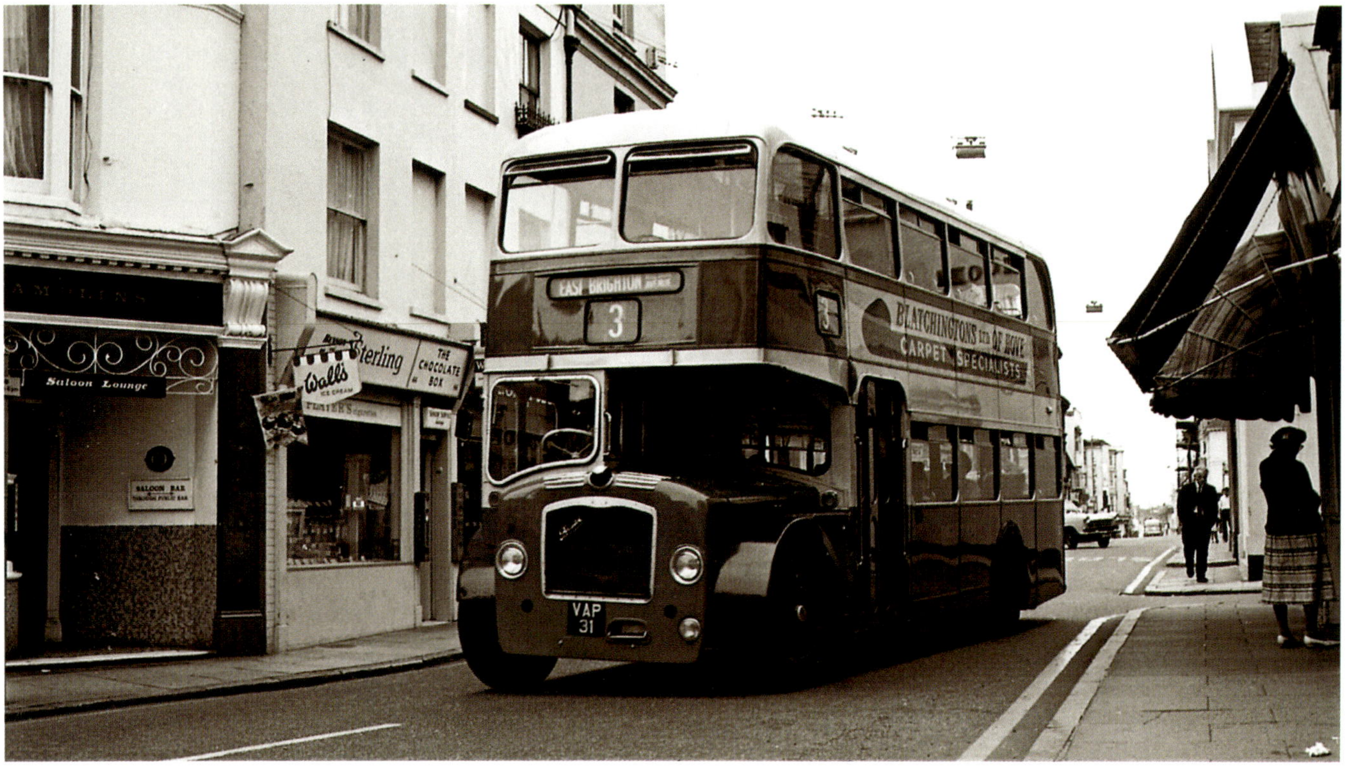

Brighton Hove & District 31 (VAP 31) negotiates the narrow streets of Brighton as it proceeds on Service 3 to East Brighton. (Peter Hirst)

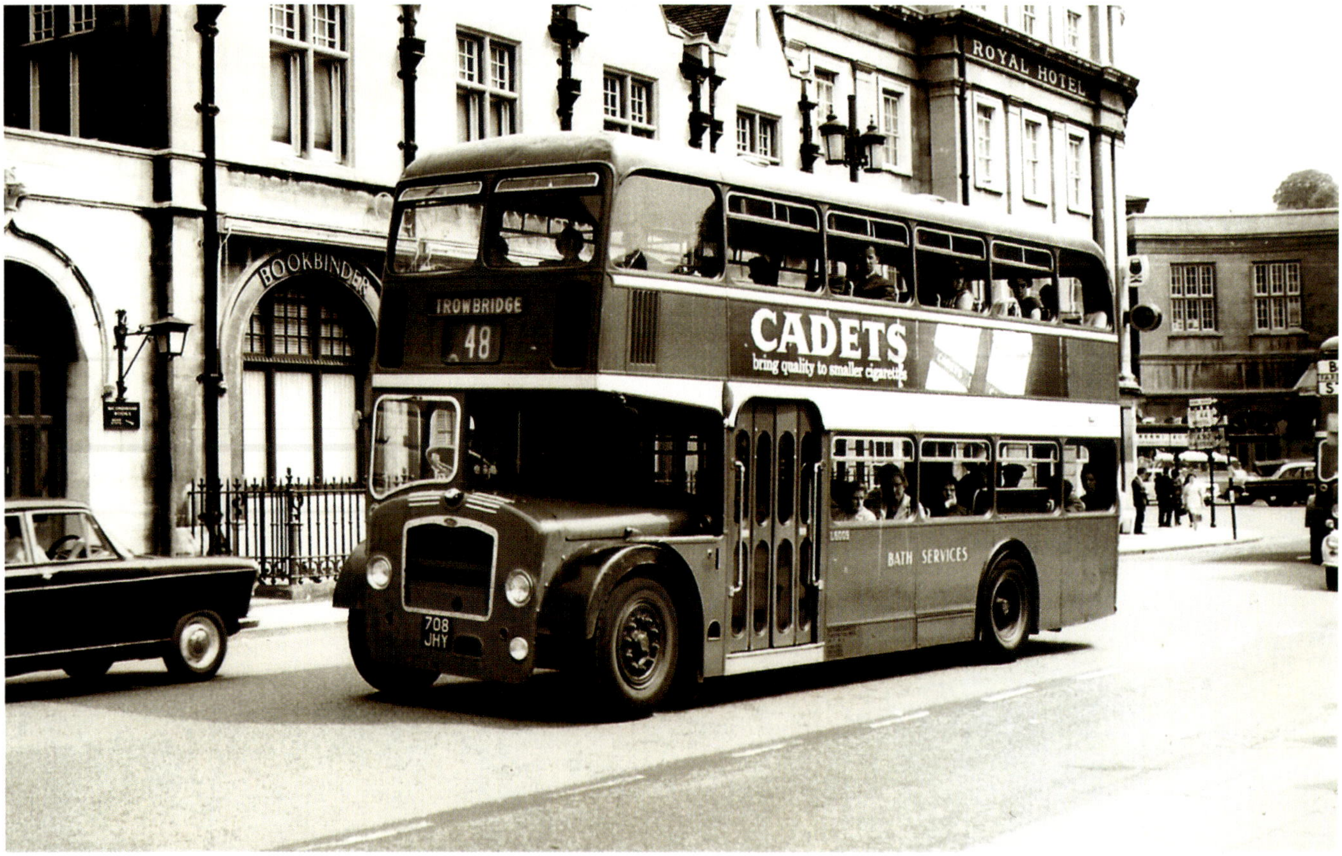

Departing Bath Bus Station with a reasonable number of passengers, L6009 (708 JHY), a 1960 FSF6G with Bath Services fleet names, heads for Trowbridge on Service 48 when crew working was considered very much the normal method of operating both Bath city and country routes. (Author's collection)

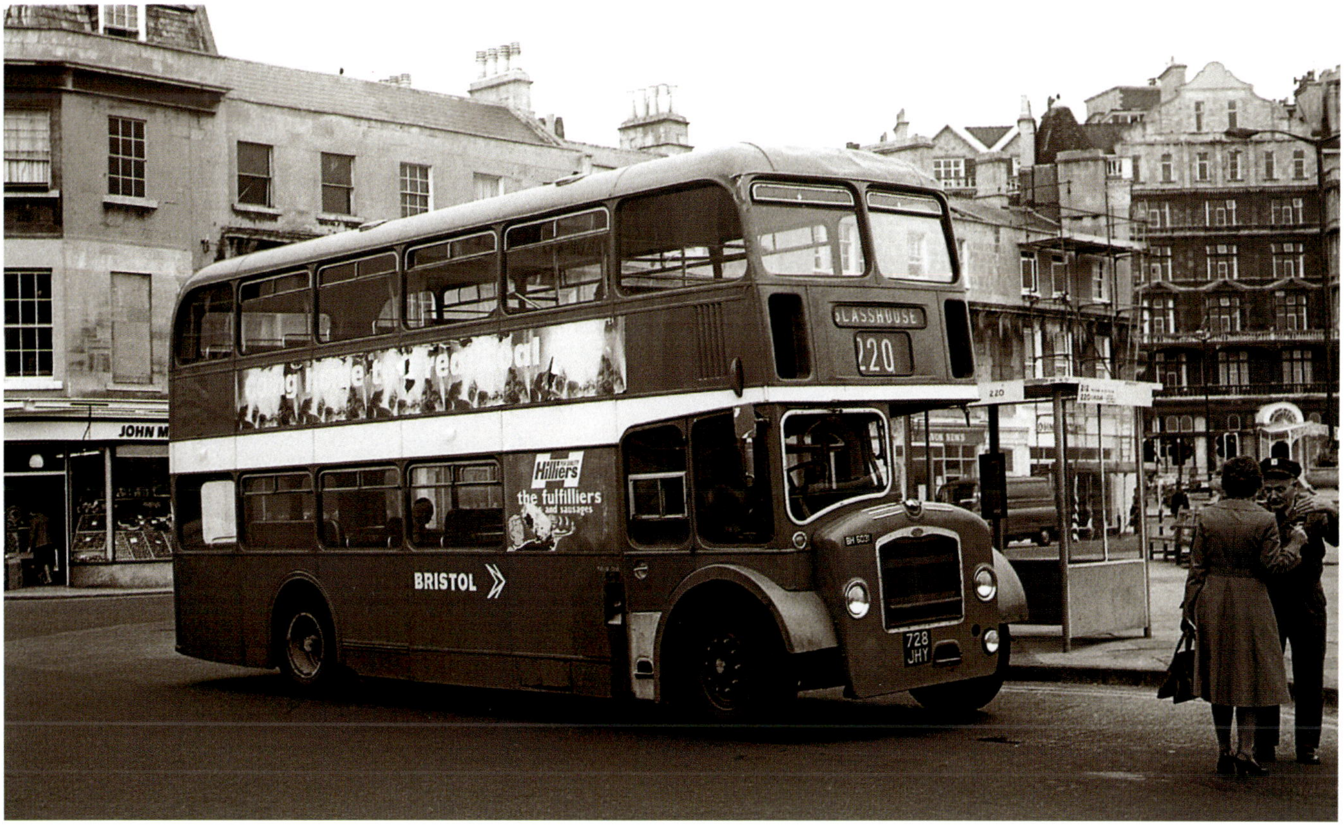

Bath based 6031 (728 JHY) stands at Terrace Walk, or Bog Island as it is commonly known to locals, looking slightly frayed at the edges with tatty paper adverts. It was one of a number of FSF6Gs to work at Bath and was photographed on Tuesday 21st September 1976. (Stephen Dowle)

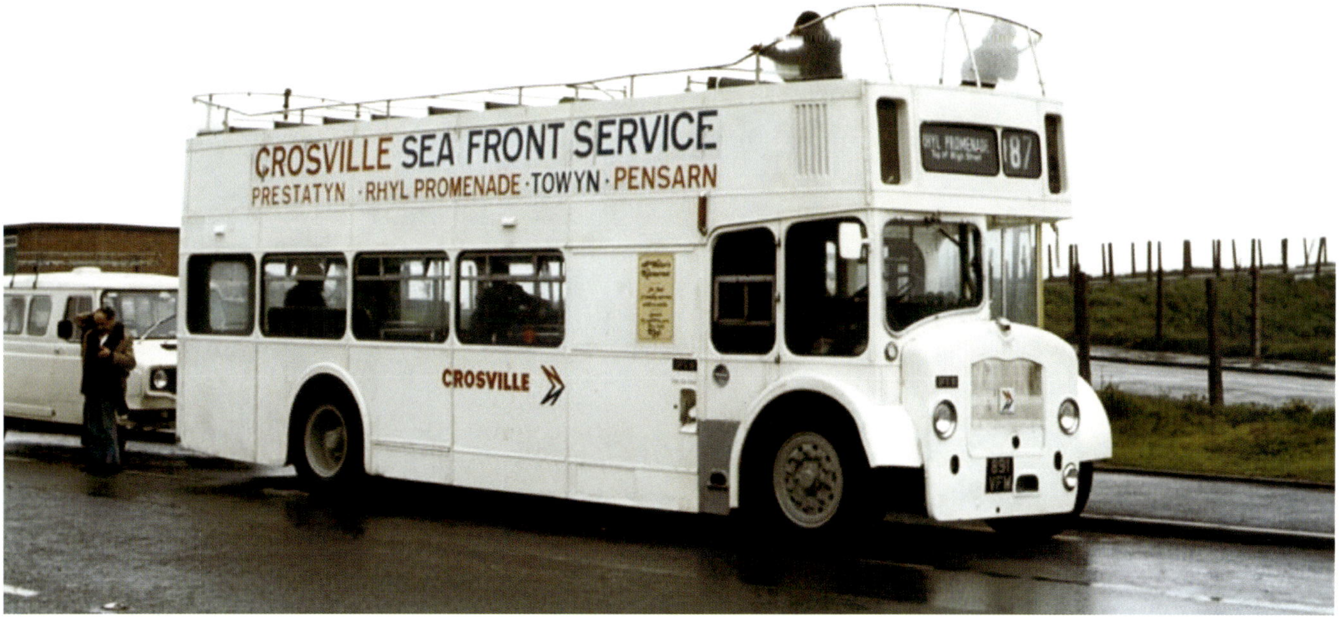

Typical British summer weather does not always deter all passengers from travelling on the upper deck of Crosville DFG81 (891 VFM) seen in Rhyl working a journey on Service M87 on 15th August 1983. (Dave Mant)

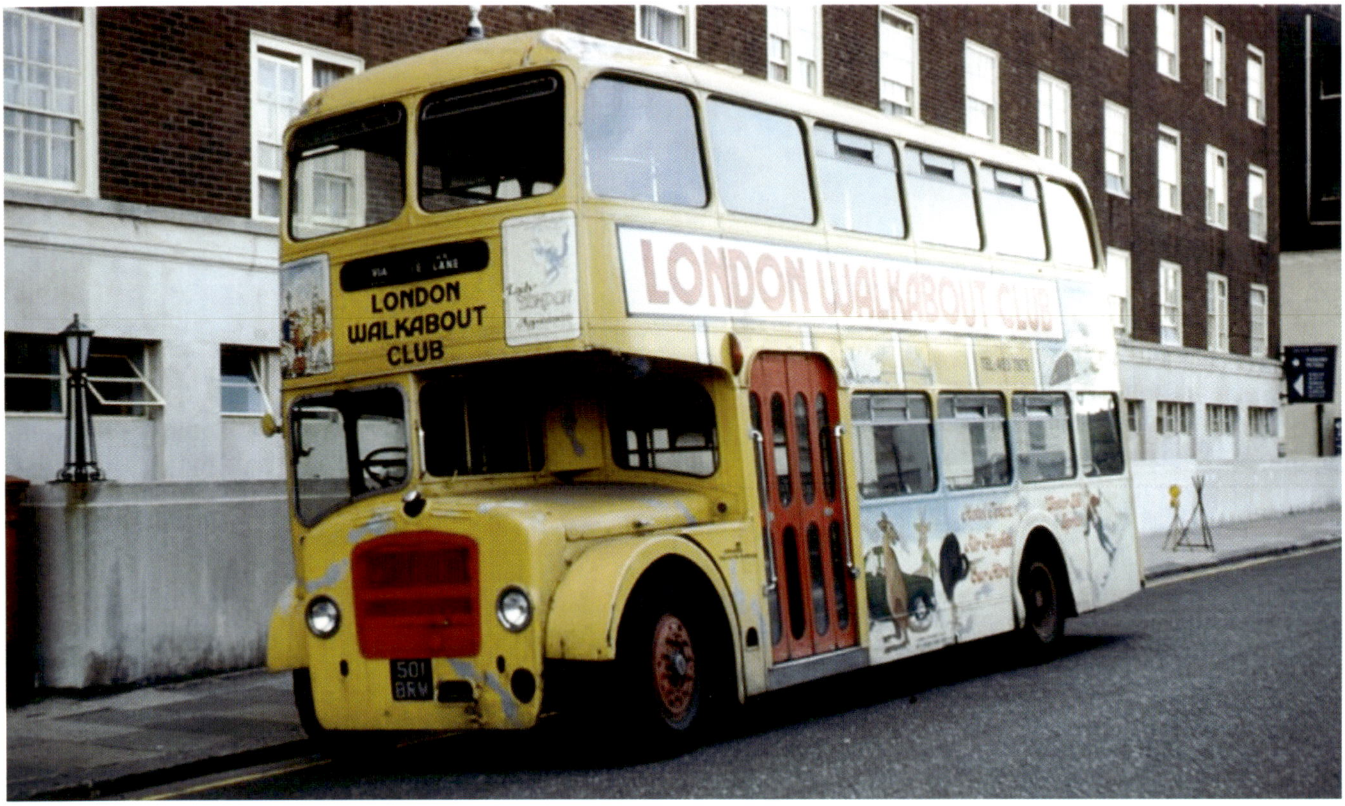

Originally with Cumberland Motor Services from new in October 1960 as C404 (501 BRM) this FSF6G was renumbered 500 in December 1961 until it was withdrawn in 1972 and went to Martin, a dealer in Weaverham, in April 1973. Green Bus of Rugeley purchased the vehicle in July 1973 and allocated fleet number 37 only to be renumbered 2176 when Midland Red took over in November 1973 but was not used after the takeover. It was purchased by Ensign, a dealer at Silver End, in March 1974 and in the following month sold to Lady London Appointments Limited who operated under the name "London Walkabout Club" as seen here on 22nd October 1977. It was transferred to Walkabout Travel Ltd in 1978 and remained there until withdrawn in February 1981. (Dave Mant)

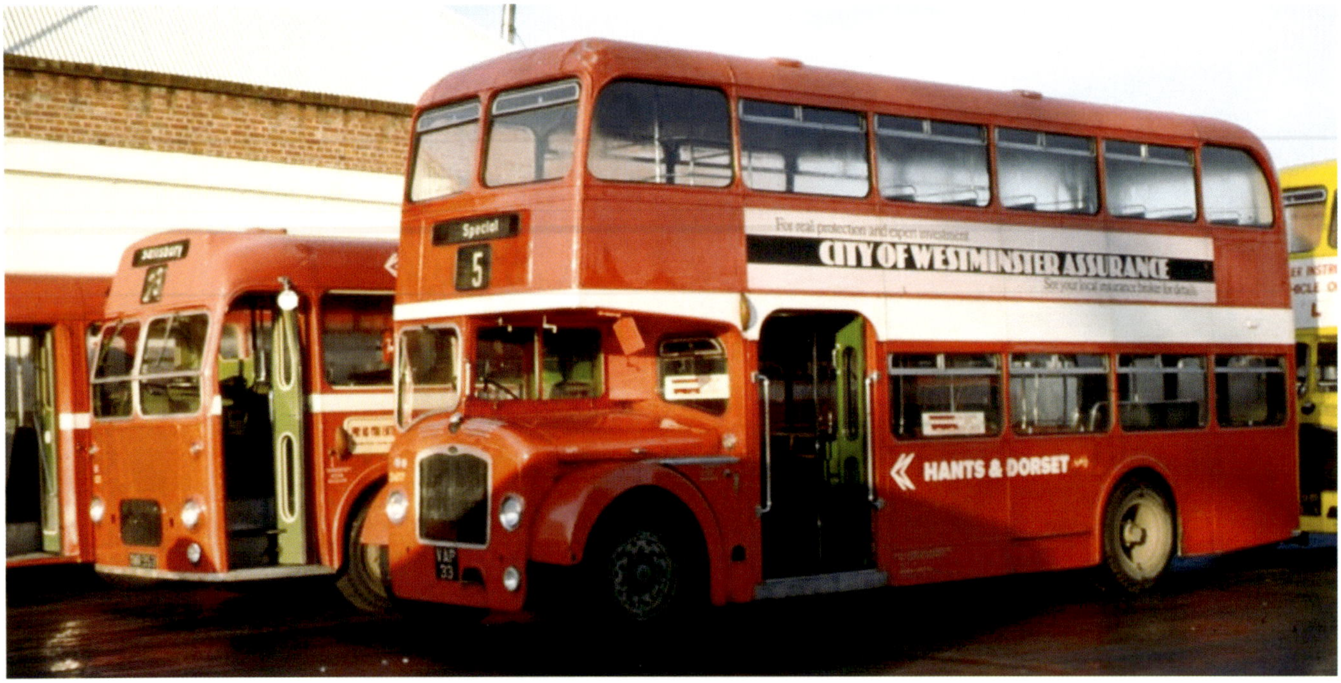

Still looking good after fourteen years Hants & Dorset 3477 (VAP 33), a 1961 ex Southdown FSF6B but new to Brighton Hove & District, stands in the yard at Castle Street Depot in Salisbury on 29th November 1975. (Dave Mant)

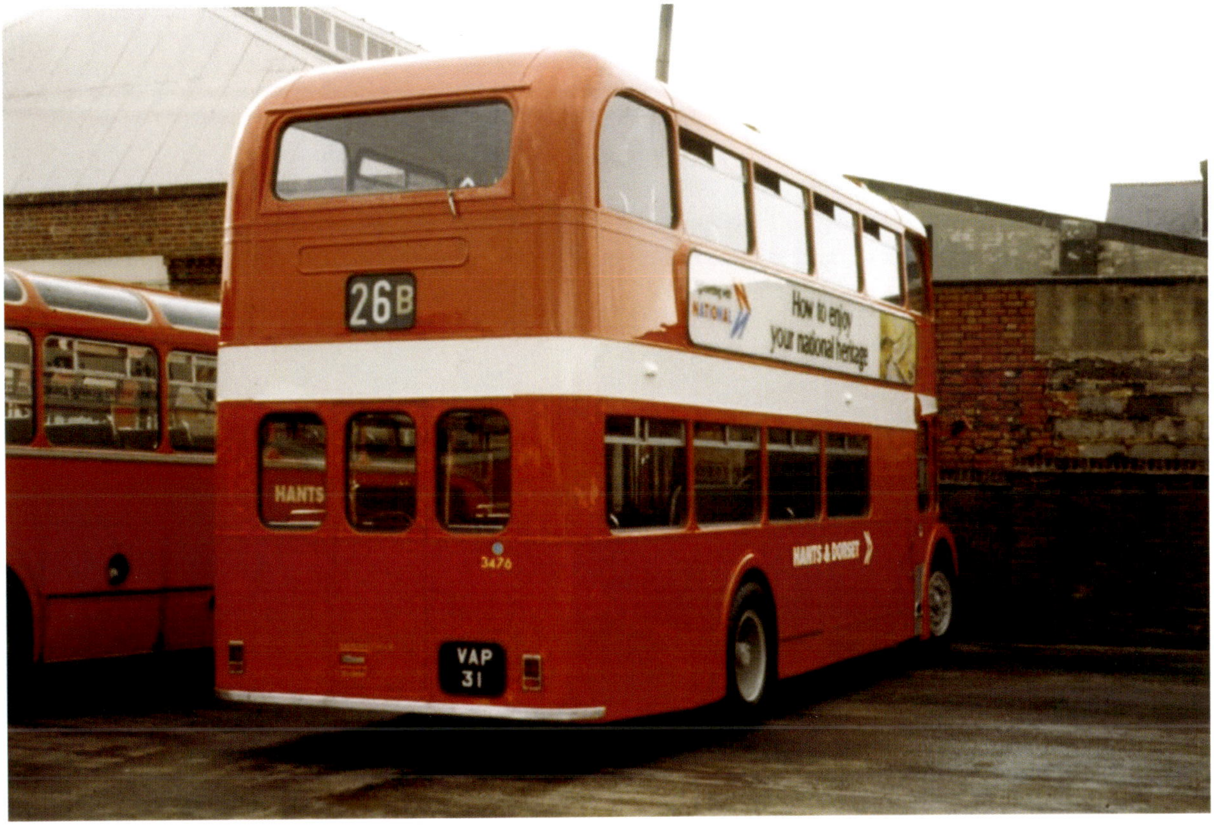

A rear view of Hants & Dorset 3476 (VAP 31), a 1961 ex Southdown former Brighton Hove & District FSF6B, looking ultra-smart with offside illuminated advertisement panel and rear service number box in use at Castle Street Garage in Salisbury on 1st February 1975. (Dave Mant)

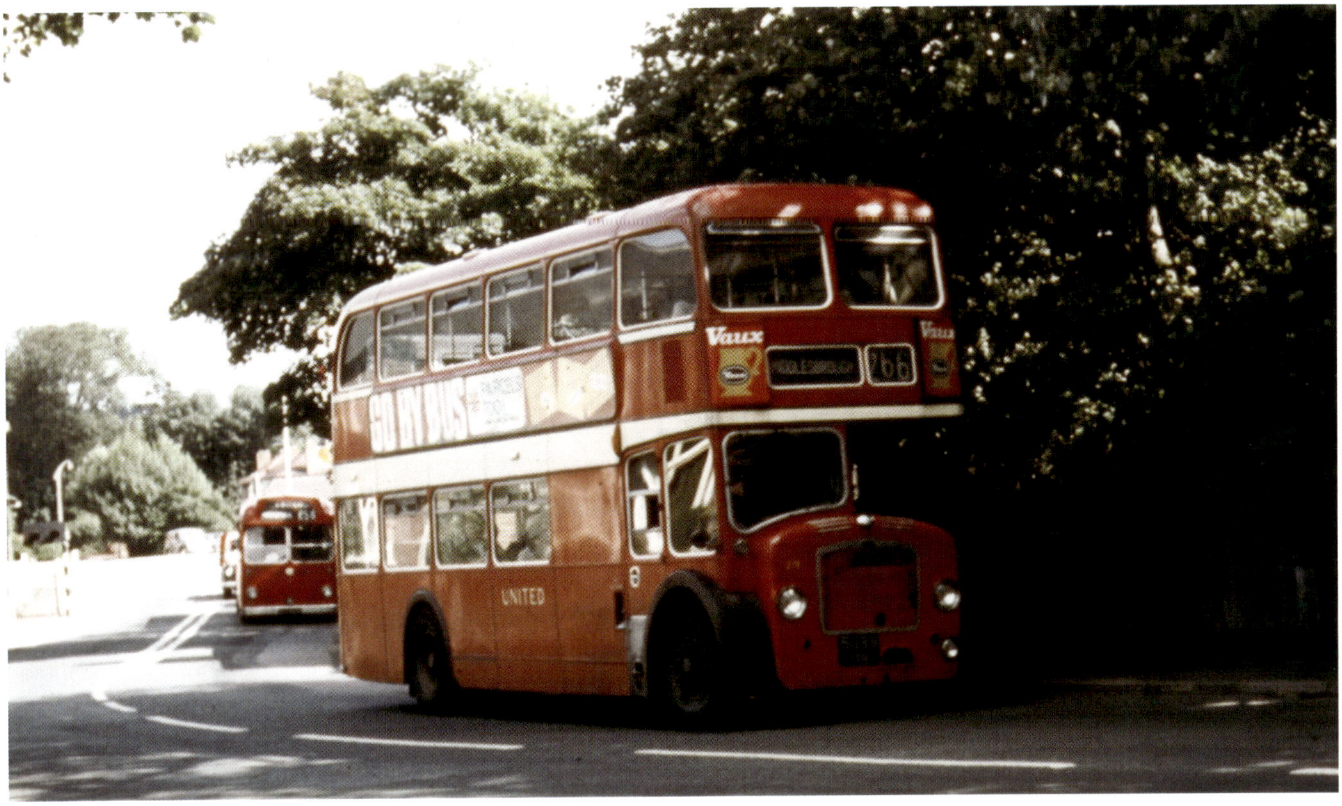

Passing through the leafy attractive suburb Nunthorpe during a pleasant day in August 1969 United Auto 279 (5099 HN) is followed by a Bristol LS when working a trip on Middlesbrough Circular Service 266. (Donald Hudson)

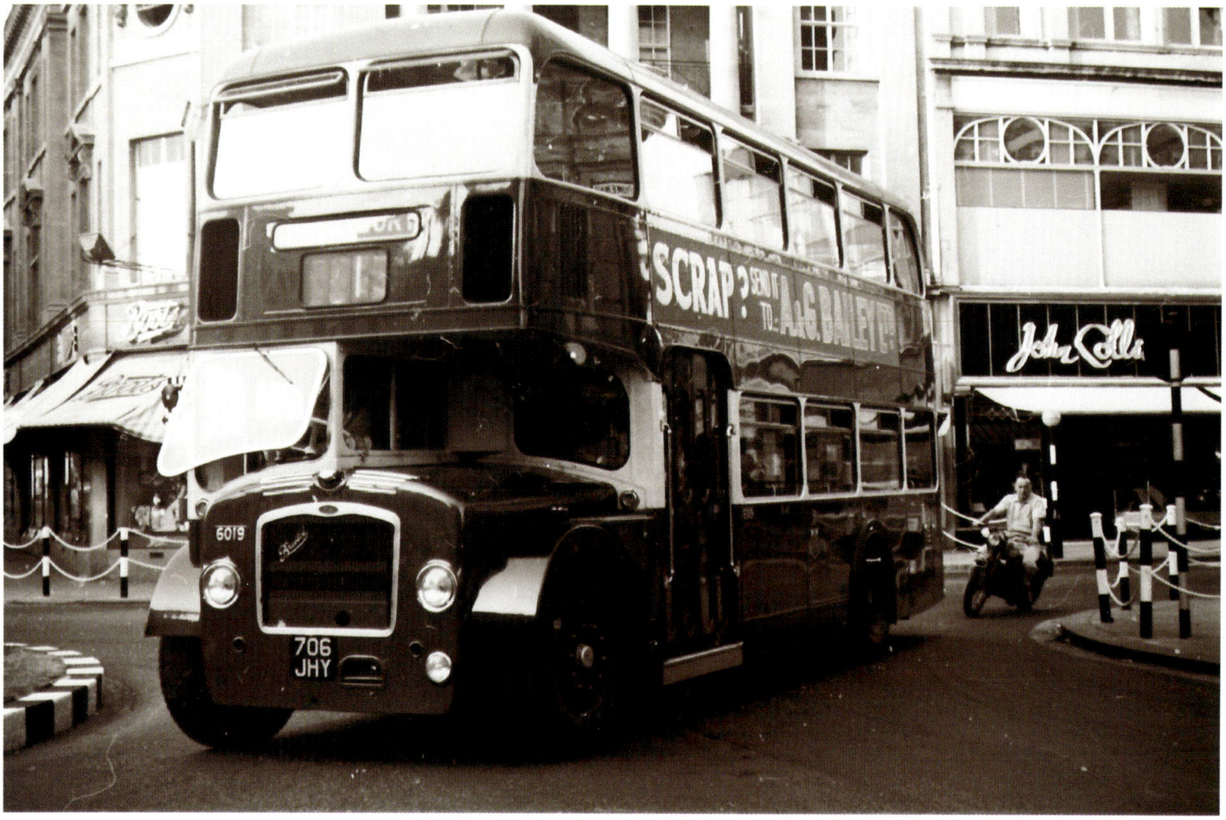

Fine weather sees Cheltenham District 6019 (706 JHY) negotiating Boots' roundabout in the central area of the town when on a positioning move. Obviously a warm day as the driver has the windscreen open the bus will work a short working on Service 1 that ran only between Centre and Prestbury. Note the following motorcyclist who is riding legally without wearing a crash helmet. (Bristol Vintage Bus Group)

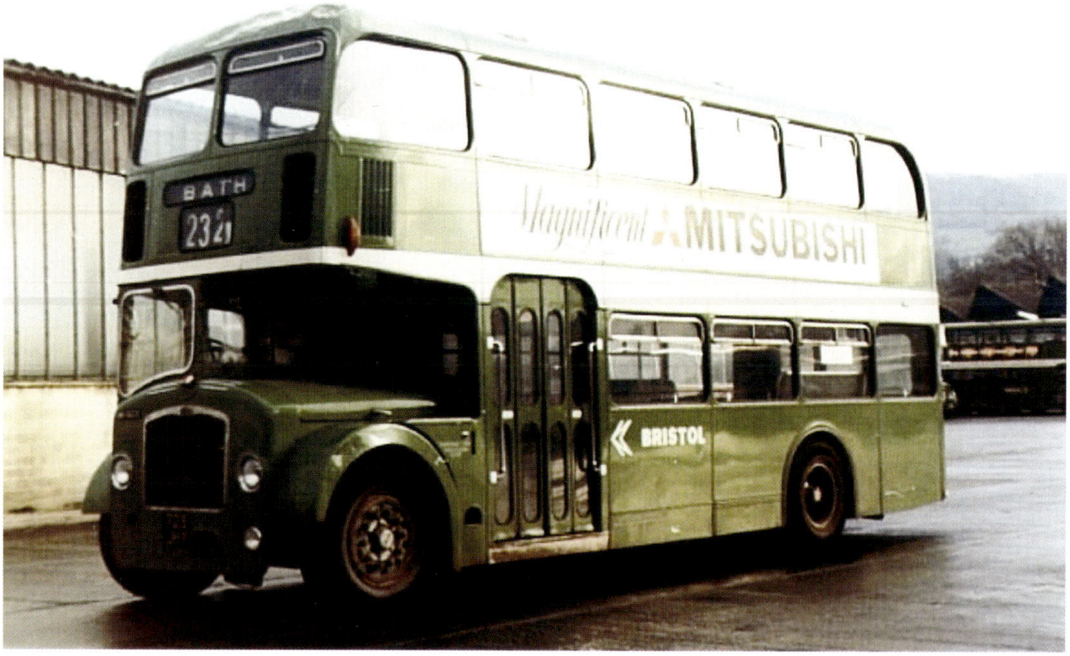

Although allocated to Totnes Depot for most of its short time with Western National between August 1967 and January 1970 1004 (728 JHY) was inexplicably transferred to Trowbridge a few days prior to Bristol Omnibus taking over the responsibility of Wiltshire services and fleet. Here it is seen at Kensington Depot in Bath in the open yard after refuelling having finished its morning peak trip on Service 232 from Chippenham (or the Corsham area if the bus had worked a Service 286 journey for "Ministry of Defence" workers from Boxfields to Monk's Park). (Stephen Dowle)

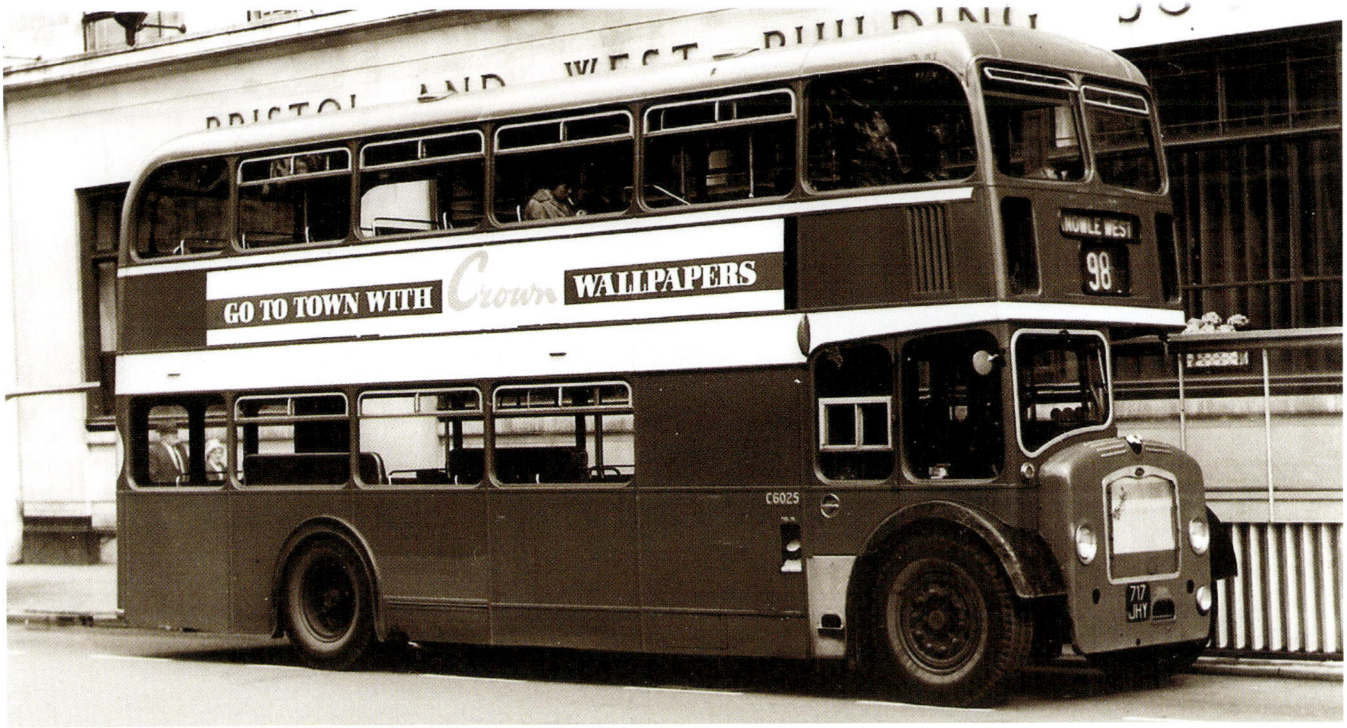

Bristol Omnibus C6025 (717 JHY) stands in central Bristol on 30th May 1964 waiting for passengers and departure time to operate on Service 98 to Knowle West. (Gerry Mead)

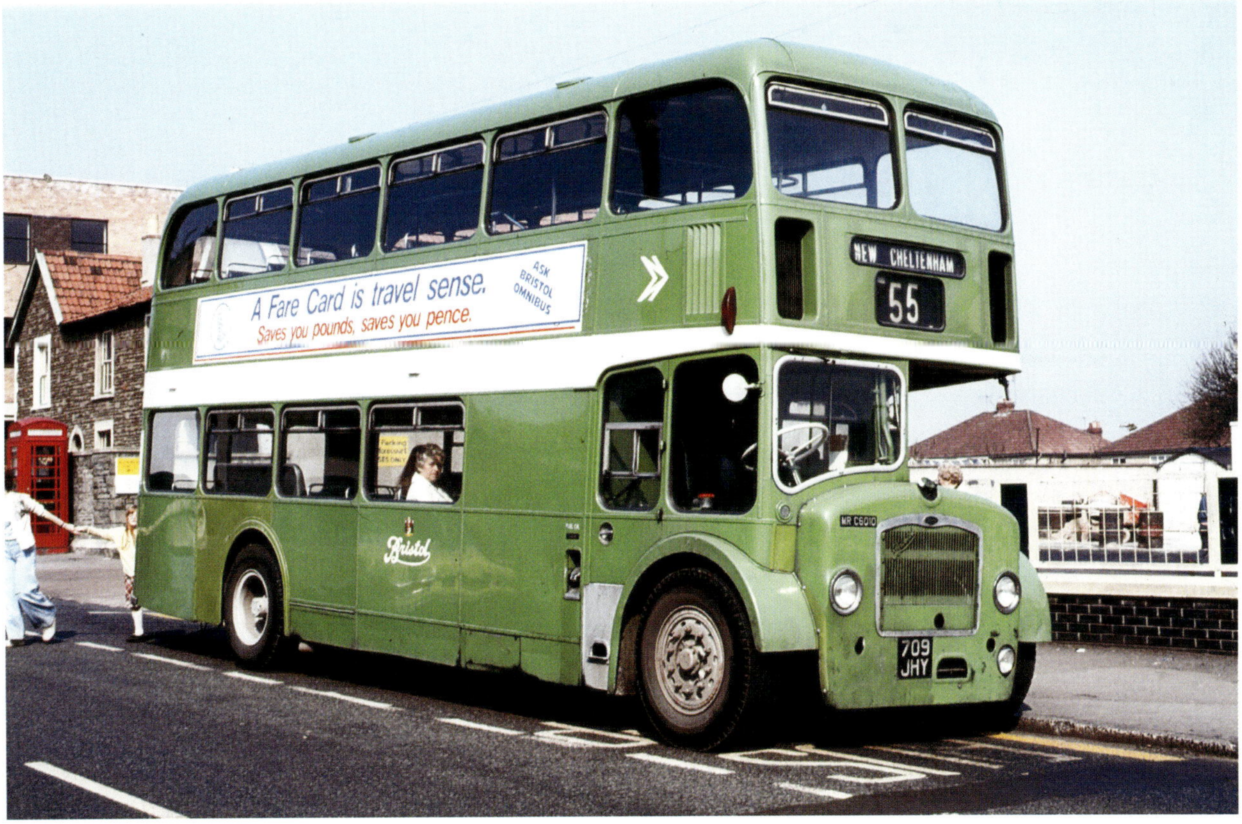

Outside the now closed Staple Hill Depot C6010 (709 JHY) allocated to Muller Road Depot waits for its driver and conductor to take the bus forward to New Cheltenham on Bristol City Service 55. A "casualty" of the major service cuts introduced on 27th June 1976 it was sold to Paul Sykes, a Barnsley vehicle dealer, and very quickly purchased by Wiltshire Area Health Authority for use by hospital staff and patients travelling between Salisbury Infirmary and Odstock Hospital from September 1976 until it was withdrawn and sold at auction in March 1979. (Geoff Gould)

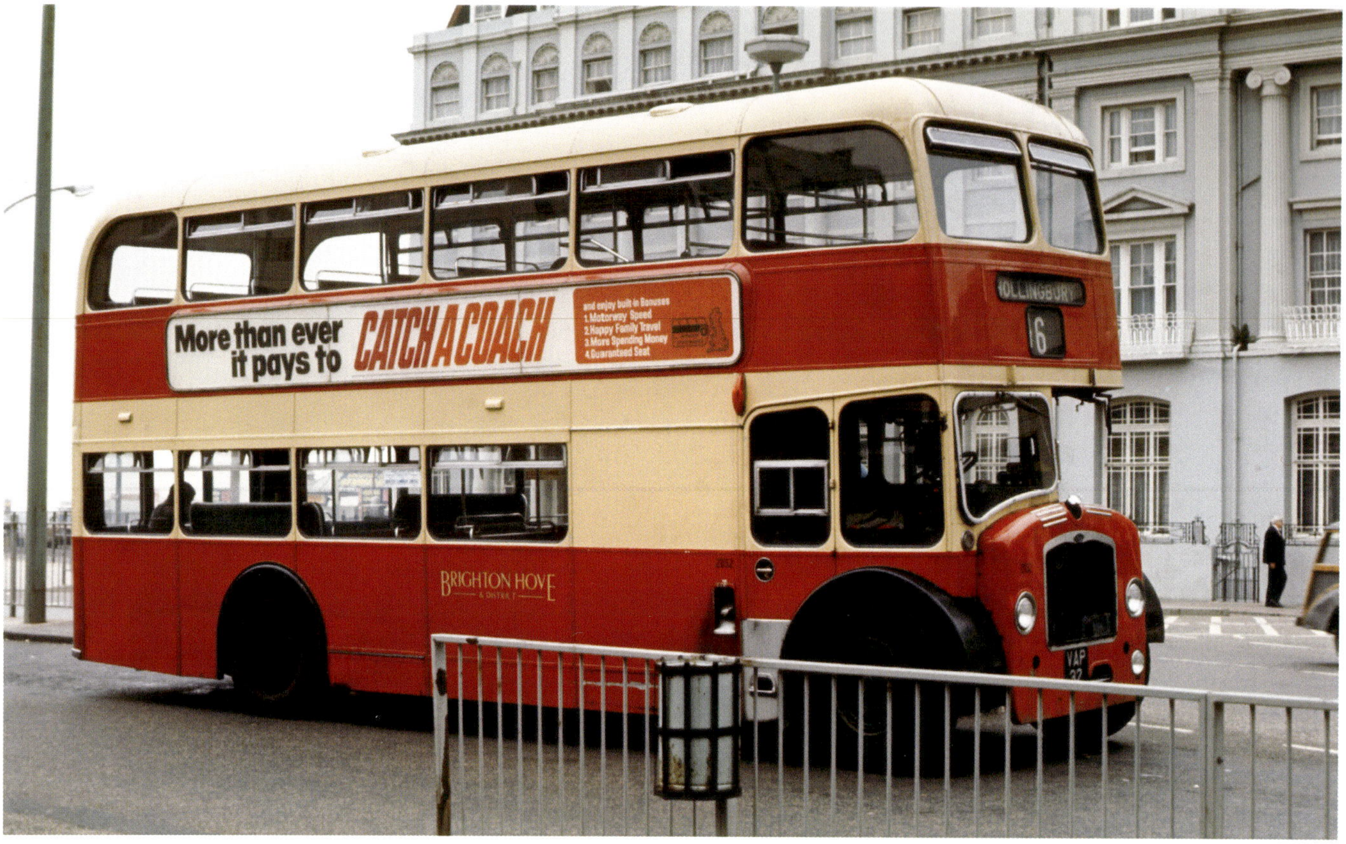

Old Steine in Brighton on 23rd August 1973 sees 2032 (VAP 32), one of five 1962 FSF deliveries to Brighton Hove & District, in traditional red and cream livery and fleet names but with its updated Southdown fleet number on Service 46 to Hollingbury. (M. R. Hodges)

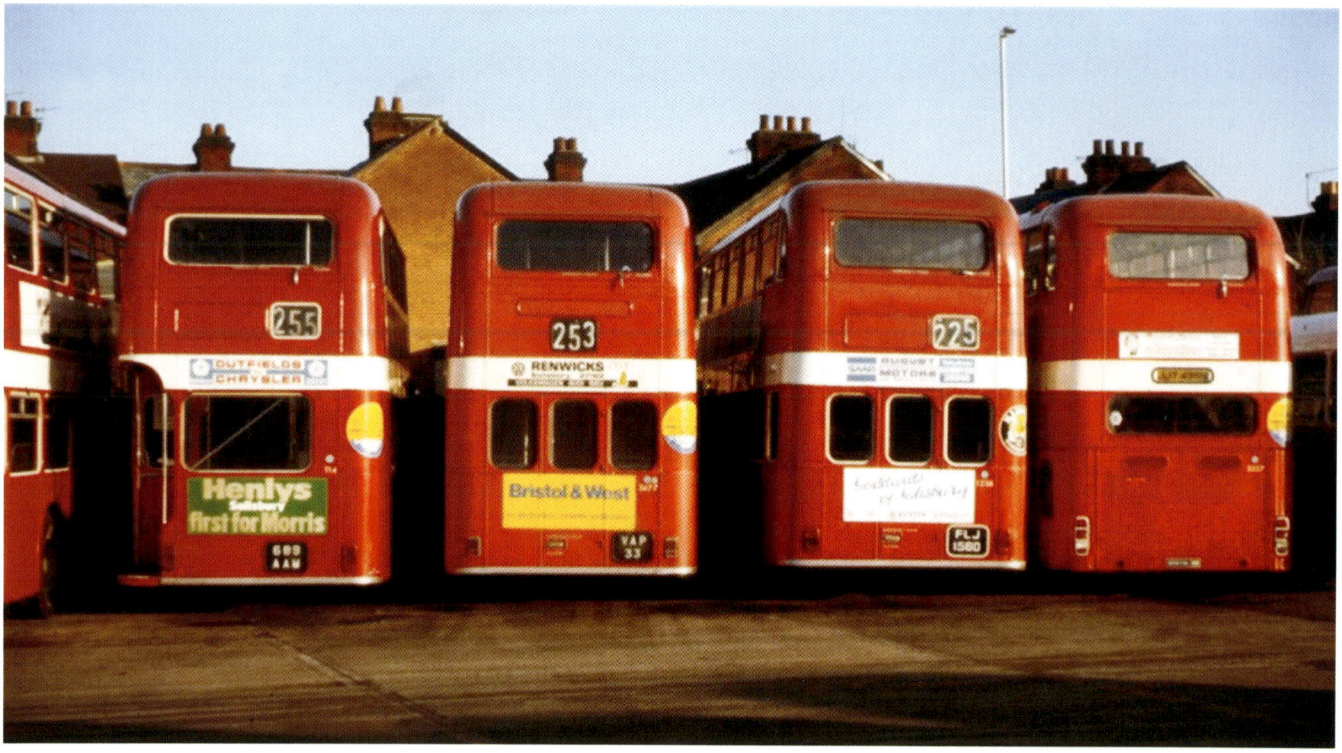

Spot the FSF in this rear view line up at Castle Street Garage in Salisbury on 4th January 1977 with 114 (689 AAM) a 1960 Bristol FS6G; 3477 (VAP 33) a 1961 ex Brighton Hove & District FSF6B; 1236 (FLJ 156D) a 1966 Bristol FLF6B and 3327 (JJT 439N) a 1975 Bristol VRT. (Dave Mant)

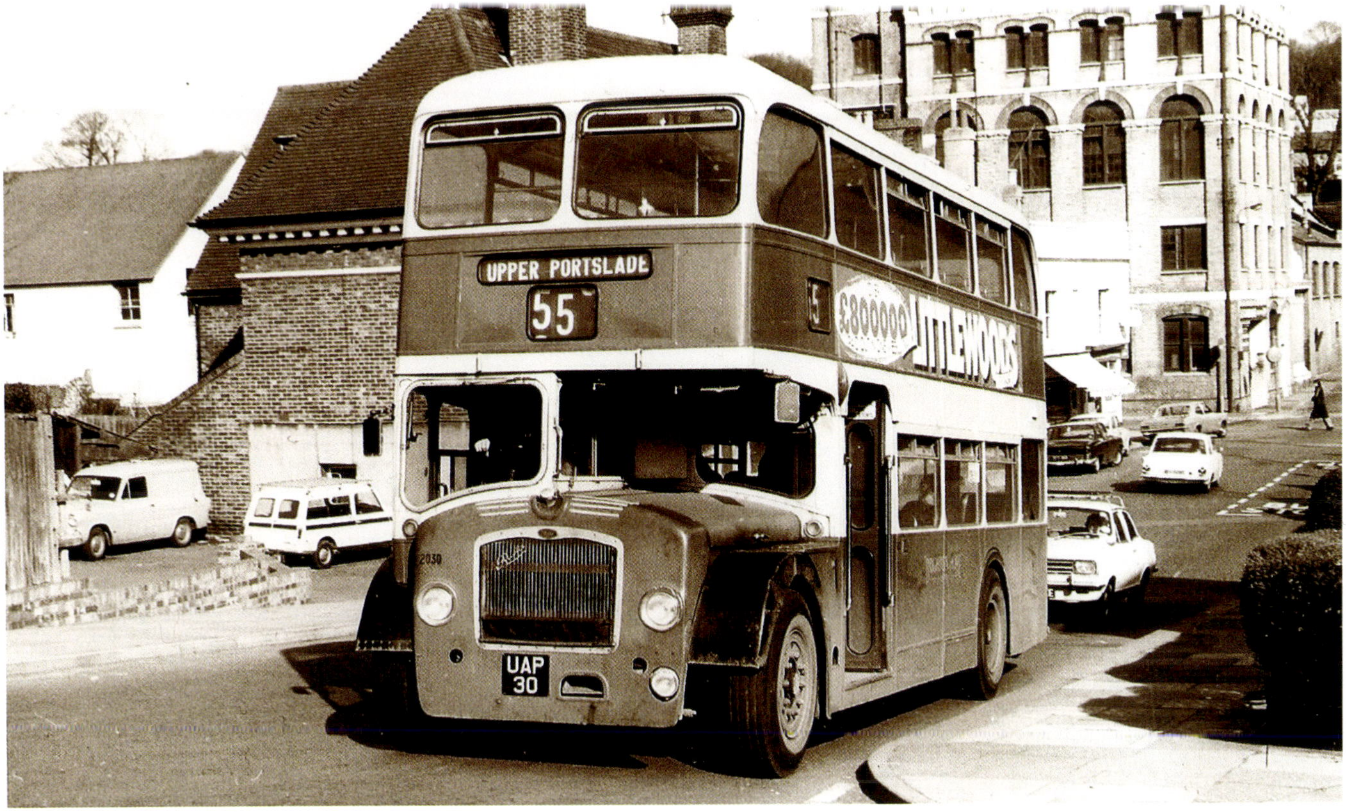

The driver of Brighton Hove & District 2030 (UAP 30), renumbered for the full takeover of the company by Southdown on 1st January 1969, drives his bus with little apparent regard for the safety of the few passengers travelling on Service 55 to Upper Portslade by leaving the platform doors open. (Denis Clark)

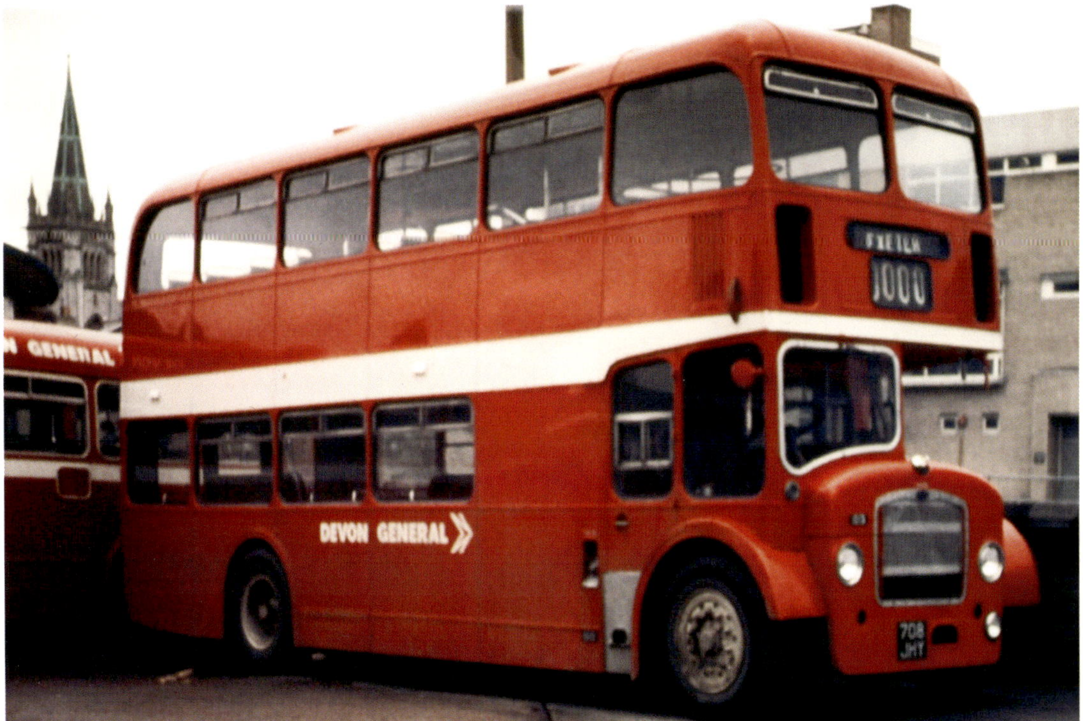

One of just two FSFs to receive Devon General red livery was 1013 (708 JHY) ex Bath Electric Tramways L6009. This FSF6G, seen here at Newton Abbot, was new in November 1960 and was originally L8567 until renumbered L6009 in January 1961. Purchased by Southern National in August 1967 it was repainted into National Bus Company "poppy red" livery in November 1976 that it carried until withdrawn from service in February 1978. (Bristol Vintage Bus Group)

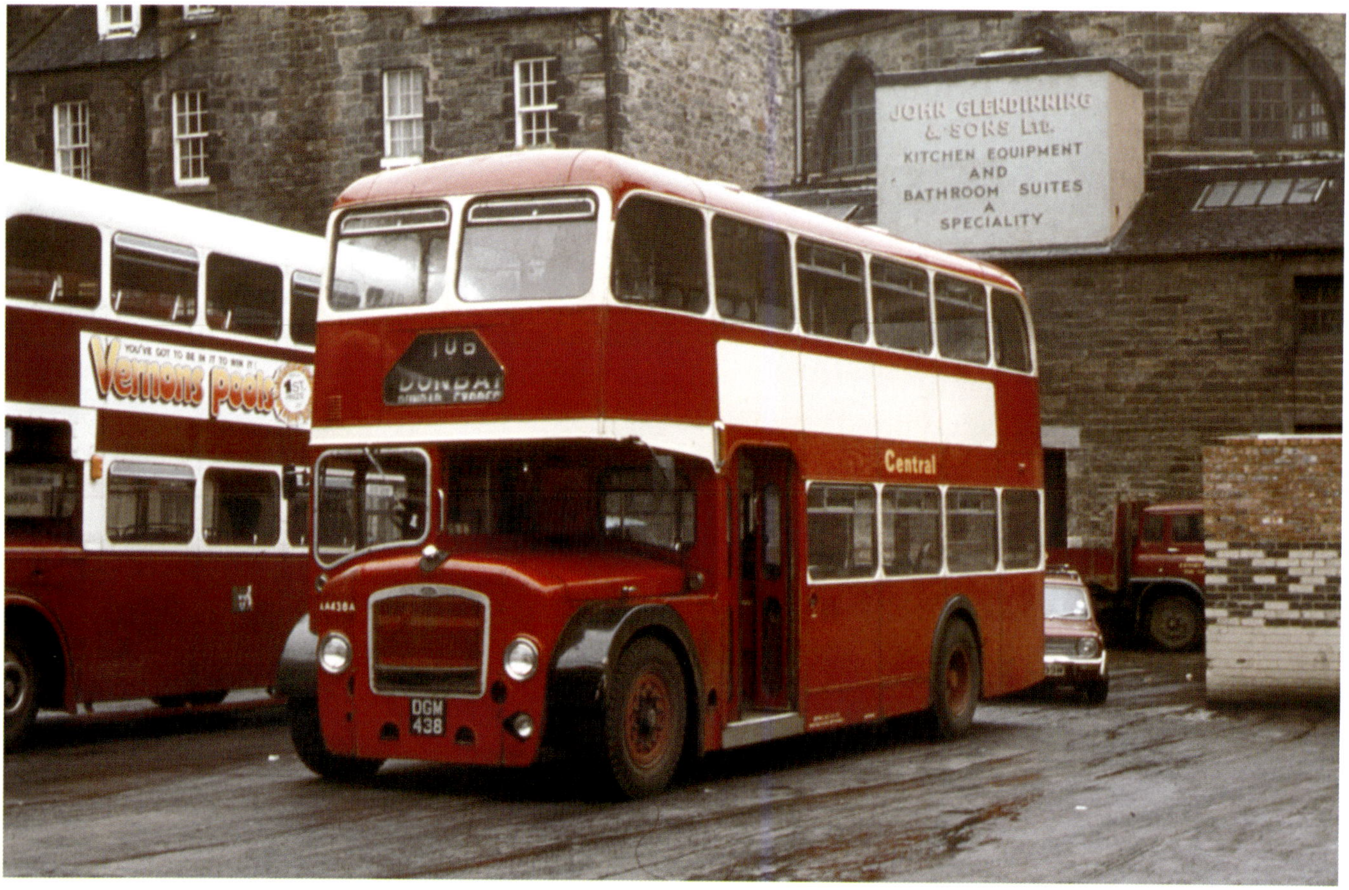

Unsure of its ownership and identity Eastern Scottish AA438 (DGM 438) is still in Central SMT livery but with its new fleet numbers at Edinburgh Bus Station during July 1977. (Donald Hudson)

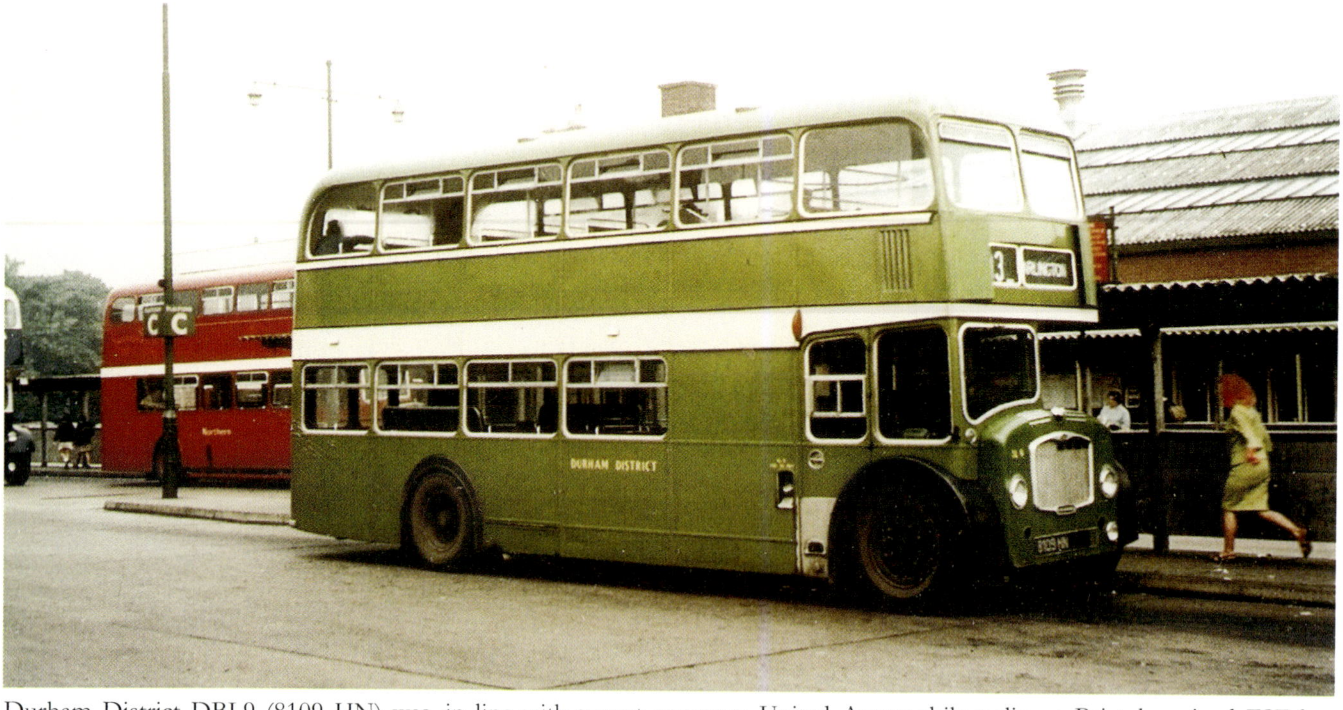

Durham District DBL9 (8109 HN) was, in line with parent company United Automobile policy, a Bristol engined FSF but differed from the vehicles in the general United fleet with reversed destination display layout, white window rubbers and additional lower deck window slider. Received in September 1962 this bus together with the other four were absorbed by United Automobile in July 1969. (E. A. Wood)

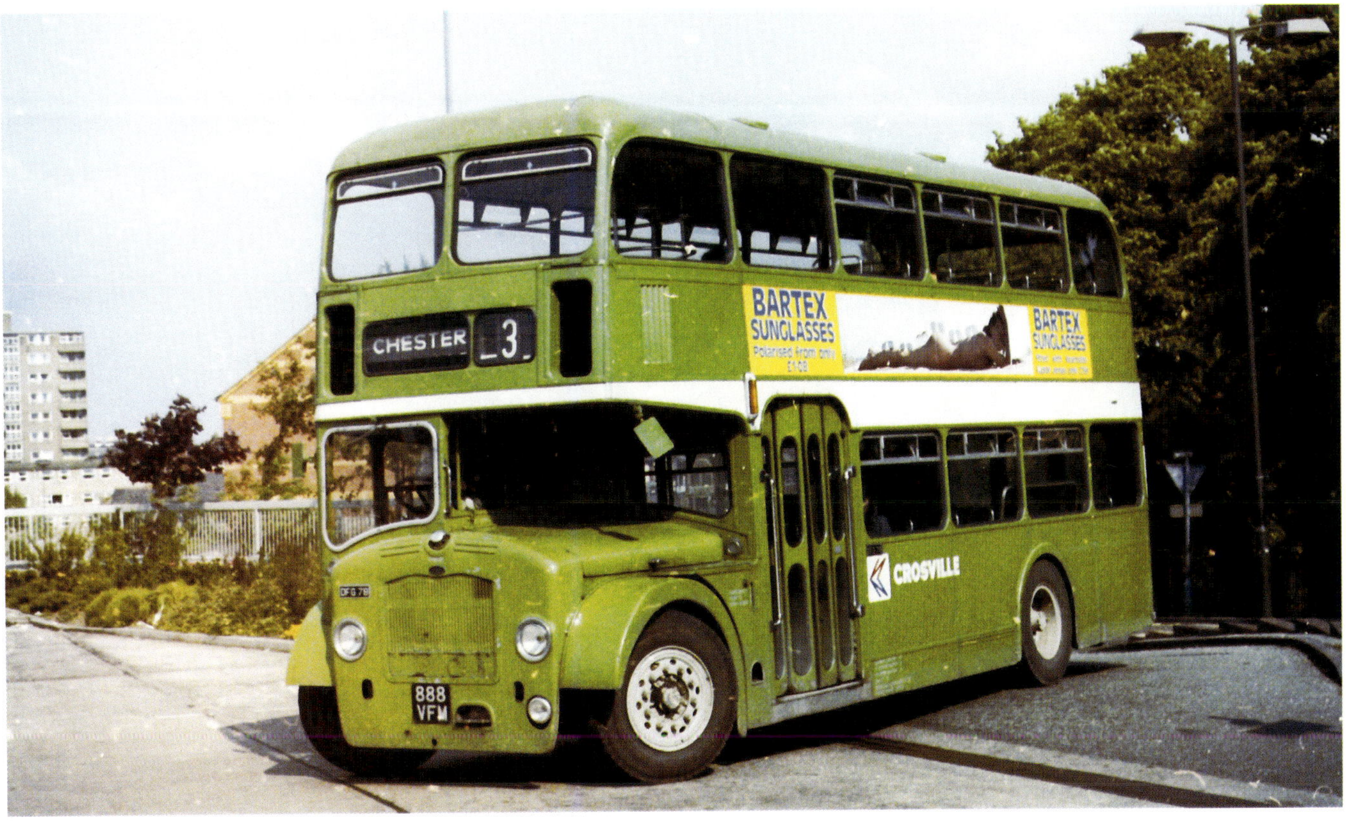

Crosville DFG78 (888 VFM) arrives at Chester Bus Station on a journey from Mold on Service B3, although the number blind of the first track has broken, and was one of the final nine FSFs for the company. (Author's collection)

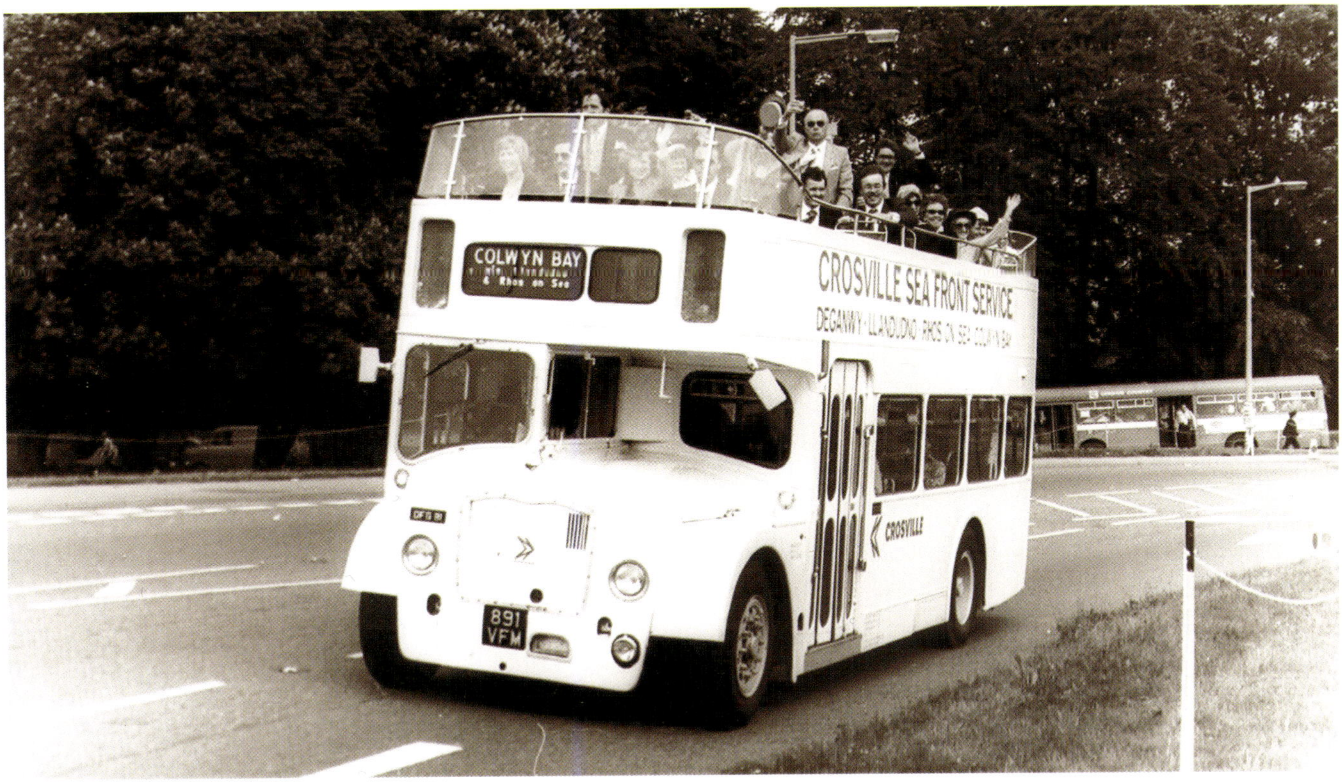

Crosville DFG81 (891 VFM), a 1962 FSF6G, was converted to open top O34+26F by the company in February 1977 and is seen here on "Derby Day" on its way to Epsom Racecourse. Vehicles such as this were often hired to be used as grandstands at events such as this in the days before "tachograph" laws affected private hire arrangements. Open top double deckers were popular for hosting and pampering influential and highly regarded guests by many businesses. (Author's collection)

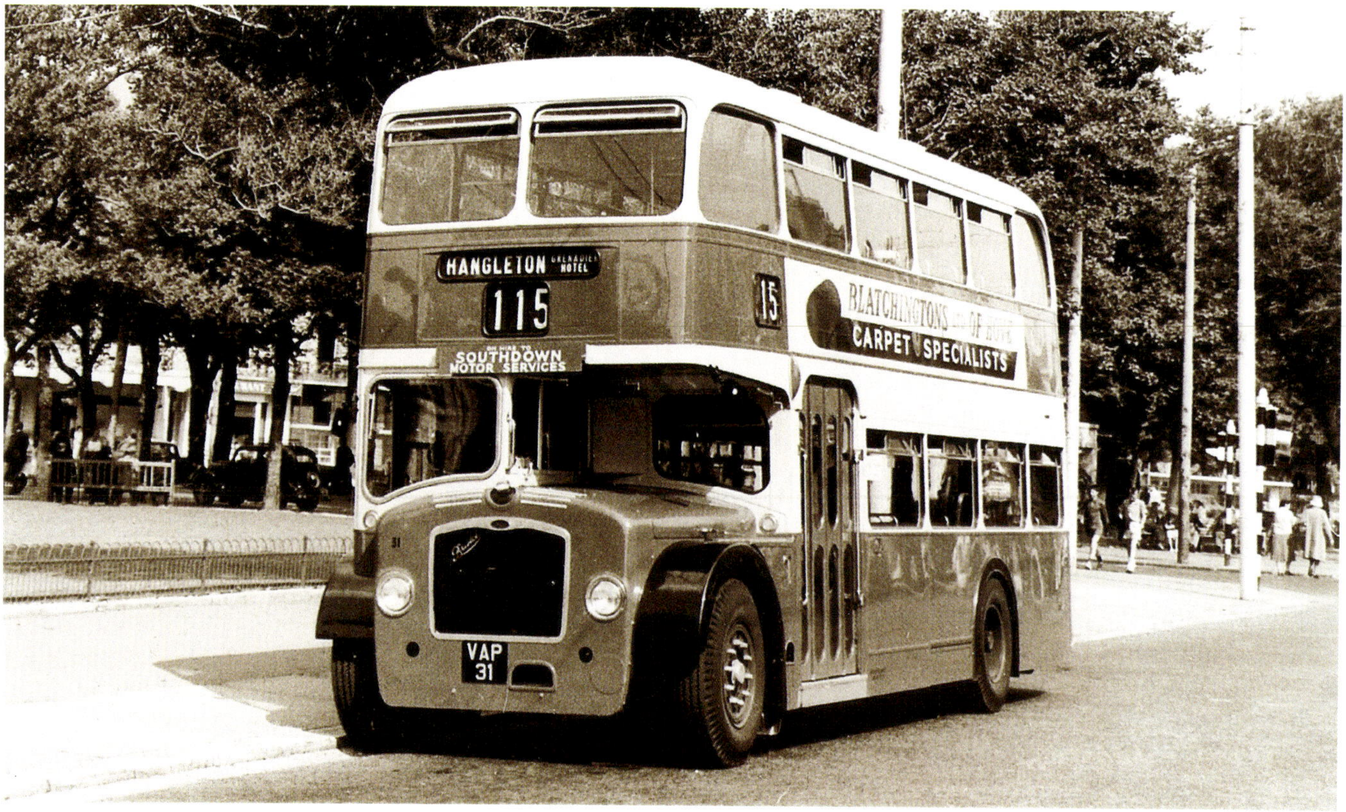

On hire to Southdown Motor Services is indicated on the "slip board" below the destination display on Brighton Hove & District 31 (VAP 31) as it stands at Old Steine in Brighton waiting to operate to Hangleton (Grenadier Hotel) on Service 115. (Denis Clark)

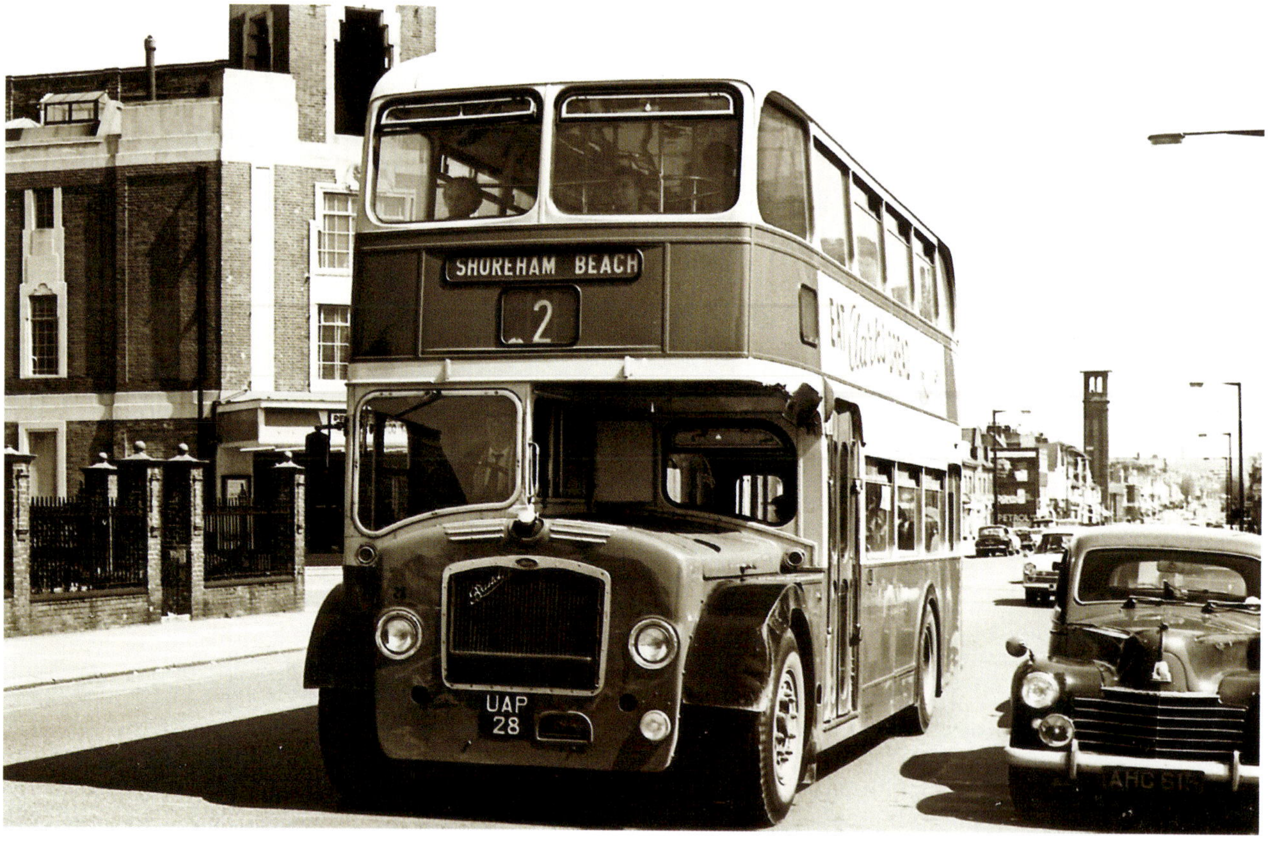

Brighton Hove & District 28 (UAP 28) passes a number of "classic" cars on Service 2 to Shoreham Beach but the lazy conductor has failed to use the canopy service number box that remains blank. (Peter Hirst)

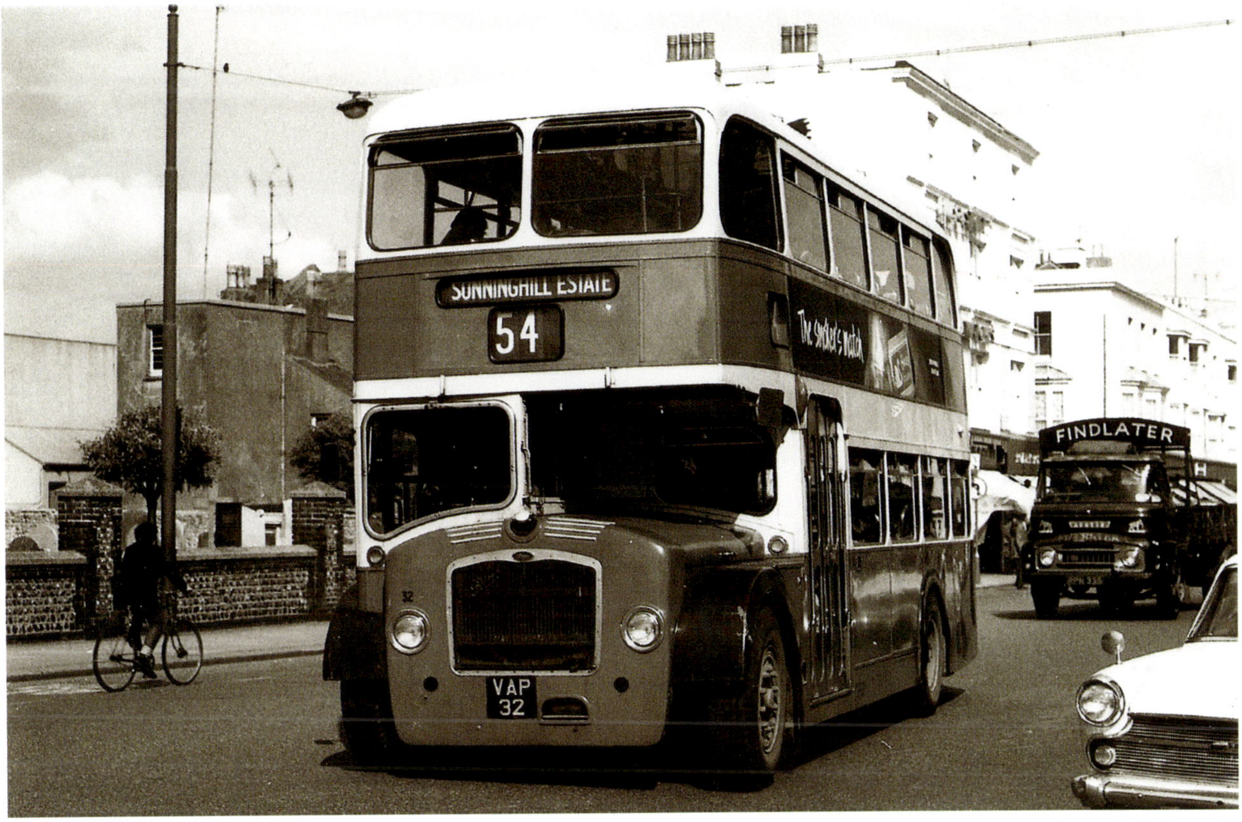

Oozing with 1960s atmosphere, including the street furniture, Brighton Hove & District 32 progresses through light traffic on Service 54 to Sunninghill Estate. (Peter Hirst)

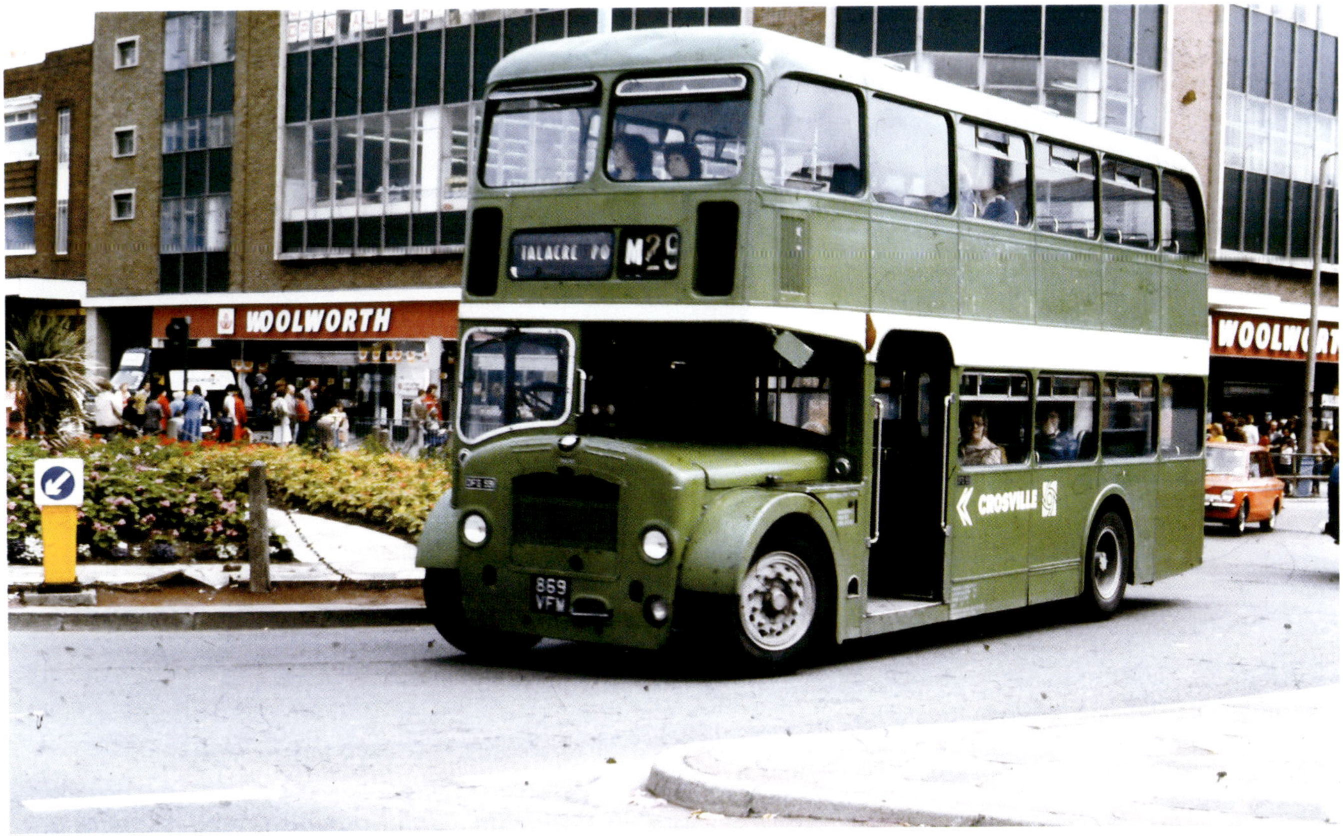

Crosville DFG59 (869 VFM), a 1961 FSF6G, tackles a roundabout in Rhyl on Service M29 to Talacre in August 1978. (Author's collection)

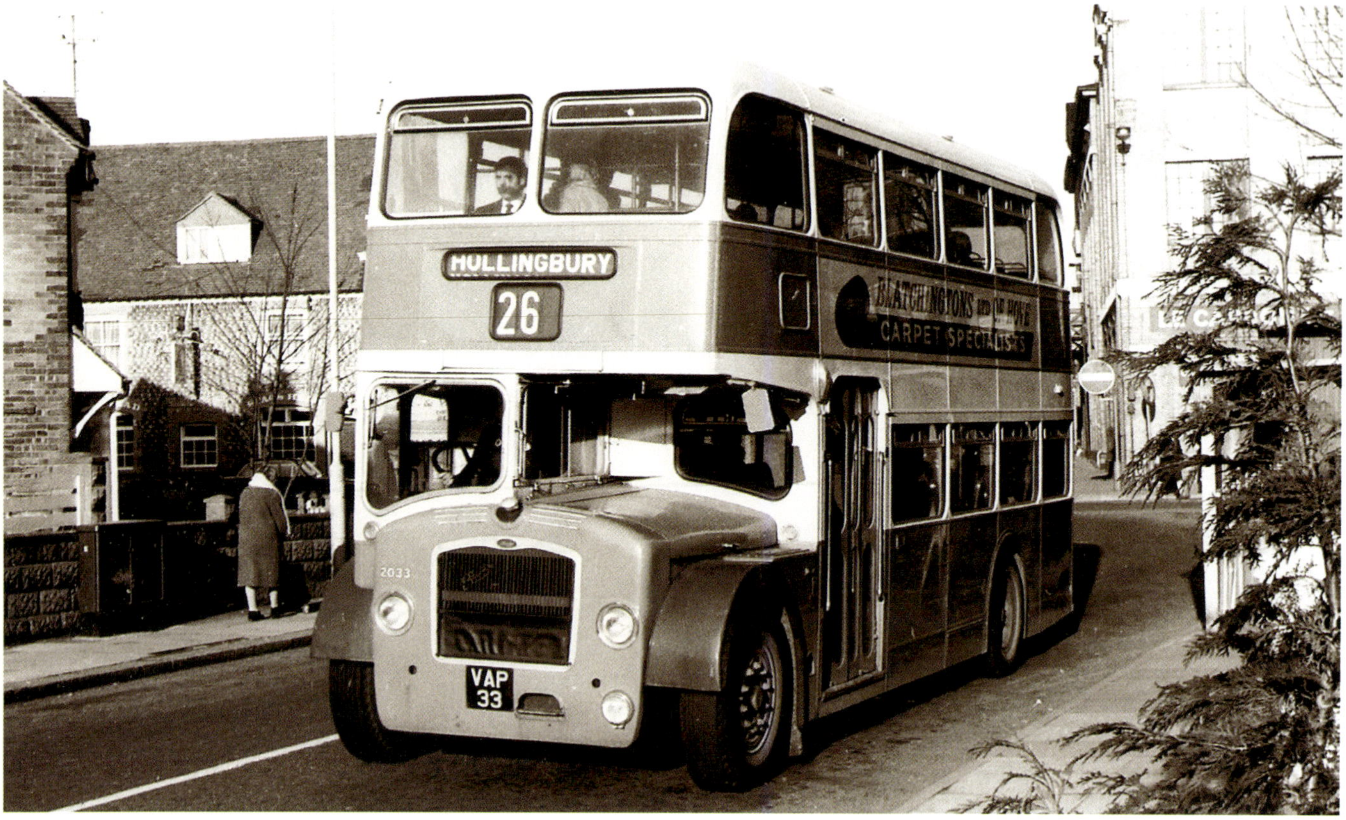

Although the canopy service number box has been painted over it has yet to be panelled over on Brighton Hove & District 33 (VAP 33) as it is seen heading for Hollingbury on Service 26. (Denis Clark)

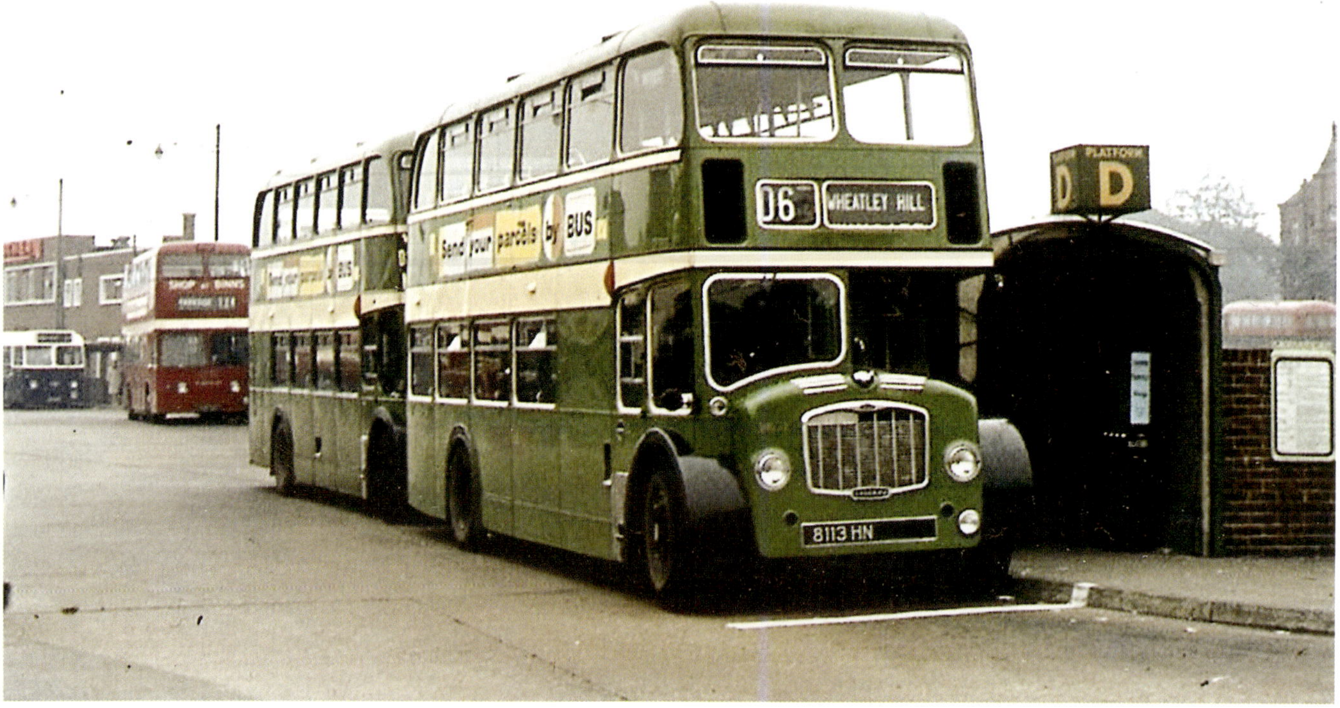

Durham District DBL13 (8113 HN) was the last FSF for English operators with subsequent deliveries being eight for United Welsh in November 1962 and eleven for Central SMT in September 1963. (Author's collection)

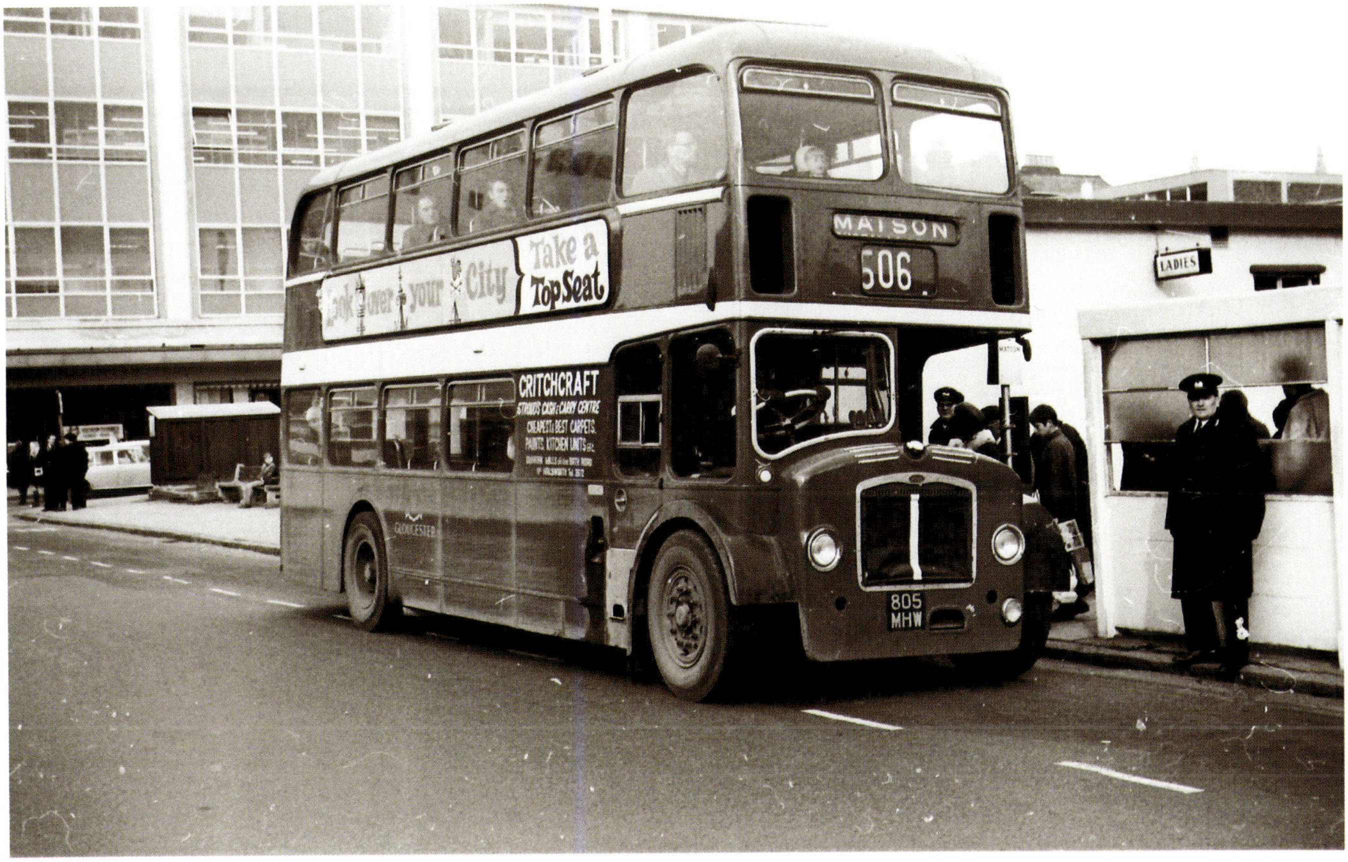

A Bristol Omnibus Company Inspector observes the photographer as this picture of G6040 (805 MHW), a 1961 FSF6G, was taken at King's Square in Gloucester when it was working a Gloucester City Service 506 journey to Matson. (Author's collection)

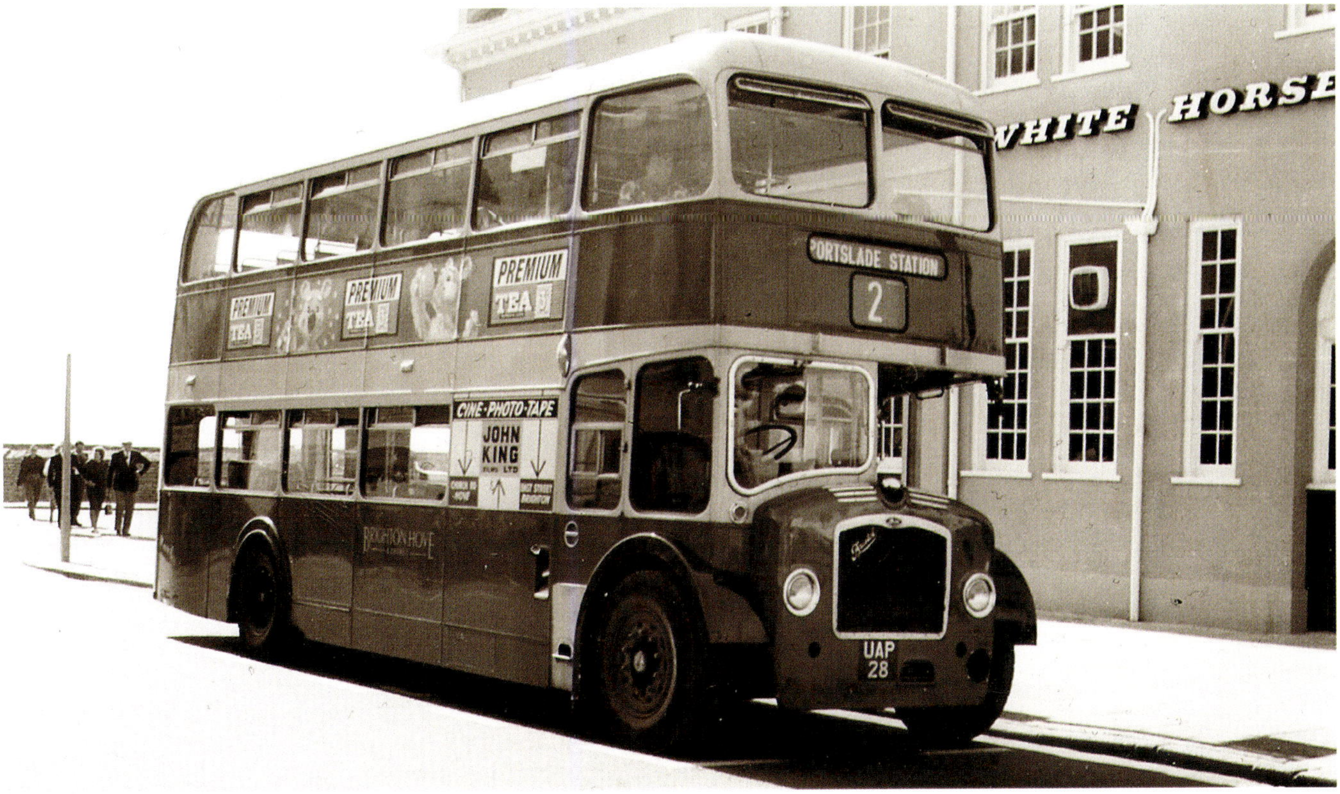

Brighton Hove & District 28 (UAP 28) was one of three FSFs delivered to the company in February 1961 and is seen at work on Service 2 to Portslade Station. (Bristol Vintage Bus Group)

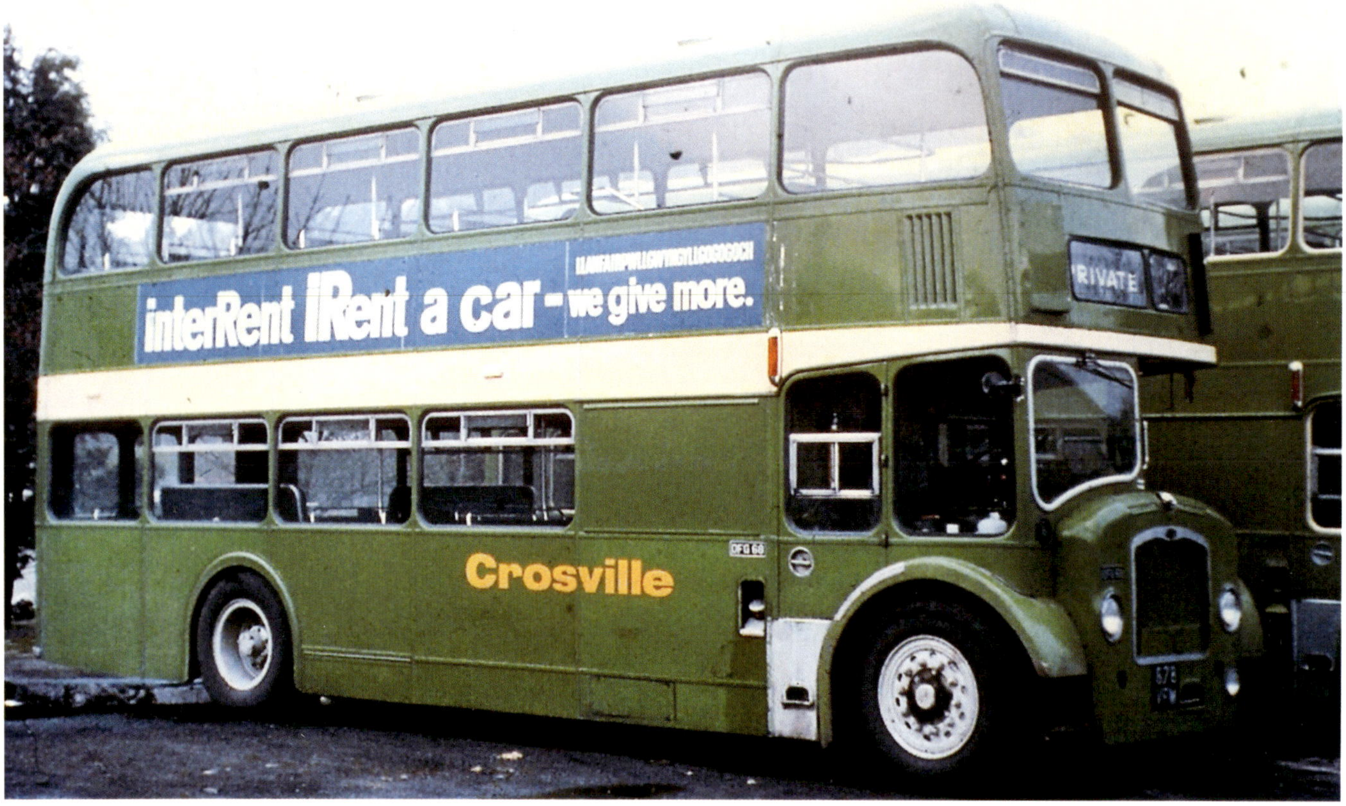

Carrying the final large upper and lower case pre-NBC fleet name DFG68 (878 VFM) stands next to what can only be described, in my opinion, as the most drab and totally uninspiring bus livery ever. In fact, it was pleasing to see advertisements to break up this boring look. (Author's collection)

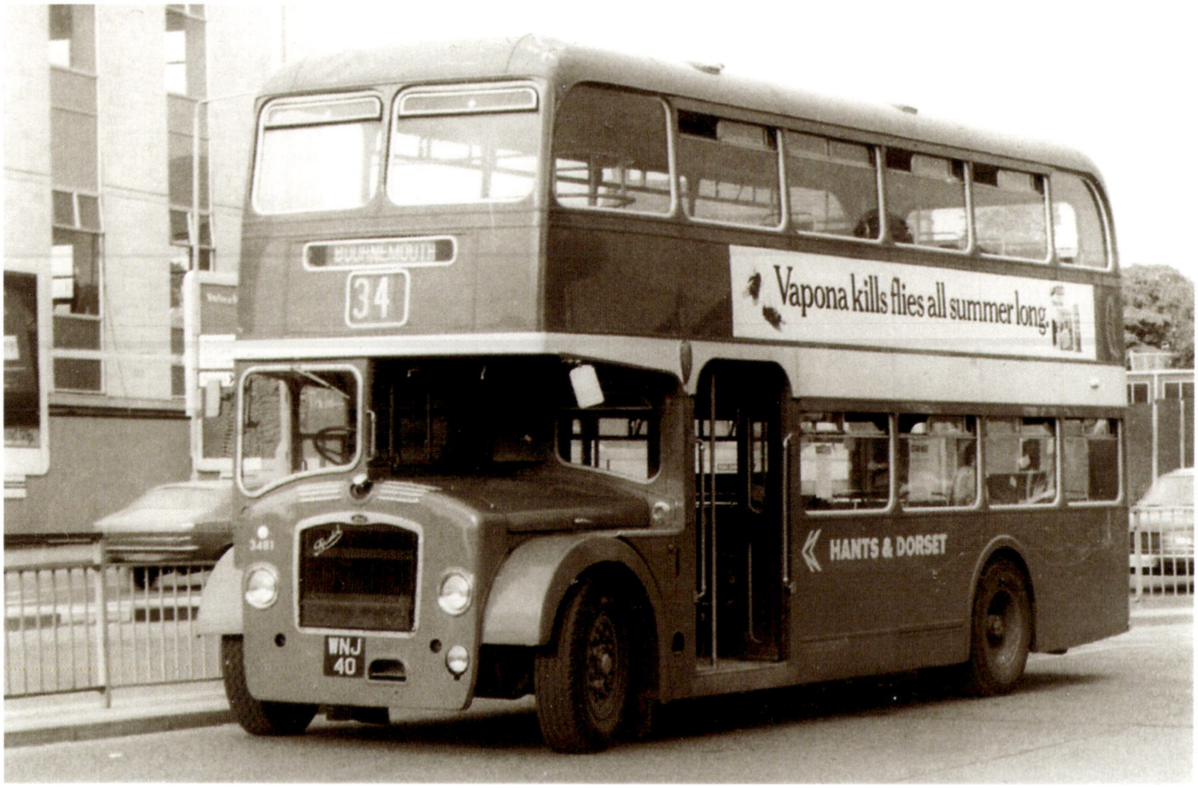

Seen at Poole Bus Station resting between duties is Hants & Dorset 3481 (WNJ 40) ex Southdown FSF6B that was the last purchased by Brighton Hove & District in April 1962 and bought by H&D in 1974. (Brian Botley)

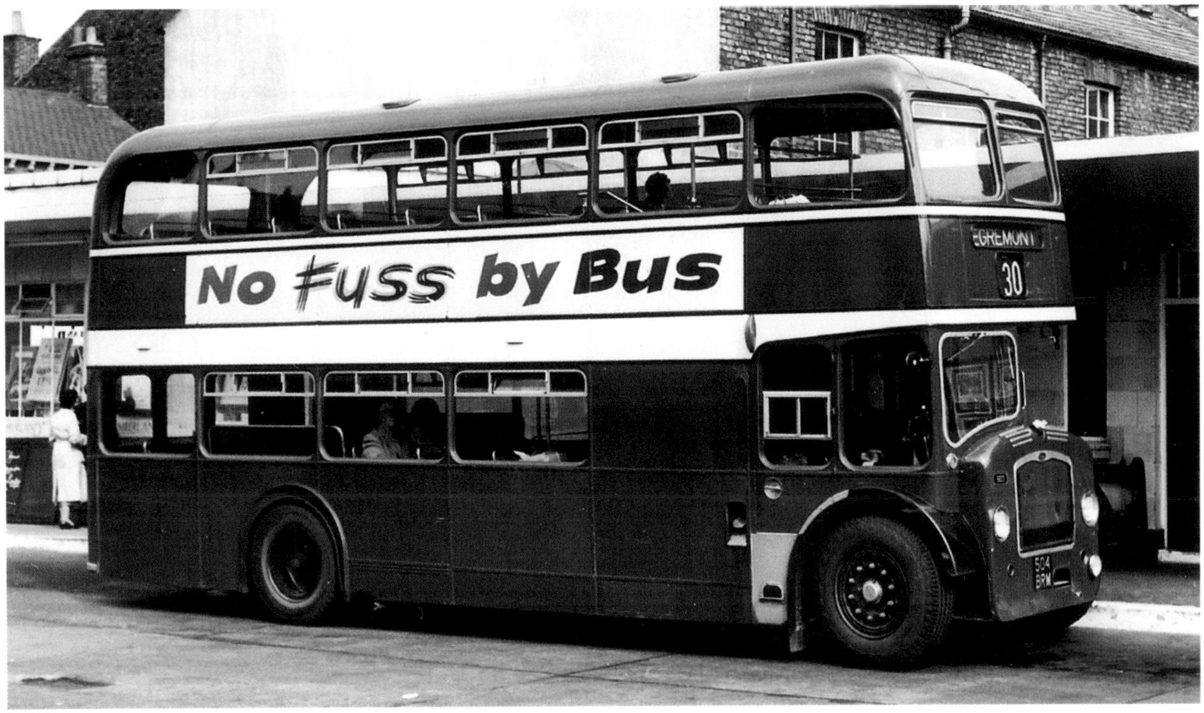

Cumberland 503 (504 BRM) a 1960 FSF6G seen at Carlisle Bus Station on 29th June 1962 was numbered C407 when delivered but renumbered in December 1961. Withdrawn from the fleet in 1973 it was bought by Martin, a dealer at Weaverham, in April 1973 and sold on to Green Bus Company in July 1973 who gave it fleet number 36. After the takeover by Midland Red it was numbered 2175 in November 1973 but not used and passed to Ensign, dealer at Silver End, in March 1974. It was exported to Holland in April 1974 and later registered 14-19 FB for use as a showroom in Sweden. (Gerry Mead)

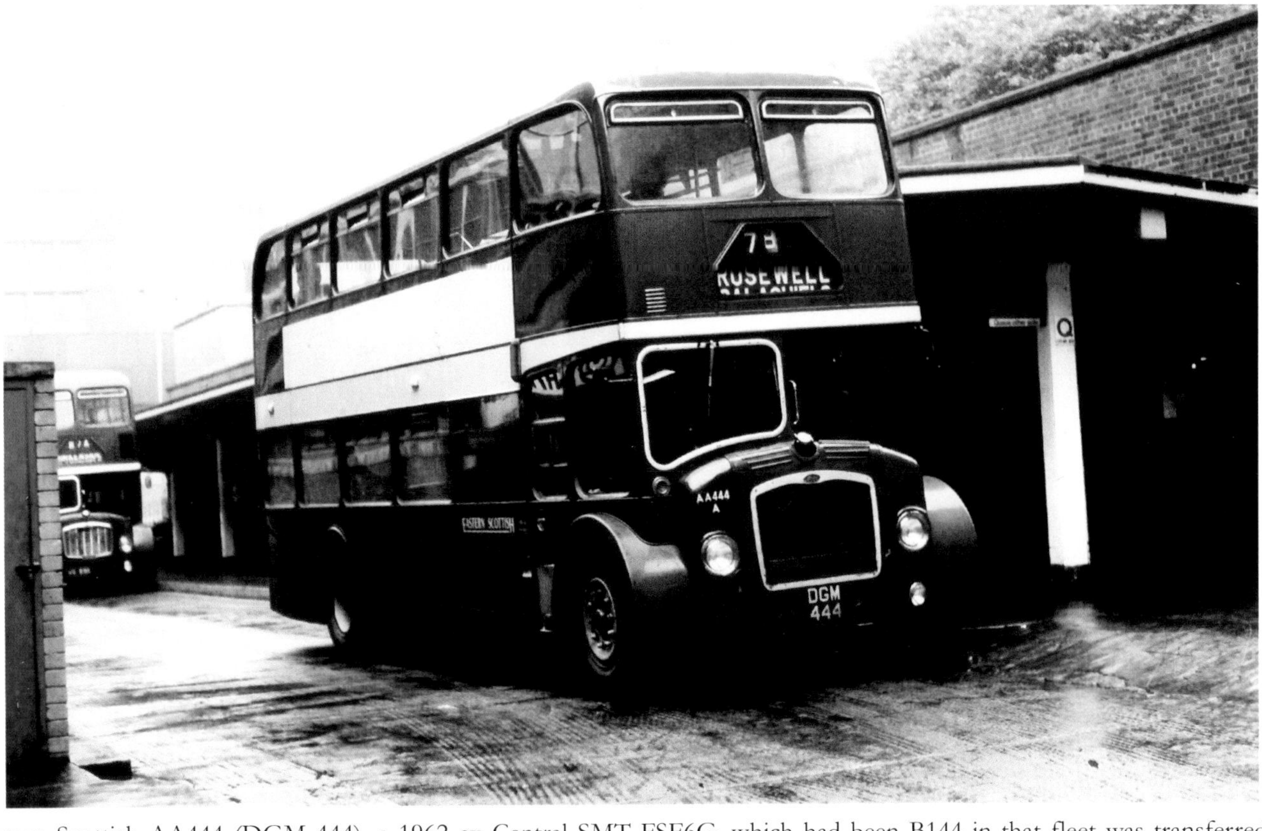

Eastern Scottish AA444 (DGM 444), a 1962 ex Central SMT FSF6G, which had been B144 in that fleet was transferred to Eastern Scottish in July 1977 together with five other FSFs. It was withdrawn in 1979 and sold to Muir, a Kirkcaldy dealer, in October of that year. (Kevin Lane)

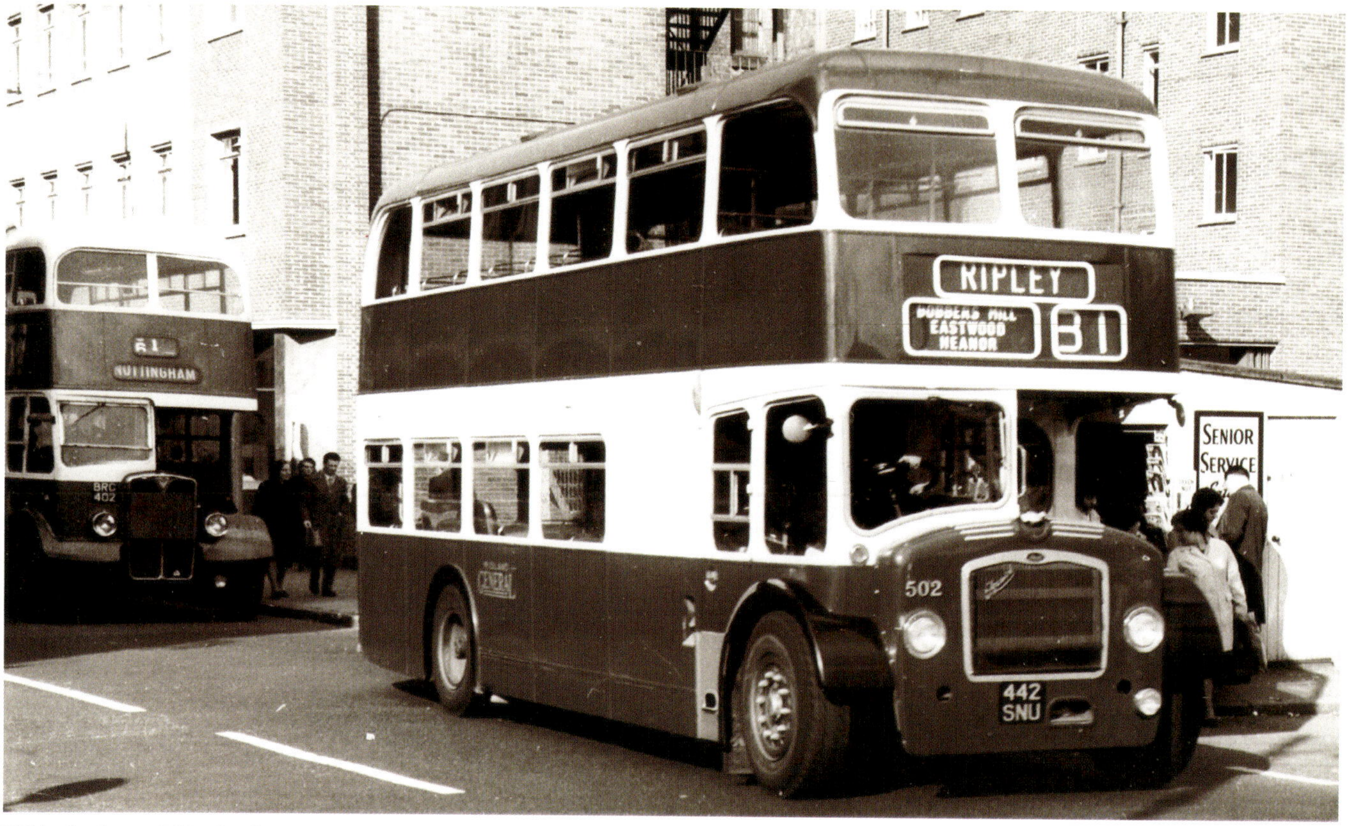

With the later ECW body style of no below window upper deck beading but with extra lower deck slider window ventilation and white glass rubbers Midland General 502 (442 SNU) looks in "fine fettle" on Service B1 to Ripley and had completed 15 years of service when withdrawn from the fleet during 1976. (Bristol Vintage Bus Group)

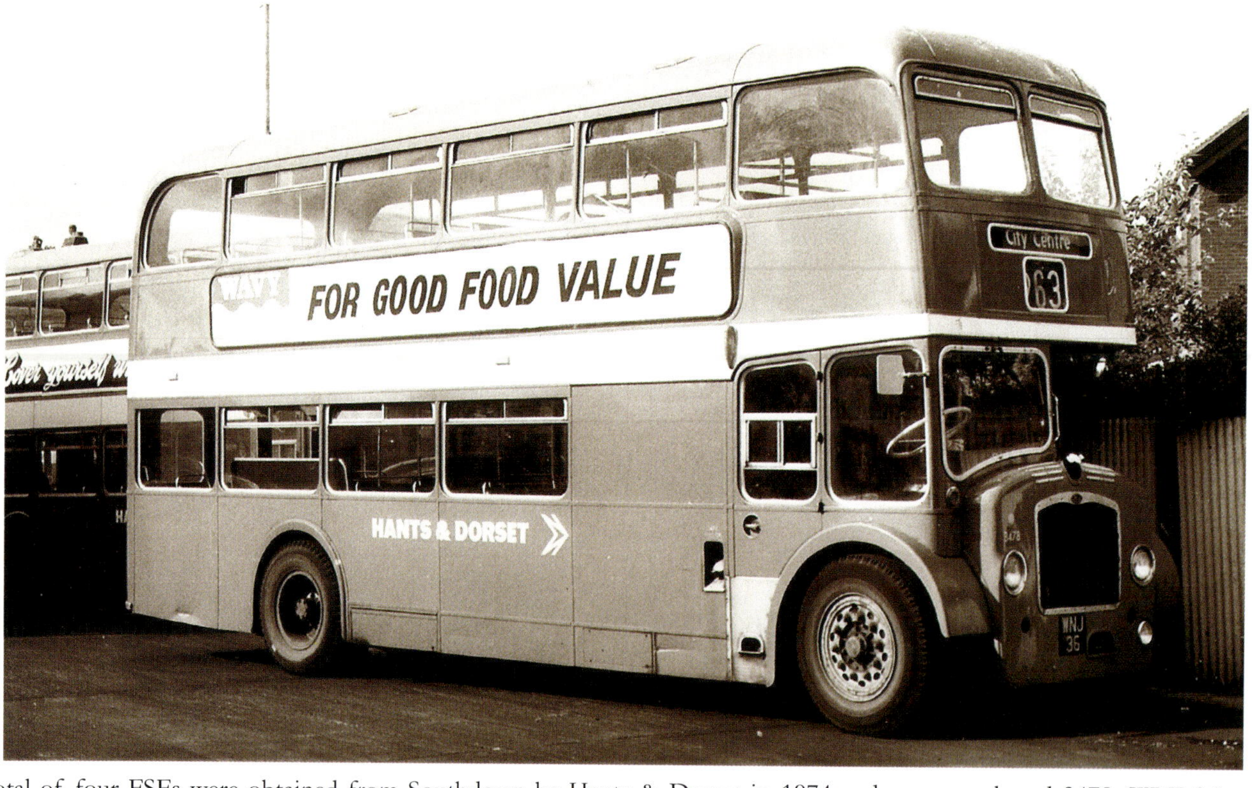

A total of four FSFs were obtained from Southdown by Hants & Dorset in 1974 and were numbered 3478 (WNJ 36), seen standing in Salisbury Garage between duties, and 3479–3481 (WNJ 38–40) with two more arriving in 1975 and numbered 3476 and 3477 (VAP 31/33). They were used on various routes including Salisbury City Services. (Denis Clark)

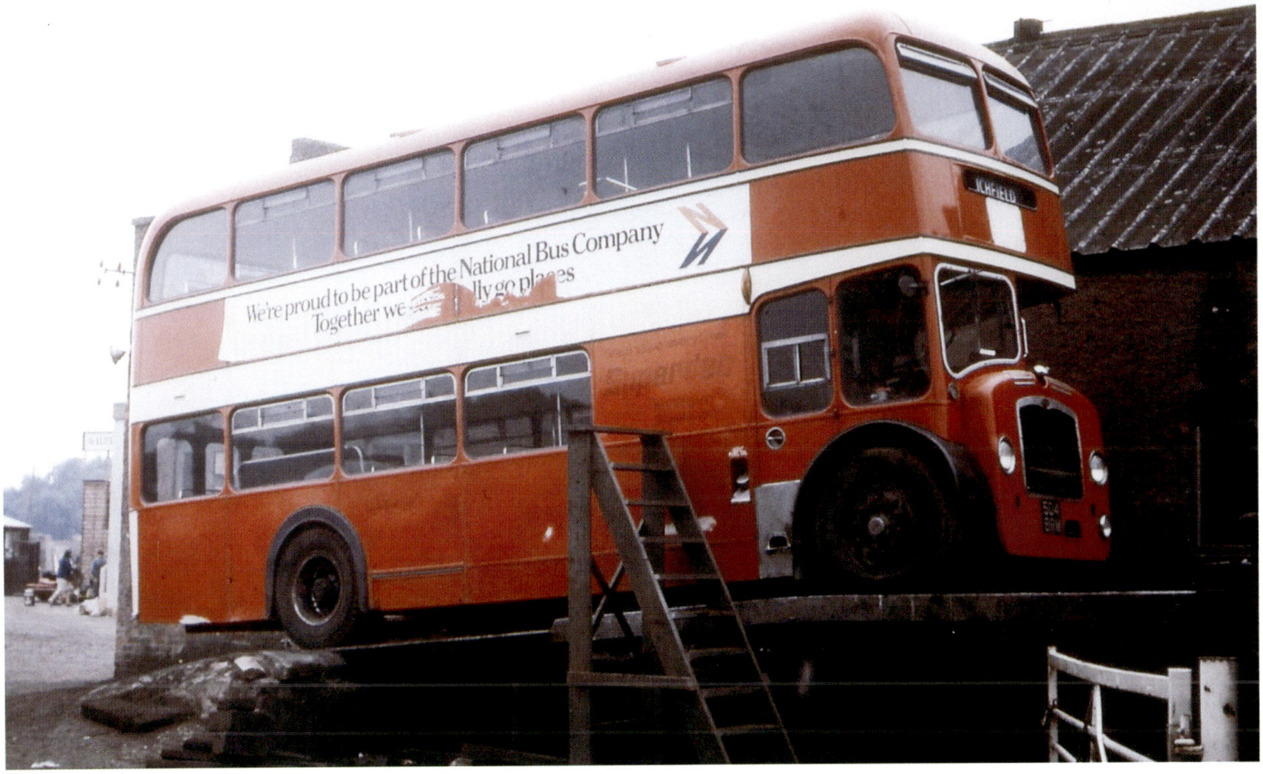

The last traces of its former NBC identity are being removed from Green Bus Company 36 (504 BRM) an ex-Cumberland Bristol FSF6G that was bought in July 1973. It is seen parked on the ramp at the depot at Taylors Lane in Rugeley, Staffordshire prior to entering service with its new owners. (Tony Robbins collection)

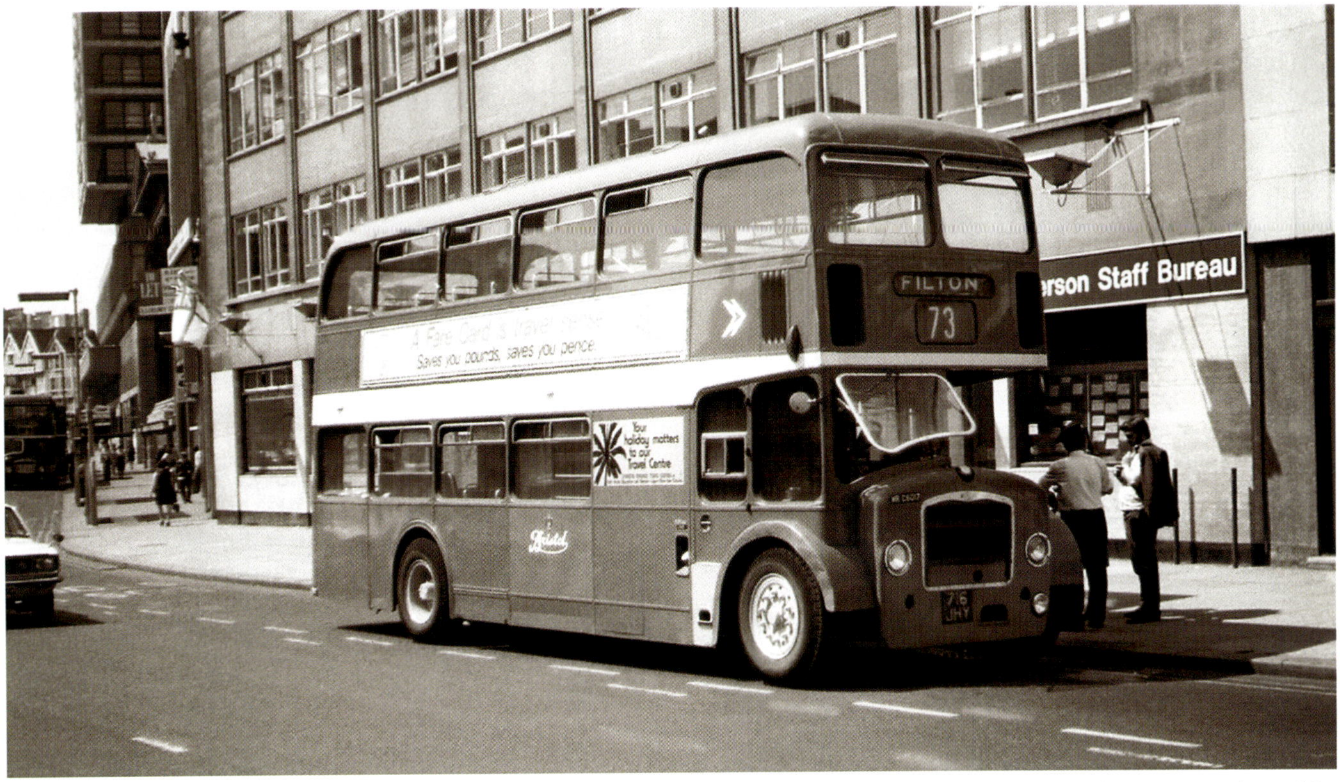

During 1976 Britain experienced a long, very hot and extremely dry summer with serious drought conditions as evidenced by nearly all windows, including the driver's, being open on Bristol Omnibus C6017 (716 JHY) on Tuesday 8th June 1976. Due to the drought bus washing was abandoned and many vehicles looked shabby as a result. (Stephen Dowle)

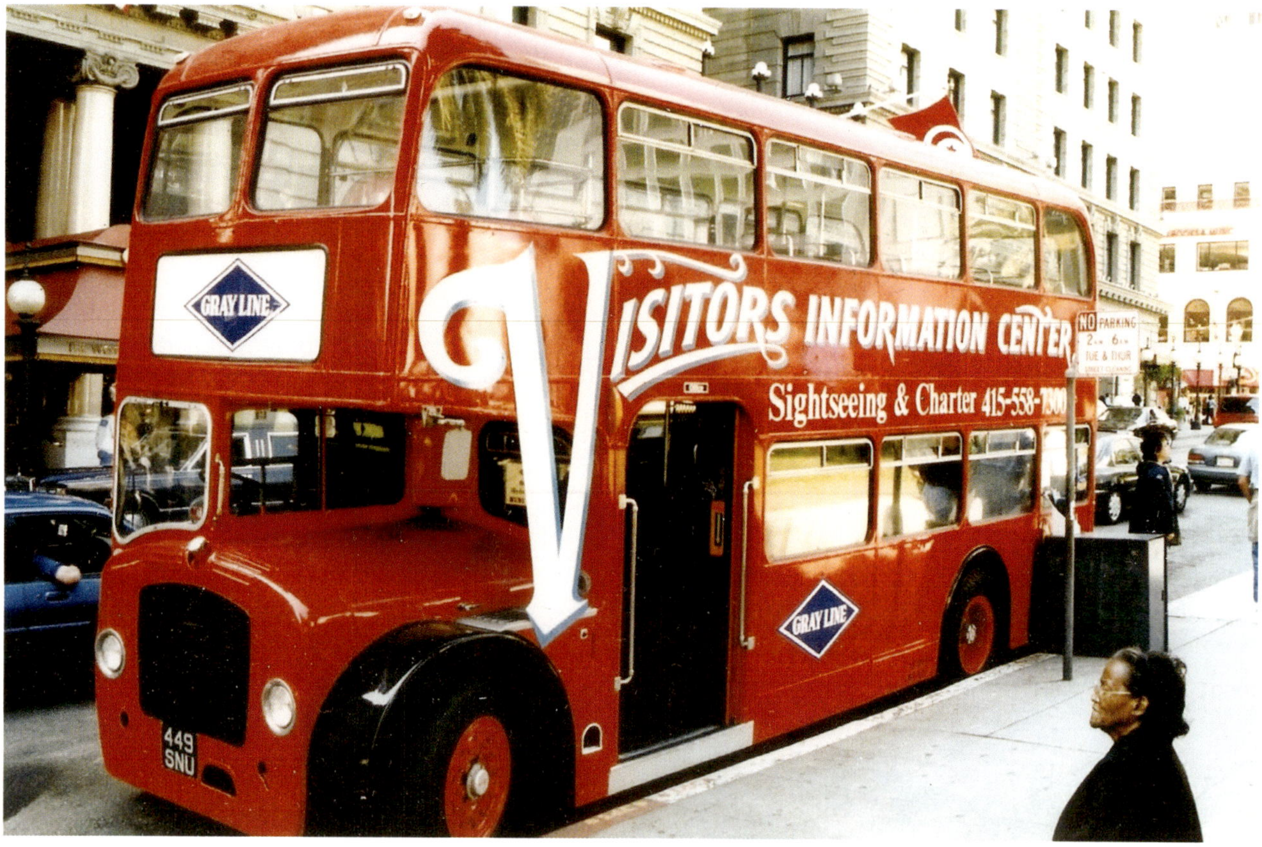

Gray Line used former Midland General 449 SNU as an information centre in San Francisco during 1997 to attract passengers for charter – or as we call it, private hire work – and sightseeing tours. (Leigh Quinell)

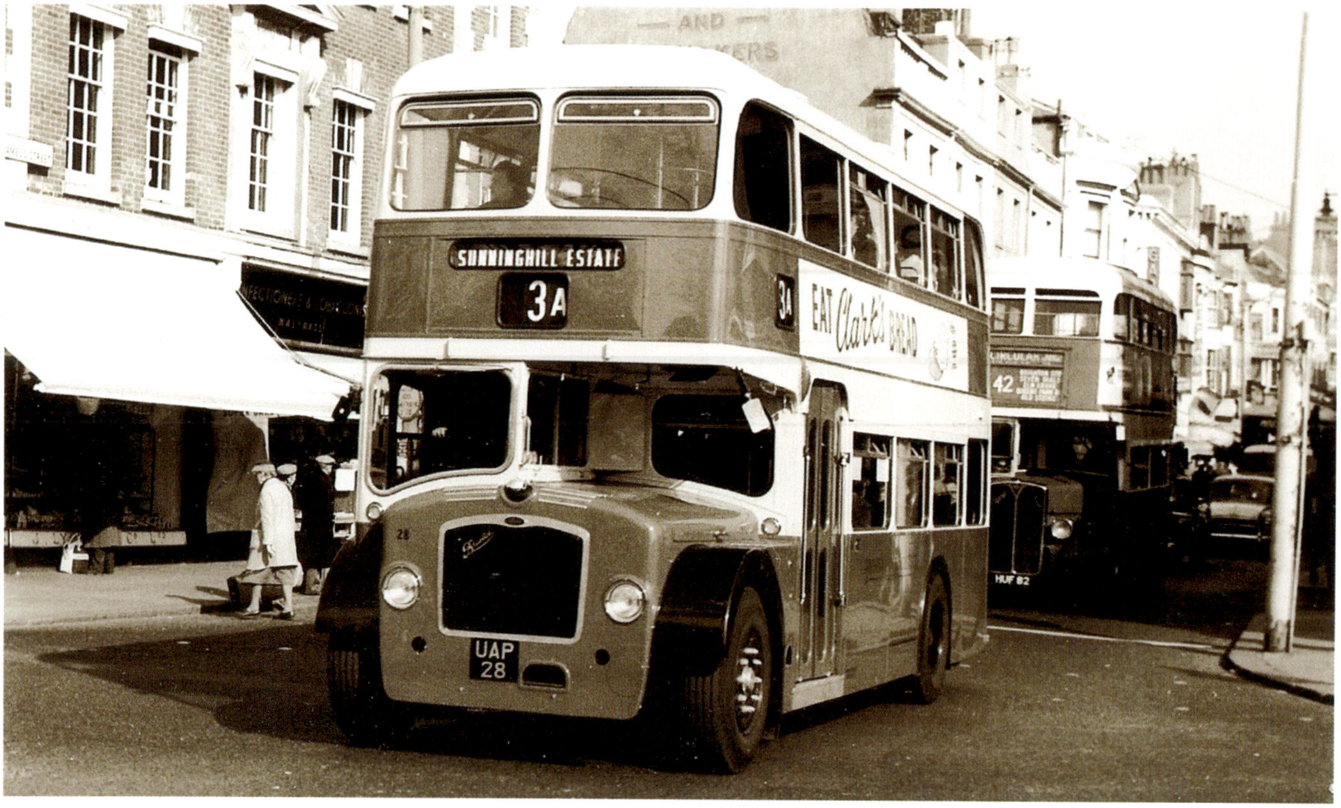

Brighton Hove & District 28 (UAP 28) on Service 3A to Sunninghill Estate appears to be chased by Brighton Corporation 82 (HUF 82), a 1947 AEC Regent III with Weymann H30+26R bodywork operating on Circular Service 42. (Denis Clark)

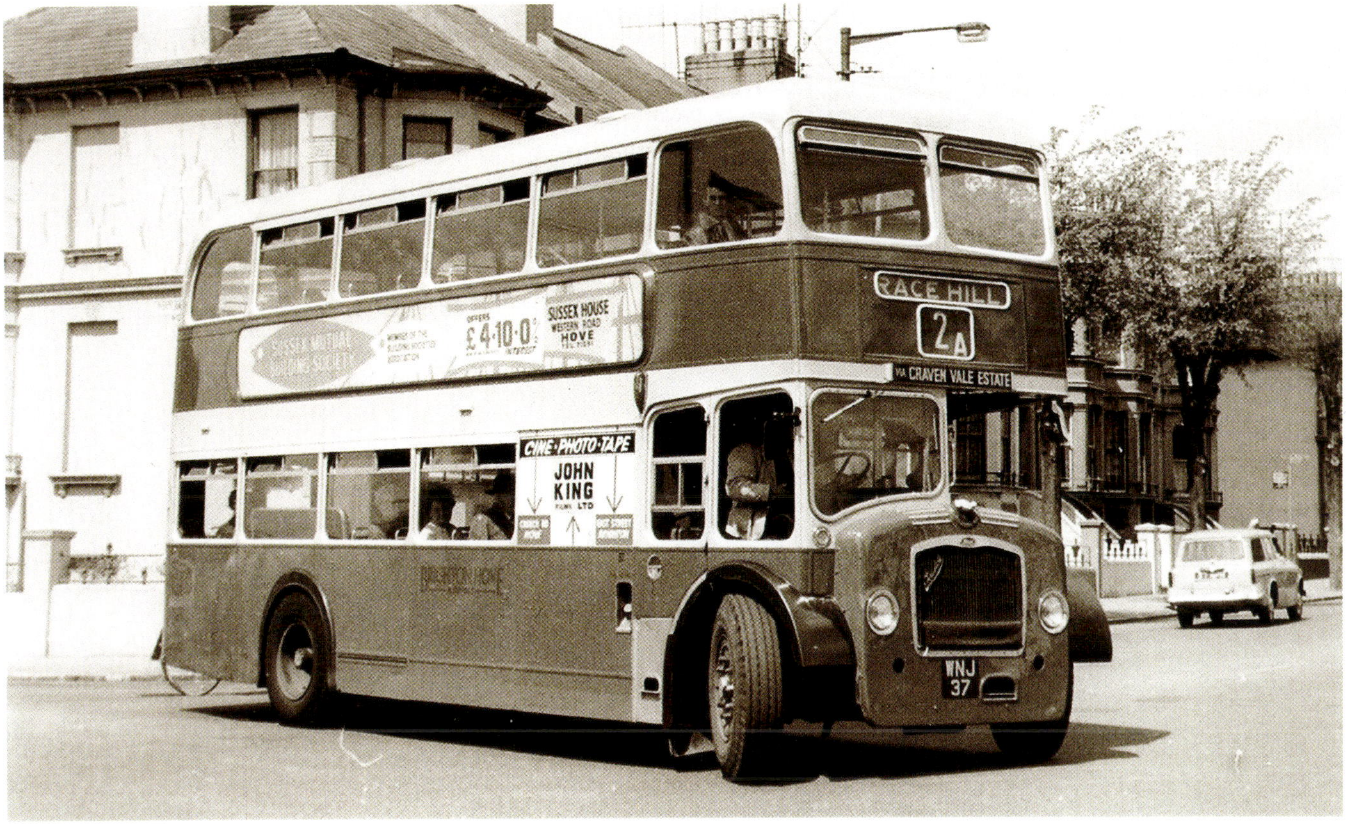

Smart looking Brighton Hove & District 37 (WNJ 37) carries a 'via Craven Vale Estate' slip board on a journey to Race Hill on Service 2A. (Denis Clark)

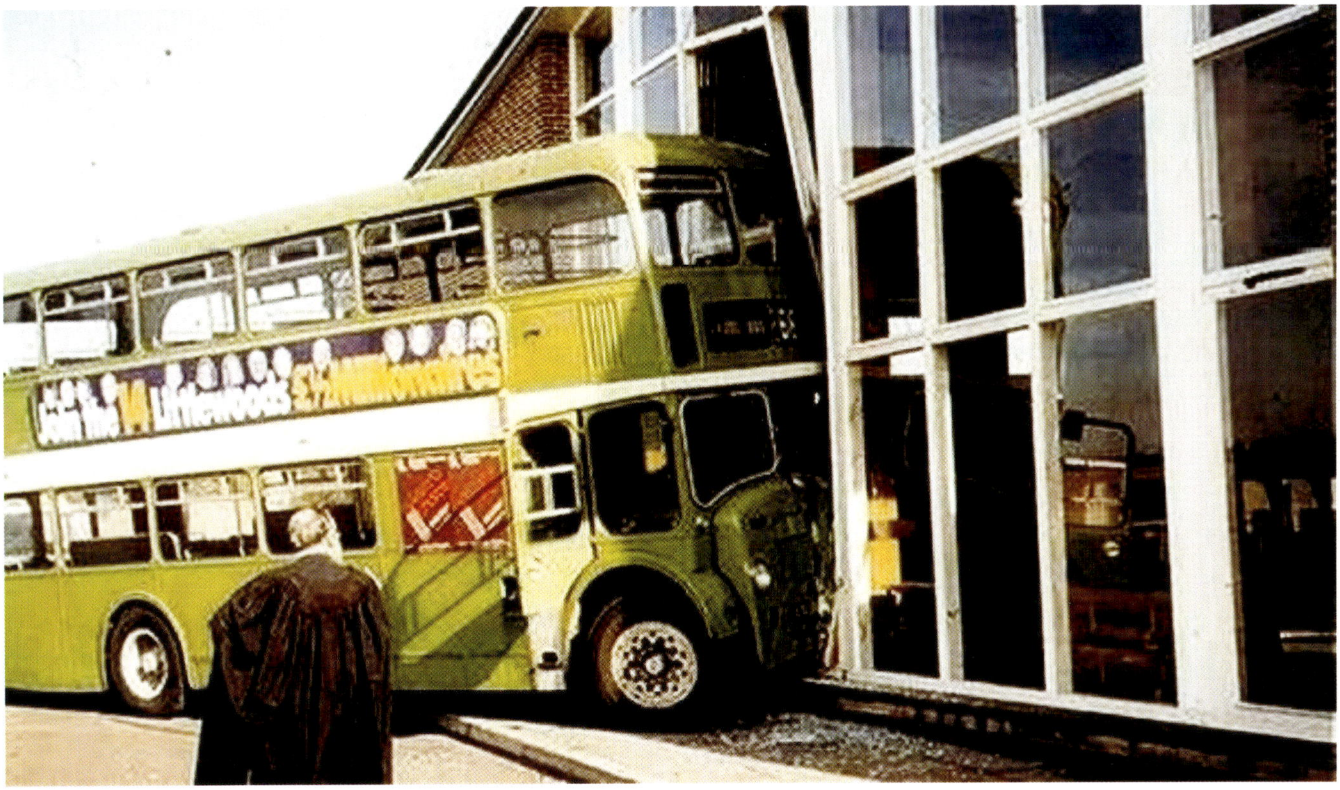

After Crosville DFG66 (876 VFM) had dropped off pupils at King's School in Chester it mounted the kerb and caused quite significant damage to the gymnasium, much to the concern of the headmaster viewing the aftermath but creating much entertainment for the children. (Rob Sly)

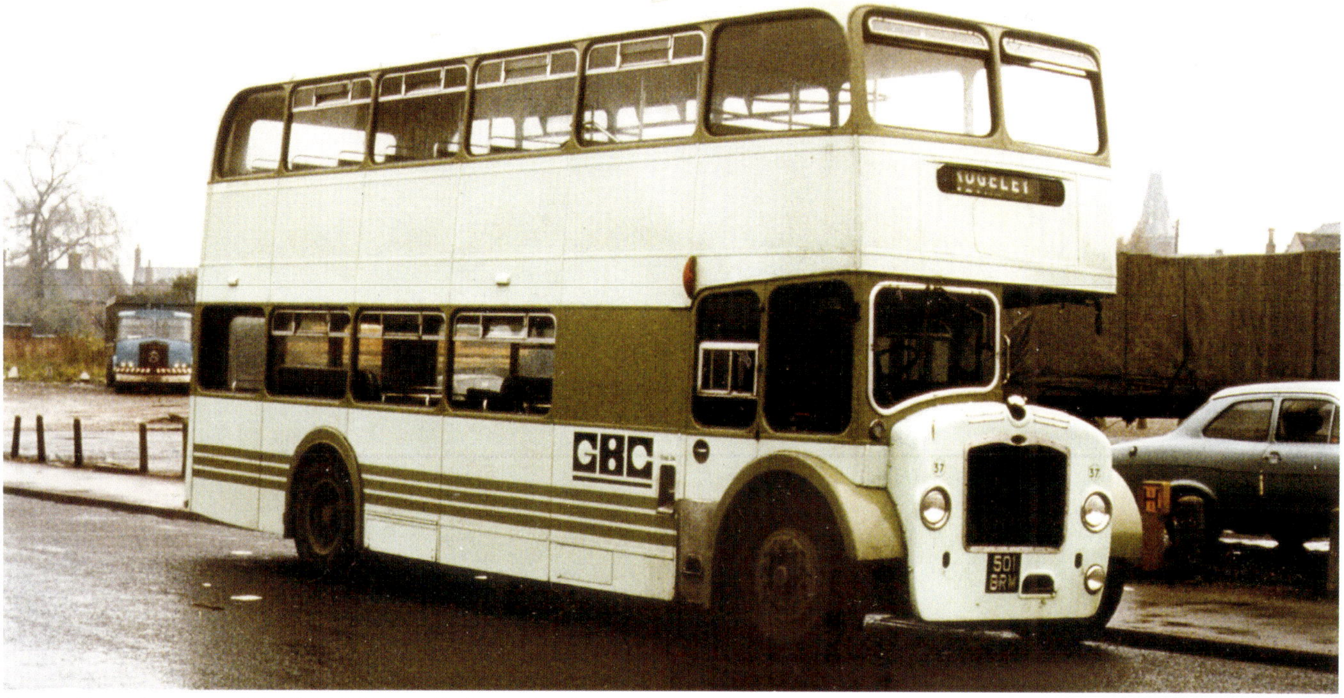

Green Bus Company 37 (501 BRM), a 1960 ex Cumberland FSF6G, was purchased in July 1973 only to be withdrawn five months later in November when the company was taken over by Midland Red. It is pictured in Rugeley during its short period with Green Bus. (Bristol Vintage Bus Group)

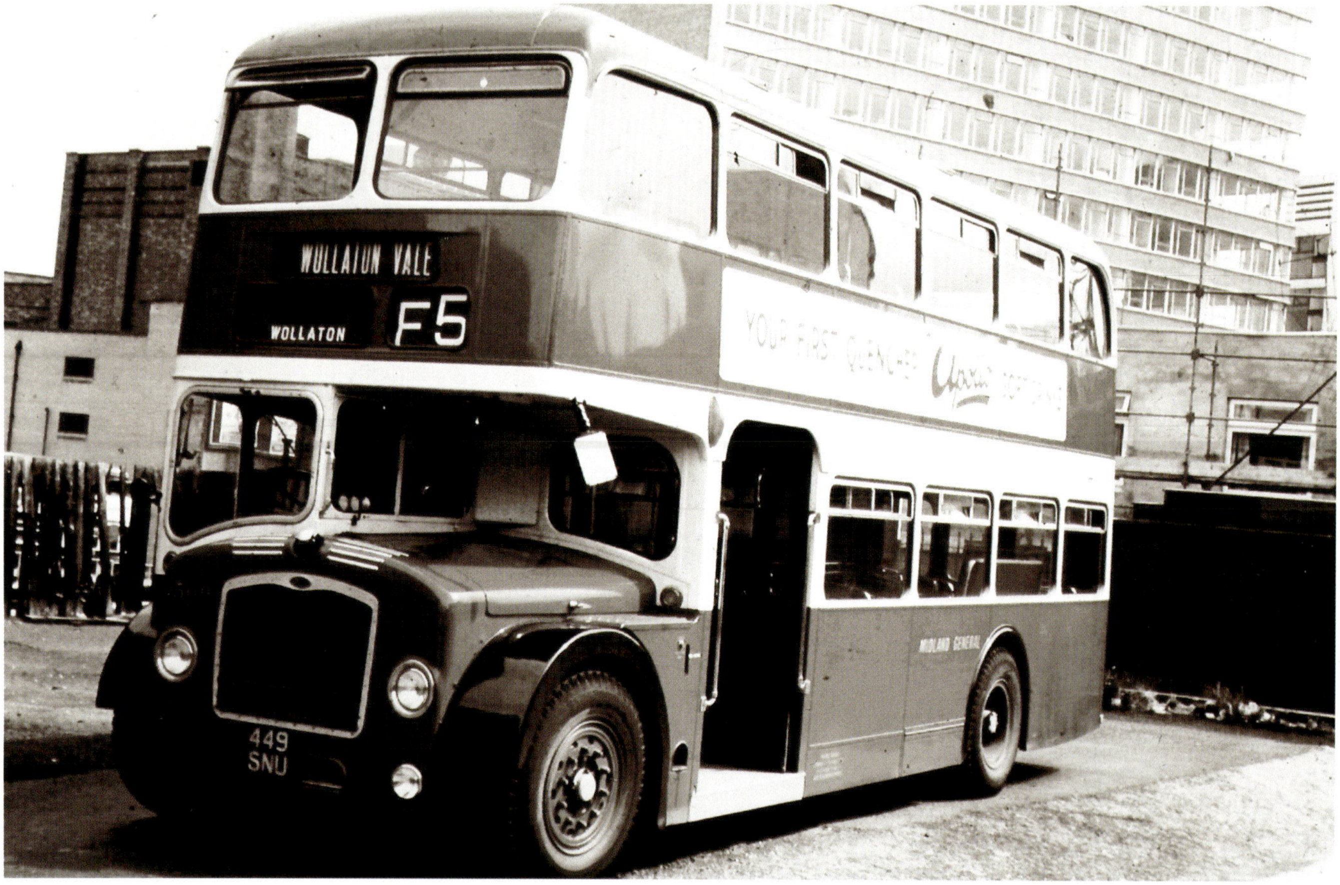

The unusual blue livery gives a pleasant look to Midland General 509 (449 SNU), a 1962 FSF6G standing at Nottingham, ready to work a journey to Wollaton Vale on Service F5. (Author's collection)

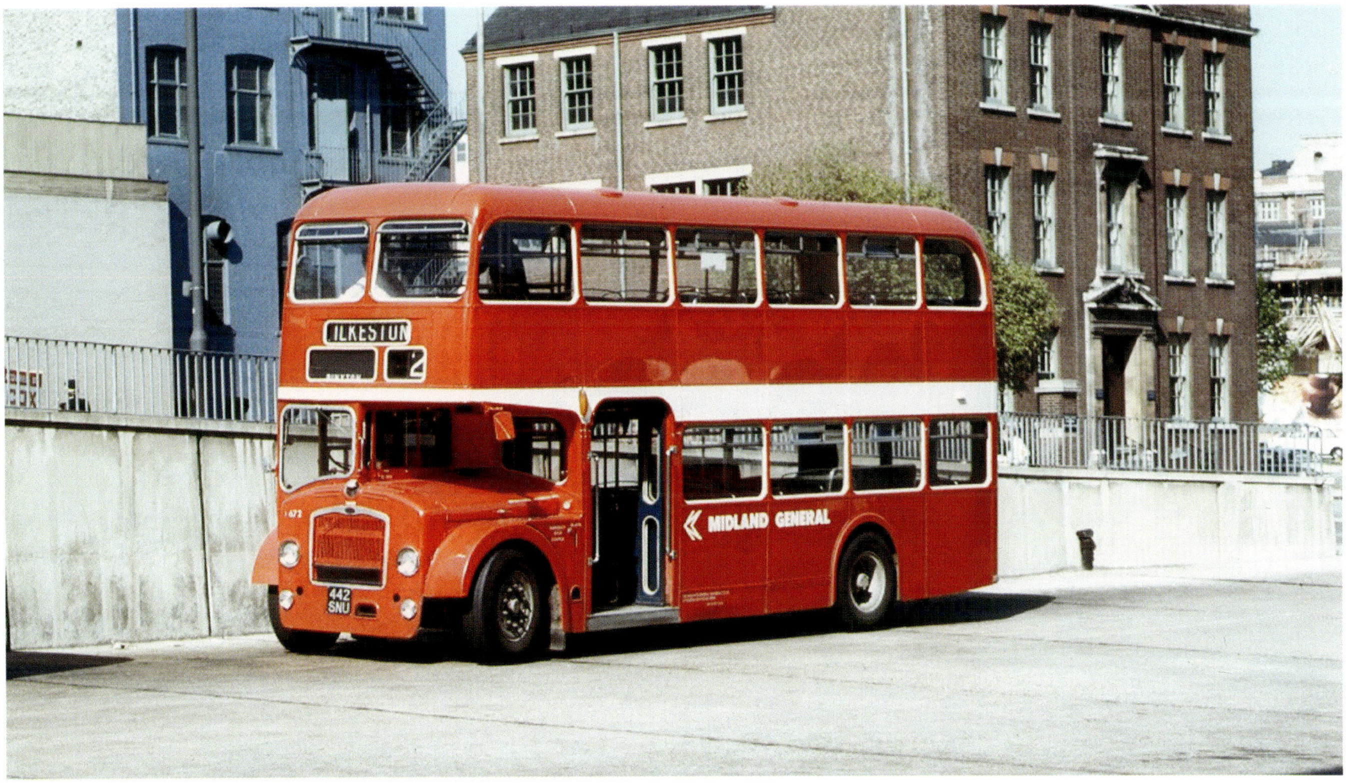

Even NBC poppy red livery doesn't detract from the clean lines and style of the Eastern Coach Works body on Midland General's 672 (442 SNU) one of five FSF6Gs received by the company in November 1961. (Cliff Essex)

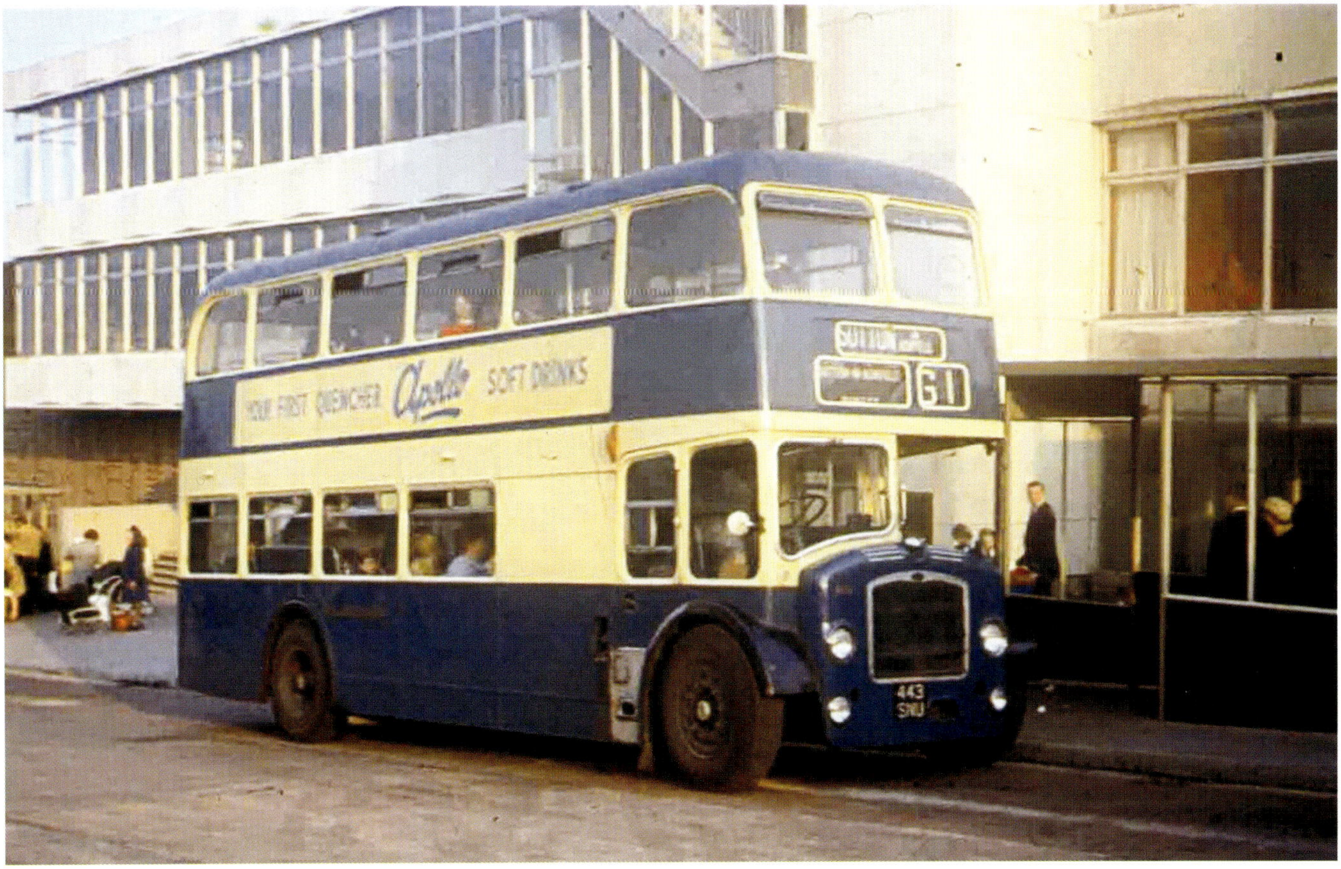

Midland General 673, originally 503 (443 SNU), has a reasonable tally of passengers when working Service G1 at Sutton in Ashfield during September 1972. (Cliff Essex)

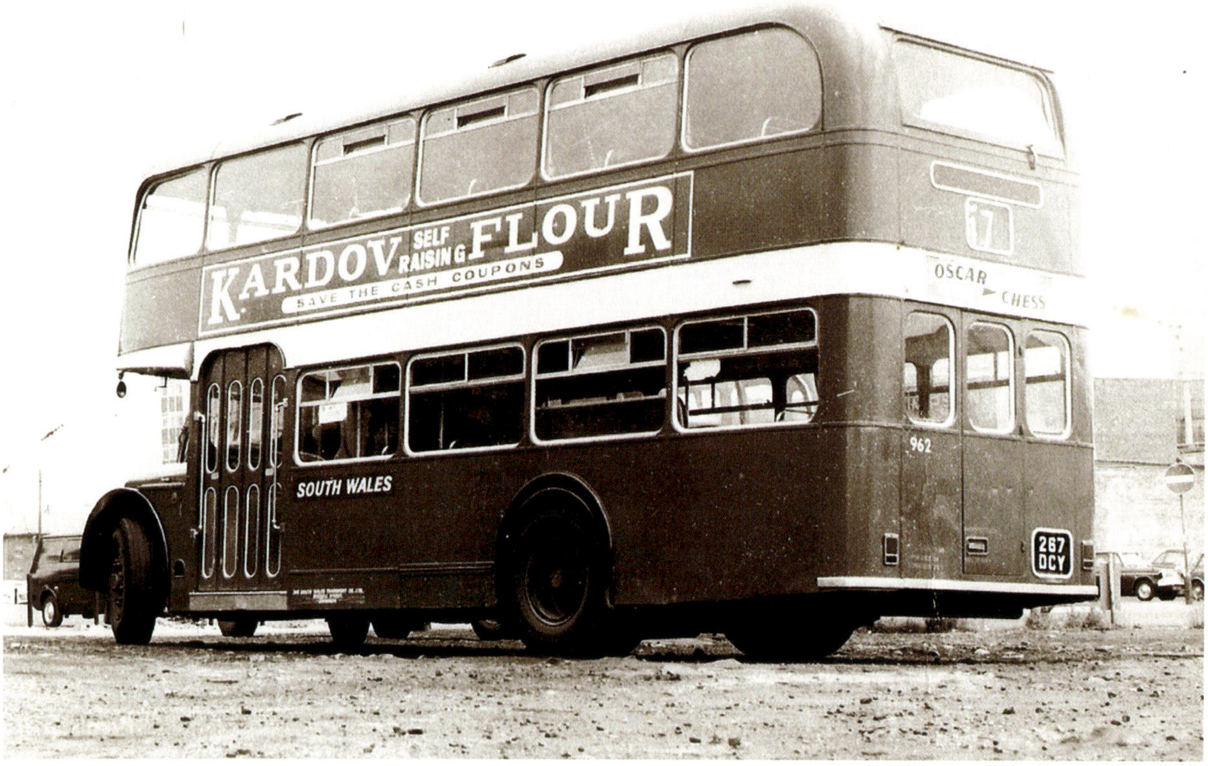

An unusual low aspect rear view of South Wales 962 (267 DCY), a 1962 ex United Welsh, clearly shows the temporary vinyl fleet name and additional lower deck sliding ventilator. As with many NBC operators the painting over of the rear destination aperture and using the service number box was the prelude to the complete removal of destination information on the backs of buses. (Bristol Vintage Bus Group)

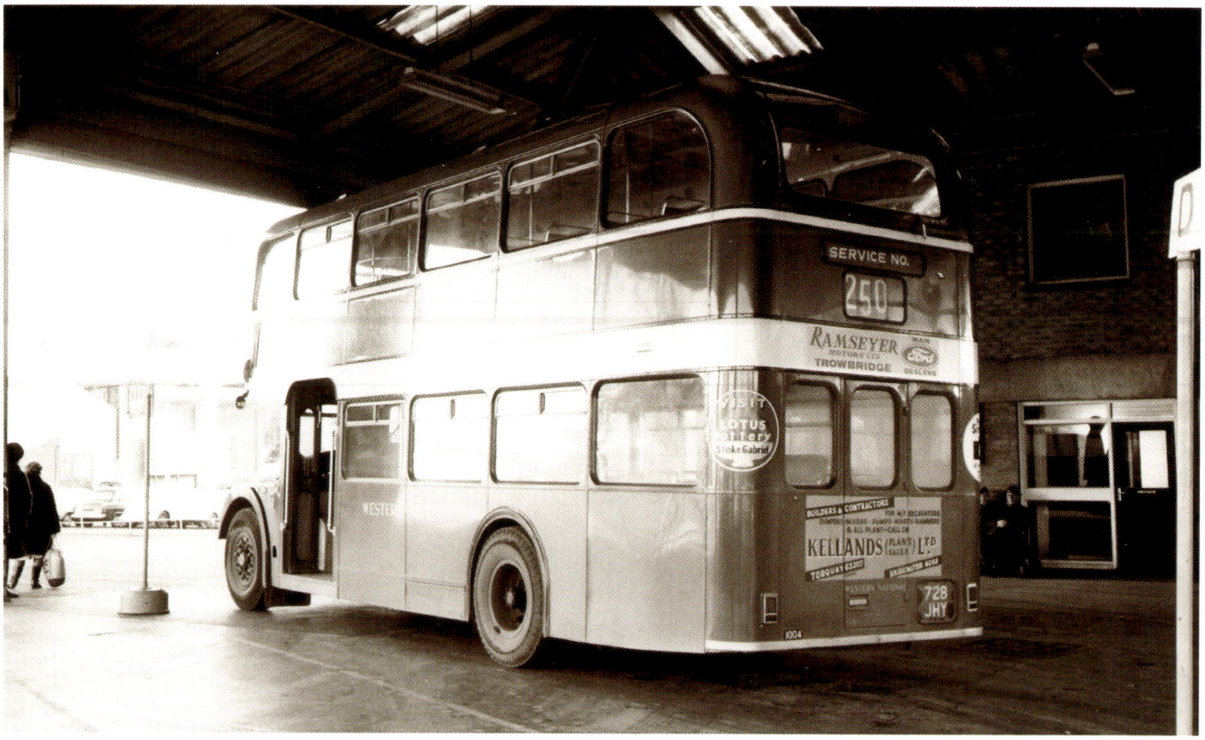

Displaying "SERVICE NO." was invariably seen in the 1960s and early 1970s on the rear of Southern National and Western National buses. Western National 1004 (728 JHY), a 1961 ex Bristol Omnibus FSF6G, is no exception to this as seen inside Trowbridge Bus Station when working Town Service 250 to Studley Green. (Bristol Vintage Bus Group)

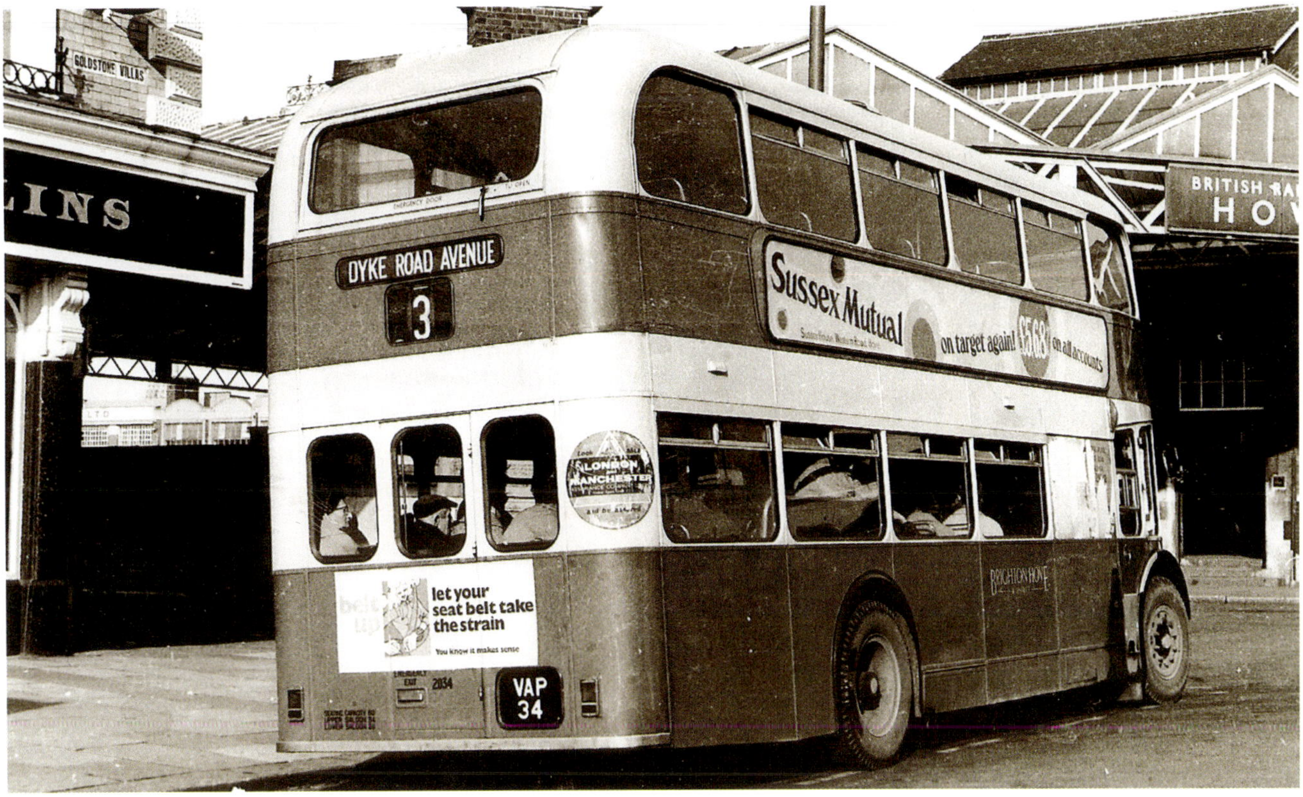

Full use of the rear destination boxes is emphasised in this rear view of Brighton Hove & District 34 (VAP 34) at Hove Railway Station. It has already been renumbered with its Southdown fleet number 2034 and is recorded working on Service 3 to Dyke Road Avenue. (Denis Clark)

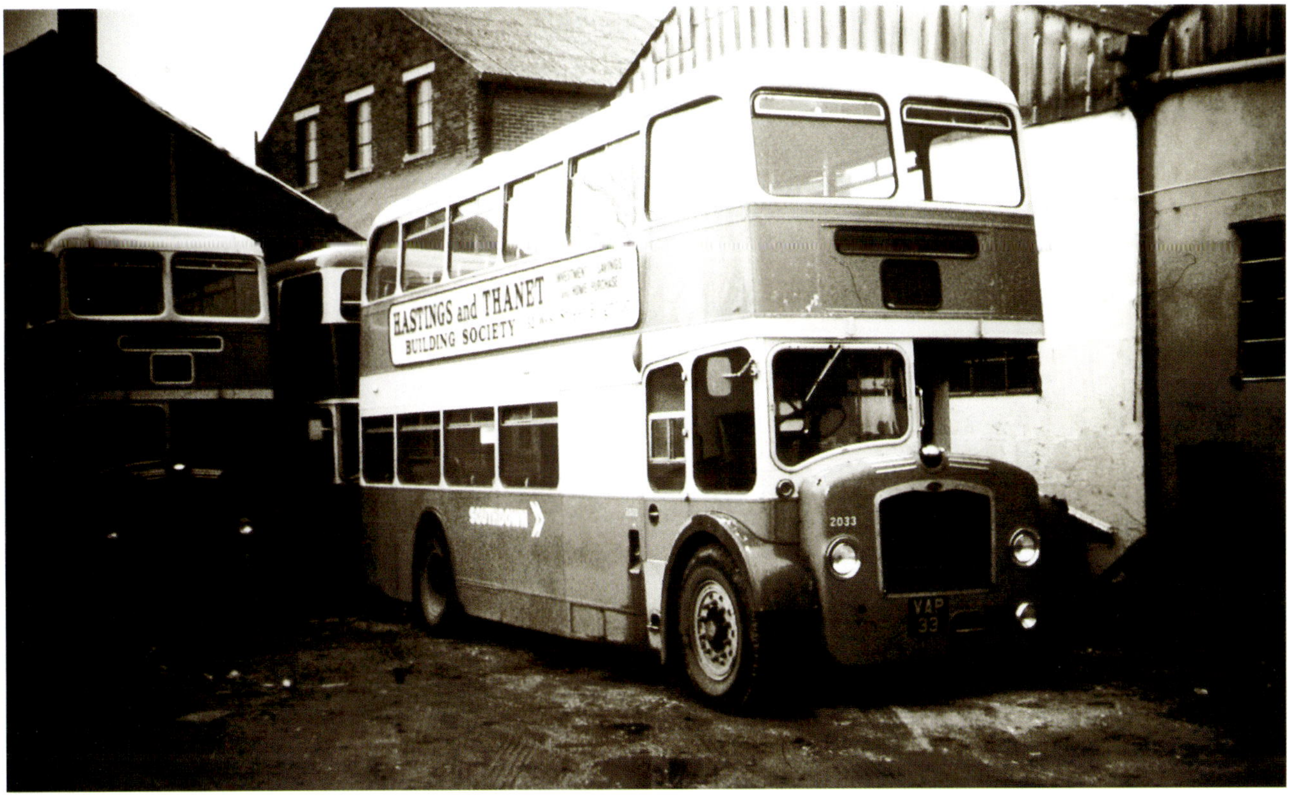

Waiting for preparation and painting in NBC poppy red livery to become 3477 in the Hants & Dorset fleet at Southampton on 11th January 1975, Southdown 2033 (VAP 33), a 1961 former Brighton Hove & District (No. 33) FSF6B, would be allocated to Salisbury. (Author's collection)

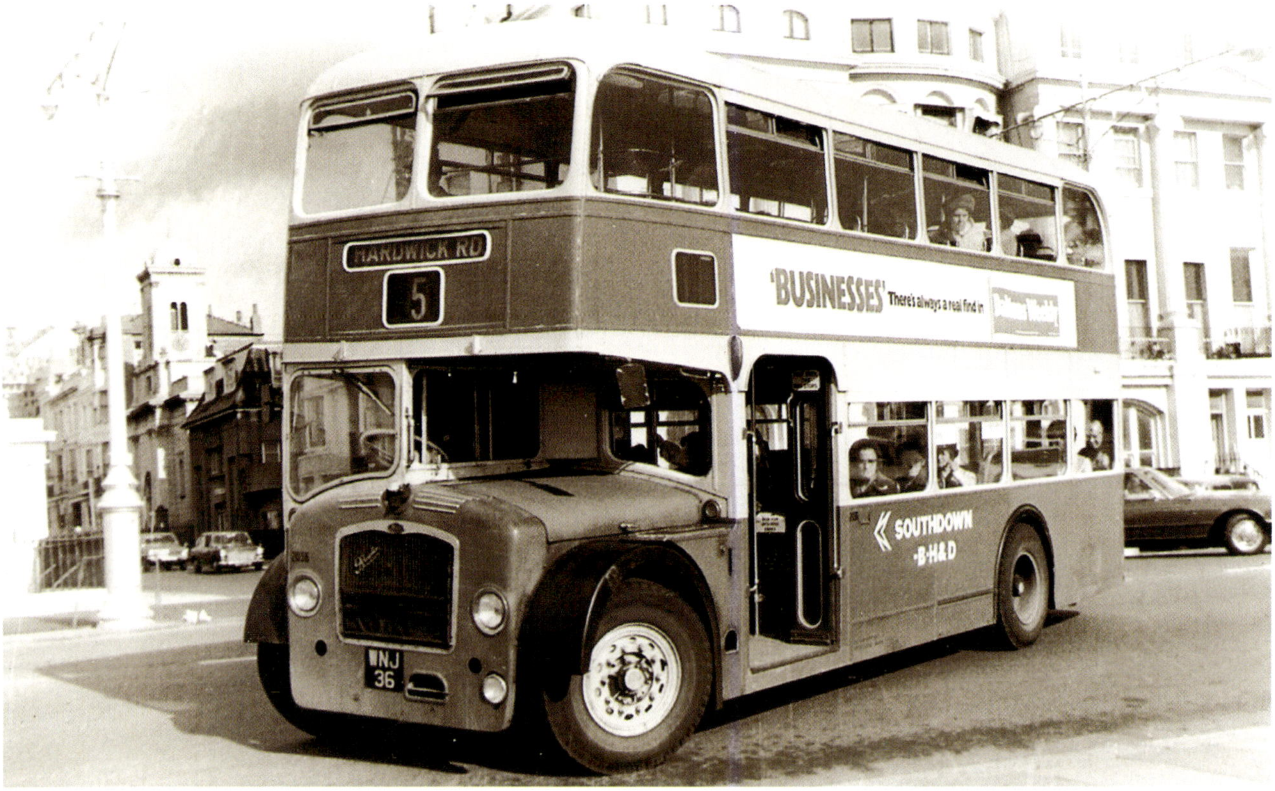

Southdown-BH&D fleet names are carried on 2036 (WNJ 36) still in original BH&D livery and canopy route number box that hasn't been used by the conductor on Service 5 to Hardwick Road. The platform doors should have been closed to prevent any passengers, or even the conductor, falling out as it turns out of the side road with possible serious injuries. (Denis Clark)

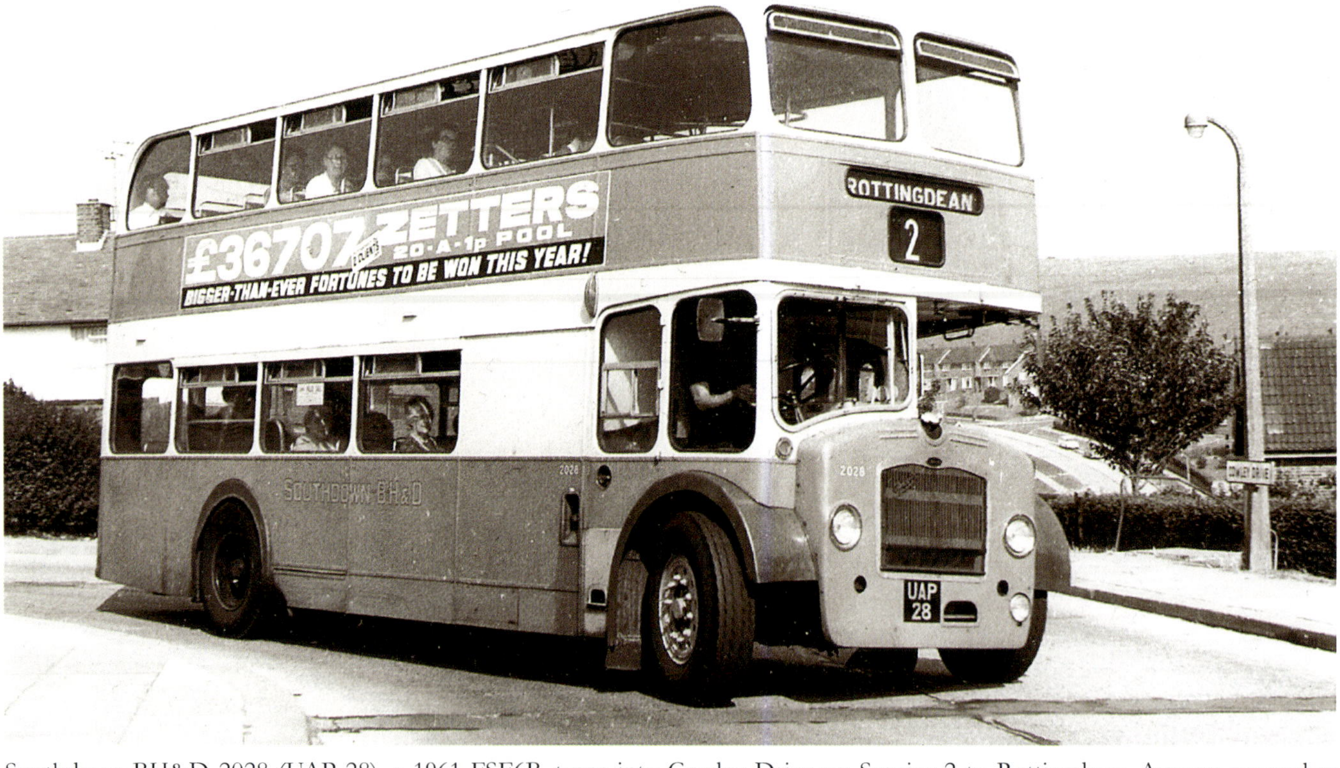

Southdown-BH&D 2028 (UAP 28), a 1961 FSF6B, turns into Cowley Drive on Service 2 to Rottingdean. Anyone remember Zetters Football Pools and what was probably a "tidy" win of £36,707 at the time? (Denis Clark)

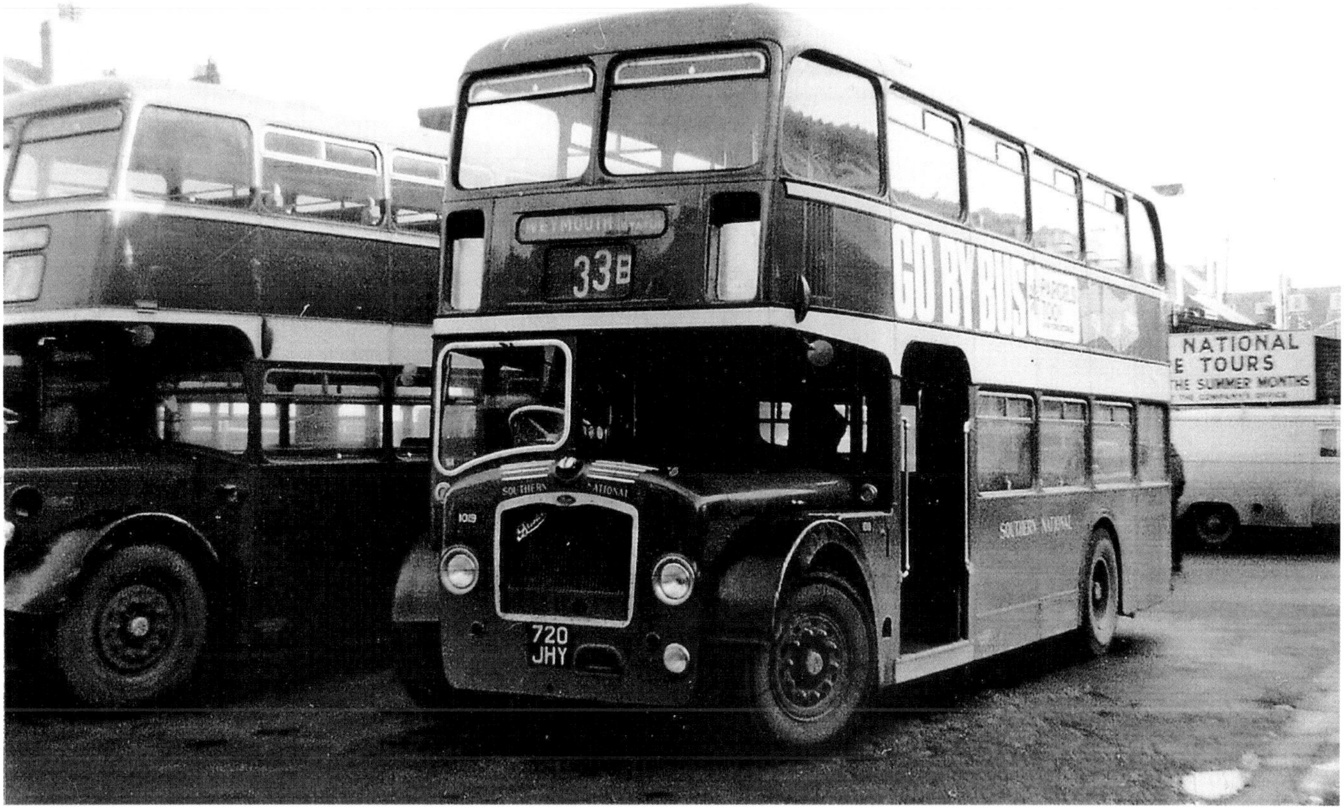

A hint of saloon heating problems appears to have occurred with Southern National 1019 (720 JHY), a 1961 FSF6G with an "in house" solution with freshly over-panelled CBC radiators, at Weymouth Depot. (Brian Botley)

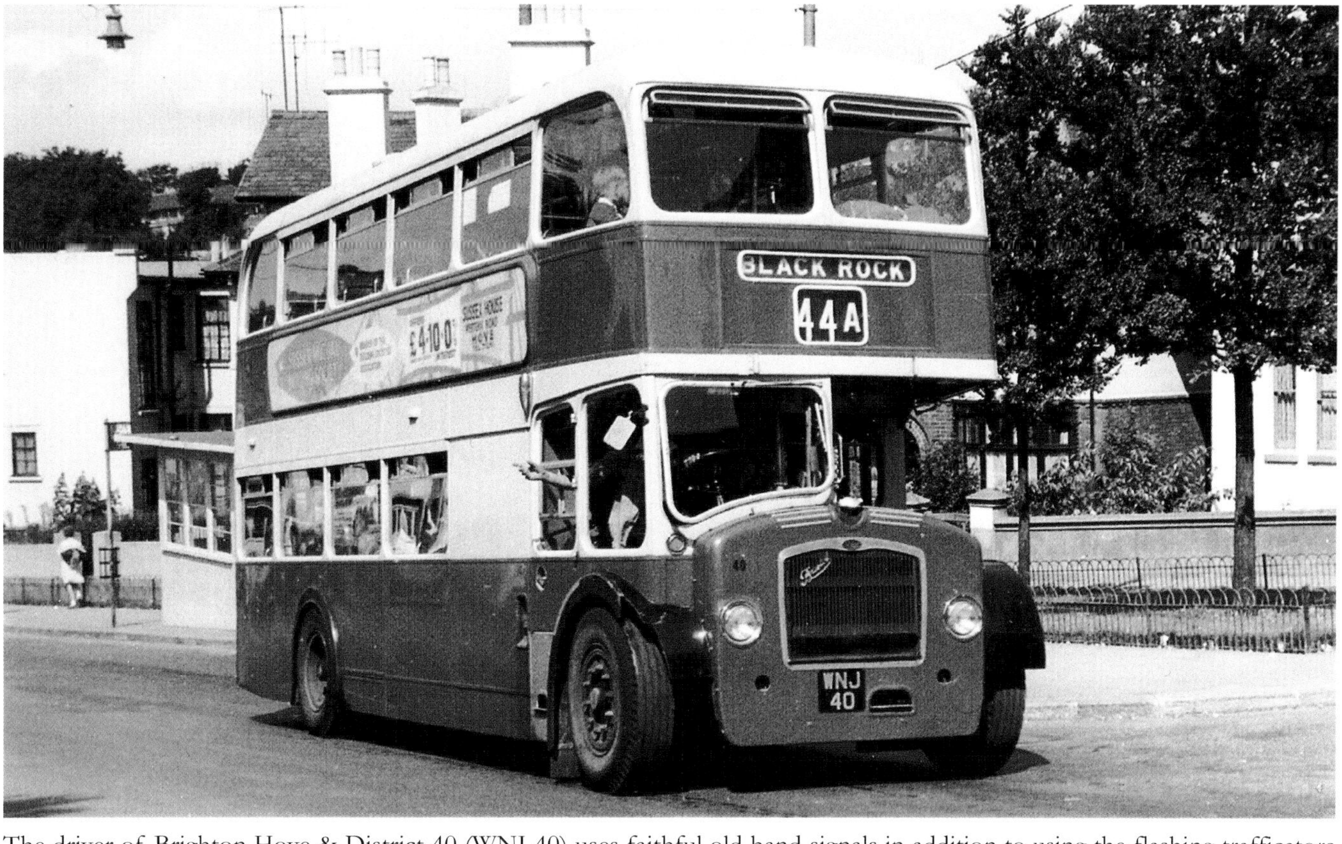

The driver of Brighton Hove & District 40 (WNJ 40) uses faithful old hand signals in addition to using the flashing trafficators on a journey to Black Rock on Service 44A. (Denis Clark)

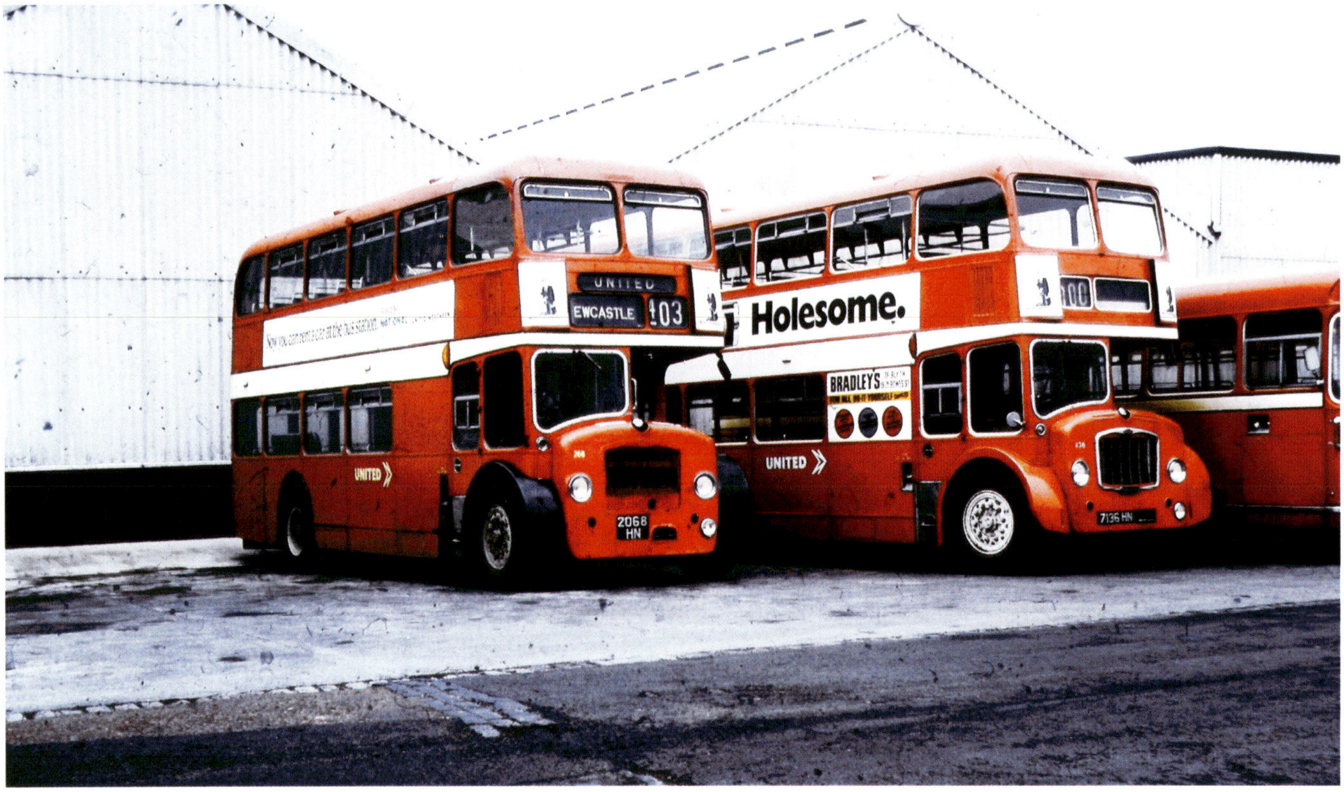

United Automobile 268 (2068 HN) was delivered with fleet number BL68 in March 1961 and was one of nine FSFs received that month. A good comparison of body finishes can be seen in the open yard at Newcastle in July 1973 436 (7136 HN) a 1962 FLF6B with later radiator grille, destination layout and white glass rubbers. (Kevin Lane)

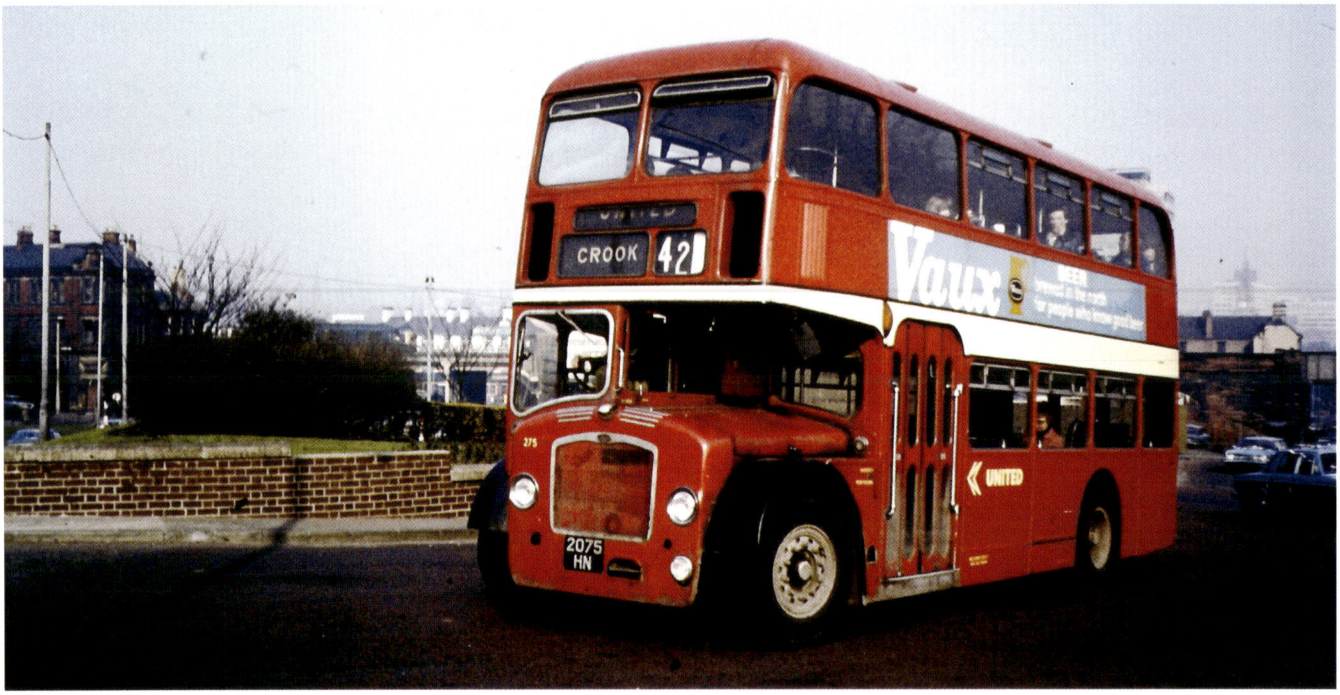

Passengers are few and well spread out on United Automobile 275 (2075 HN) a 1961 FSF6B, originally numbered BL75, seen here on Service 42 which in September 1960 was jointly operated with Northern General. Journeys ran half hourly between Newcastle (Worswick Street) and Crook (Market Place) with further half hourly journeys between Durham Omnibus Station and Crook, even on Sundays. On Saturdays according to the United timetable book dated 1st June–30th September 1960 with a cover price of 1/- for 321 pages there were additional journeys every half an hour from Crook to Willington Railway Station from 11.27 am until 9.57 pm offering passengers six departures an hour at those times. (Author's collection)

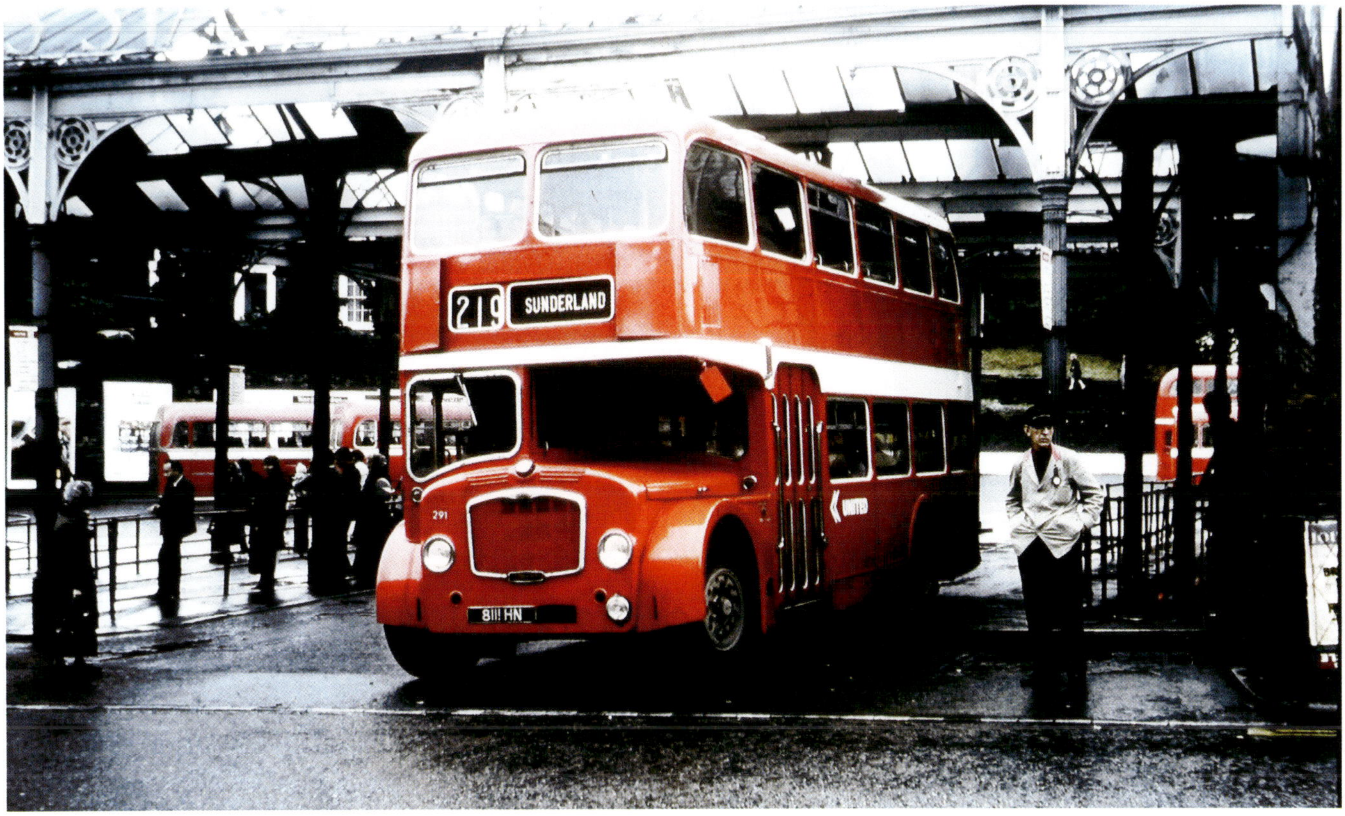

United 291 (8111 HN), a 1962 ex Durham District FSF6B, departs Durham Bus Station on a wet day in August 1974; note the driver or conductor to the right in pre-NBC uniform. (Kevin Lane)

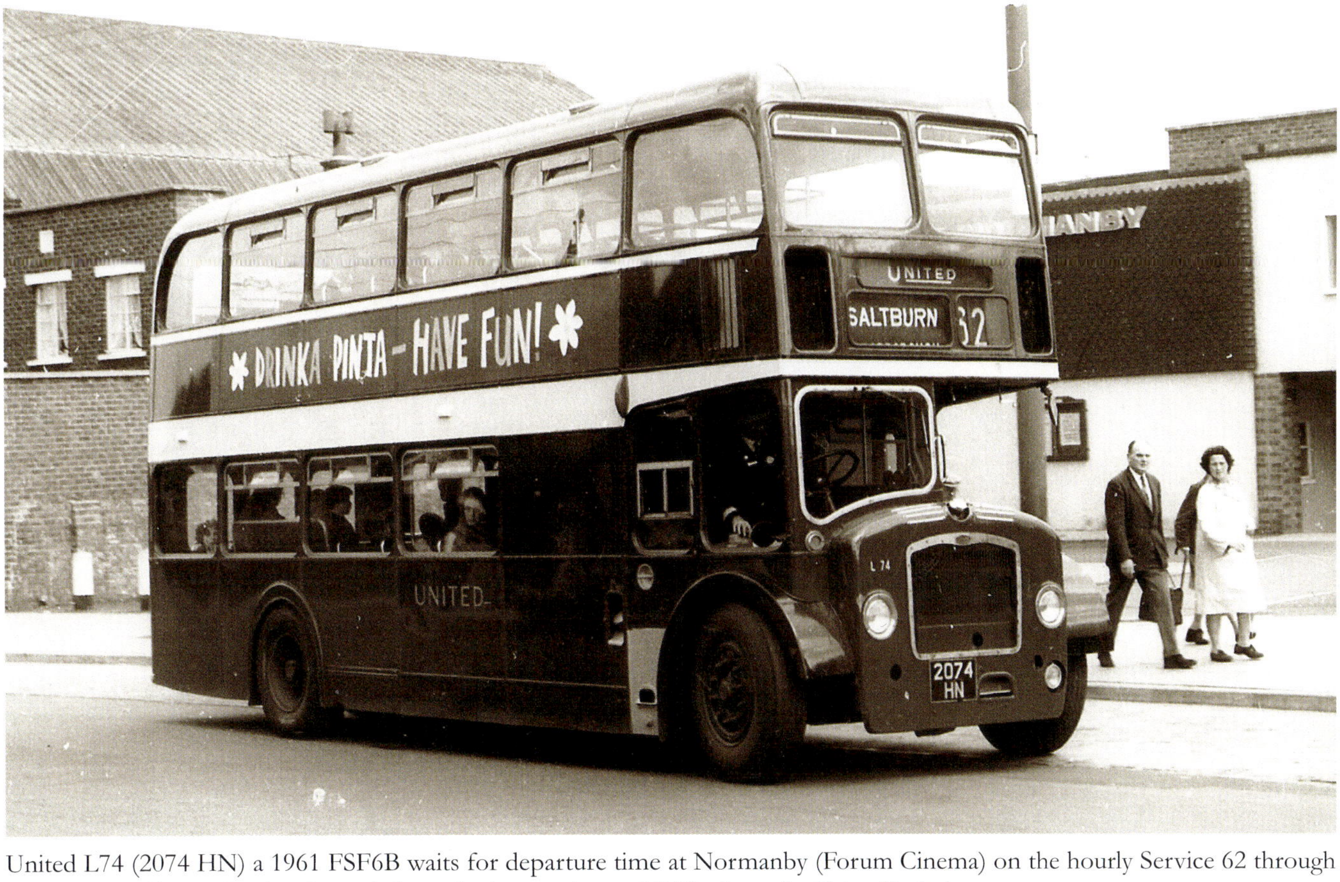

United L74 (2074 HN) a 1961 FSF6B waits for departure time at Normanby (Forum Cinema) on the hourly Service 62 through journey to Saltburn (Station Square) from the bus station at Middlesbrough. (Brian Botley)

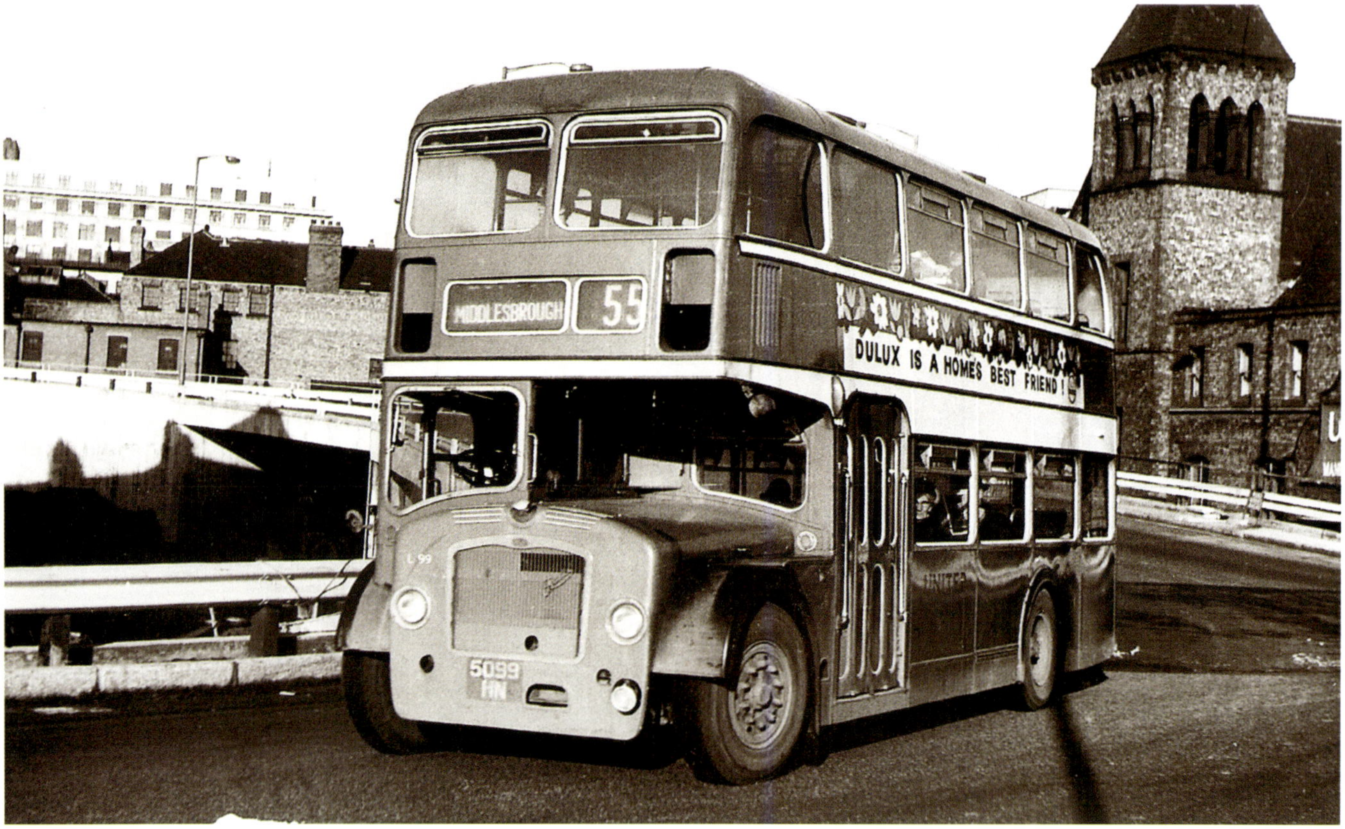

With partly masked CBC radiators United L99 (5099 HN), a 1961 FSF6B, works a Service 55 journey to Middlesbrough Bus Station from Newcastle (Worswick Street) via Durham when relatively new with lined out cream band livery. (Brian Botley)

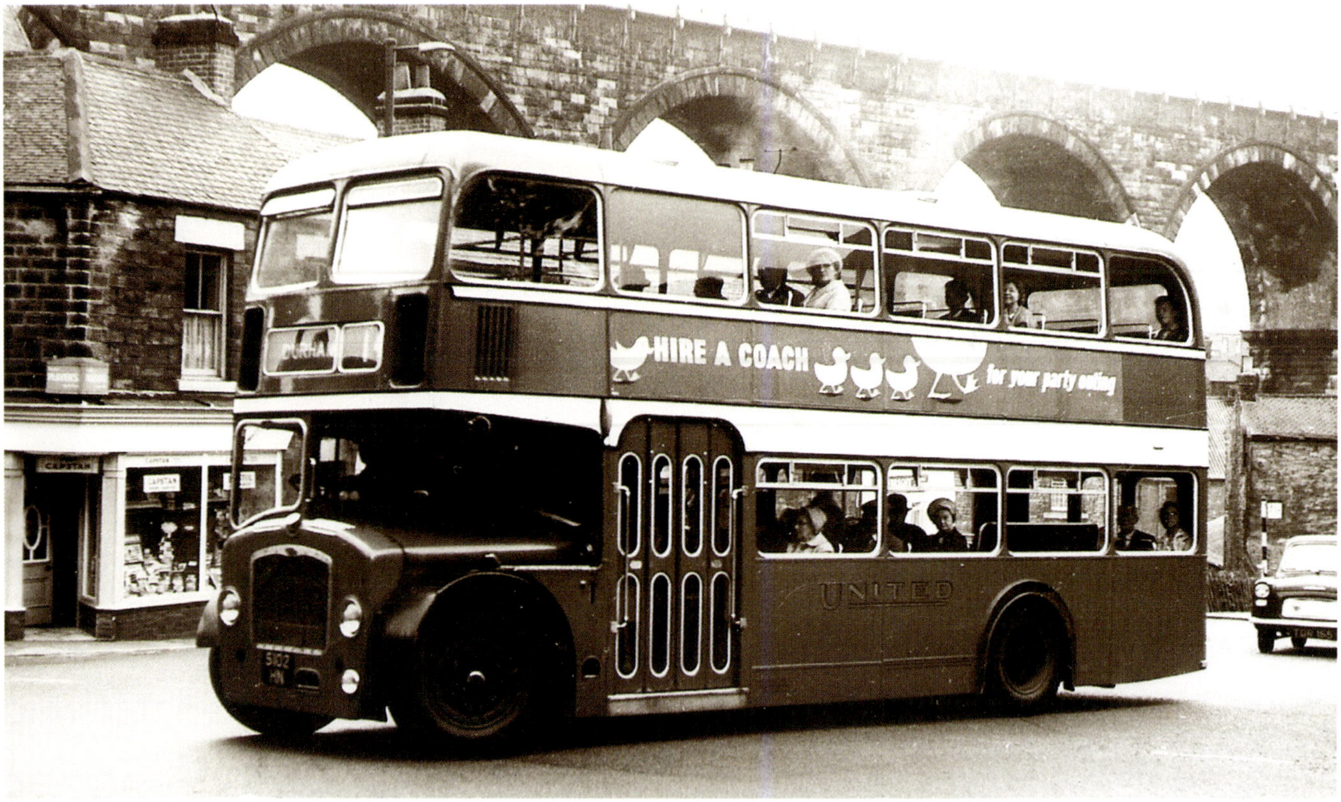

United L102 (5102 HN) a 1961 FSF6B arrives in its destination city of Durham on Service 14 from Darlington with relatively few passengers travelling. (Brian Botley)

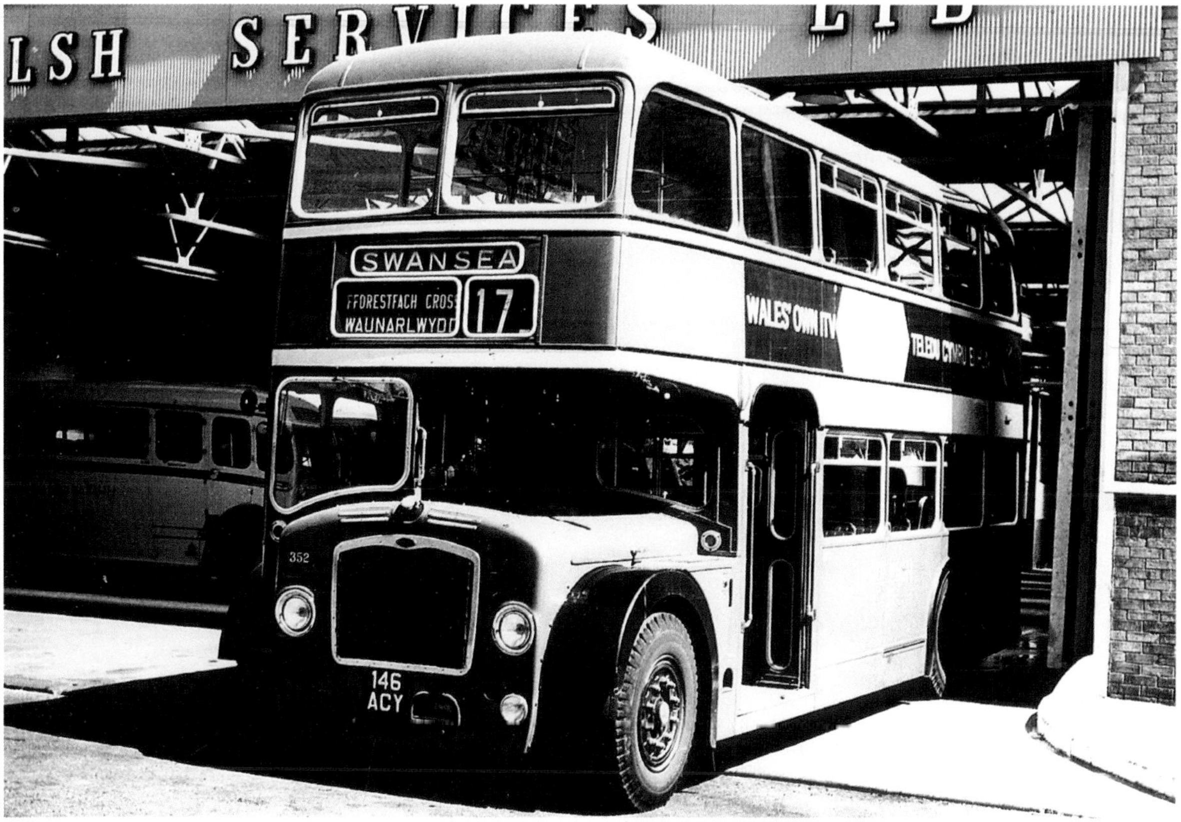

Peering out from the protection of the depot through the entrance doors at Swansea United Welsh 352 (146 ACY), a 1961 FSF6G, was one of 28 FSFs delivered to the company in 1961 and 1962. (Robert F. Mack)

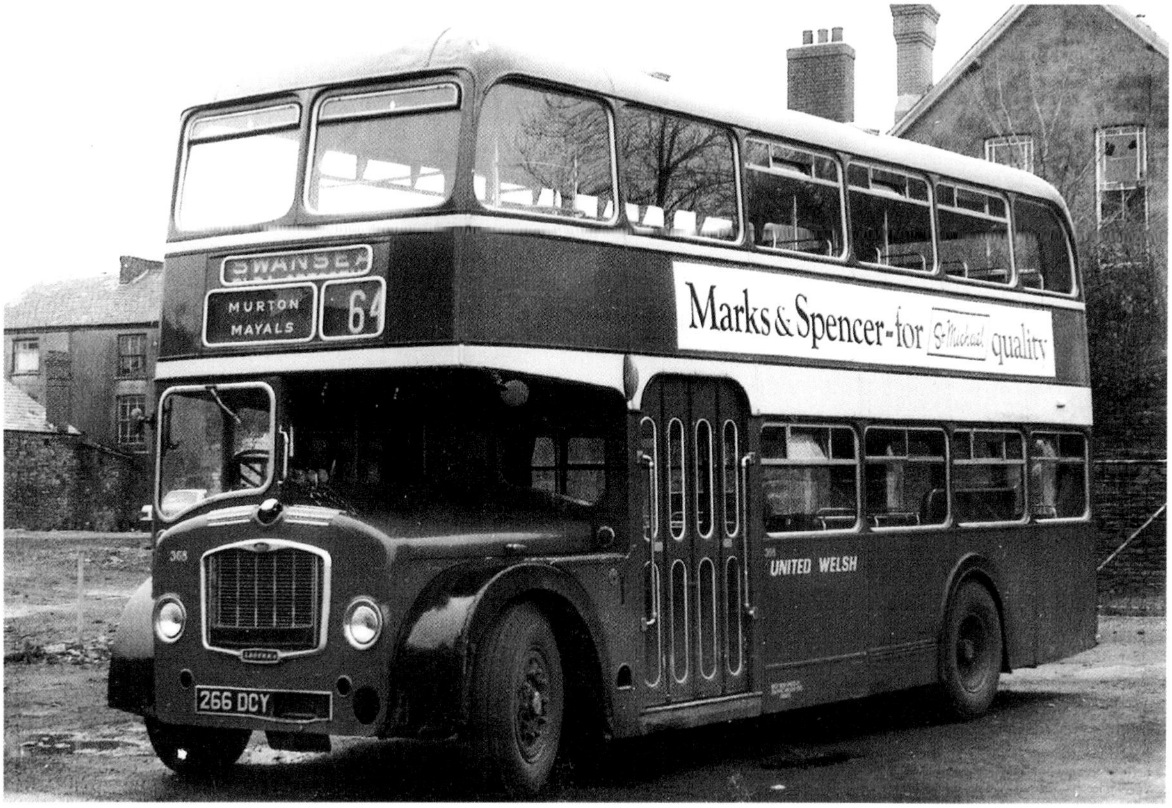

Among the final 17 FSFs received in November 1962 was United Welsh 368 (266 DCY), a 1962 FSF6G pictured in Swansea on 17th April 1970. (Robert F. Mack)

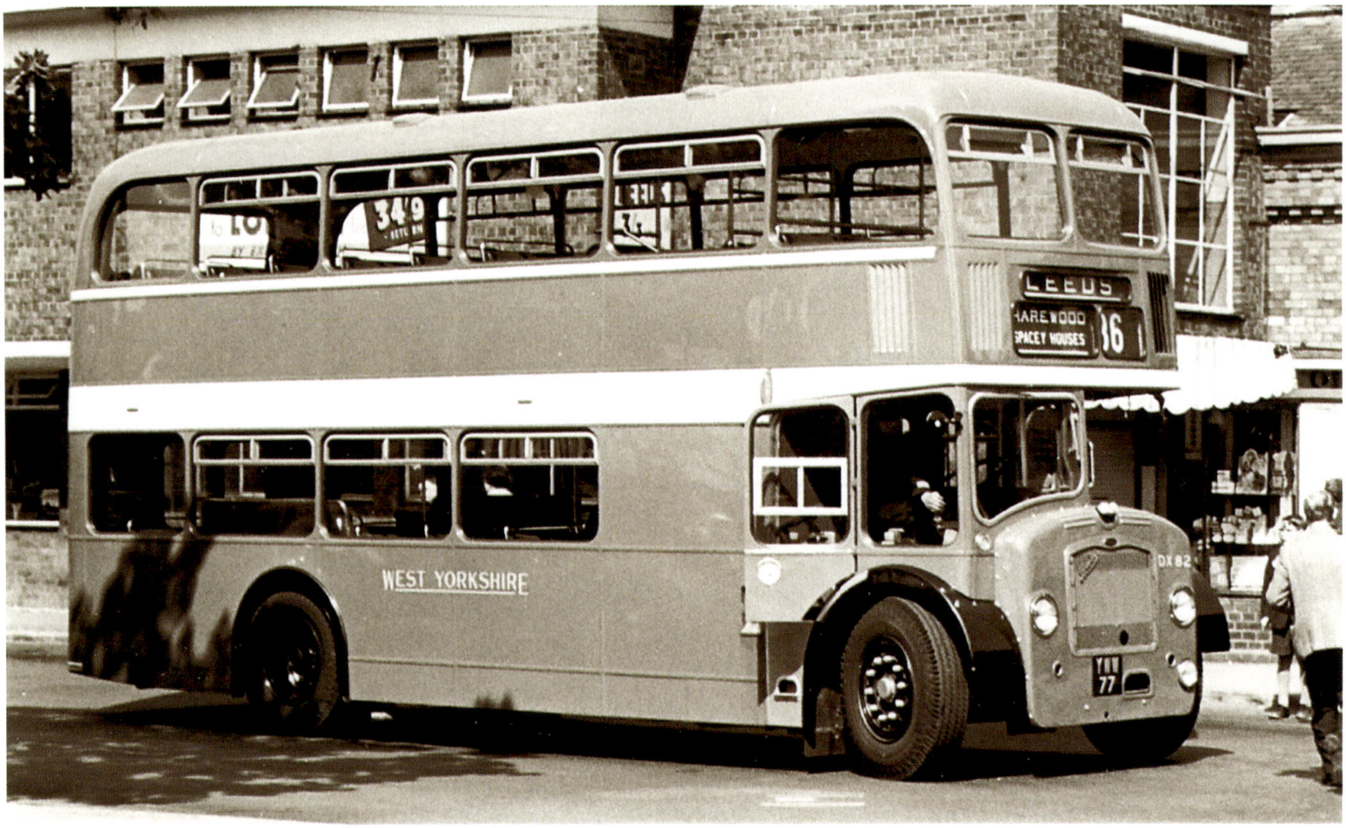

In pristine condition West Yorkshire DX82 (YWW 77), the 1960 prototype FSF, was allocated to Leeds Depot and was this company's sole FSF exchanged in 1967 for a similar aged FS from United Automobile. (Robert F. Mack)

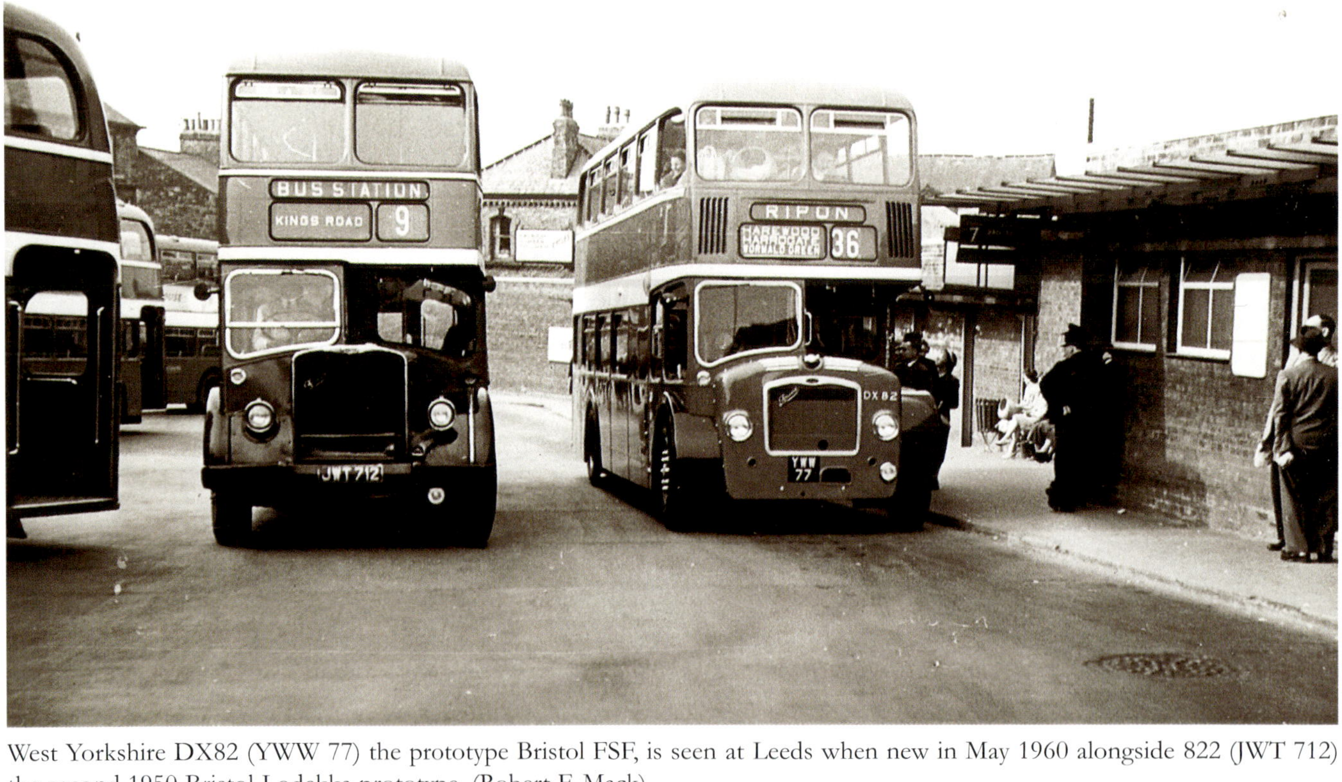

West Yorkshire DX82 (YWW 77) the prototype Bristol FSF, is seen at Leeds when new in May 1960 alongside 822 (JWT 712) the second 1950 Bristol Lodekka prototype. (Robert F. Mack)

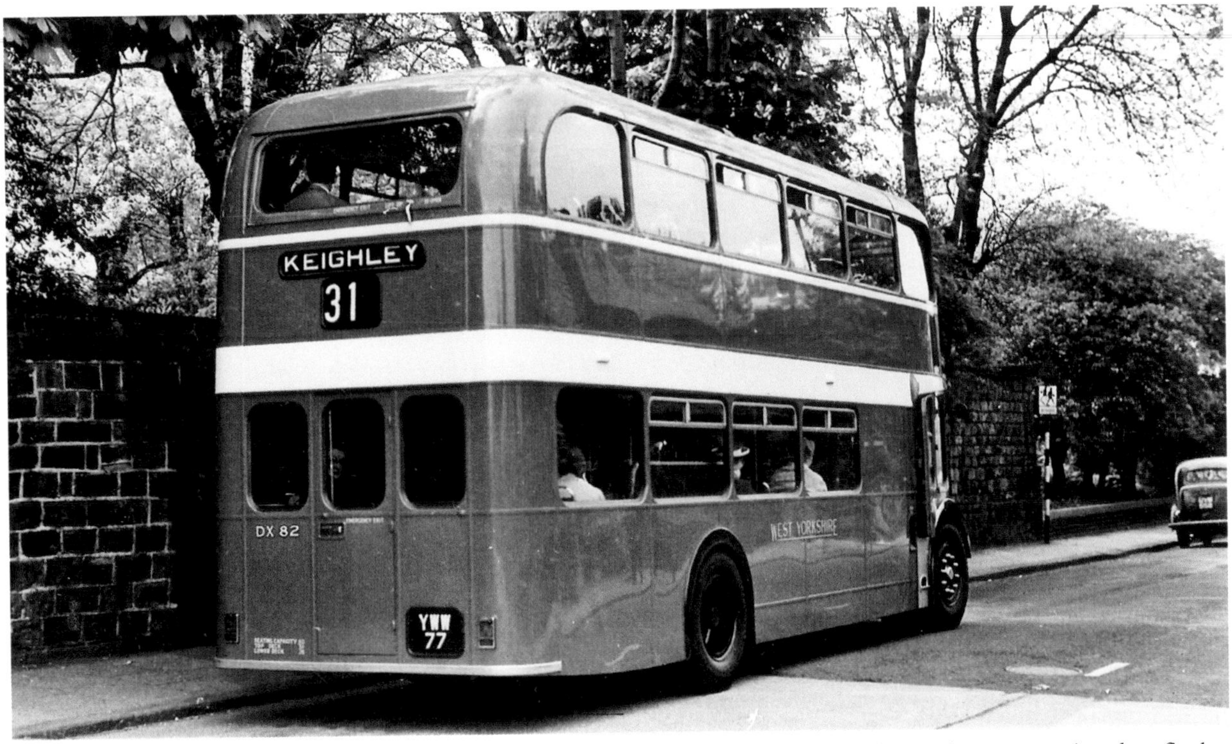

The position of the emergency door handle on the earlier FSFs resulted in adverts needing to be cut or painted to fit the space but later vehicles had the handle in line with the registration plate. West Yorkshire DX82 (YWW 77) shows the original arrangement in this view taken soon after entry into service in May 1960. (Robert F. Mack)

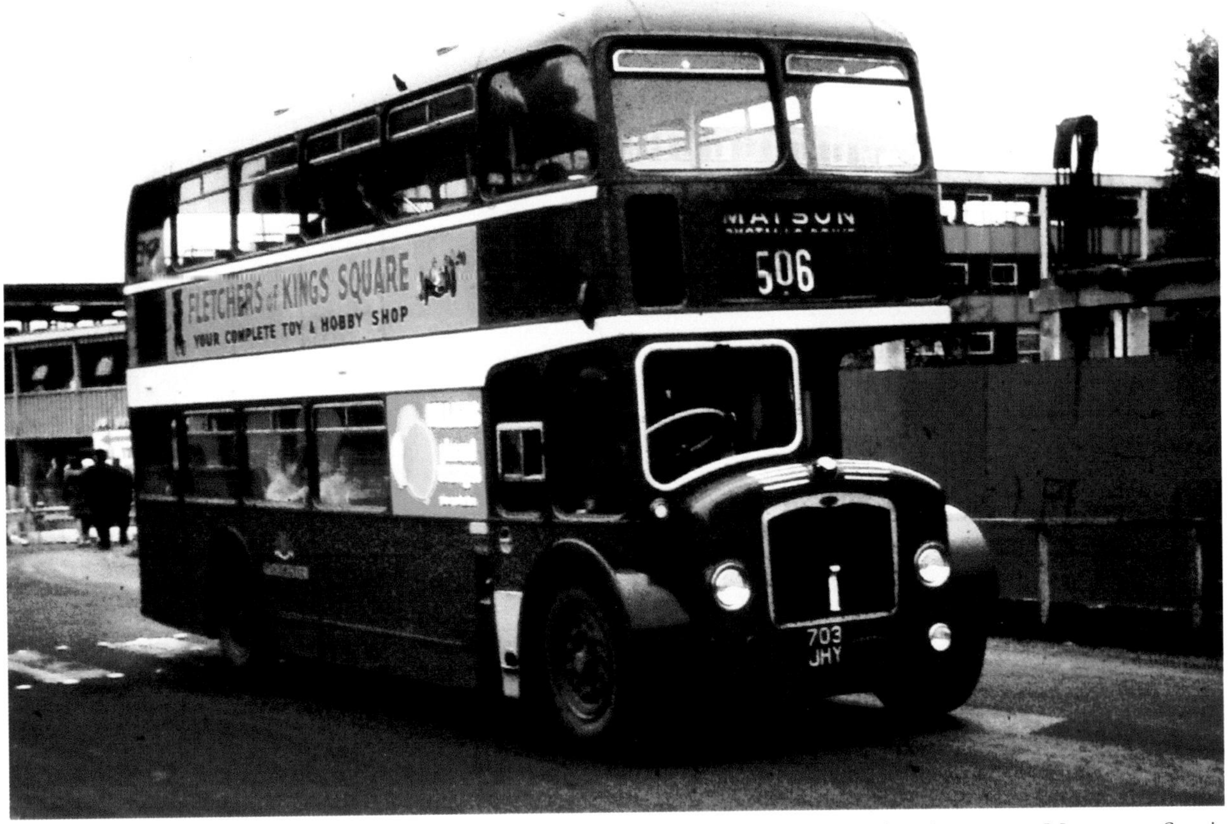

Gloucester G6006 (703 JHY), a 1960 FSF6G with Gloucester crest and fleet names, works a journey to Matson on Service 506 sometime after 1967 when Gloucester City Services were renumbered into the 500s. This vehicle was transferred to Bath in April 1972. (Author's collection)

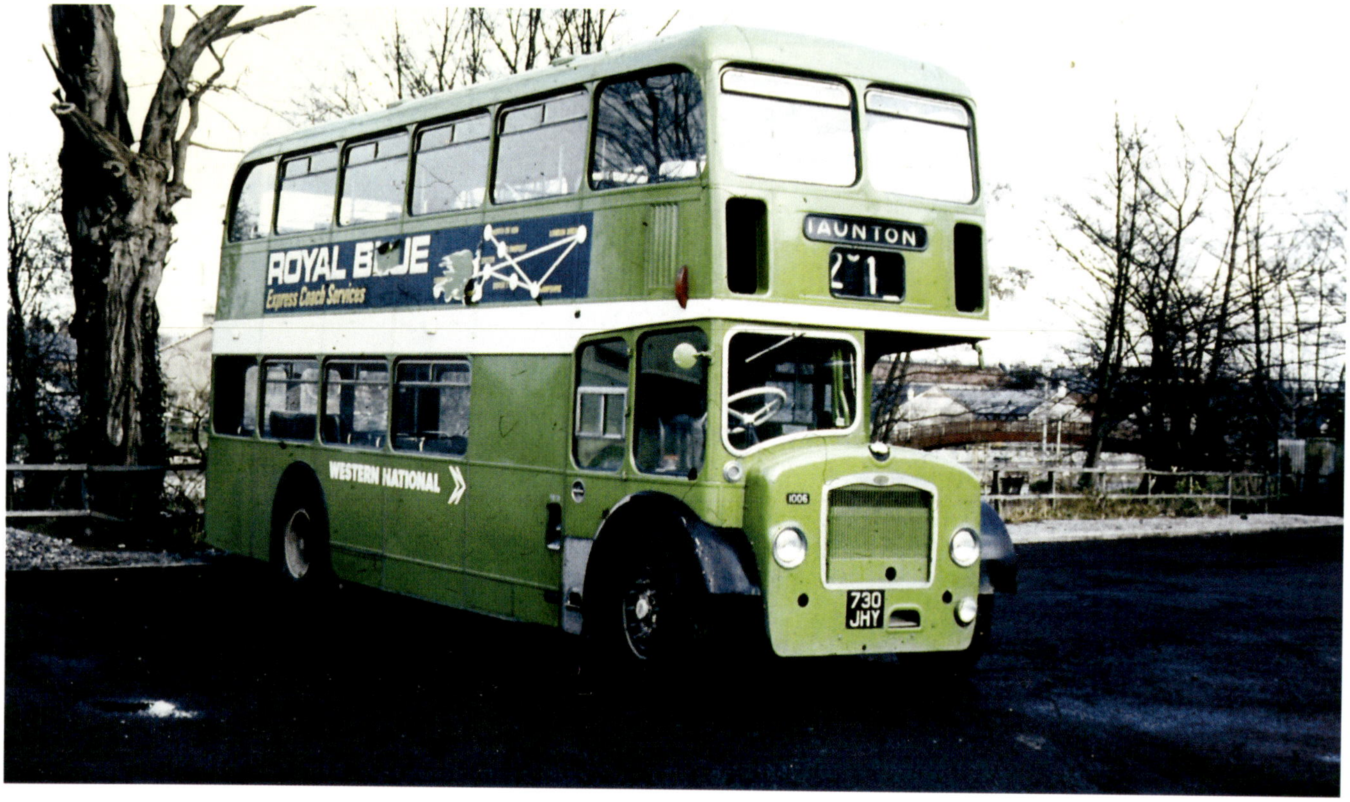

Western National 1006 (730 JHY), a 1961 former Bristol Country area FSF6G, is seen at Taunton on 10th August 1976. During its six years with Bristol Omnibus it spent most of its time allocated to Swindon. (Hugh Jones)

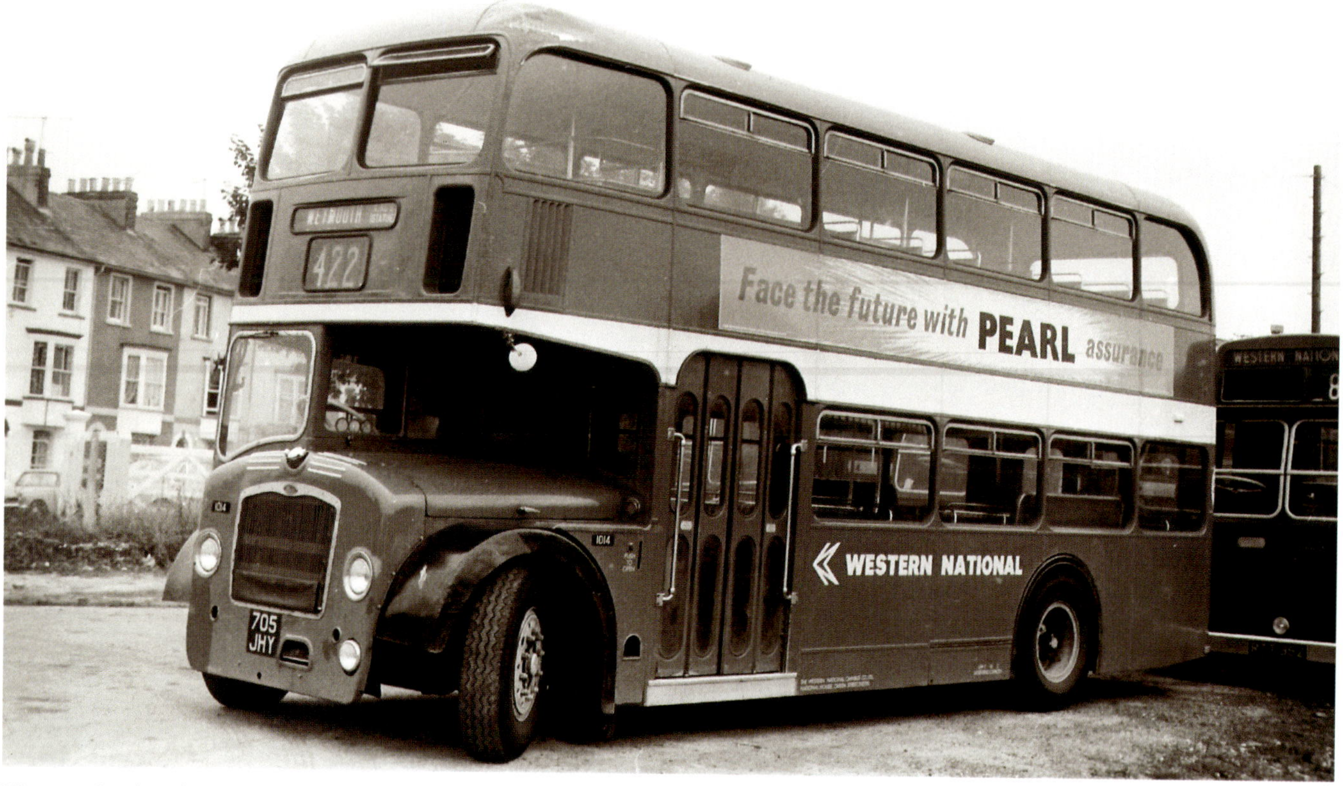

Western National 1014 (705 JHY), a 1960 ex Cheltenham District FSF6G 6018 originally numbered L99 between November 1960 and 26th March 1961, was purchased by Southern National in May 1967, transferred to Western National in November 1969 and withdrawn during August 1978. (Hugh Jones)

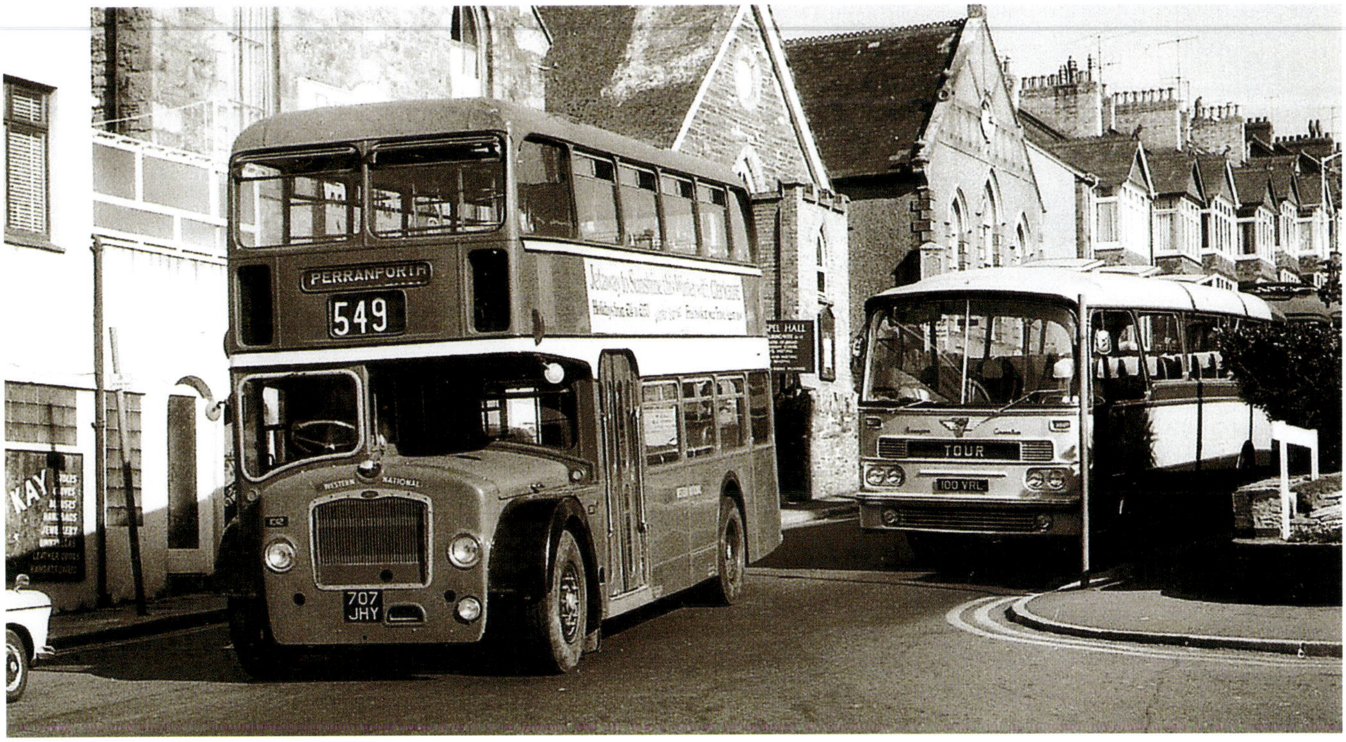

Western National 1012 (707 JHY), a 1960 ex Bath Electric FSF6G, was sold to Southern National in June 1967 and is seen on Service 549 to Perranporth soon after transfer to Western National in November 1969. (P. M. Photography)

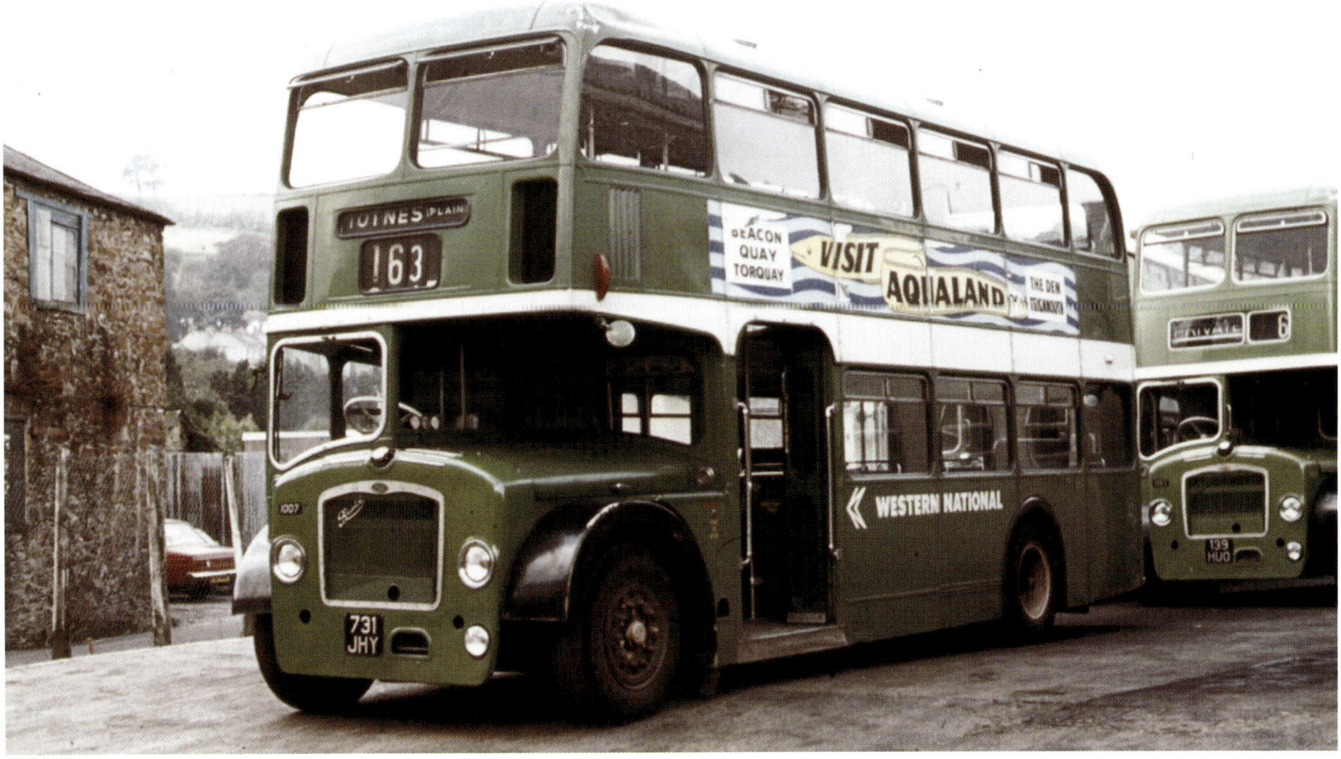

One positive attraction of the ex Bristol Omnibus vehicles for Western National crews was that neither the driver nor the conductor needed to hang on to the front of the outside of the bus to change the destination and service number blinds. The author well remembers that this was an acceptable and enjoyable task when working the ex Western National Bristol FLFs that had been transferred to Bath with the West Wiltshire services in dry sunny weather. It was, however, quite the opposite when it was raining or wintry and there was only one way for the water to go… down the handles and soak your sleeves! 1007 (731 JHY) stands in the open yard at Totnes Depot in September 1976. (Donald Hudson)

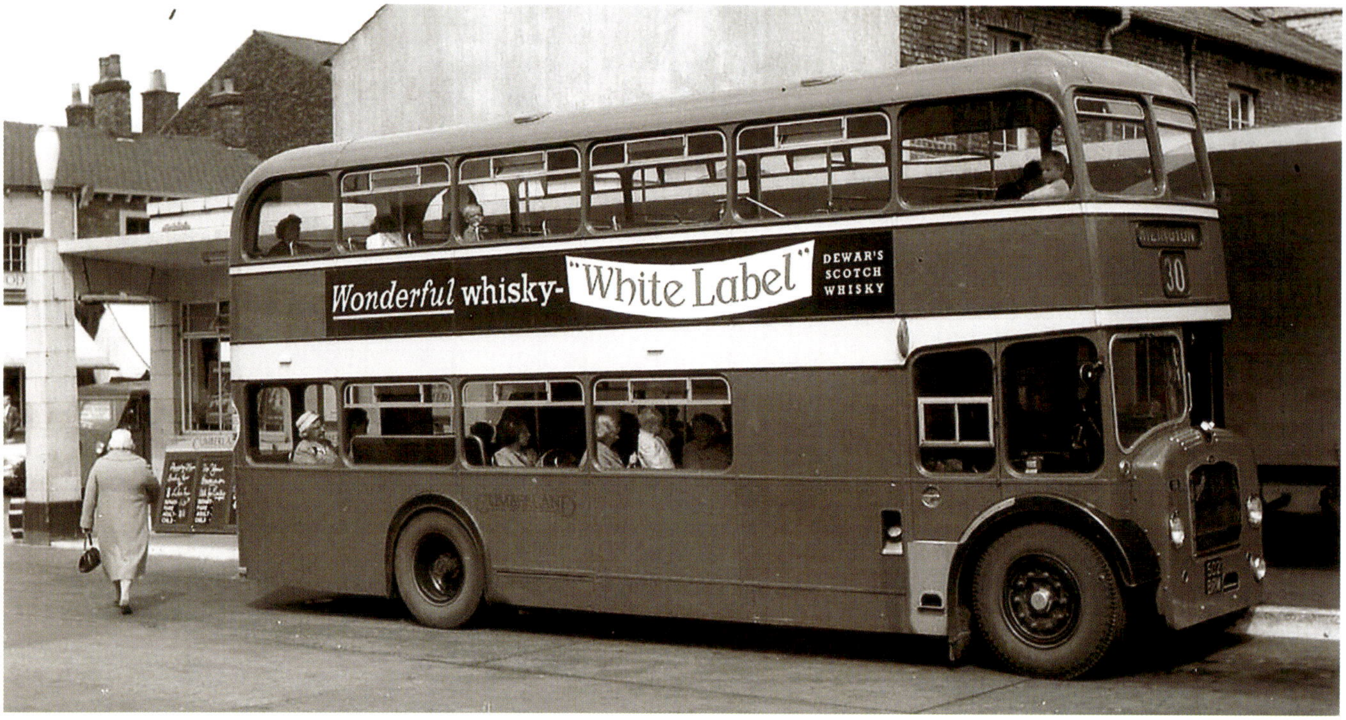

Cumberland 501 (502 BRM), a 1960 FSF6G at Carlisle waiting to depart the bus station for Workington on Service 30, was originally numbered C405 where the C indicated "country" in complete contrast to those operating for Bristol Omnibus where the letter C indicated that the vehicle was allocated to Bristol City Services. (P. M. Photography)

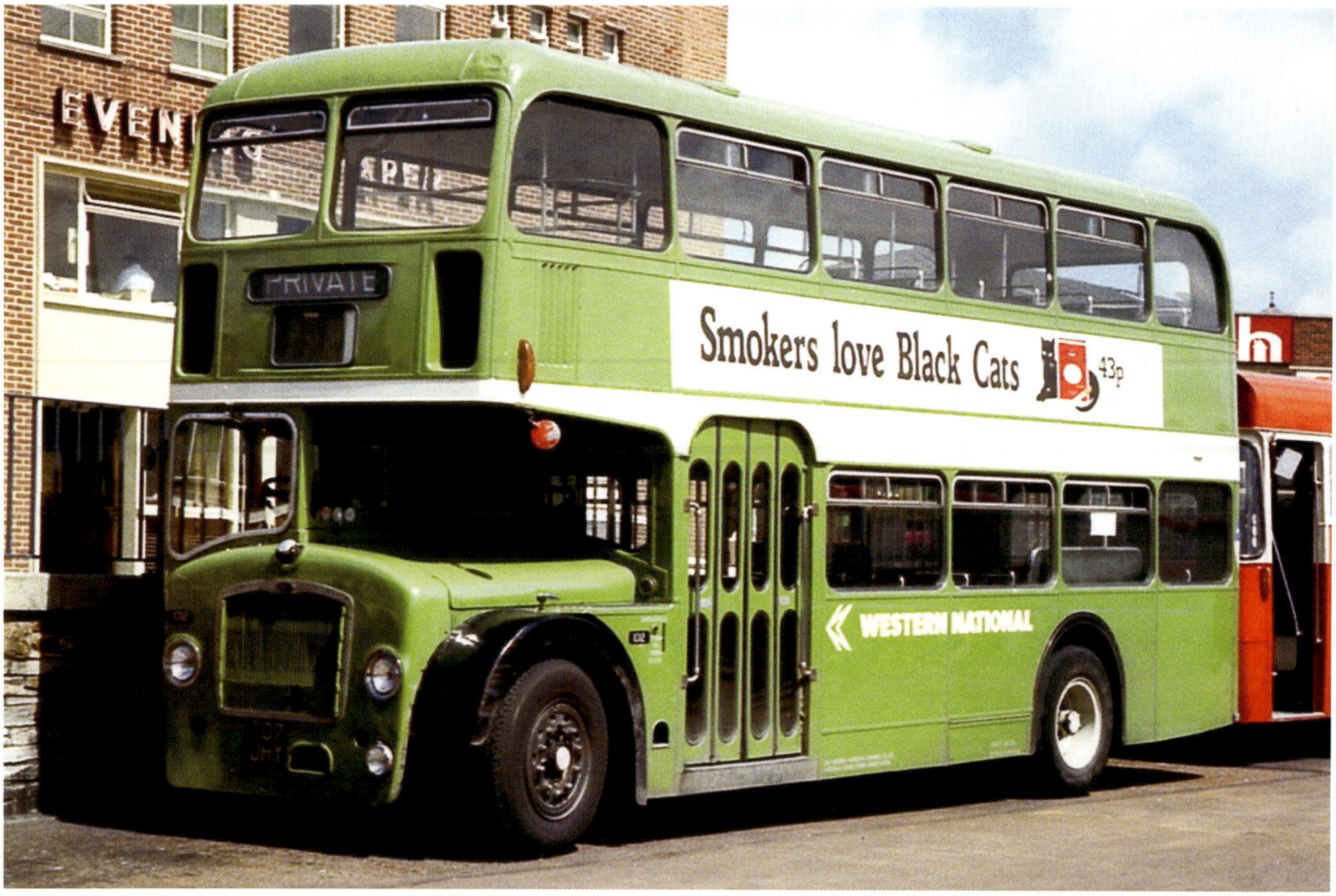

Western National 1012 (707 JHY), an ex Bath Tramways Motor Company FSF6G, is seen at Exeter Bus Station on 25th May 1976 carrying, what would now be considered illegal, cigarette advertising. (Steve Thoroughgood)

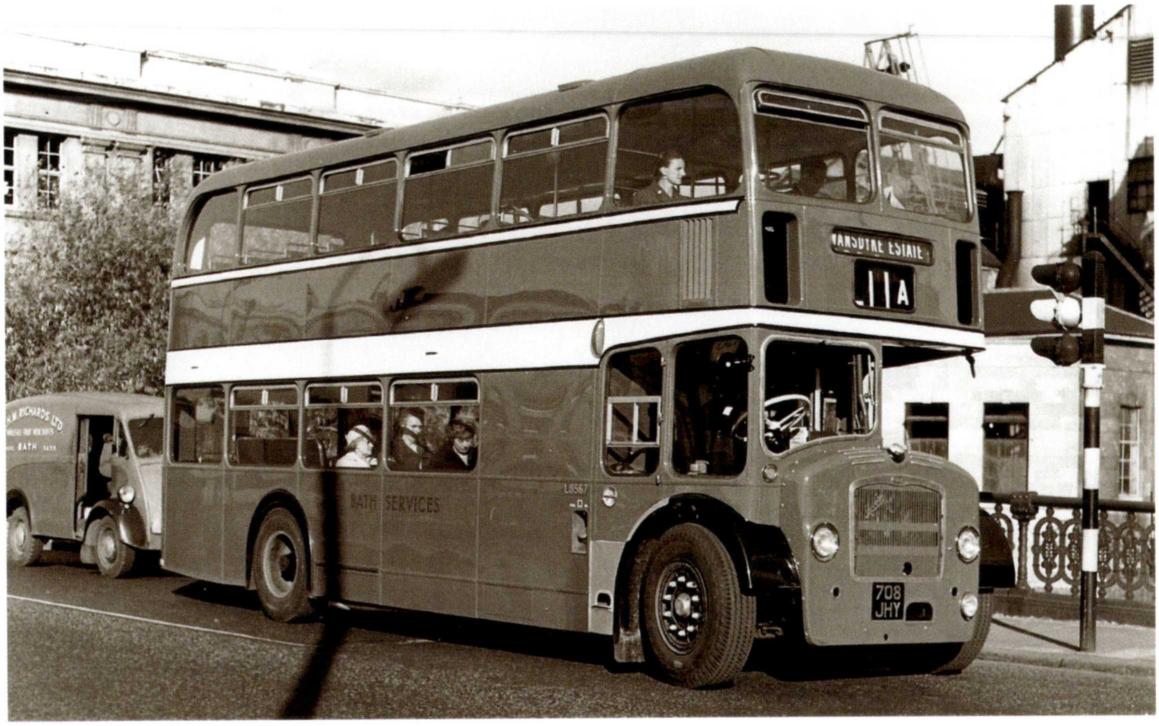

Bath Services L8567 (708 JHY), a 1960 FSF6G, was renumbered L6009 in January 1961 only to be sold on to Southern National in August 1967 where it was numbered 1013. In November 1976 it was one of just two repainted into National Bus Company "poppy red" livery with Devon General fleet names until it was withdrawn from the fleet in February 1978. Purchased by Martin, a vehicle dealer in Middlewich, Cheshire, only to be sold on to Goodwin, another vehicle dealer and scrap merchant in July 1978. Photographed when new and completely devoid of any exterior advertising it is working a Bath City journey to Wansdyke Estate on Service 11A. (P. R. Forsey)

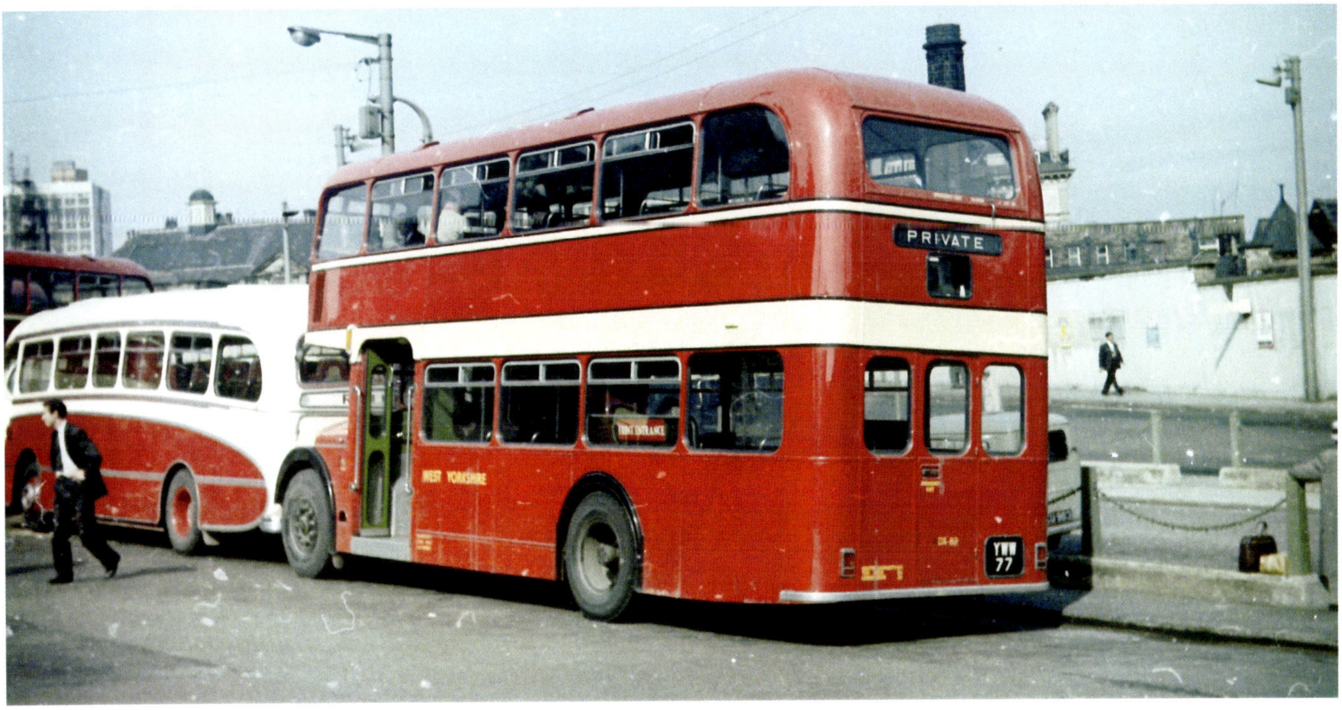

A rear view of West Yorkshire DX82 (YWW 77), the first FSF produced and considered to be the "prototype", new in May 1960 complete with a driver operated sliding door that was replaced with the standard four leaf folding door before entry into service. The original position of the emergency door handle on early FSFs is clear to see and the unusual 'front entrance' side window label might be an indication that as this was the only front entrance vehicle in this fleet passengers had to be reminded of where to find the door! (Author's collection)

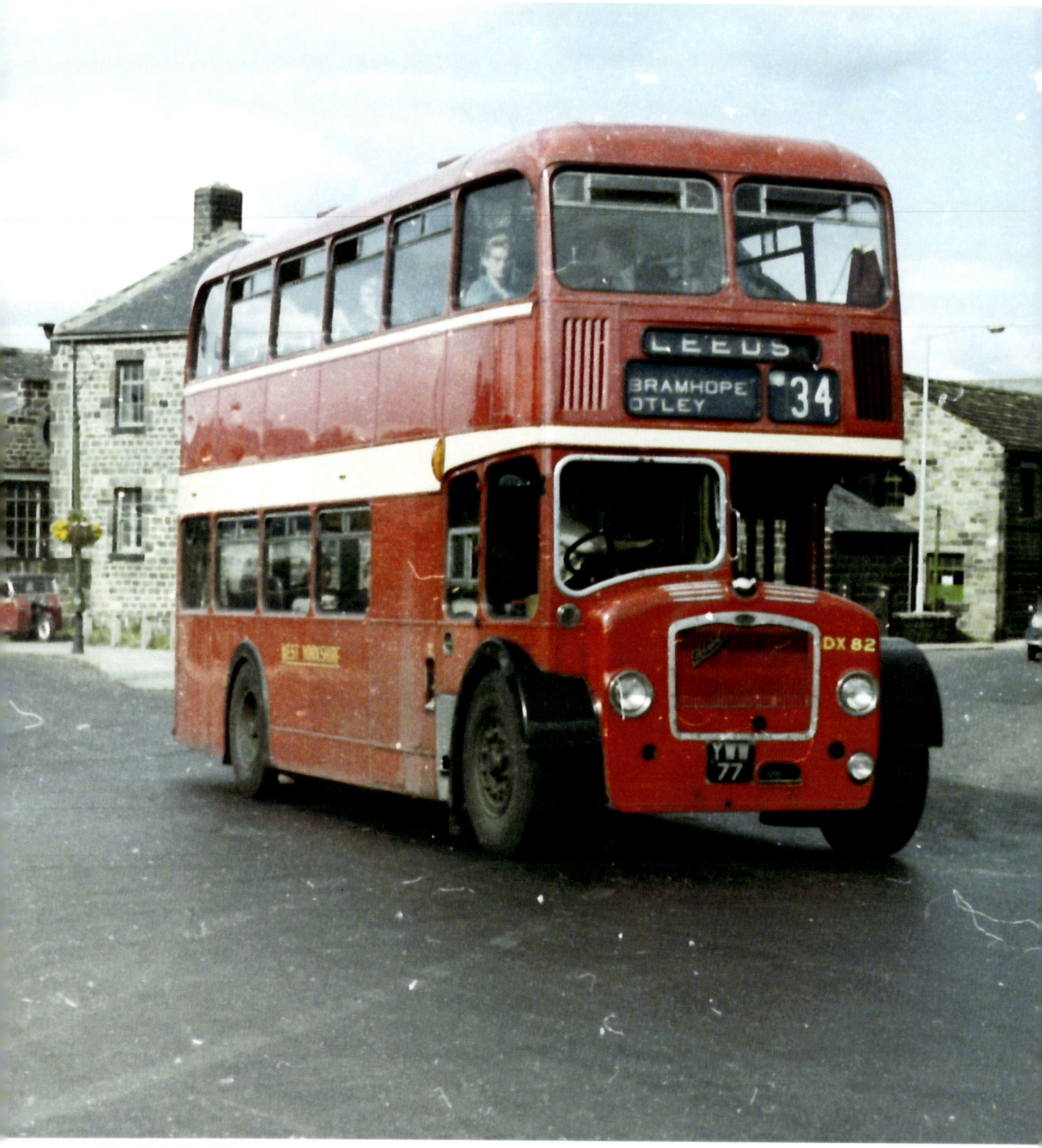

West Yorkshire DX82 (YWW 77) was the only front entrance Lodekka ever owned by the company and was extremely unpopular with drivers at Leeds Depot and exchanged in 1967 for a similar aged rear entrance United Automobile Lodekka as a result. It is pictured heading back to Leeds via Bramhope and Otley on its usual route on Service 34. (Author's collection)

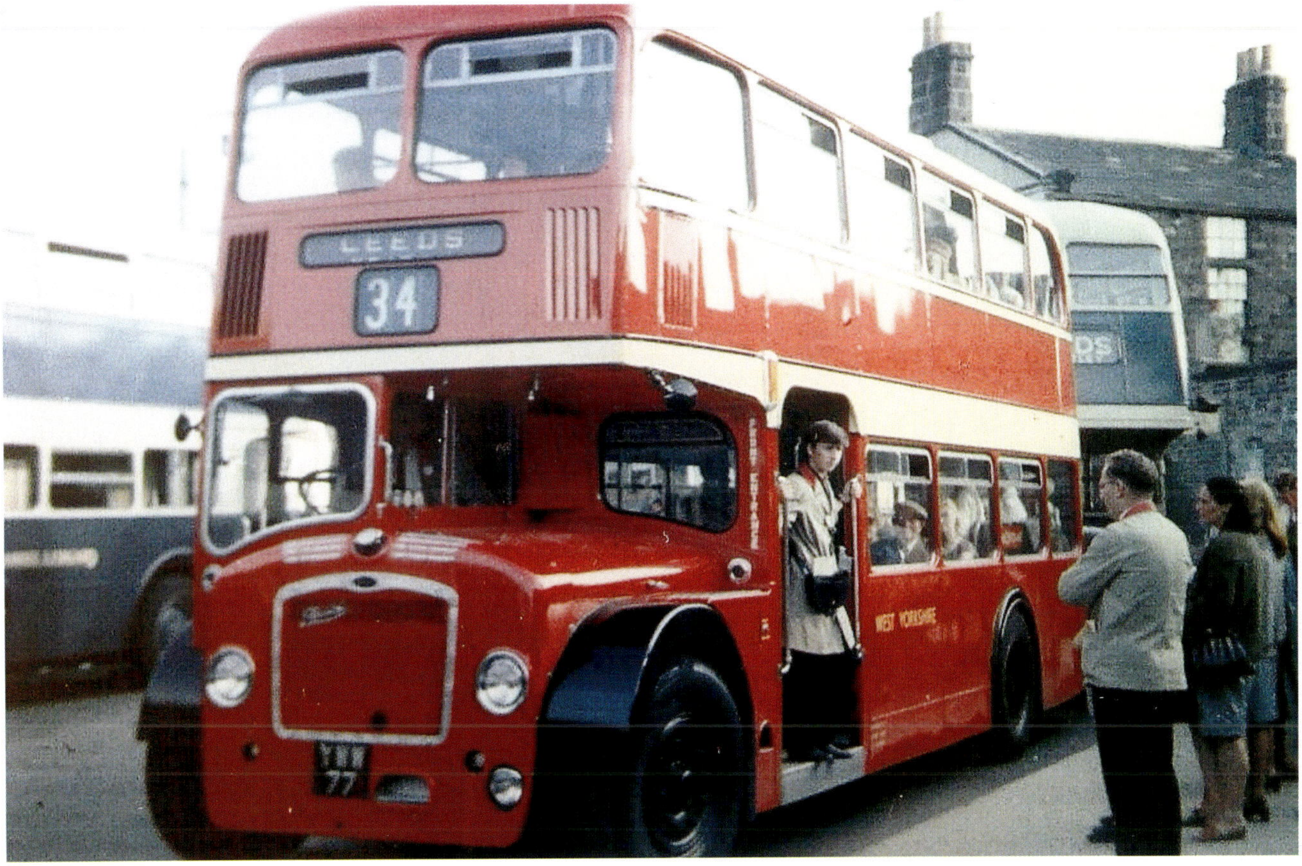

A very young looking conductor stands on the platform of West Yorkshire DX82 (YWW 77) at Otley when new but after alterations to the platform door and destination display had been completed working a journey to Leeds on Service 34. (Author's collection)

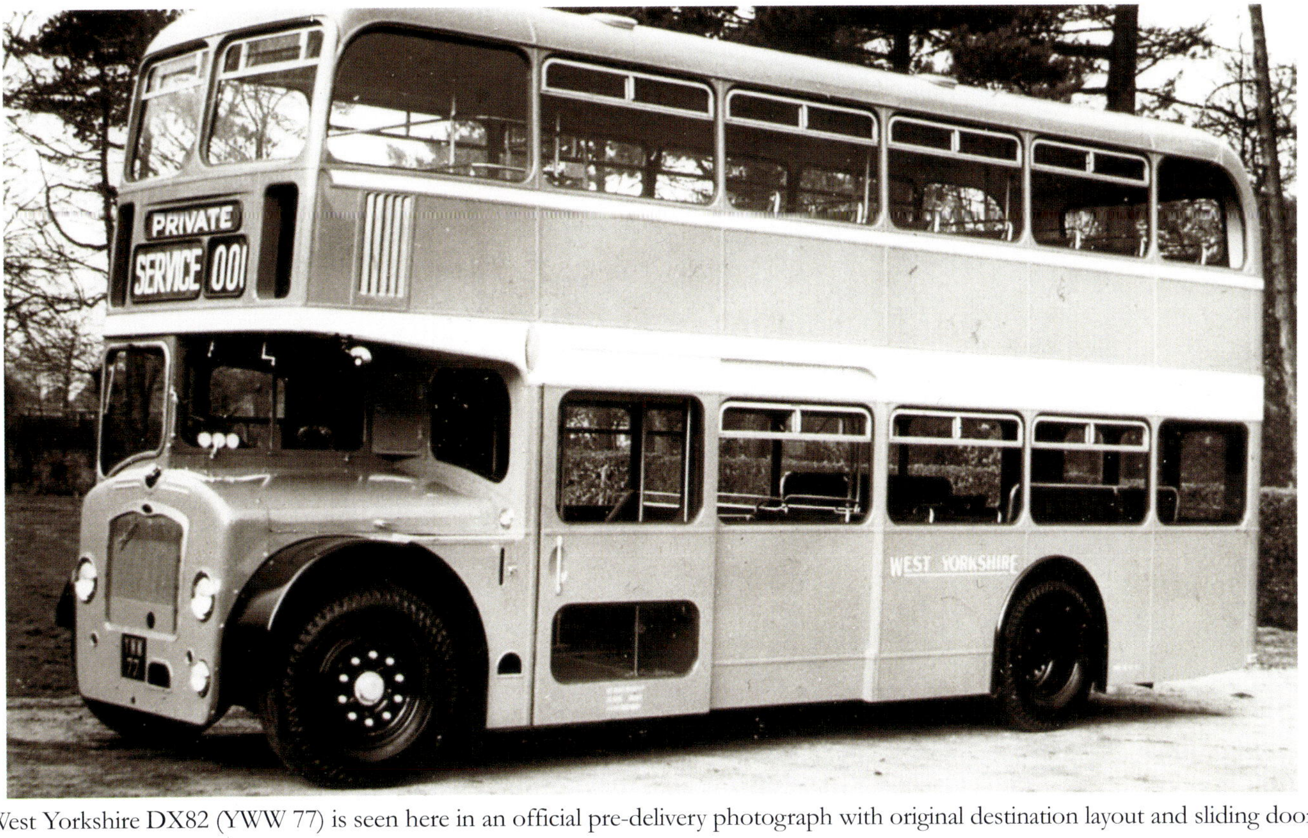

West Yorkshire DX82 (YWW 77) is seen here in an official pre-delivery photograph with original destination layout and sliding door. (Eastern Coach Works)

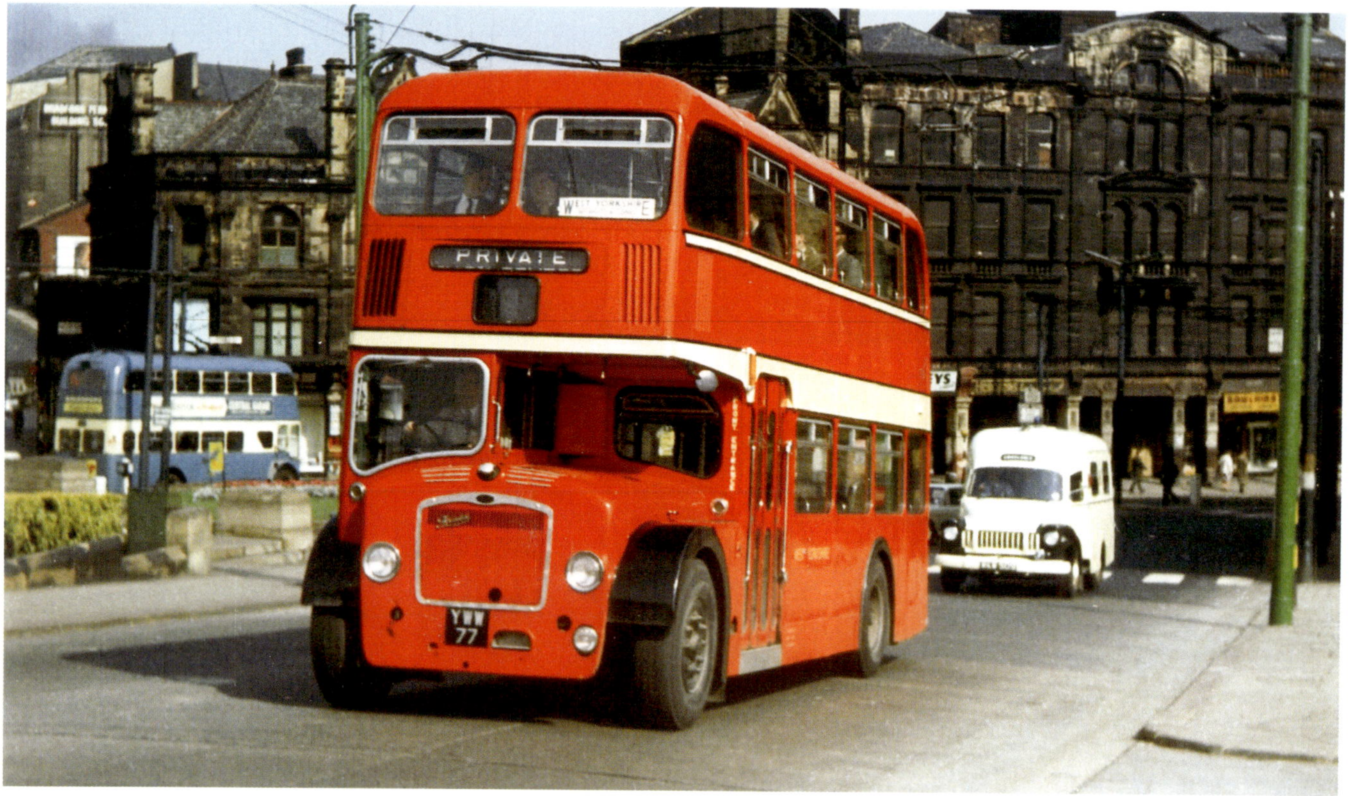

West Yorkshire DX82 (YWW 77) was the first FSF built and is seen climbing a street in Bradford beneath trolleybus wires after replacement of the original sliding door and destination equipment. The 1960s feel is emphasised by the dated appearance of the ambulance following the bus operating a bus enthusiasts' tour. (Andrew Lockwood)

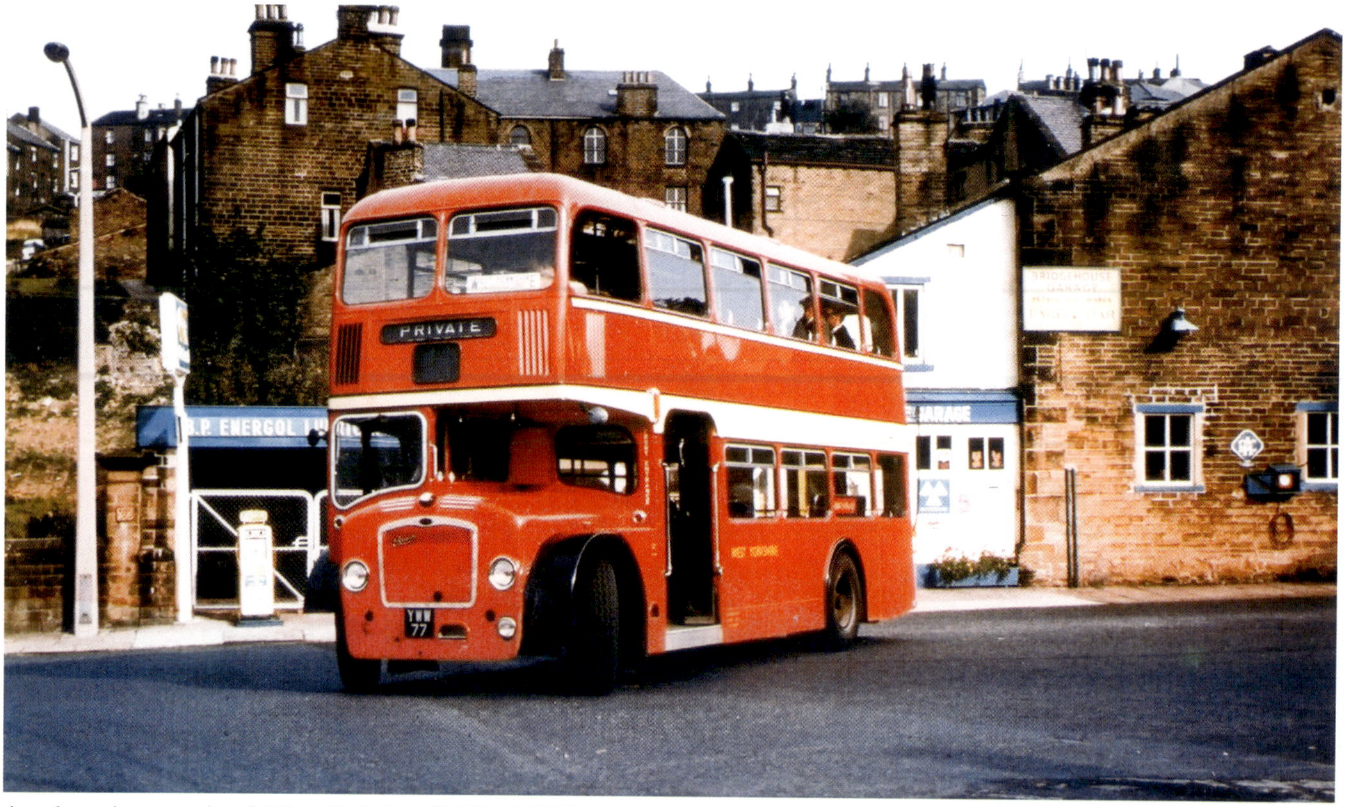

Another photograph of West Yorkshire DX82 (YWW 77) on a private hire foray with an enthusiasts' tour in Bradford. The replacement folding door can clearly be seen after the original sliding door had been converted to the usual four leaf folding option. (Andrew Lockwood)

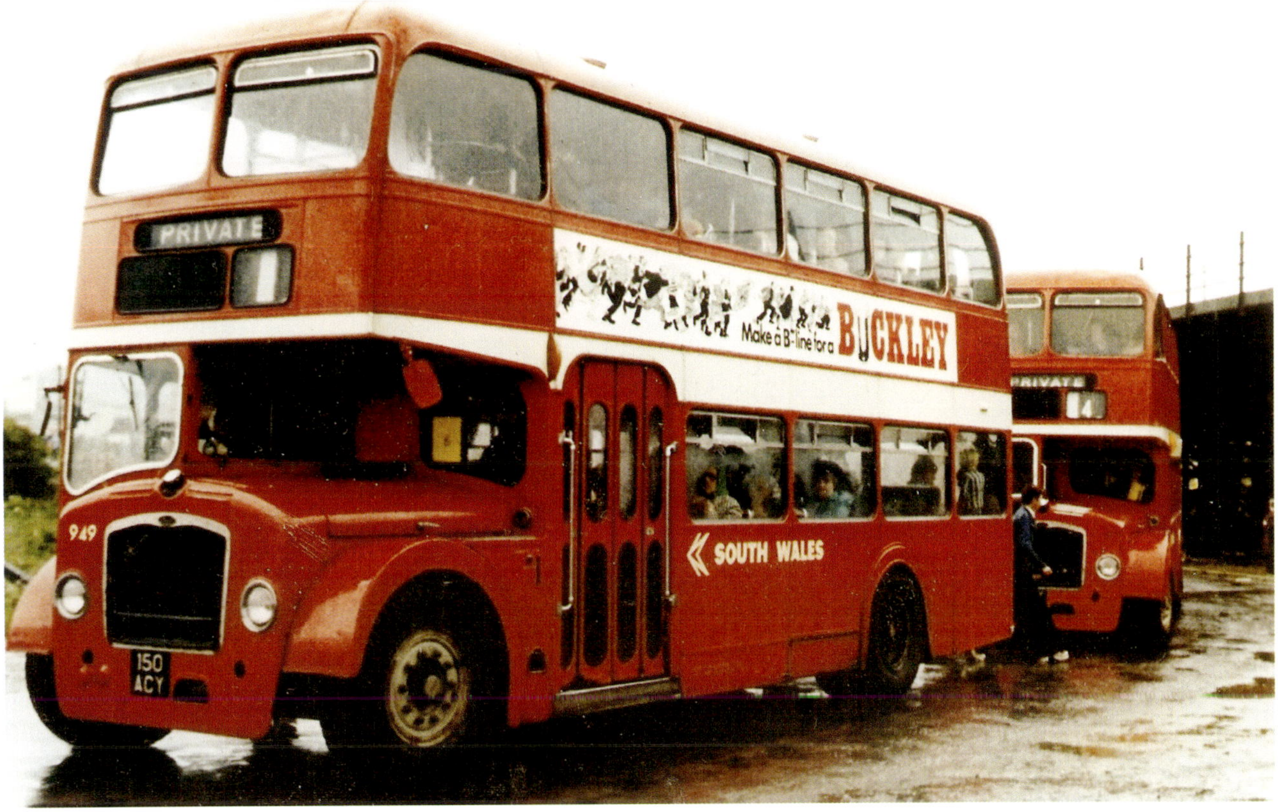

South Wales Transport 949 (150 ACY), a 1961 ex United Welsh FSF6G, on private hire duties in typical Welsh, or should that be British?, weather. (Paul Dudley)

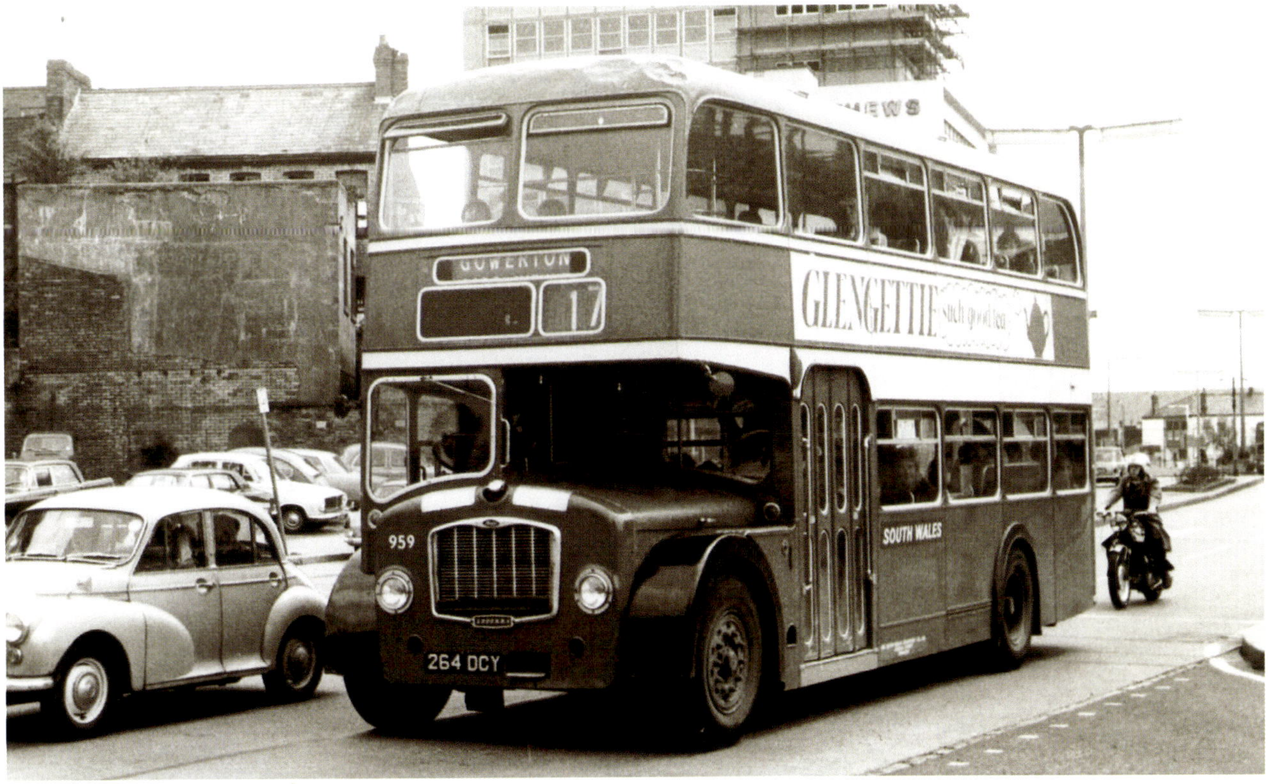

With a temporary South Wales fleet name covering its original one 959 (264 DCY), an ex United Welsh FSF6G received in November 1962, works to Gowerton on Service 17 pursued by a motorcyclist wearing a typical style of open face helmet of the late 1960s. (Tony Robbins collection)

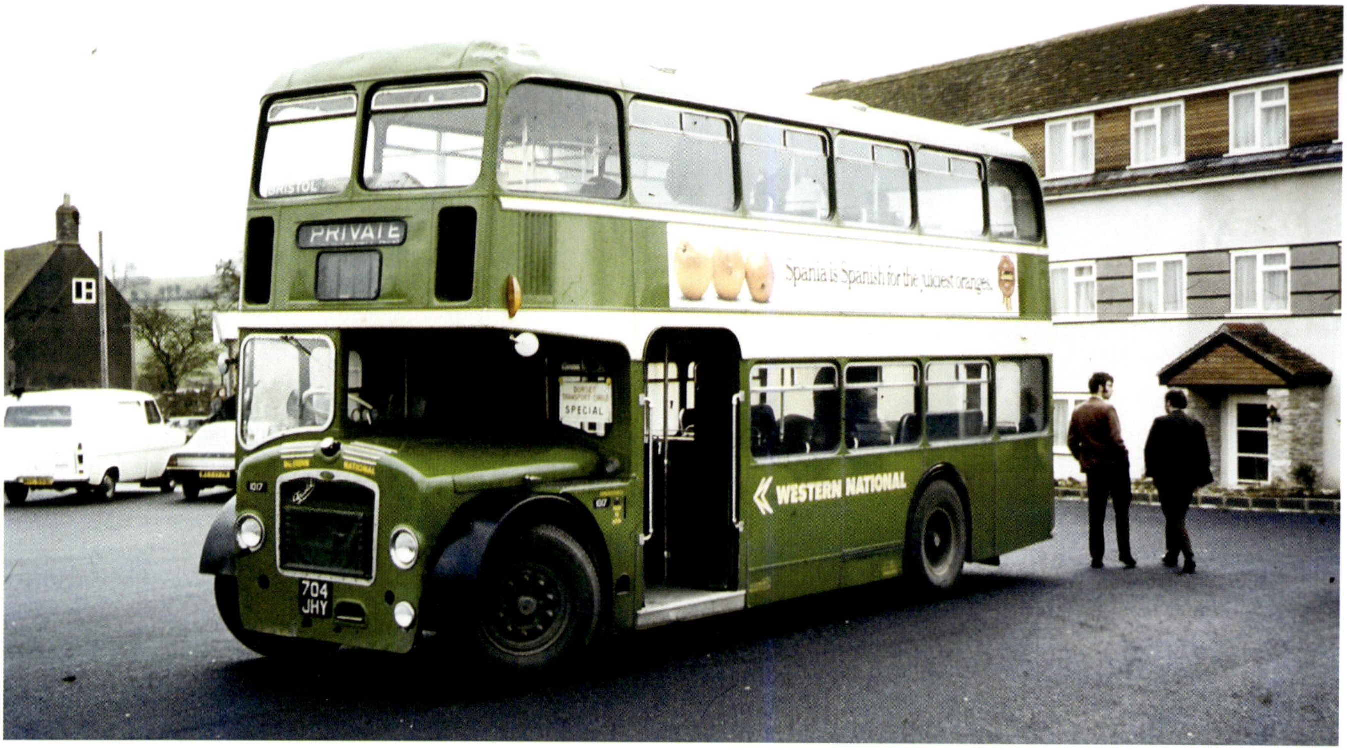

Seen here at Shepton Mallet on 10th February 1973 Western National 1017 (704 JHY) was previously with Bristol Omnibus as L6007 and based at Stroud. On this occasion it was working on private hire duties well before tachograph legislation seriously affected the ability of companies to use ordinary double deck buses on such duties. (Author's collection)

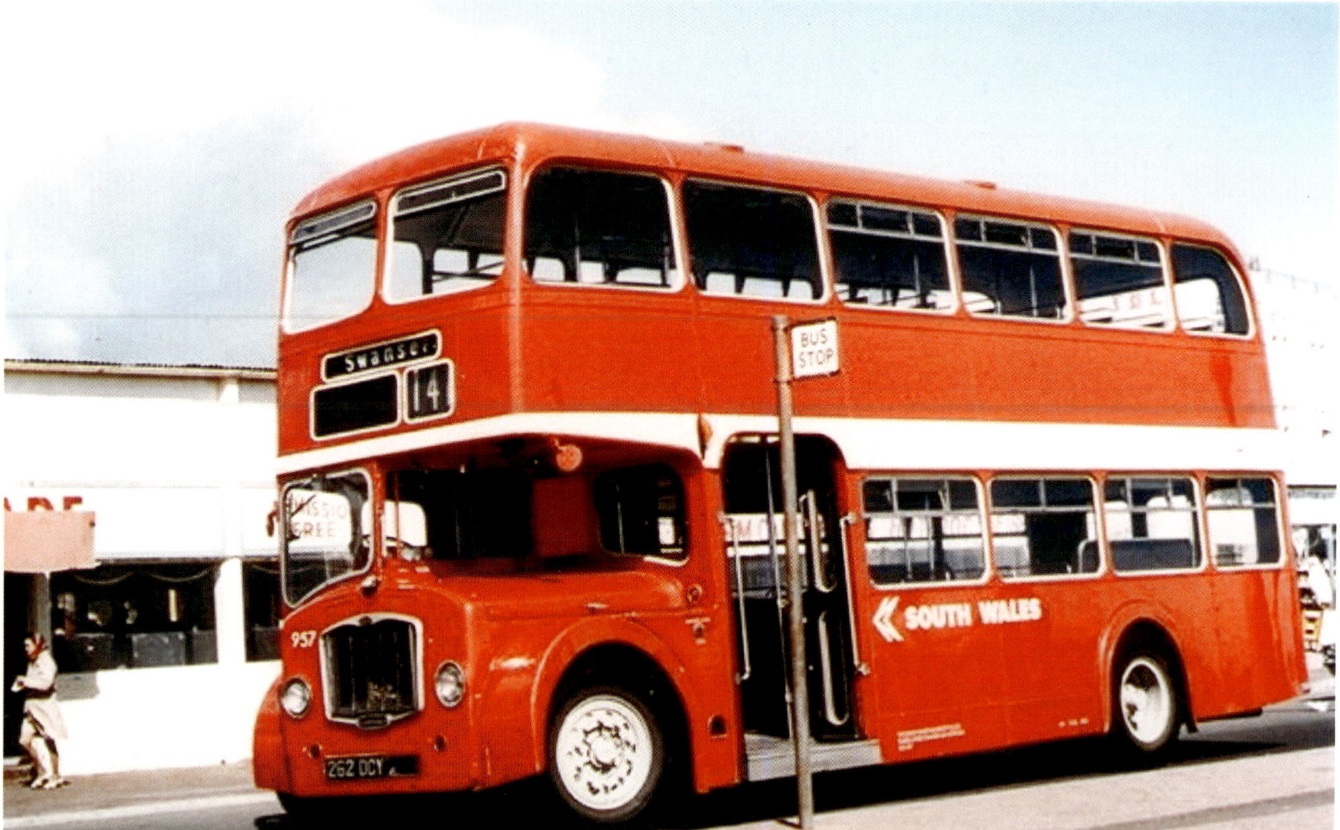

Delivered in November 1962 to United Welsh with fleet number 364 South Wales 957 (262 DCY), a 1962 FSF6G, is seen in Swansea in "poppy red" NBC livery that sits well with the white waist band and fleet names. (Tony Robbins collection)

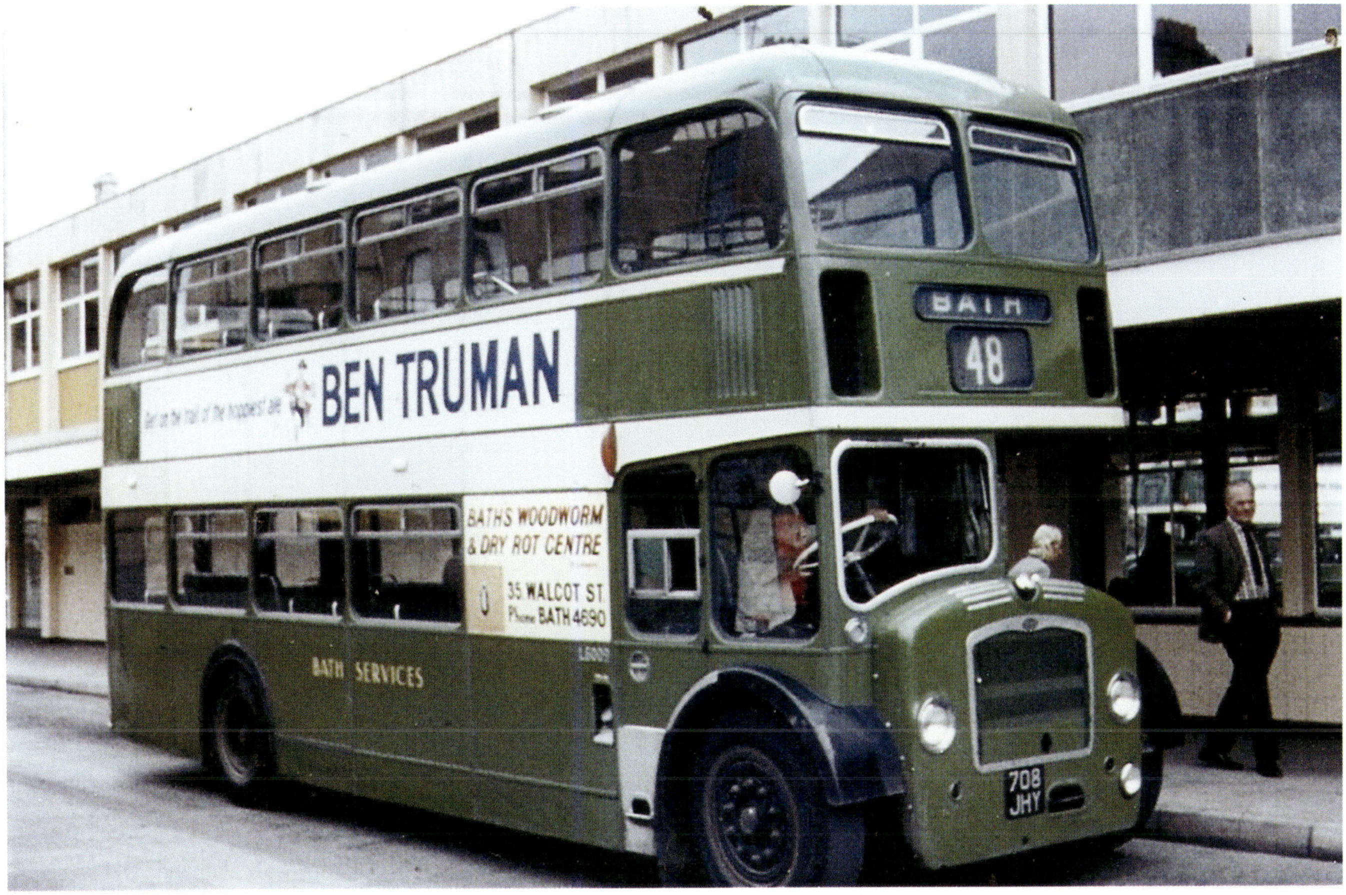

Bath Services L6009 (708 JHY), a 1960 Bristol FSF6G, arrives at the rear of Bath Bus Station from Trowbridge on Service 48, with hand painted Ben Truman beer and Bath Woodworm & Dry Rot Centre adverts. In later years the direction of traffic was reversed in Railway Street making arrivals such as this impossible and passengers having to alight on intermittent islands, on what became known as Bus Station Private Road (BSPR on duty cards), rather than the intended arrivals platform with bus doors adjacent to the bus station entrance. (Bristol Vintage Bus Group)

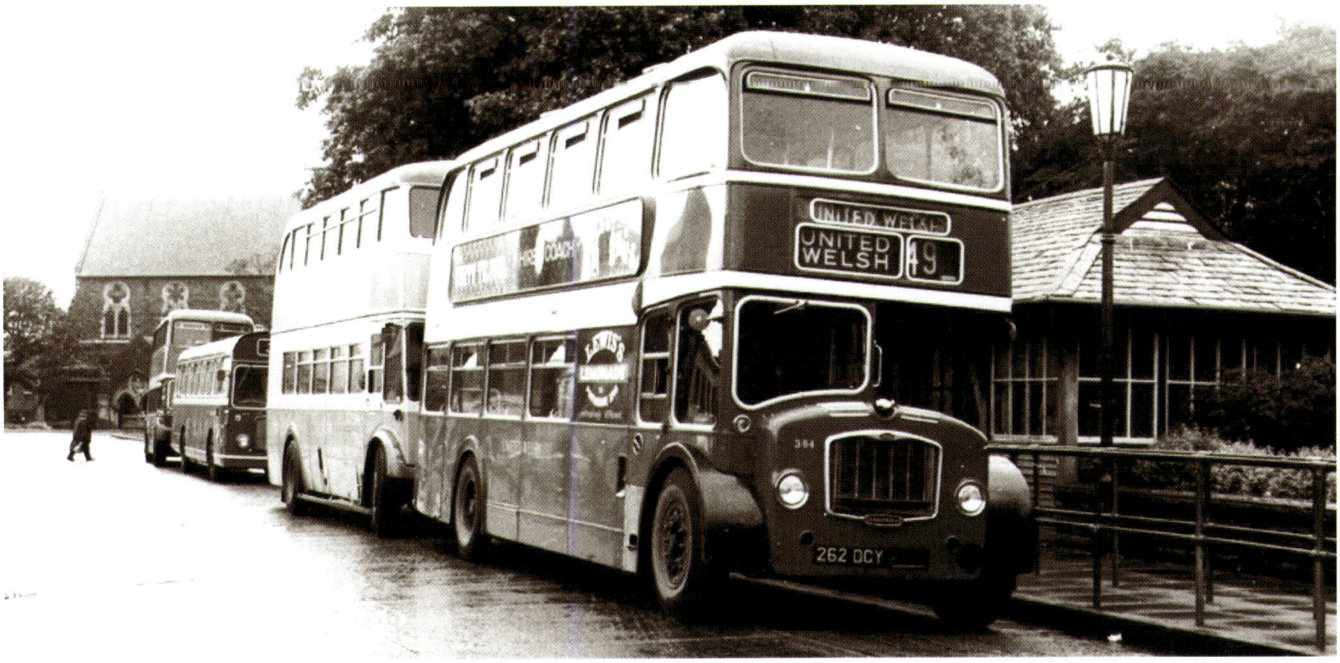

Emphasising that it's definitely owned by United Welsh FSF6G 364 (262 DCY) was photographed in Neath on 22nd June 1970 with a rather unhelpful destination blind display that tells passengers who are not locals absolutely nothing. (Bristol Vintage Bus Group)

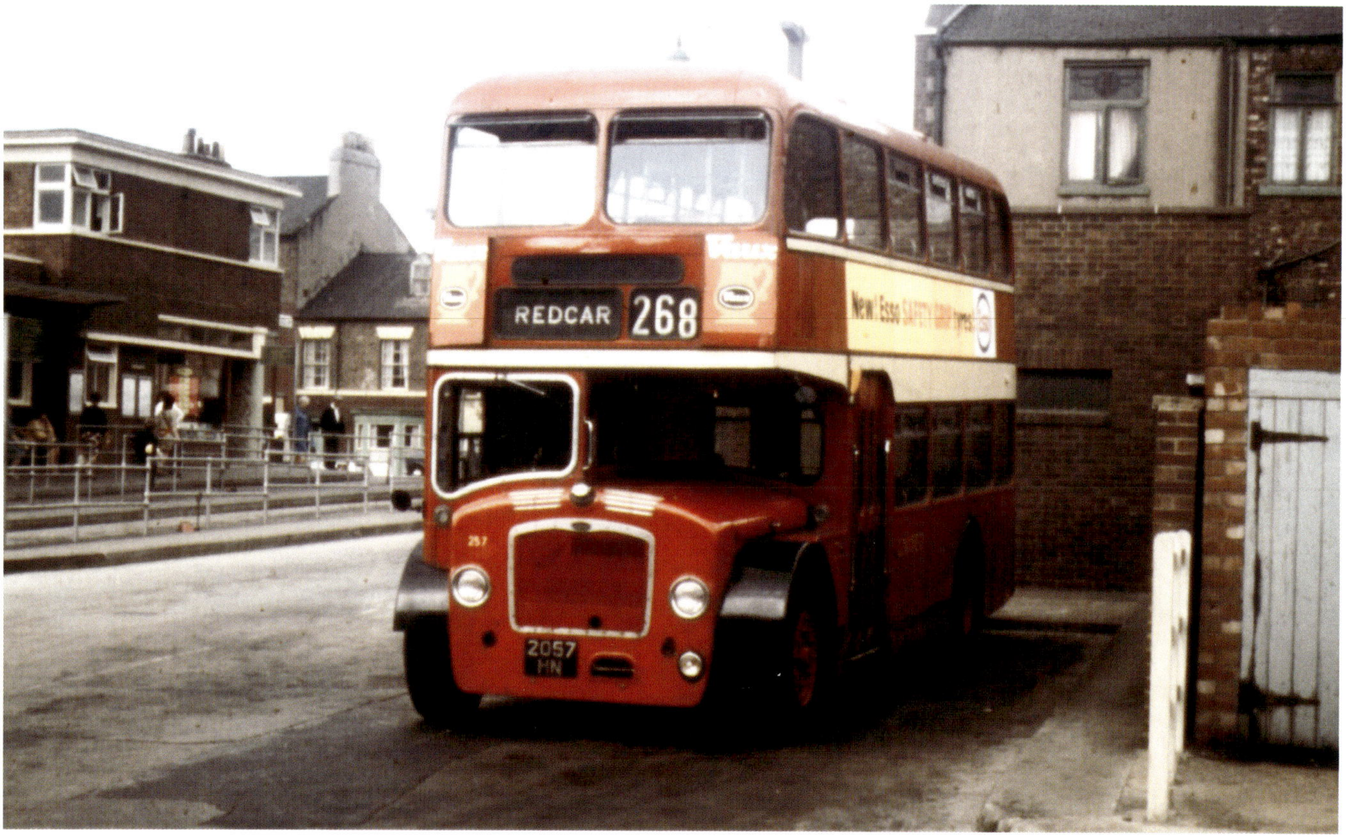

The first of a batch of 20 FSF6Bs delivered November 1960 and May 1961, United Automobile 257 (2057 HN) is pictured at Redcar Bus Station in July 1969 with CBC radiator covers after arrival from Middlesbrough. (Donald Hudson)

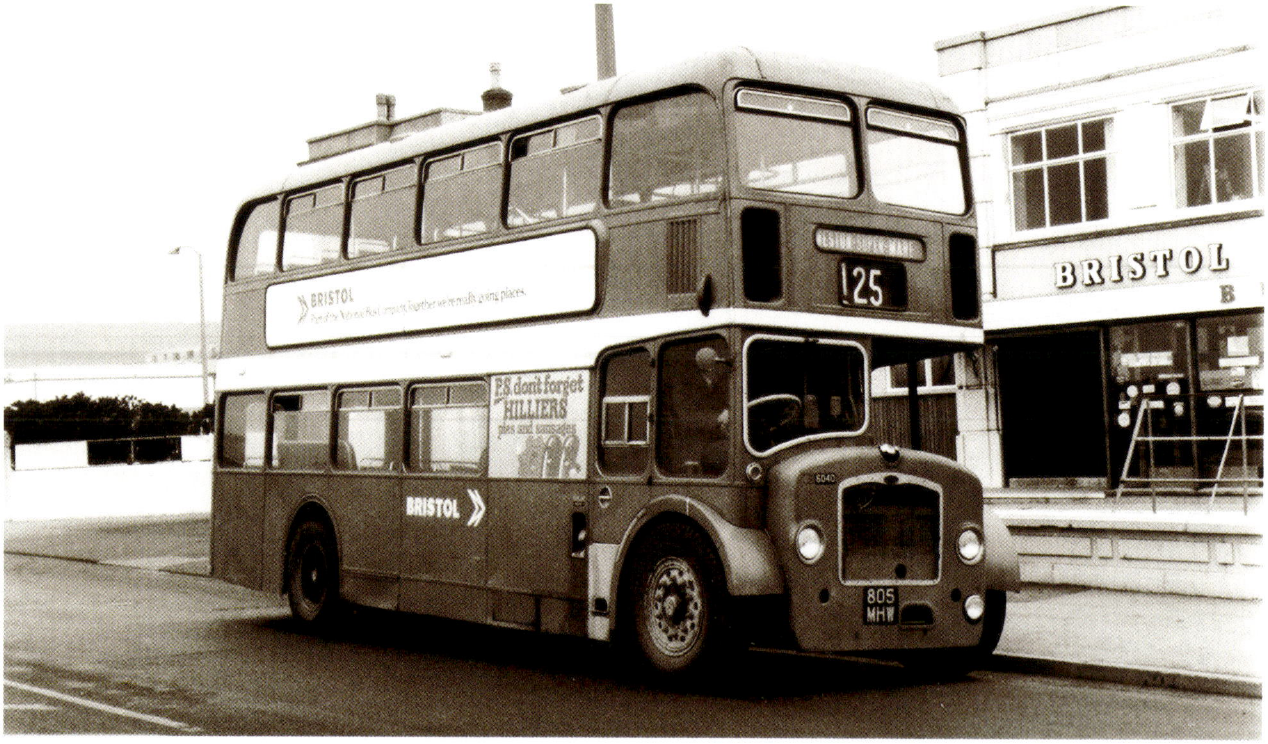

Parked outside Weston-super-Mare's Depot and Bus Station on 17th January 1977 ex Gloucester 6040 (805 MHW), a 1961 FSF6G, was exported to the United States of America in September 1977 after having spent six years at Bath prior to transfer to Weston. This bus was still active in 2008 in the USA after it had been converted into a mobile restaurant complete with a telescopic roof. (Allan Macfarlane)

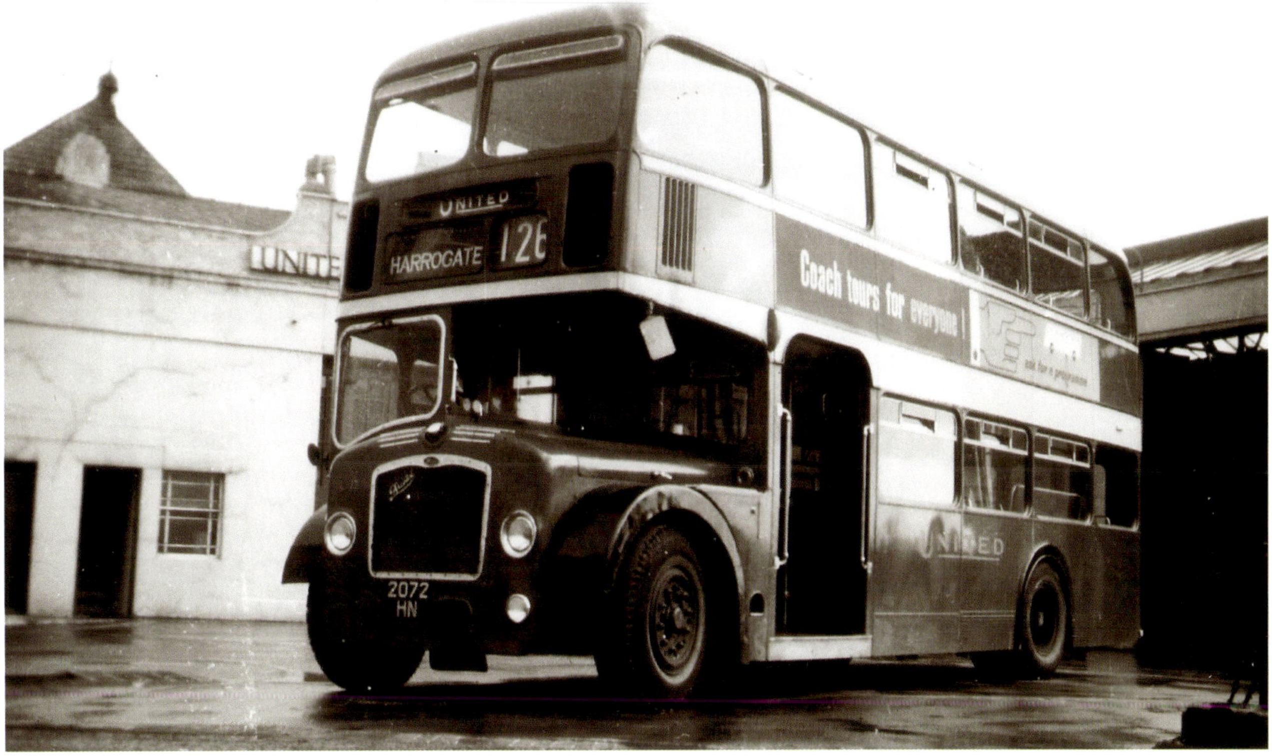

A fine low profile image of United BL72 (2072 HN) a 1961 FSF6B being prepared for a journey to Harrogate on Service 126. (Bristol Vintage Bus Group)

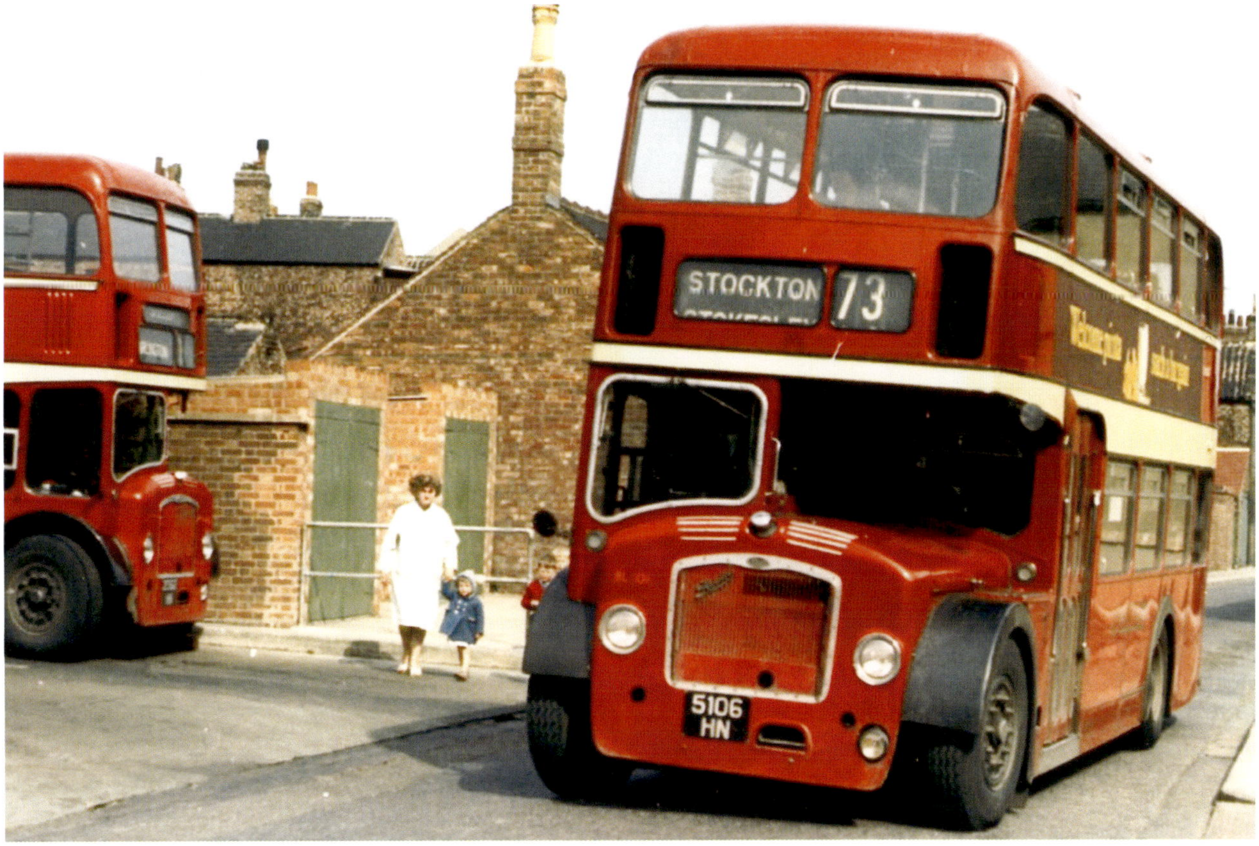

Arriving at Redcar Bus Station circa 1962 with underlined fleet names United BL106 (5106 HN) already has its destination boxes set for the return working on Service 73 to Stockton. The adult and child fashions of the period are very apparent. (Peter Horrex collection)

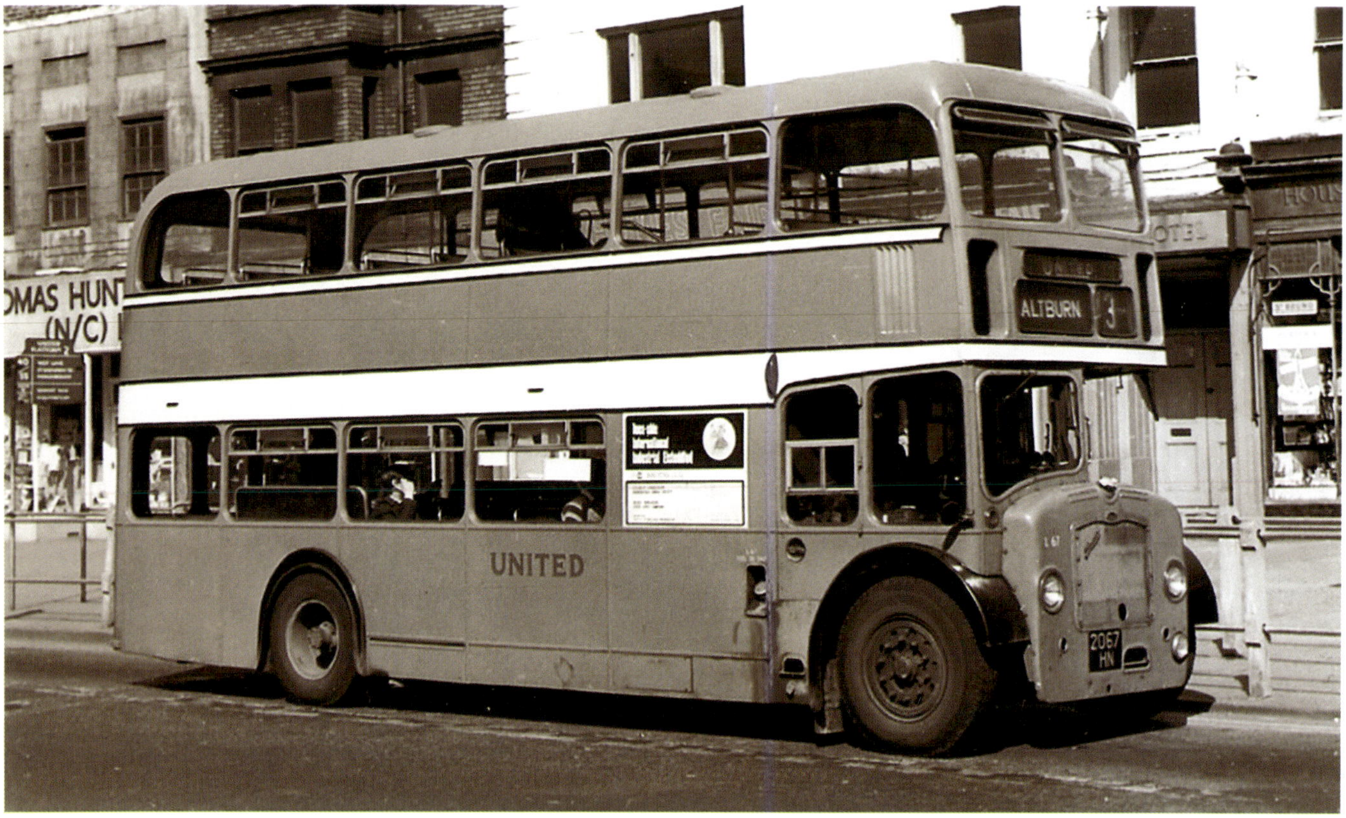

Standing in Stockton on 15th May 1966 United L67 (2067 HN), complete with smart looking lined out livery, waits for departure time to leave on Service 3 to Saltburn. (Gerry Mead)

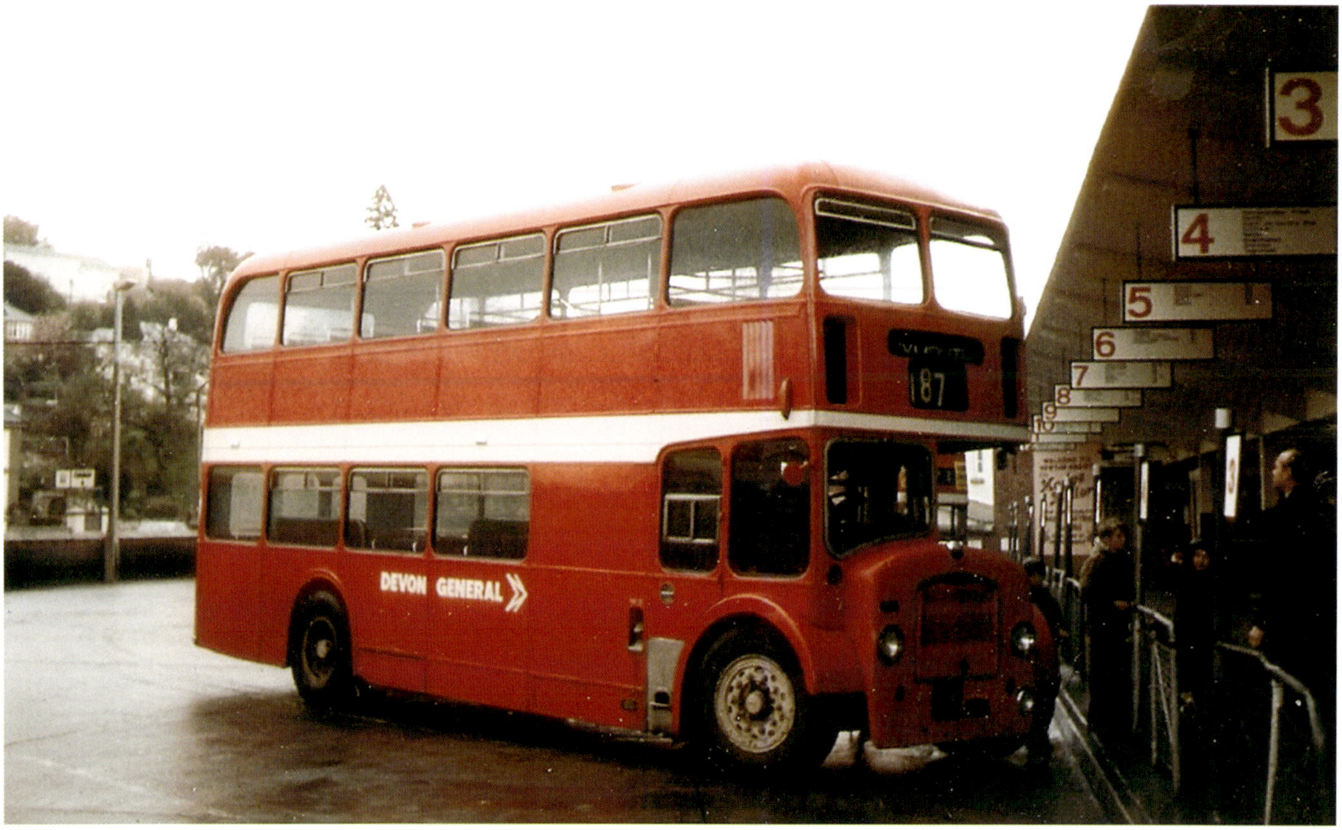

With few passengers in sight Devon General 1012 (707 JHY), a 1960 ex Bath Tramways FSF6G, stands at Paignton Bus Station prepared for a journey on Service 187 to Exmouth. (Paul Dudley)

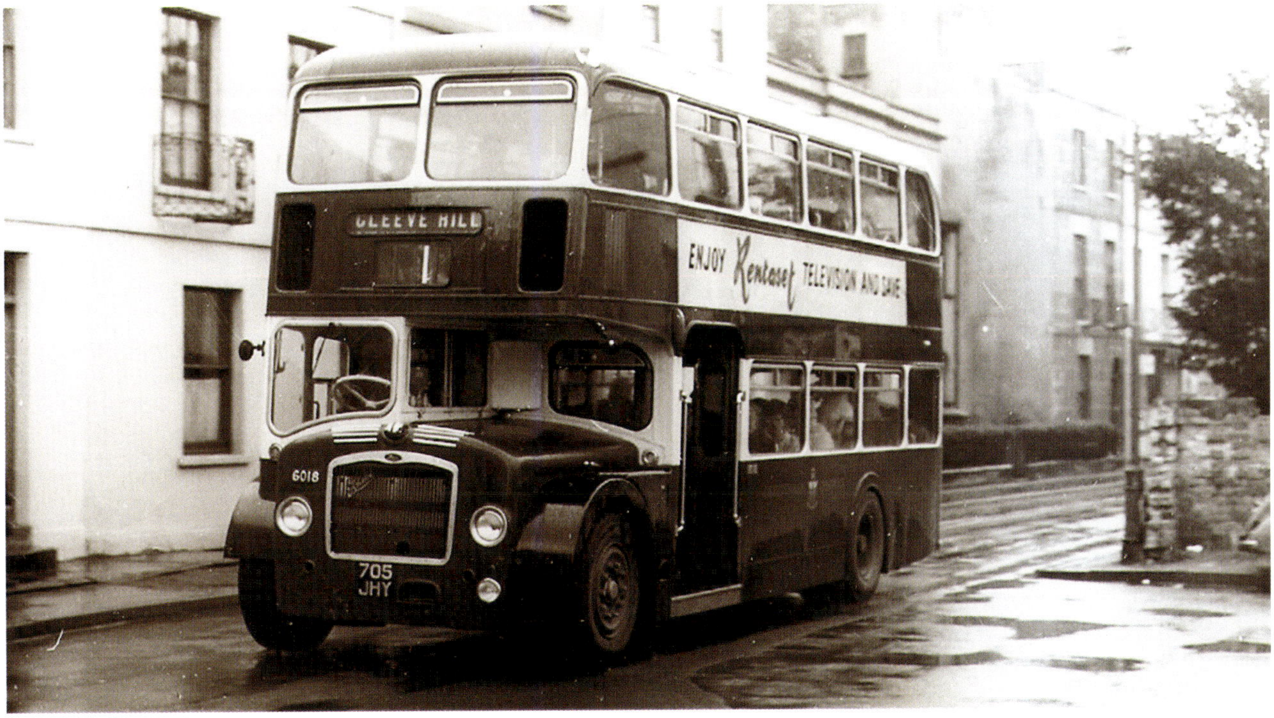

Proceeding to Cleeve Hill on Cheltenham Town Service 1 in wet and gloomy weather, Cheltenham District Traction Company 6018 (705 JHY), a 1960 FSF6G, was received as L99 until renumbered on 26th March 1961. The driver of this journey appears to want to keep the passengers and, probably, the conductor awake by driving with the platform doors open. (Tony Robbins collection)

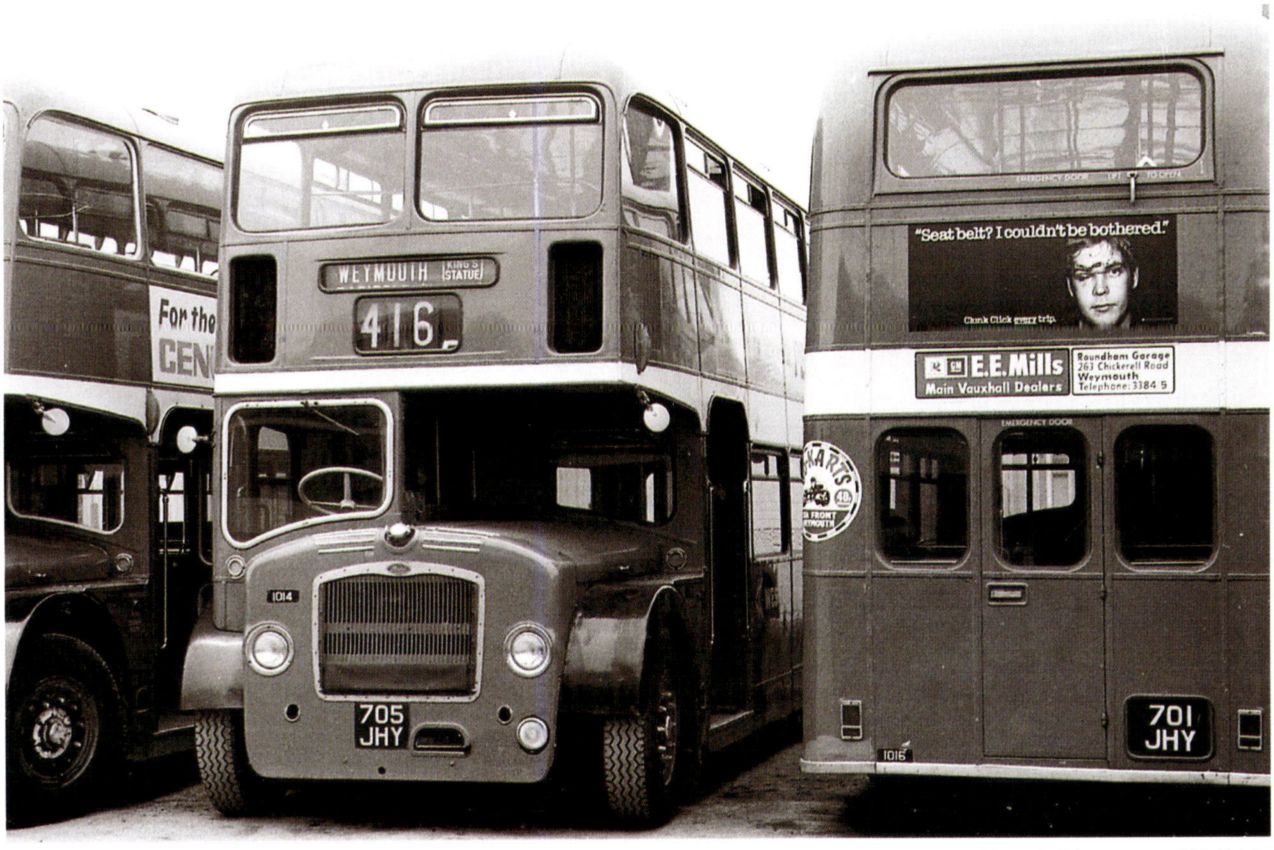

Western National 1014 (705 JHY) and 1016 (701 JHY), 1960 FSF6Gs ex Cheltenham District L99 and Gloucester GL6004, are seen at Weymouth where 1016 shows the use of the space for advertising previously showing rear destination information. The unused lower panel would have been more appropriate for the seat belt advert as it would have more easily been seen by car drivers. (P. M. Photography)

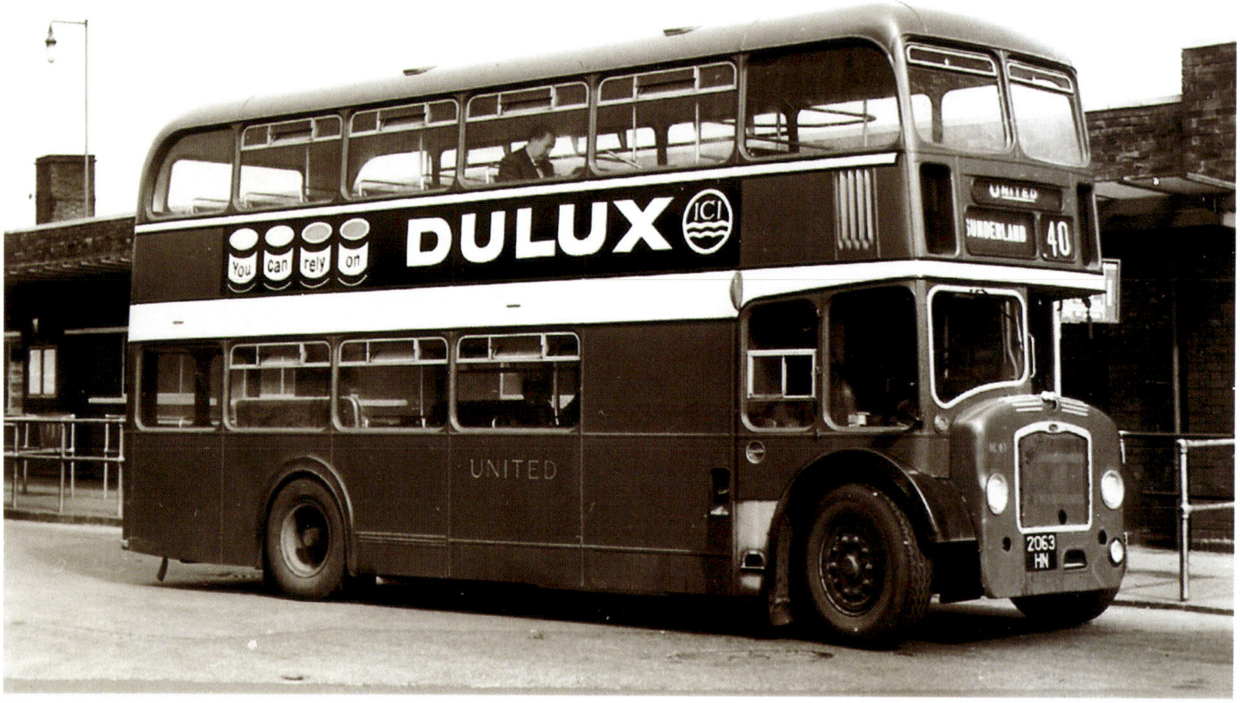

Captured on film at West Hartlepool Bus Station on 6th September 1964 United BL53 (2063 HN) waits for passengers travelling to stops on Service 40 to Sunderland. (Gerry Mead)

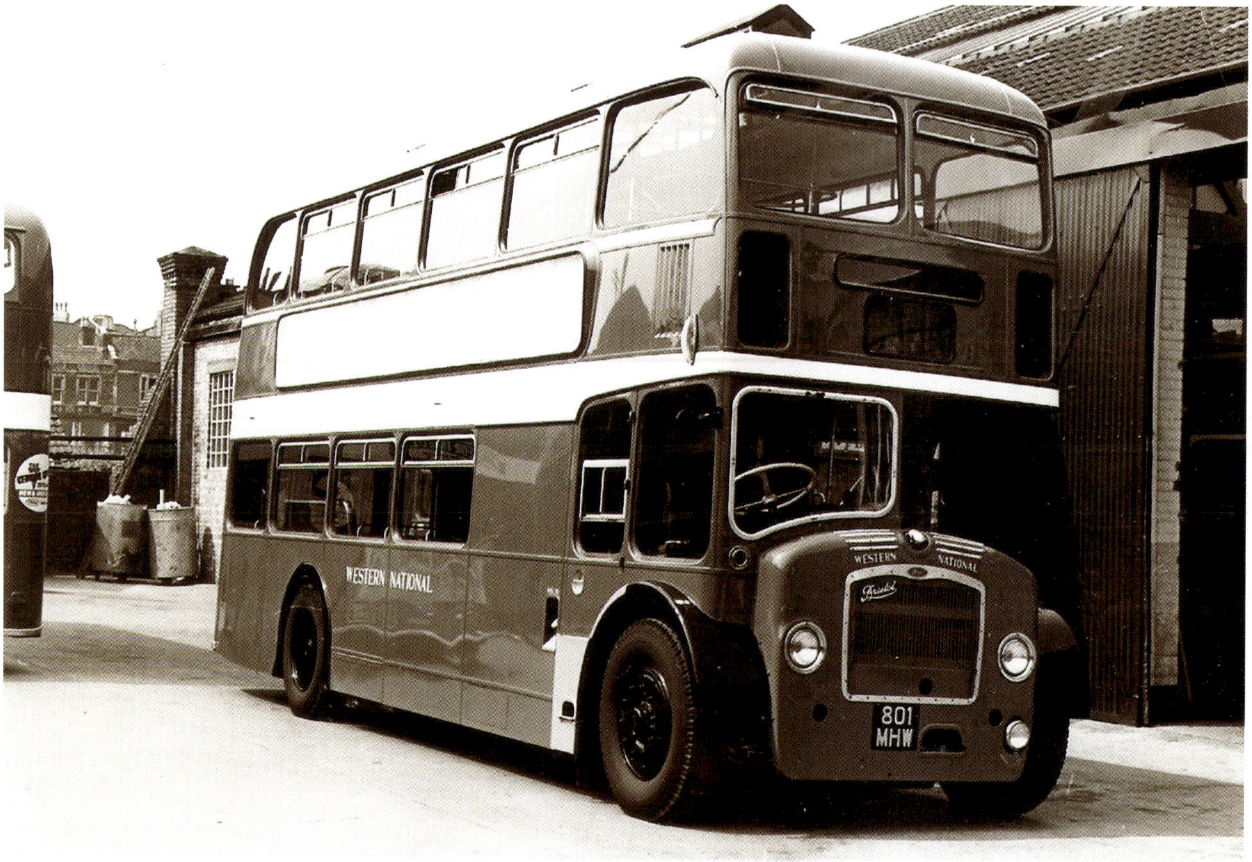

Looking as good as new Western National 1010 (801 MHW), ex Cheltenham District, has yet to receive its new owner's fleet number plates and is pictured soon after repainting at the Central Repair Works of Bristol Omnibus at Lawrence Hill in Bristol during June 1967. (Author's collection)

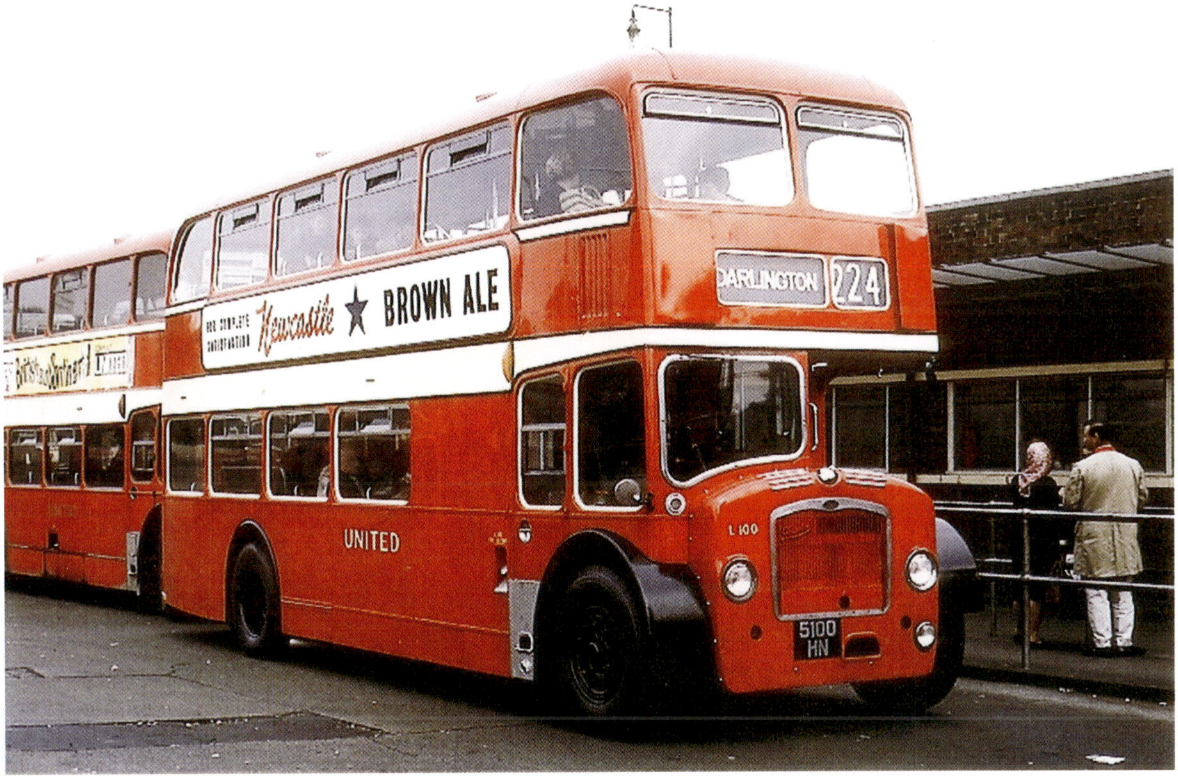

Advertising the "brew of the north", Newcastle Brown Ale, in its illuminated offside panel, United L100 (5100 HN) features covered Cave-Browne-Cave radiators. These offered valuable additional advertising space on the front of the bus that would be seen by all passengers waiting in bus queues but not in this particular instance when operating to Darlington on Service 224. (Phil Sposito collection)

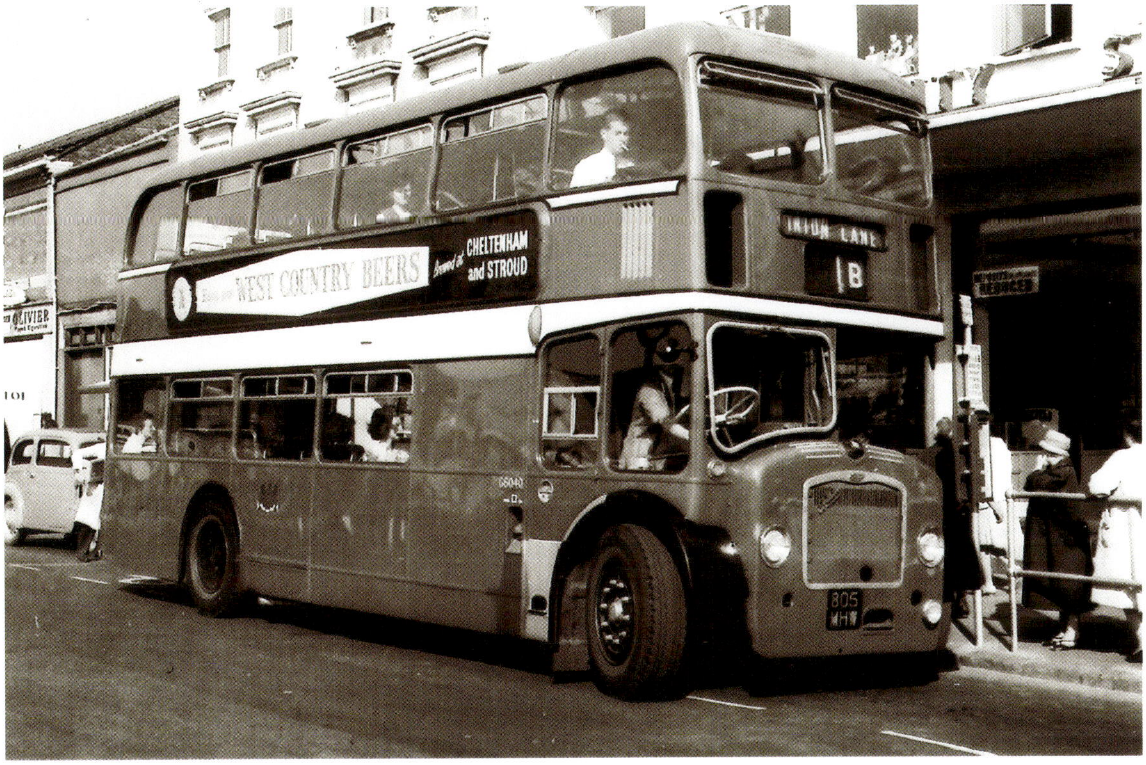

One of the six FSF6Gs built for Gloucester City Services was G6040 (805 MHW), the penultimate Bristol FSF for the Bristol Omnibus group of companies. Photographed when quite new in late 1961 it's working a journey from Tuffley to Pirton Lane on Service 1B. (Phil Sposito collection)

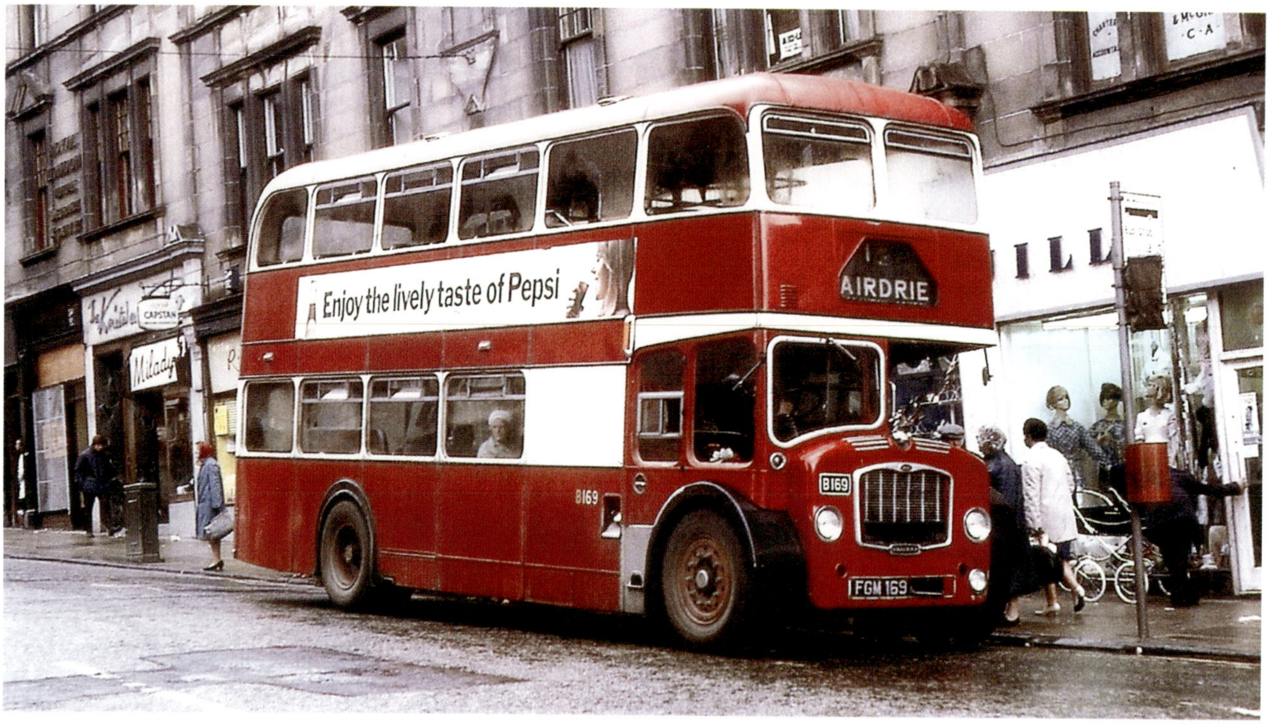

Central SMT B169 (FGM 169) was the penultimate FSF delivered in September 1963 under Sanction 215 but carries no fleet name in this view when working to Airdrie on Service 13. (Phil Sposito collection)

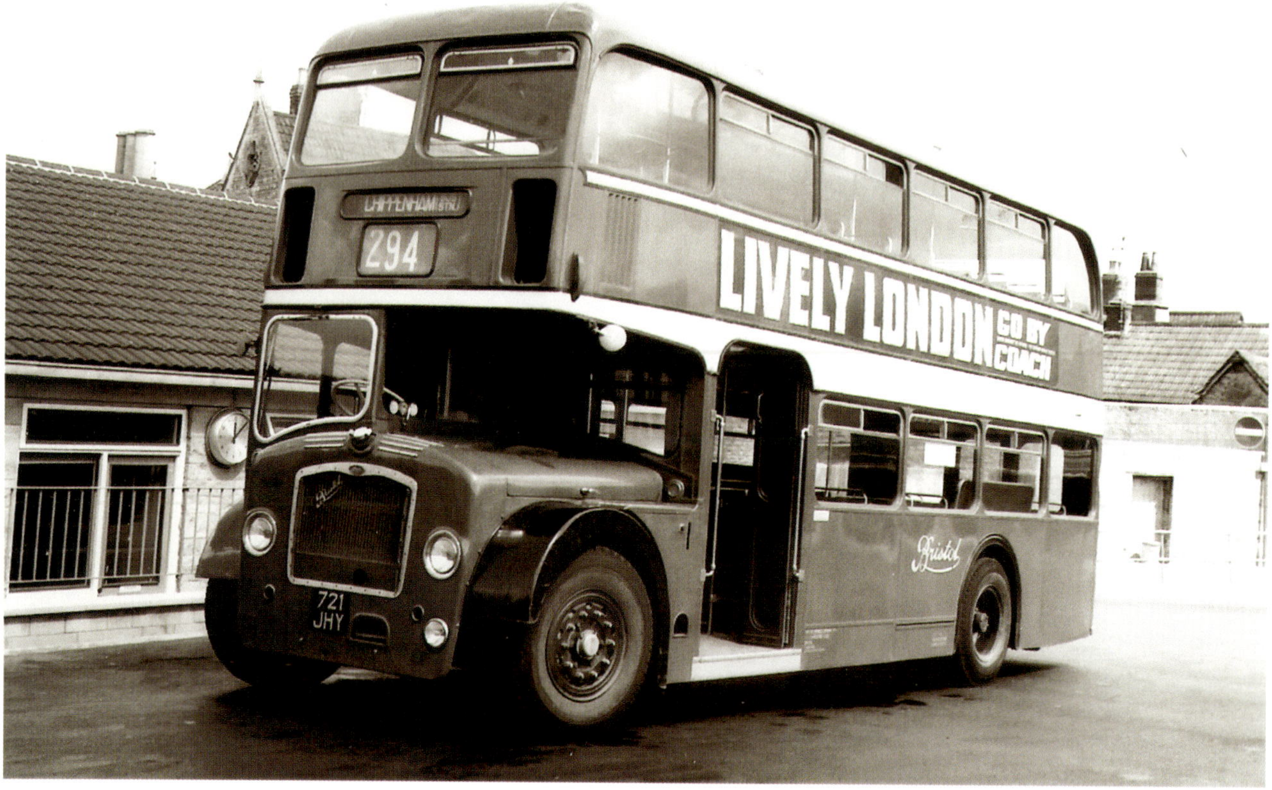

Rebranded back to Bristol Omnibus 6022 (721 JHY) with Bristol scroll fleet name from its Western National identity as 1000 this FSF6G looks to be in good external condition at Chippenham Bus Station. Originally based at Weston-super-Mare from new in February 1961 it was transferred to Bath in February 1966 until sold to Western National in August 1967. Service 294 was part of the Chippenham Town Services network operating between Rowden Hill (on school days only) or Bus Station and Monkton Park Estate. (Phil Sposito collection)

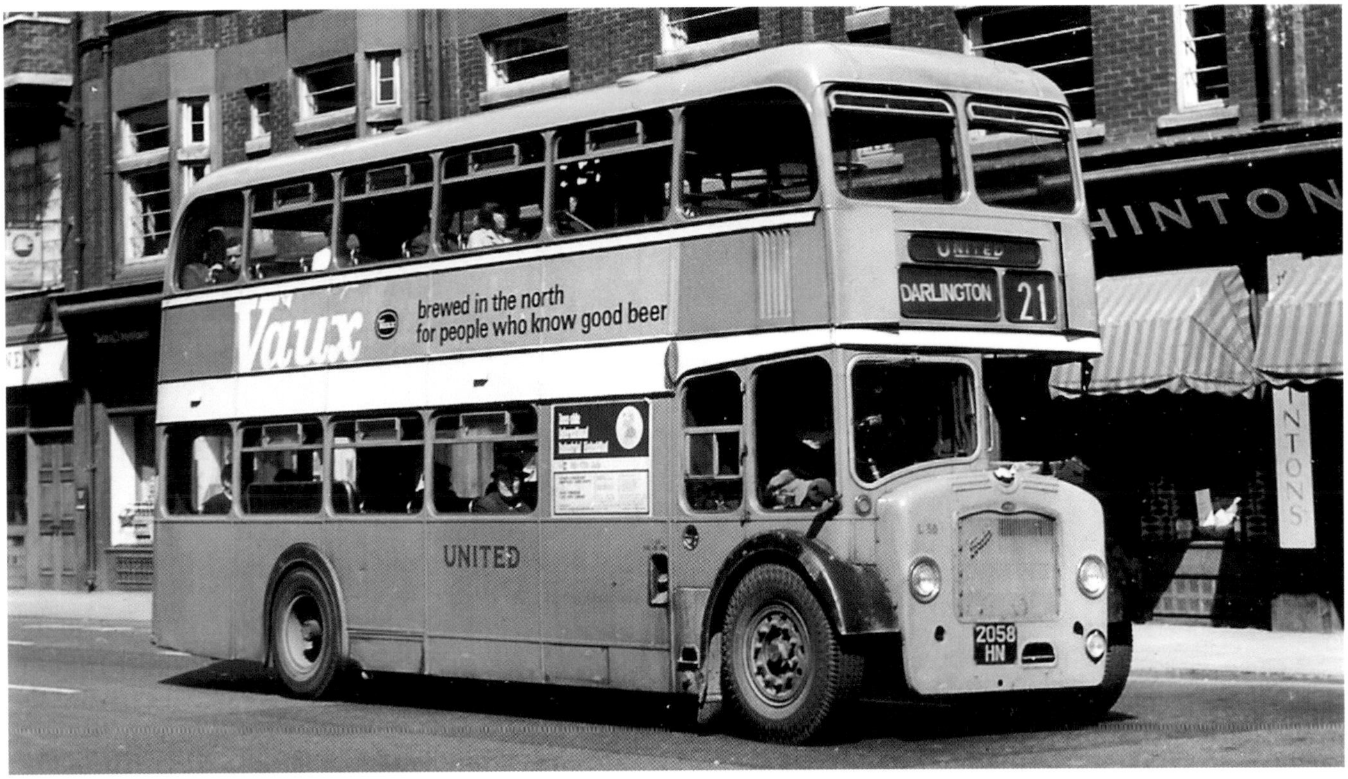

Middlesbrough is the location for L58 (2058 HN) working a journey to Darlington on Service 21 that was regarded as the midway point on the half hourly route to Redcar. This view is recorded as being taken on 15th May 1966. (Gerry Mead)

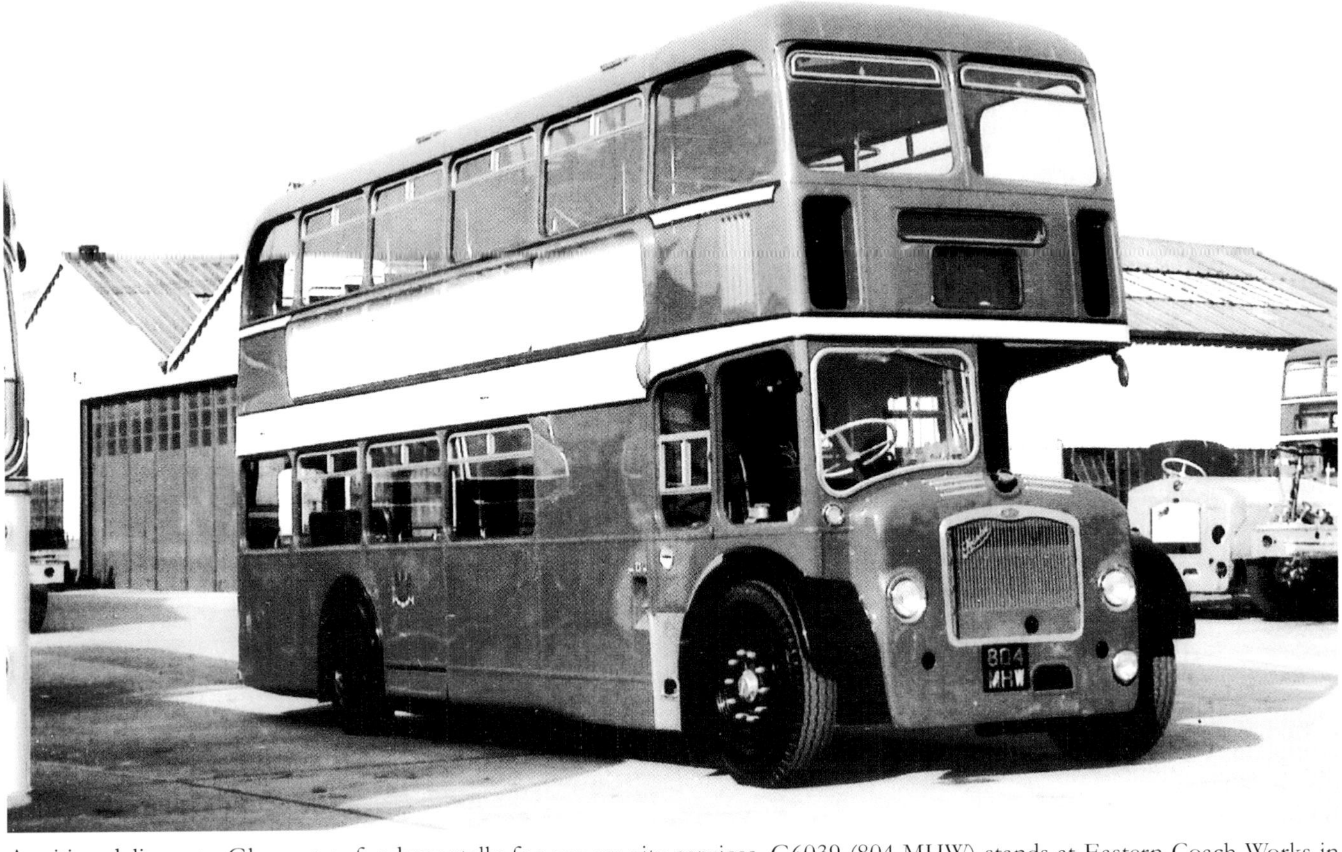

Awaiting delivery to Gloucester, fundamentally for use on city services, G6039 (804 MHW) stands at Eastern Coach Works in Lowestoft with the city crest on the unblemished fresh livery in October 1961. (Phil Sposito collection)

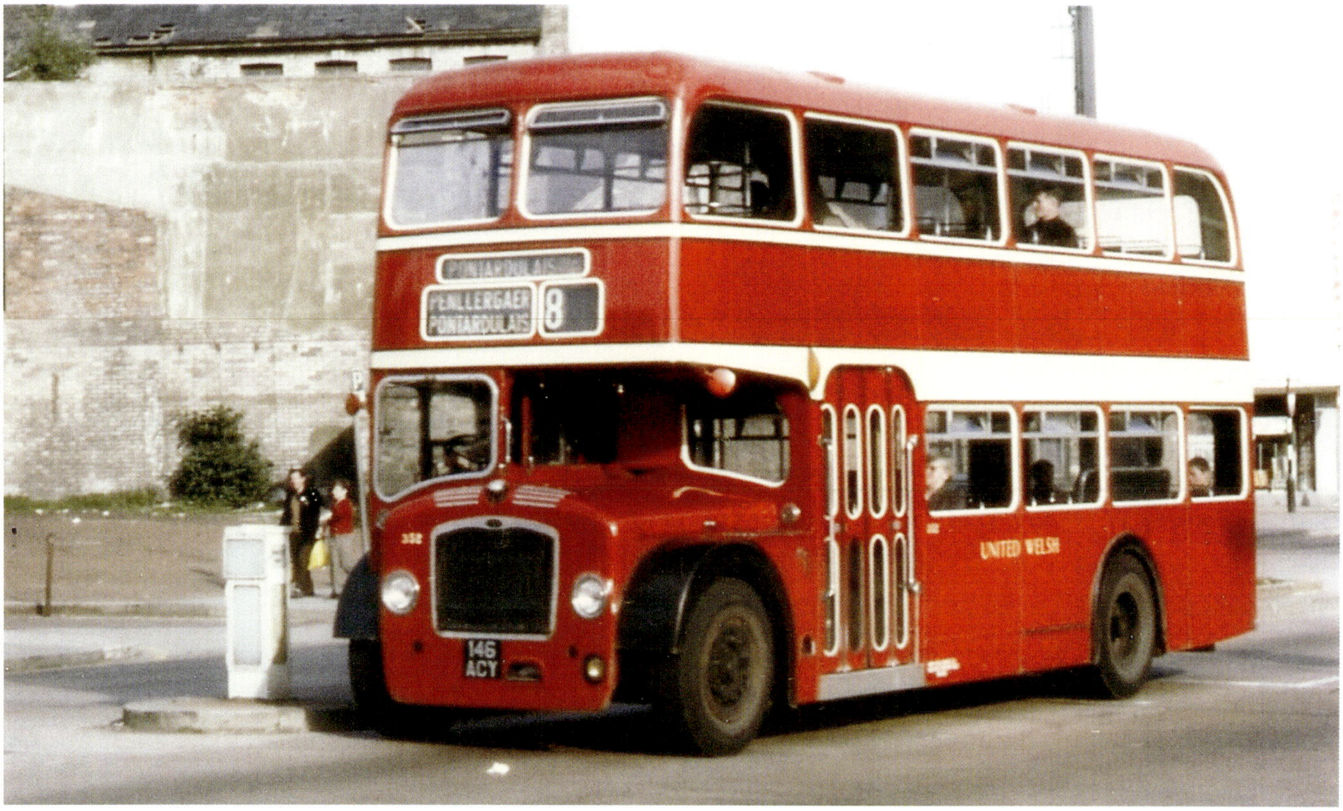

United Welsh 352 (146 ACY), a 1961 FSF6G, has very few passengers on board as it leaves Swansea for Pontardulais on Service 8. (Phil Sposito collection)

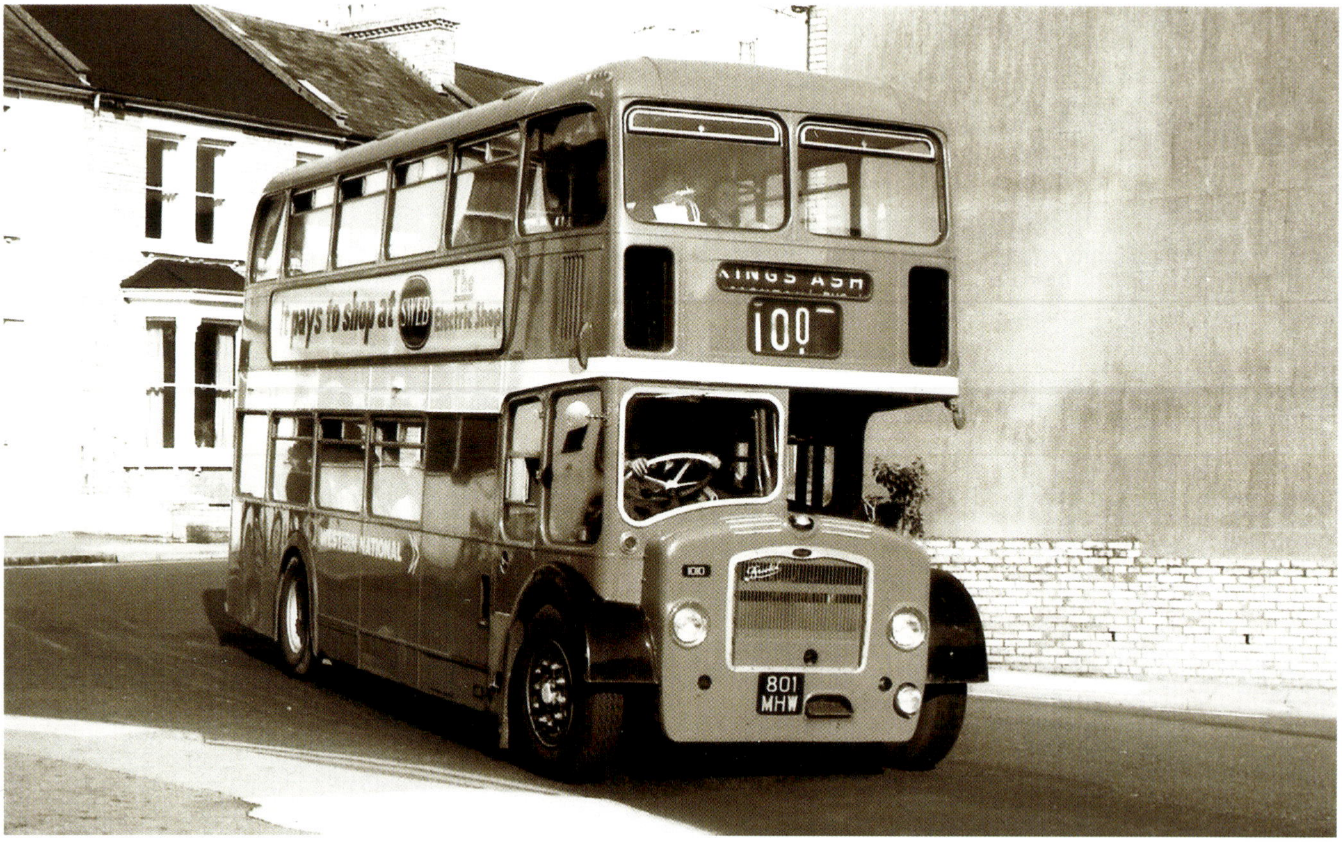

Western National 1010 (801 MHW), a 1961 former Cheltenham District FSF6G, looks in fine condition as it enters Paignton with blinds partially set for a Service 140 journey to King's Ash. (Phil Sposito collection)

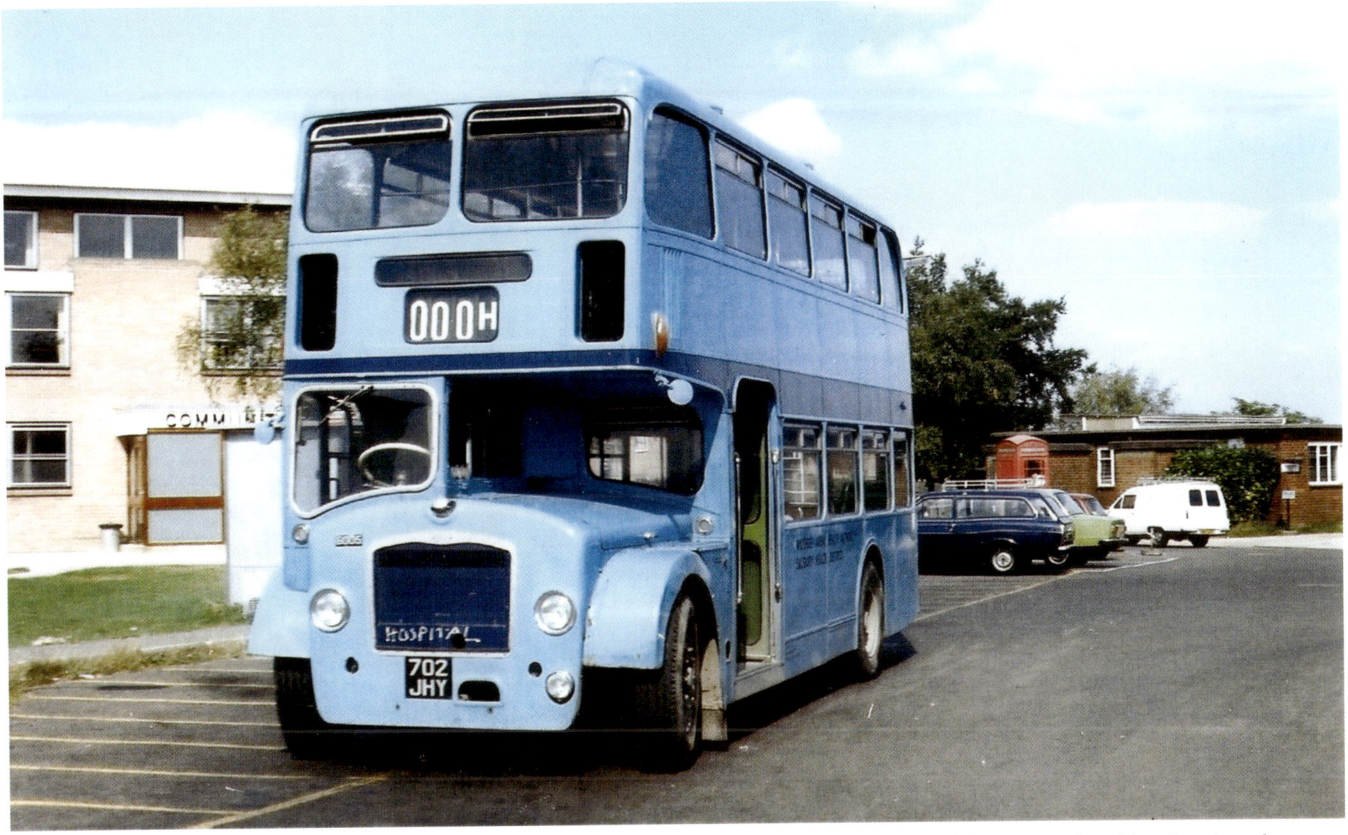

Wiltshire Area Health Authority 702 JHY, a 1960 FSF6G, was originally allocated to Gloucester for City Services but was transferred to Bath in January 1971. It's seen at Odstock Hospital still carrying its amended fleet number 6005 and 000H in the destination box in line with someone's sense of hospital humour. (Tony Robbins collection)

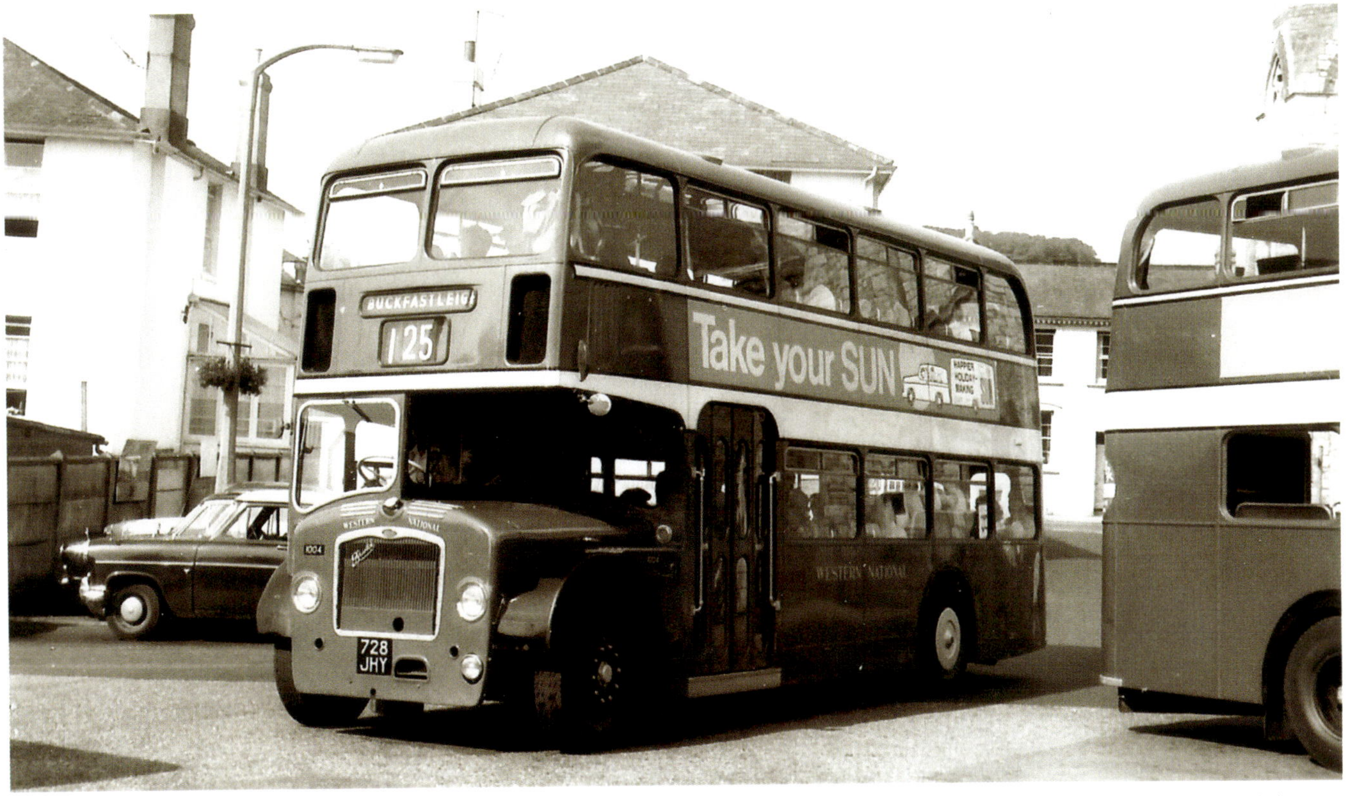

Western National 1004 (728 JHY), a 1961 ex Bristol Omnibus FSF6G, looks smart with rear wheel covers as it arrives in Paignton Bus Station with blinds already set for its next journey to Buckfastleigh. (Phil Sposito collection)

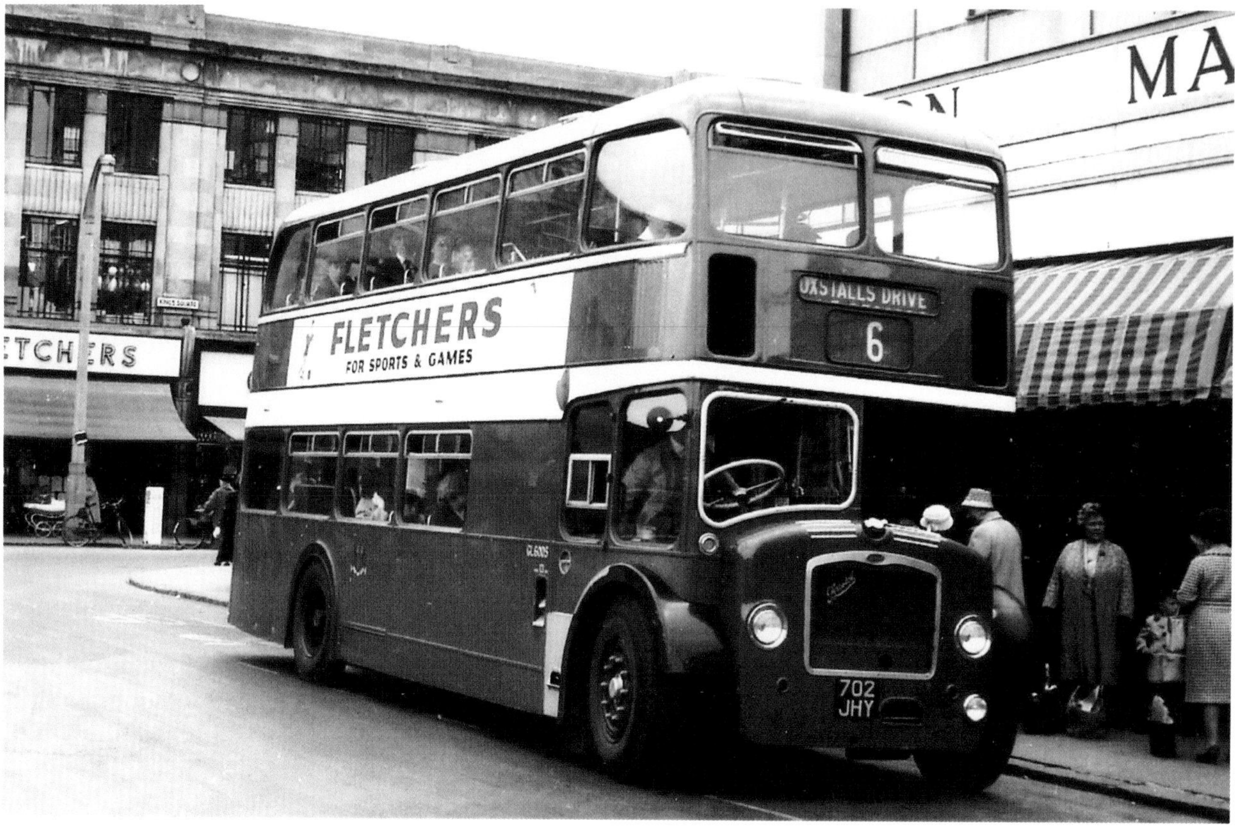

Gloucester's King's Square is the setting for GL6005 (702 JHY), a 1960 FSF6G that was delivered as GL8563 until the creation of a separate numbering series for FSFs for the Bristol Omnibus Group of companies in January 1961. (Phil Sposito collection)

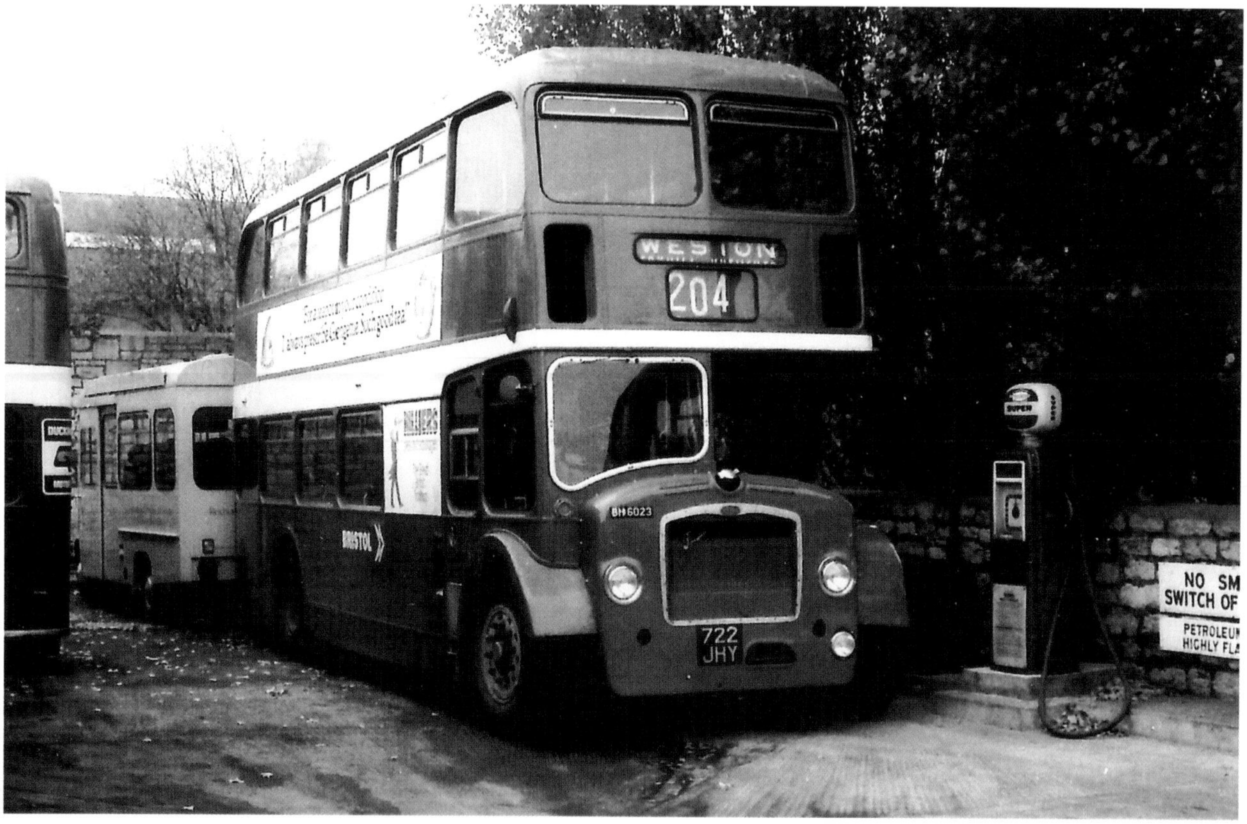

With the 'Pump Room Special' Ford Transit 16 seat minibus behind, 6023 (722 JHY) stands in the open yard at Kensington Depot, Bath. The fuel pump with classic dial and plastic globe is noteworthy as a sign of the times. (Phil Sposito collection)

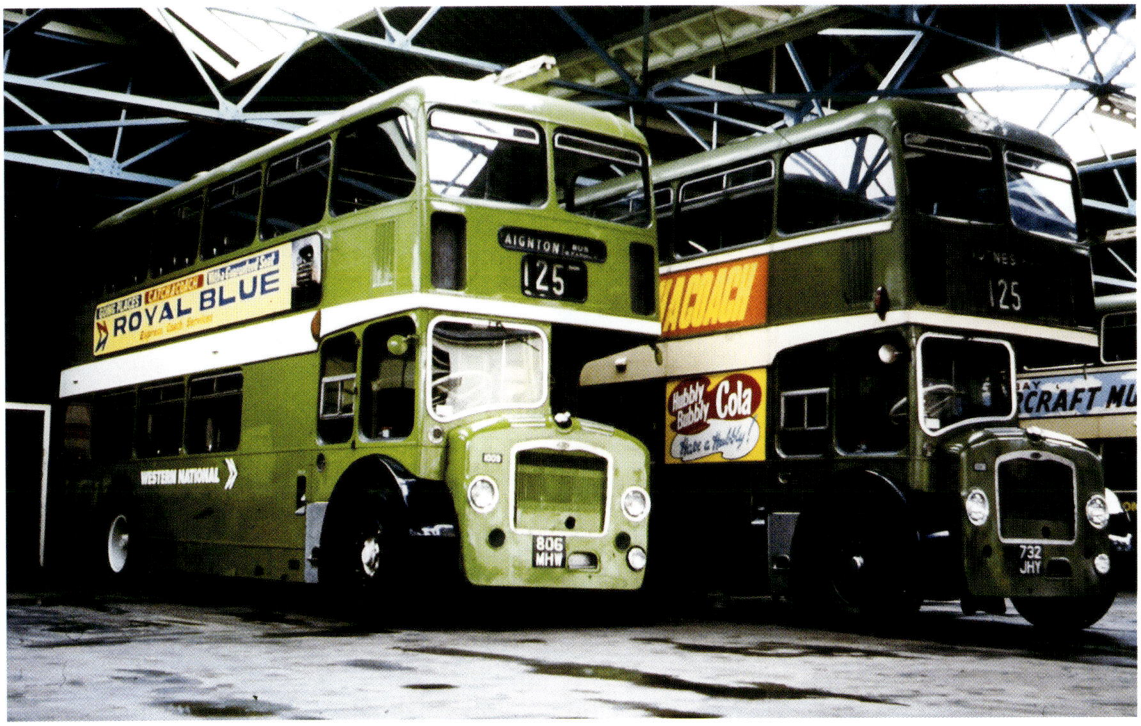

A pair of ex Bristol Omnibus FSF6Gs stand inside Totnes Depot with Western National 1009 (806 MHW) new to Bath Electric Tramways in October 1961 and sold to WN in August 1967 and 1008 (732 JHY) new in March 1961 and sold to WN in April 1967. Frequently seen around Devon they are prepared to work journeys on Service 125 that in the early 1970s operated very "seasonal" timetables. During the summer peak on weekdays between early June and early September there were eleven journeys between Paignton Bus Station and Buckfastleigh (Woodholme) reduced to four at other times and 17 journeys between Paignton and Totnes (Plains) reduced to ten at other times. On Sundays and Late Summer Bank Holiday there were four full journeys and one to Totnes but none at all advertised at other times. (Tony Robbins collection)

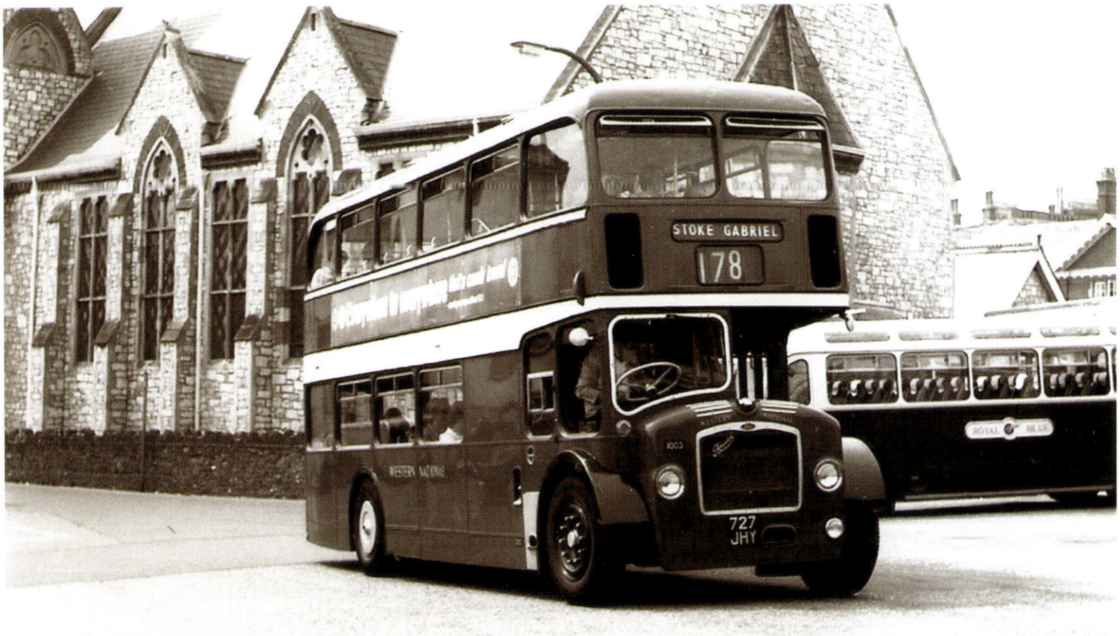

Passing in front of a Royal Blue Bristol MW coach as it arrives at Paignton Bus Station the driver of Western National 1003 (727 JHY), a 1961 former Bristol Omnibus FSF6G, has already set the blinds for a journey on Service 178 to Stoke Gabriel. Journeys in the early 1970s operated every 30 minutes from early June to early September including Sundays and Late Summer Bank Holiday but this frequency was reduced to hourly on weekdays with six journeys on the three days of Easter Sunday, Easter Monday and Spring Bank Holiday. (Author's collection)

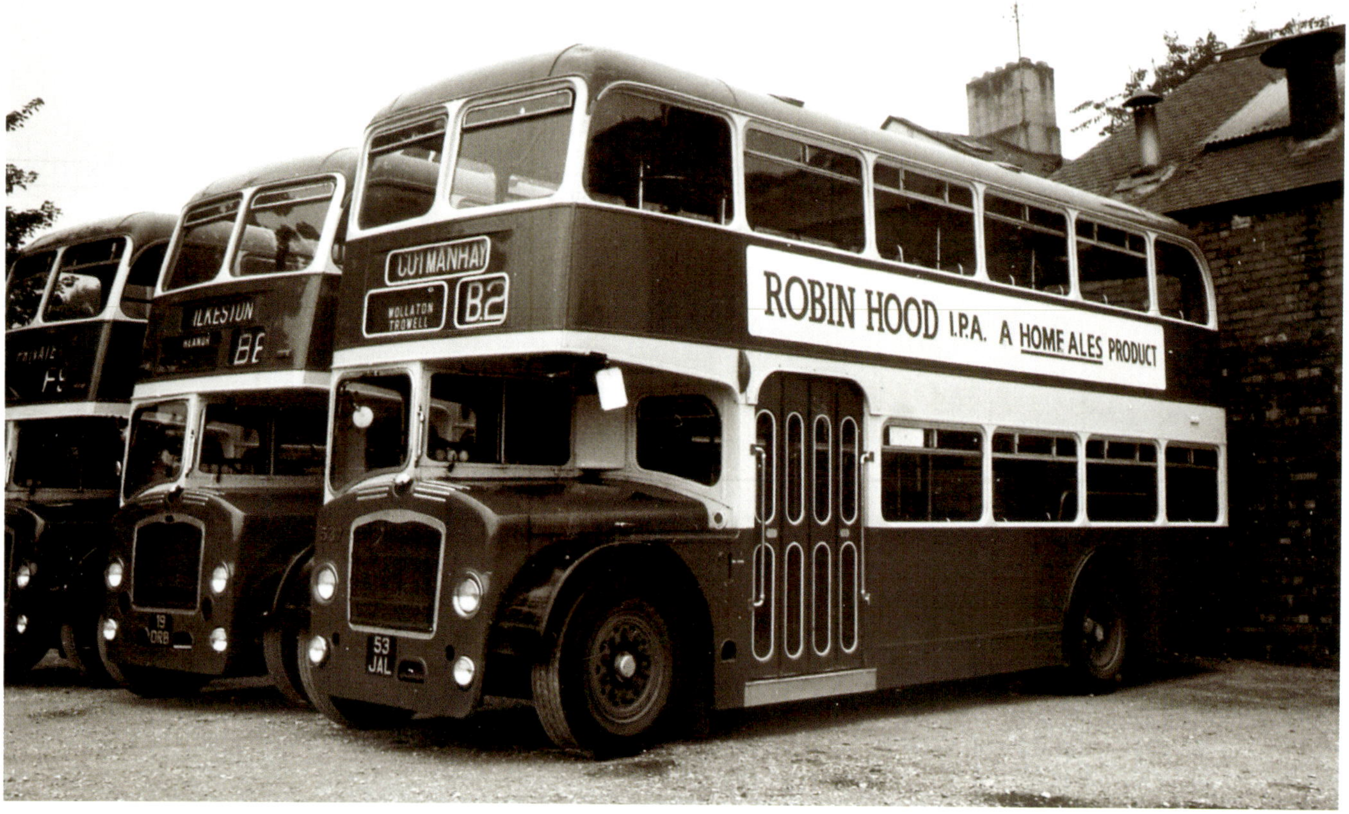

Mansfield District 537 (53 JAL), one of ten 1962 FSF6Gs for the company, is seen after May 1968 when Midland General fully took over the operations and vehicles. Seen here taking it easy between duties it has its destination set for a journey to Cotmanhay on Service B2. (Tony Robbins collection)

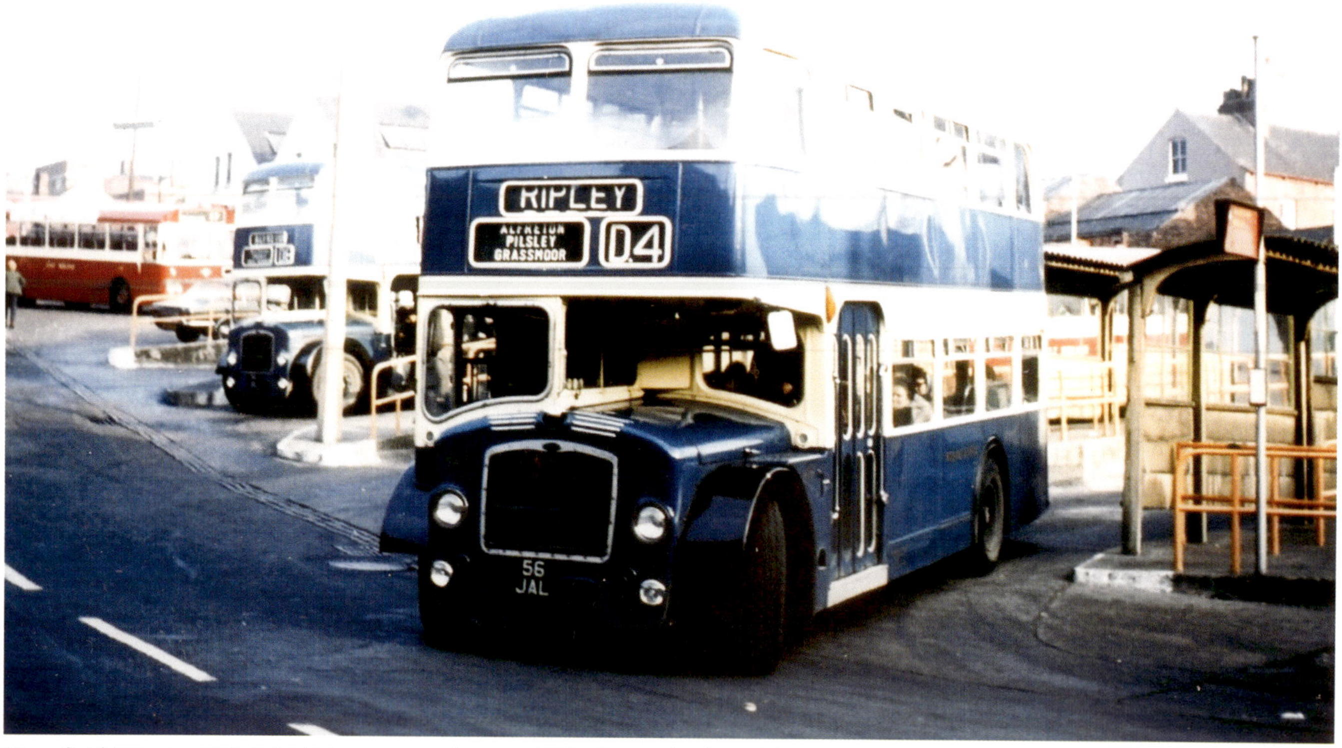

Mansfield District 540 (56 JAL) was one of seven FSF6Gs received in February 1962 and is seen in bright sunlight on Service D4 to Ripley. The blue and cream livery at that time looks pleasant on the Eastern Coach Works bodywork. (Author's collection)

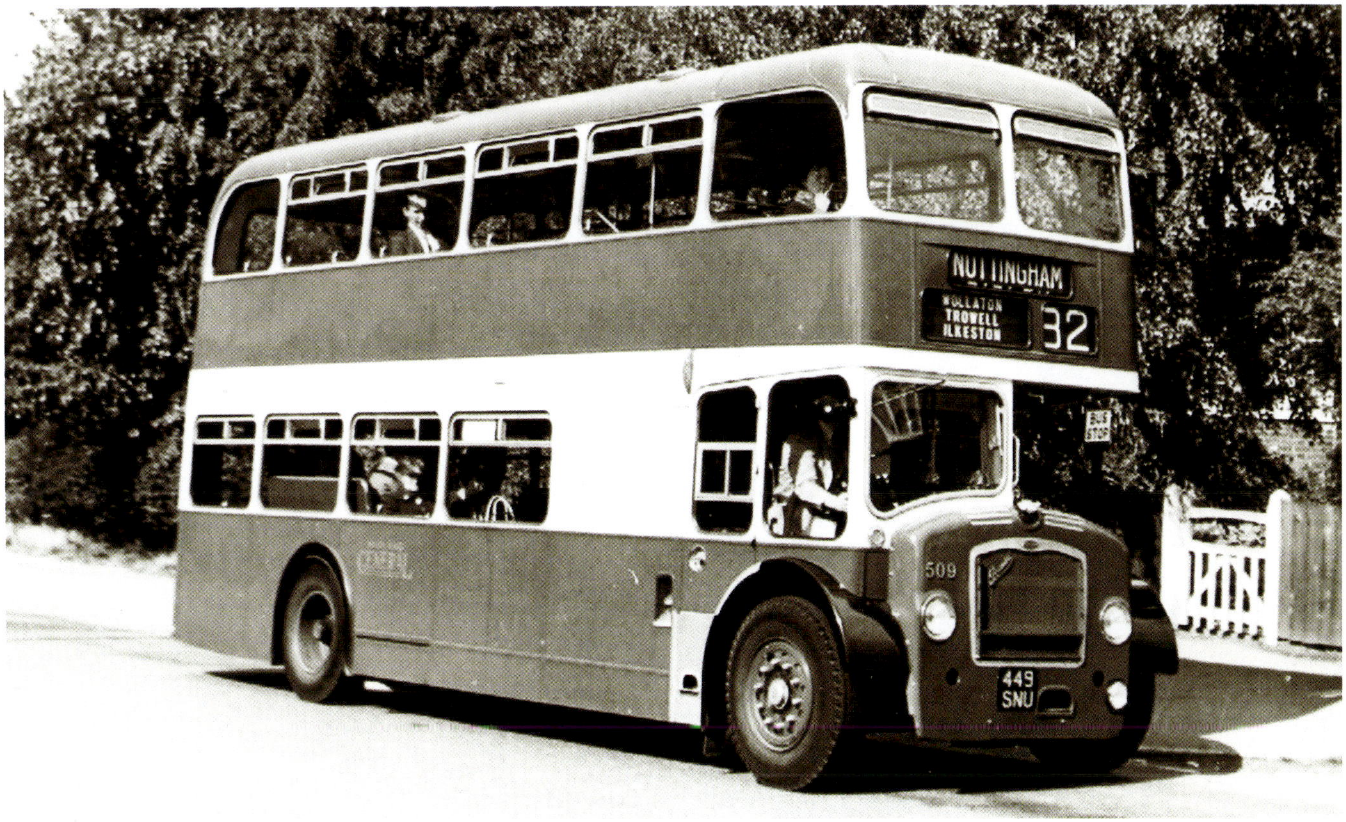

Received in June 1962 Midland General 509 (449 SNU) was one of ten FSF6Gs received new by the company. Pictured here working a journey to Nottingham on Service B2 it was joined by ten further FSF6Gs in May 1968 with the transfer of those purchased new for Mansfield District. (Steve Kelly collection)

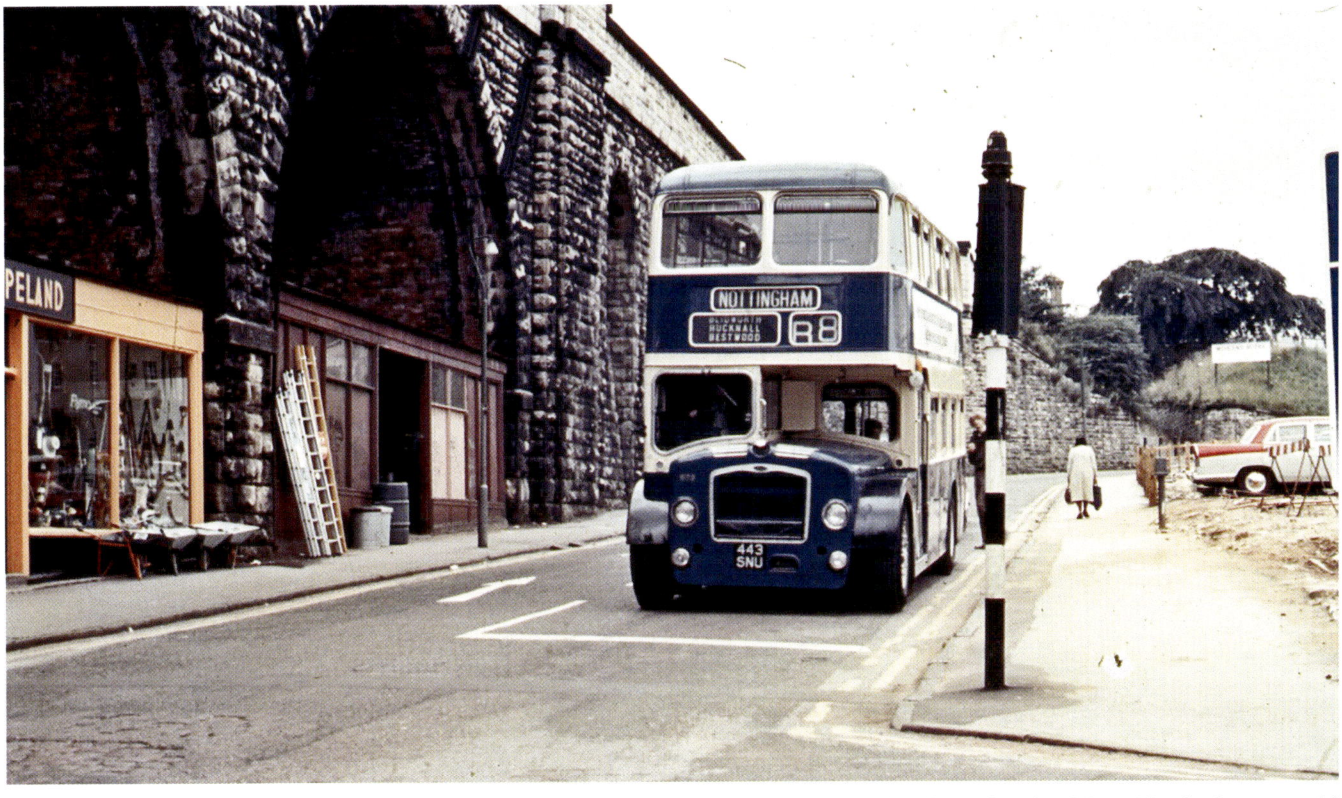

Seen in Mansfield on 3rd August 1973 Midland General 673 (443 SNU), a 1961 FSF6G on Service B8 to Nottingham, would have been 12 years with the company in November that year. (Dr. Mike Walker)

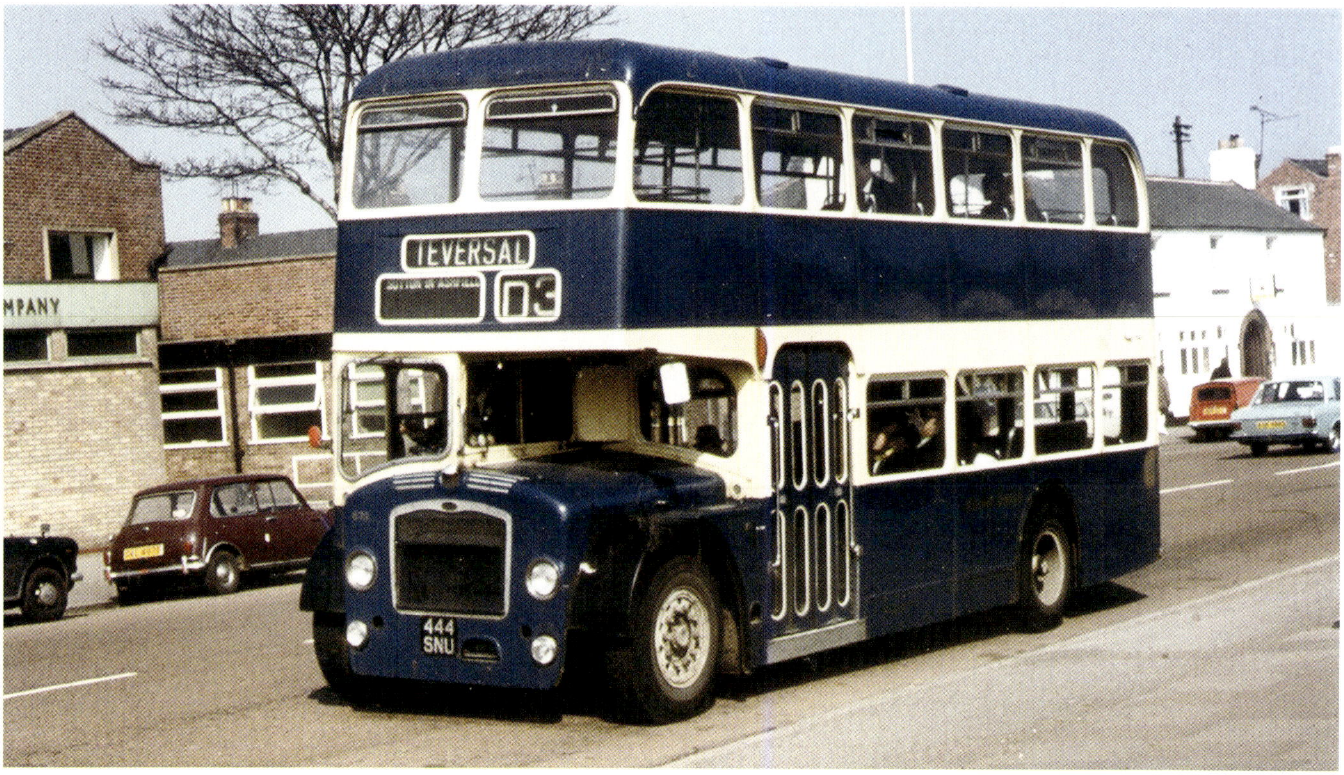

Midland General 674 (444 SNU) a 1961 FSF6G was new as 504 in November that year and has few passengers on board when working to Teversal on Service D3. (Author's collection)

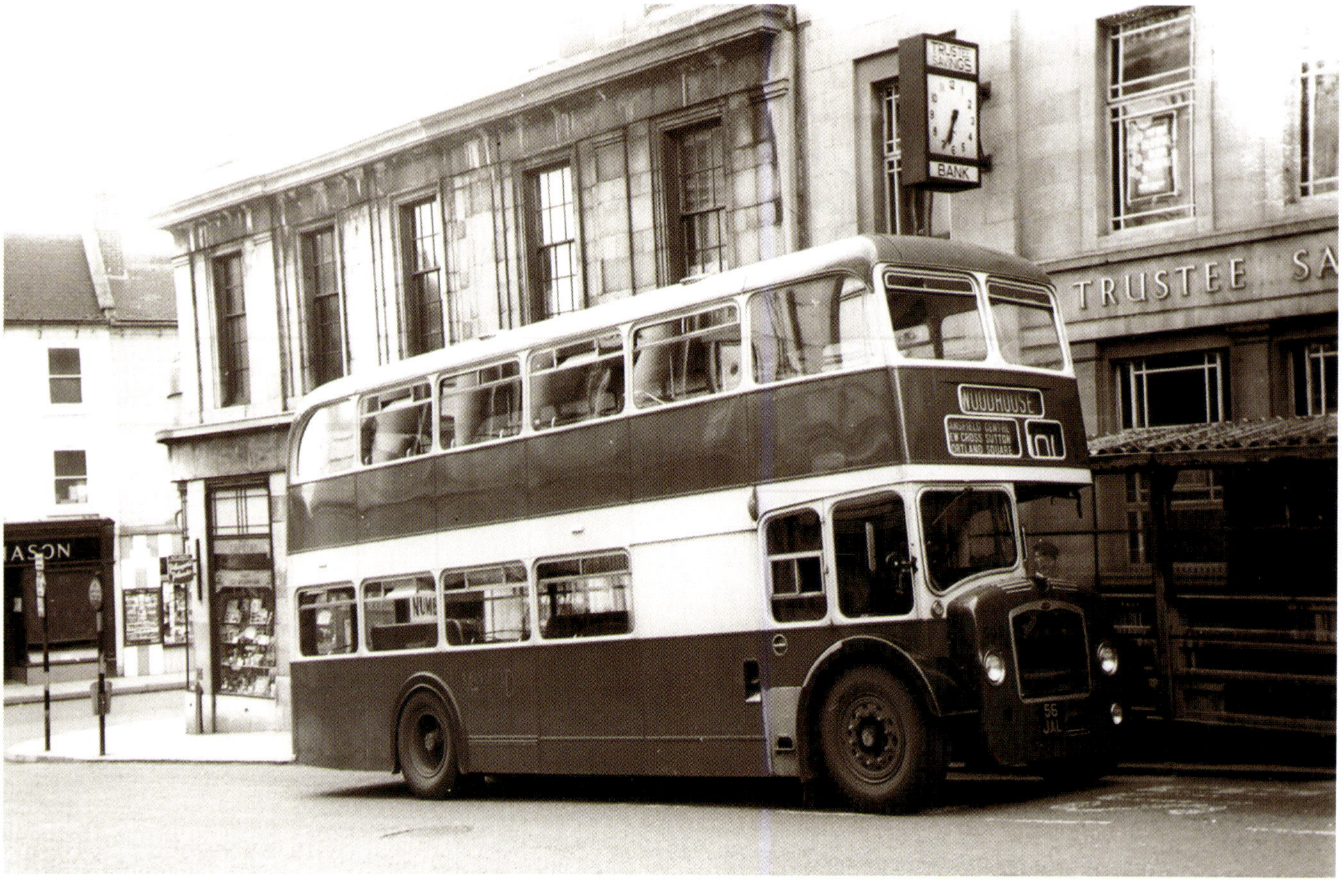

Mansfield District 540 (56 JAL), a 1962 FSF6G delivered in February of that year, waits for passengers at Mansfield Trustee Savings Bank before departing for Woodhouse on Service 101. (Tony Robbins collection)

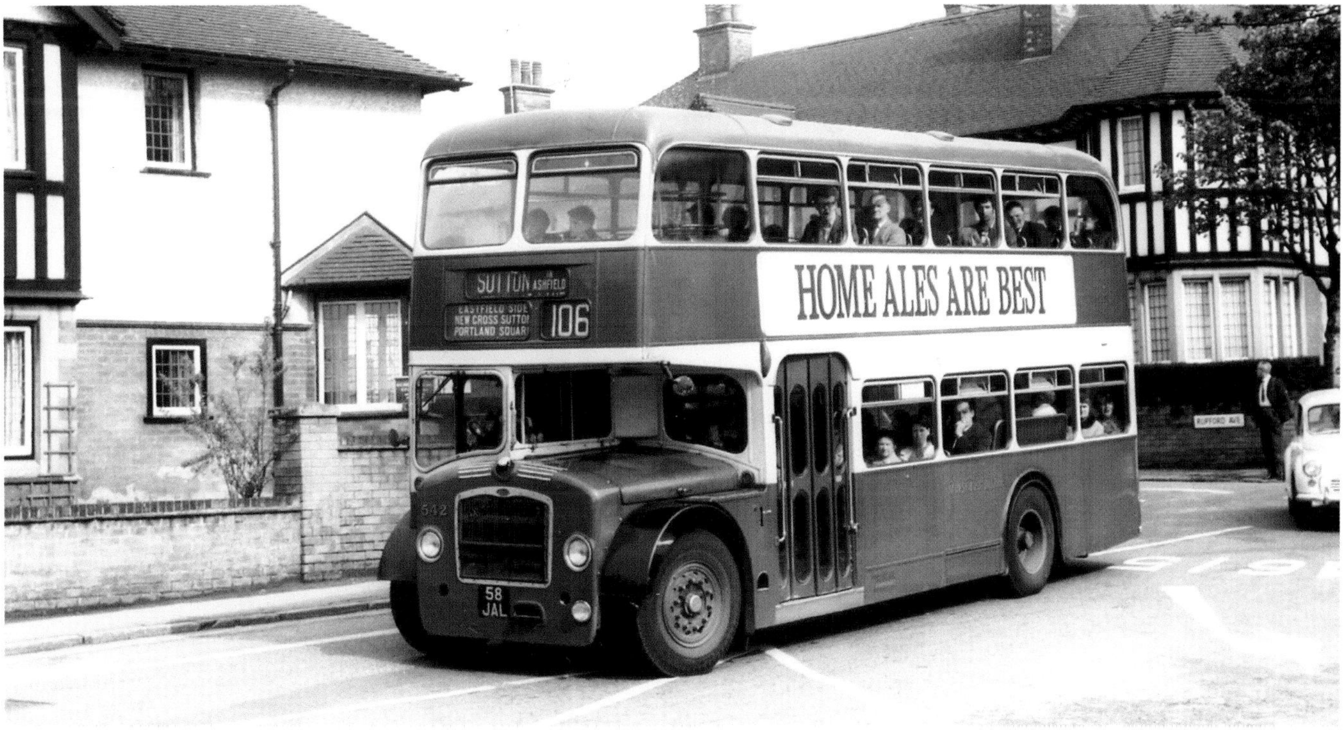

Mansfield District 542 (58 JAL), one of seven 1962 FSF6Gs delivered to the company in February that year, is seen operating a well patronised journey to Sutton via Ashfield on Service 106. (Tony Robbins collection)

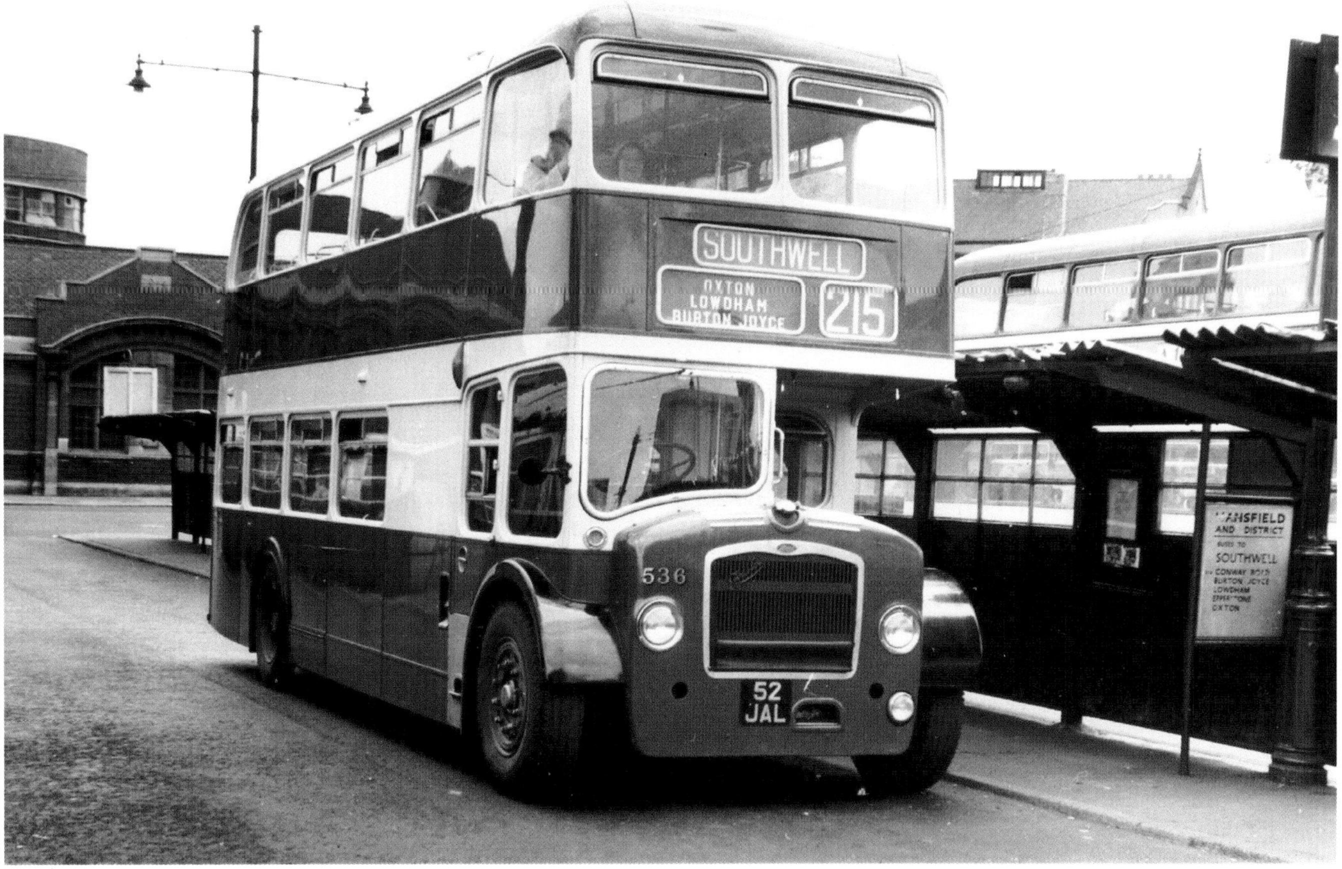

Mansfield District 536 (52 JAL), another one of the February FSF6G arrivals, stands in Mansfield's Huntingdon Street Bus Station waiting to depart on Service 215 to Southwell. (Phil Sposito collection)

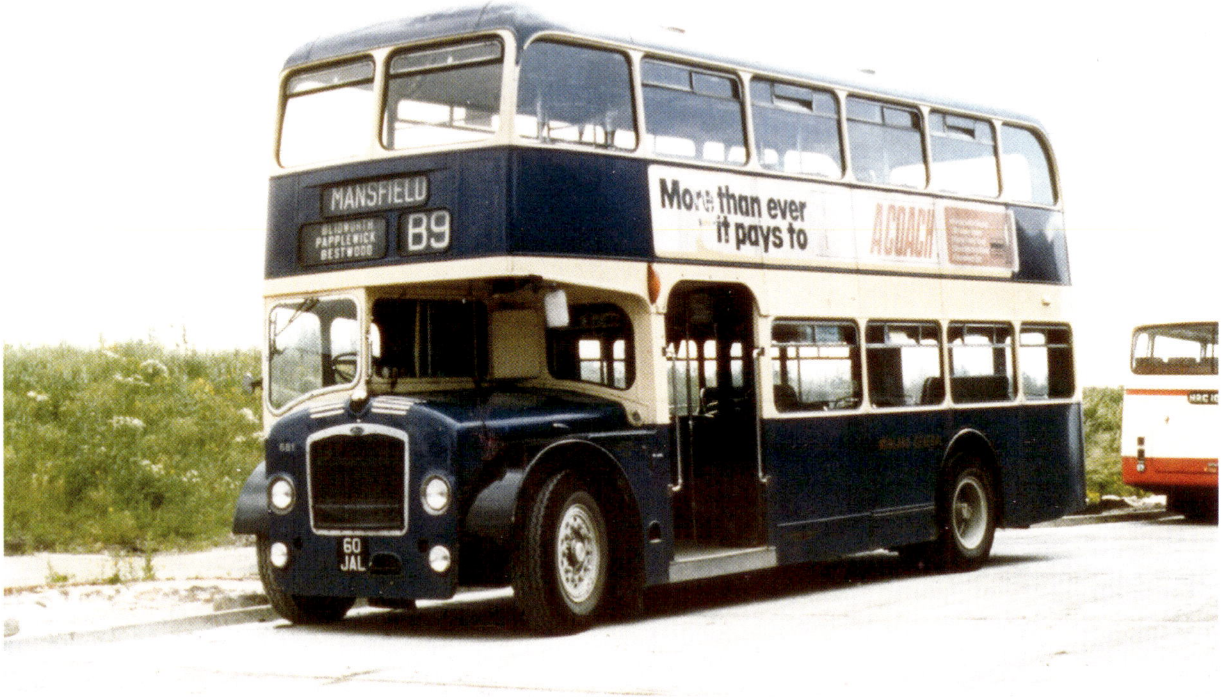

Midland General 681 (60 JAL), a 1962 FSF6G, was new as Mansfield and District 544 and was photographed before working back to its home town of Mansfield on Service B9 during 1967. In May of the following year it, along with the other nine similar vehicles, would be transferred to the Midland General main fleet. (Author's collection)

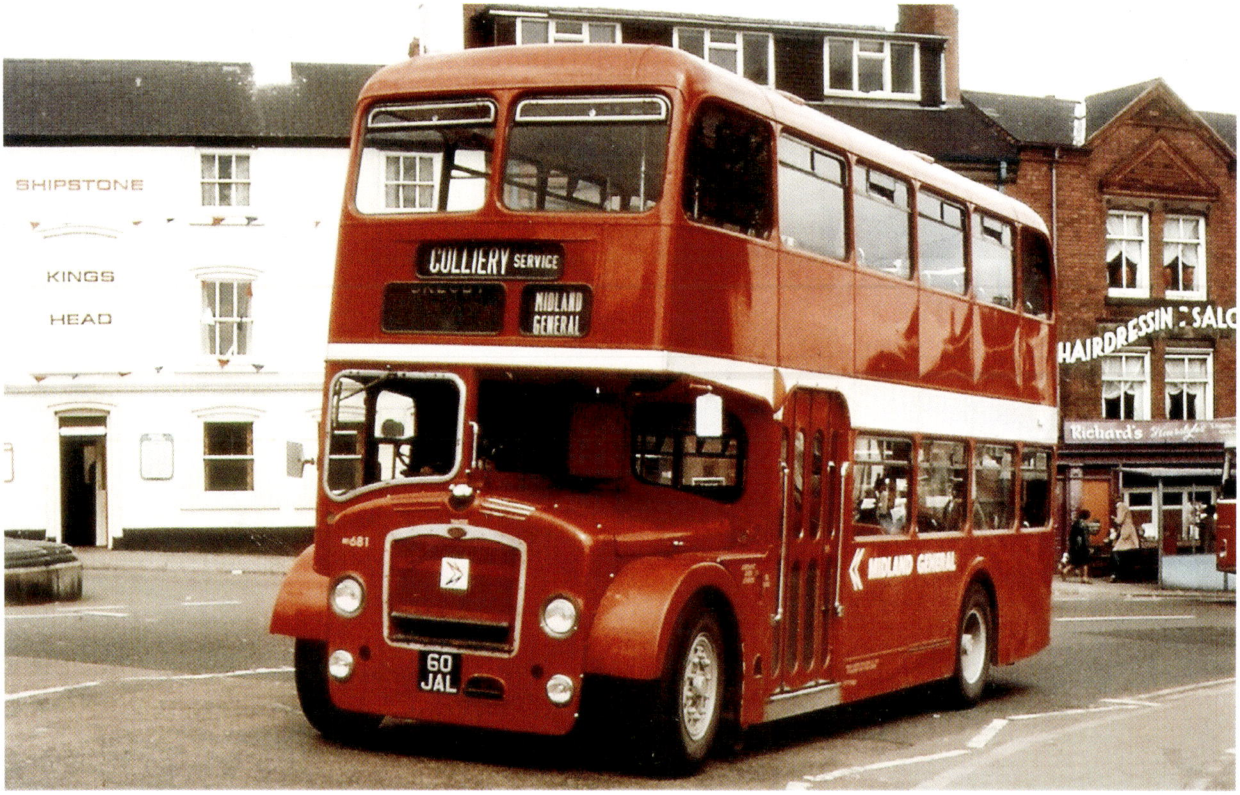

Midland General 681 (60 JAL), a 1962 ex Mansfield District FSF6G, was delivered as 544 in June that year and transferred to the Midland General fleet in August 1968 and later renumbered. The bodywork appears to be in good condition as it seems to be prepared for a colliery journey. (Cliff Essex)

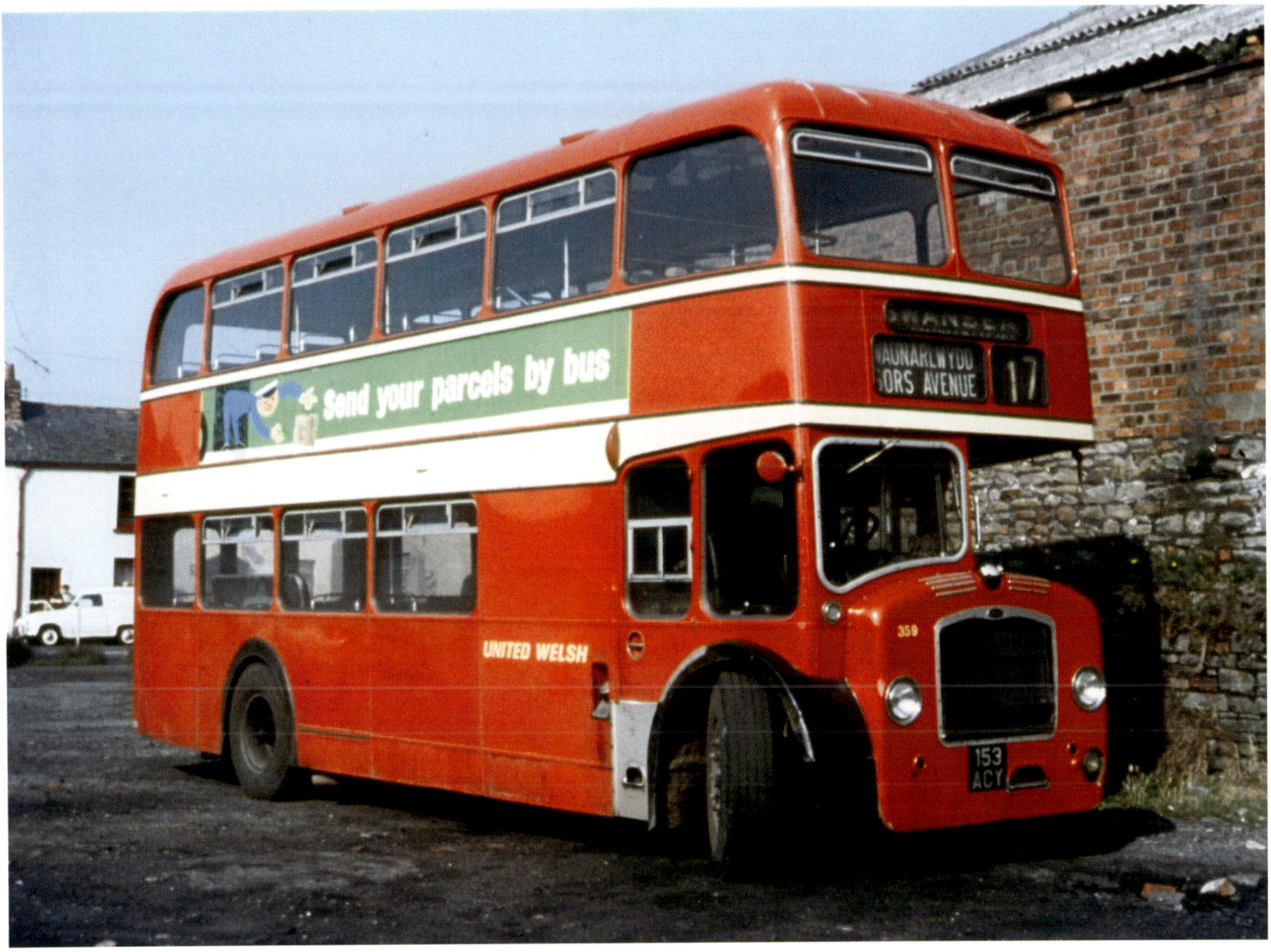

United Welsh opted for its FSFs not to be fitted with the distinctive Cave-Browne-Cave radiators next to the front destination boxes as exemplified on Gardner powered 359 (153 ACY) delivered in November 1961. (Author's collection)

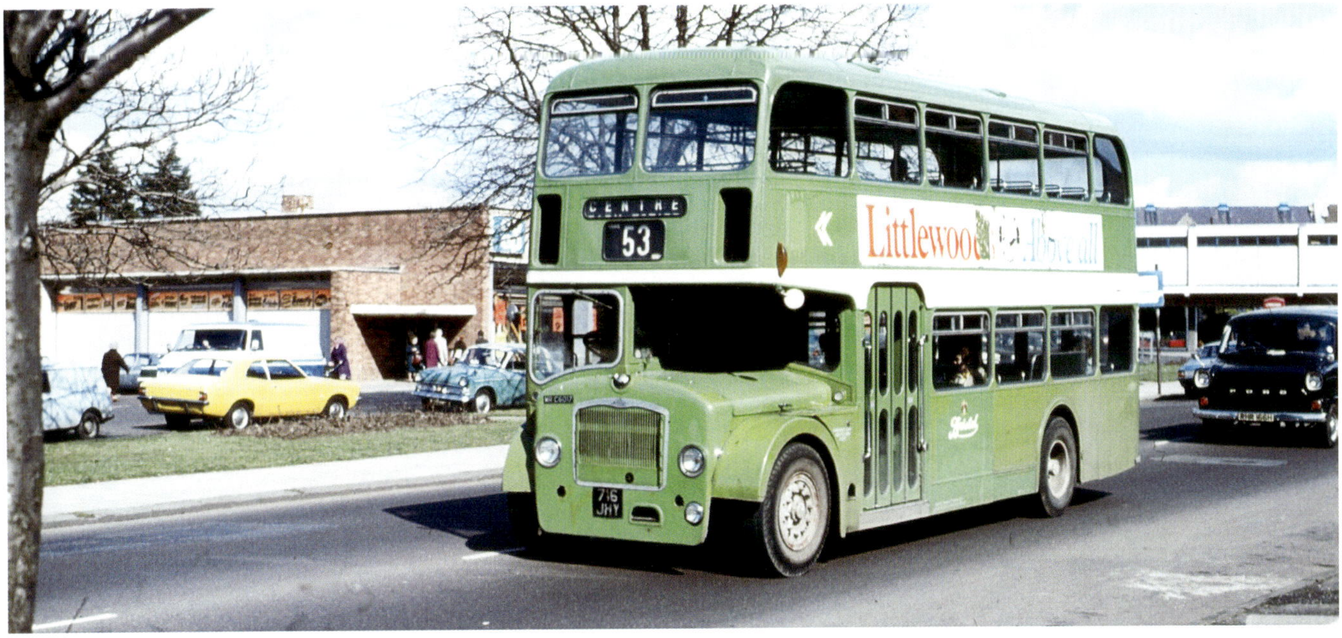

Bristol Omnibus C6017 (716 JHY), a 1960 Bristol FSF6B originally numbered LC8575, is seen with NBC double arrow symbol and scroll fleet names on a lightly loaded Service 53 journey along Fishponds Road in north Bristol. (Geoff Gould)

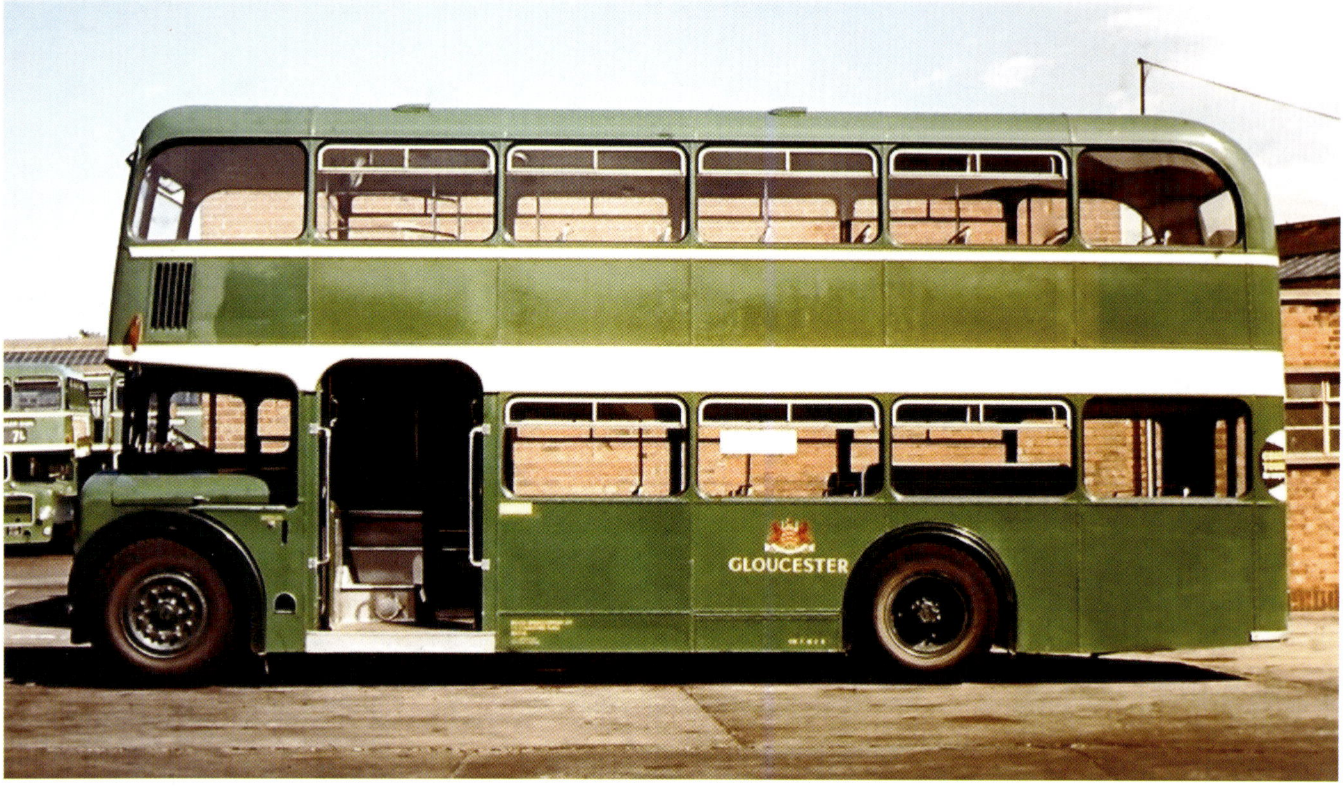

A broadside view of an unidentified Gloucester FSF6G clearly shows the pre-NBC fleet name and city crest used for buses allocated to Gloucester City Services. (Author's collection)

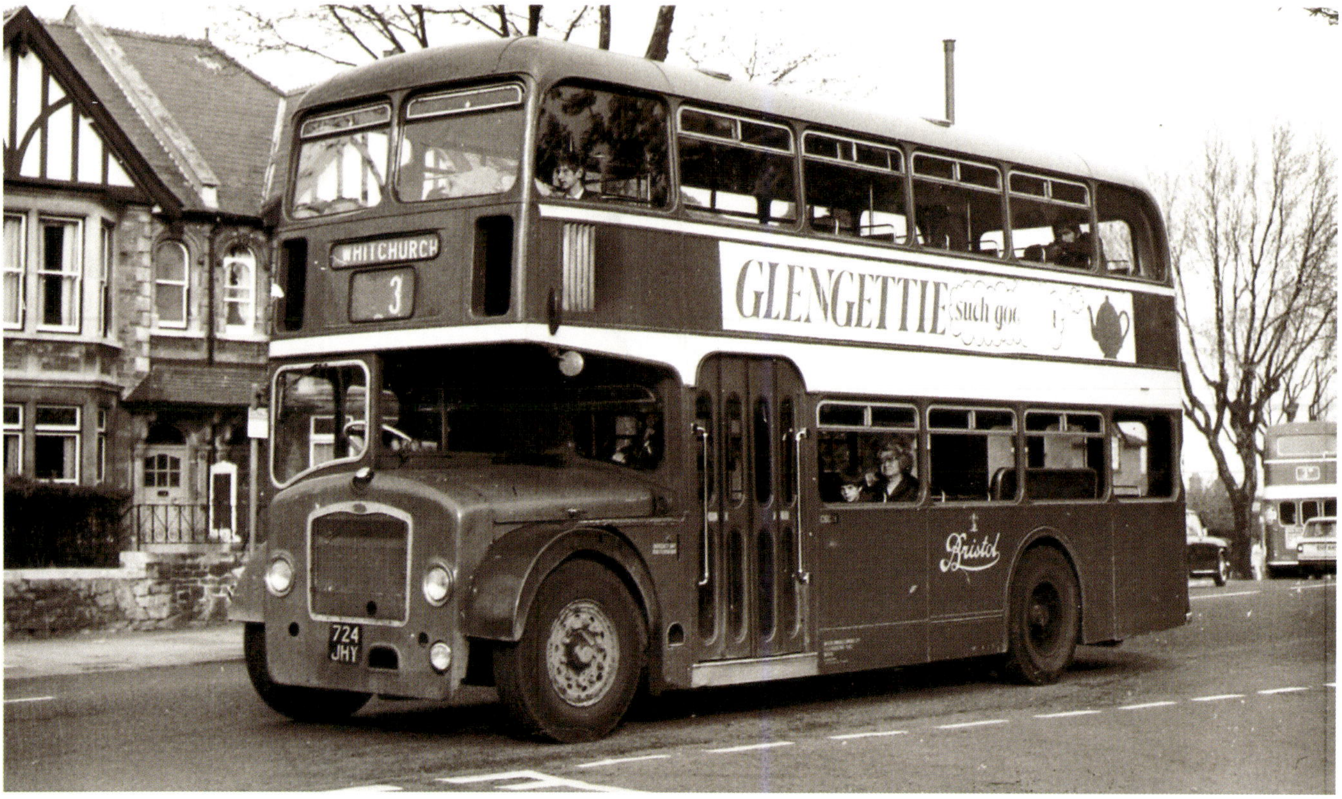

Working to Whitchurch to the south of Bristol on Bristol City Service 3 C6028 (724 JHY), a 1961 FSF6B, arrived in January of that year and remained in the Bristol Joint Services fleet until withdrawn in September 1976. It passed to P Sykes, a Barnsley dealer, who sold it for further PSV use to Merseyside Coaches Limited in May 1977 until withdrawn one year later. (Bristol Vintage Bus Group)

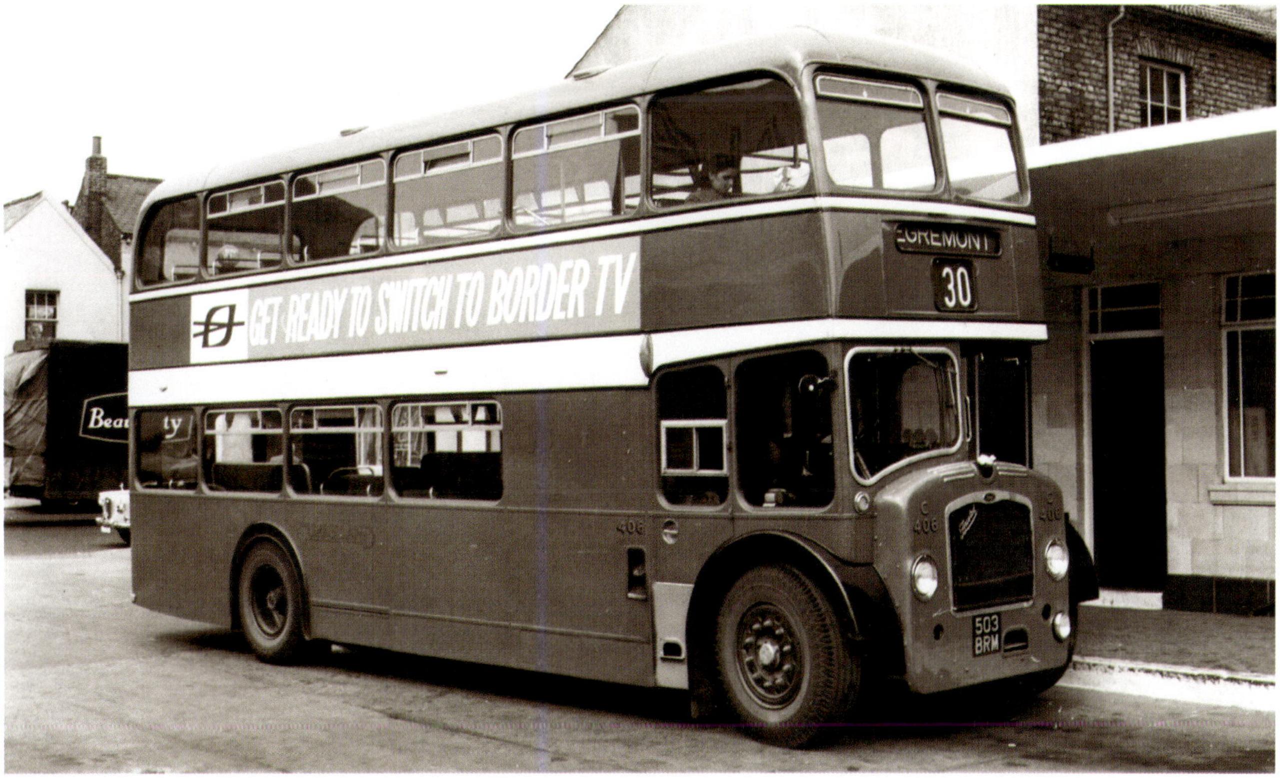

When Independent Television companies were being established throughout Britain there was considerable publicity to promote these new "commercial television" stations including bus adverts. Cumberland C406 (503 BRM) is captured on film when new at Workington Bus Station ready to depart on Service 30 to Egremont in November 1960 when Border Television was due to start transmitting local ITV programmes. (Tony Robbins collection)

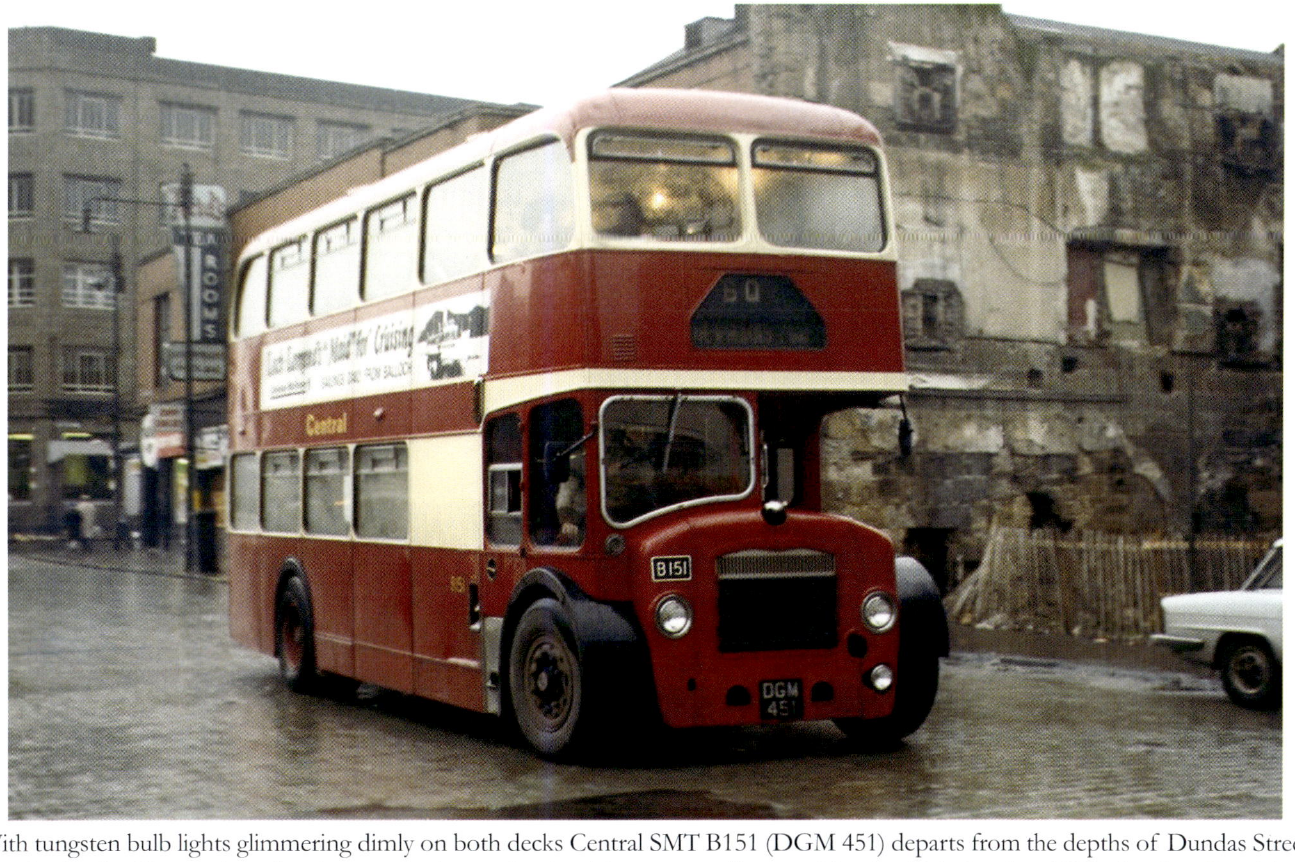

With tungsten bulb lights glimmering dimly on both decks Central SMT B151 (DGM 451) departs from the depths of Dundas Street Bus Station in Glasgow into the gloomy weather and uninspiring surroundings on Monday 18th October 1976. (Stephen Dowle)

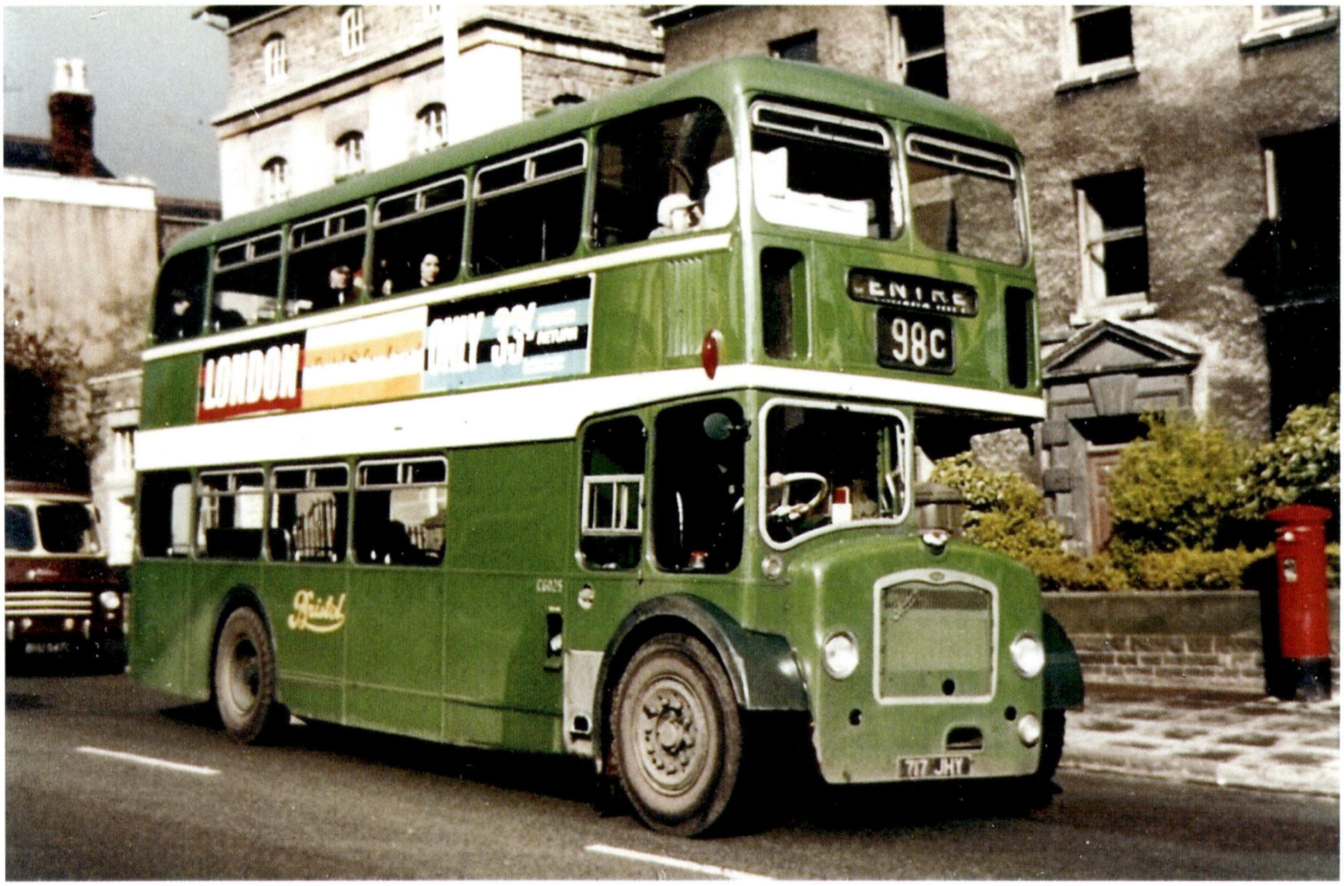

Bristol Omnibus C6025 (717 JHY), a 1961 FSF6B, was unique in the Bristol Omnibus Group fleets with an oblong registration plate as seen on a journey to Centre on Service 98C. It was withdrawn in the changes to Bristol City Services introduced on 27th June 1976 and scrapped after being bought by P Sykes, a Barnsley dealer. (Bristol Vintage Bus Group)

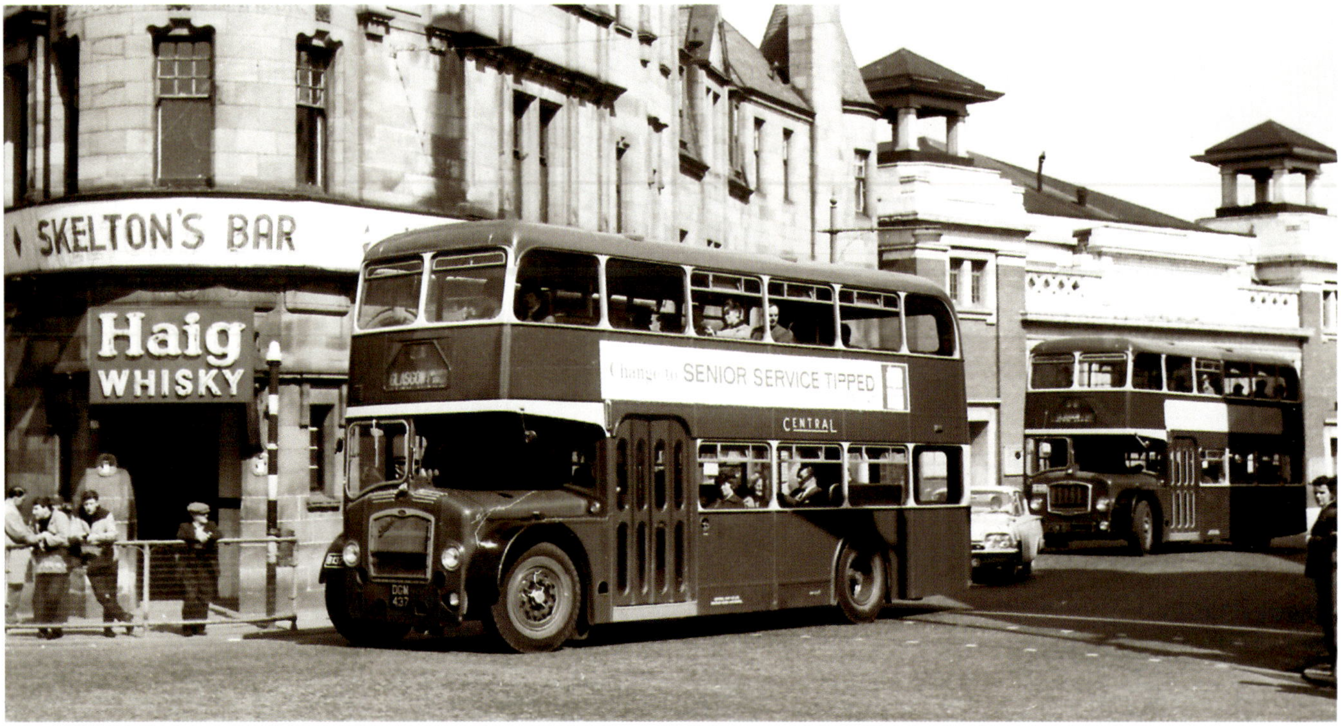

A rotating door control rather than the usual platform doors emergency button is carried by Central SMT B137 (DGM 437), a 1962 FSF6G, at Hamilton (Lower Cross) on 18th April 1964. (A. J. Douglas)

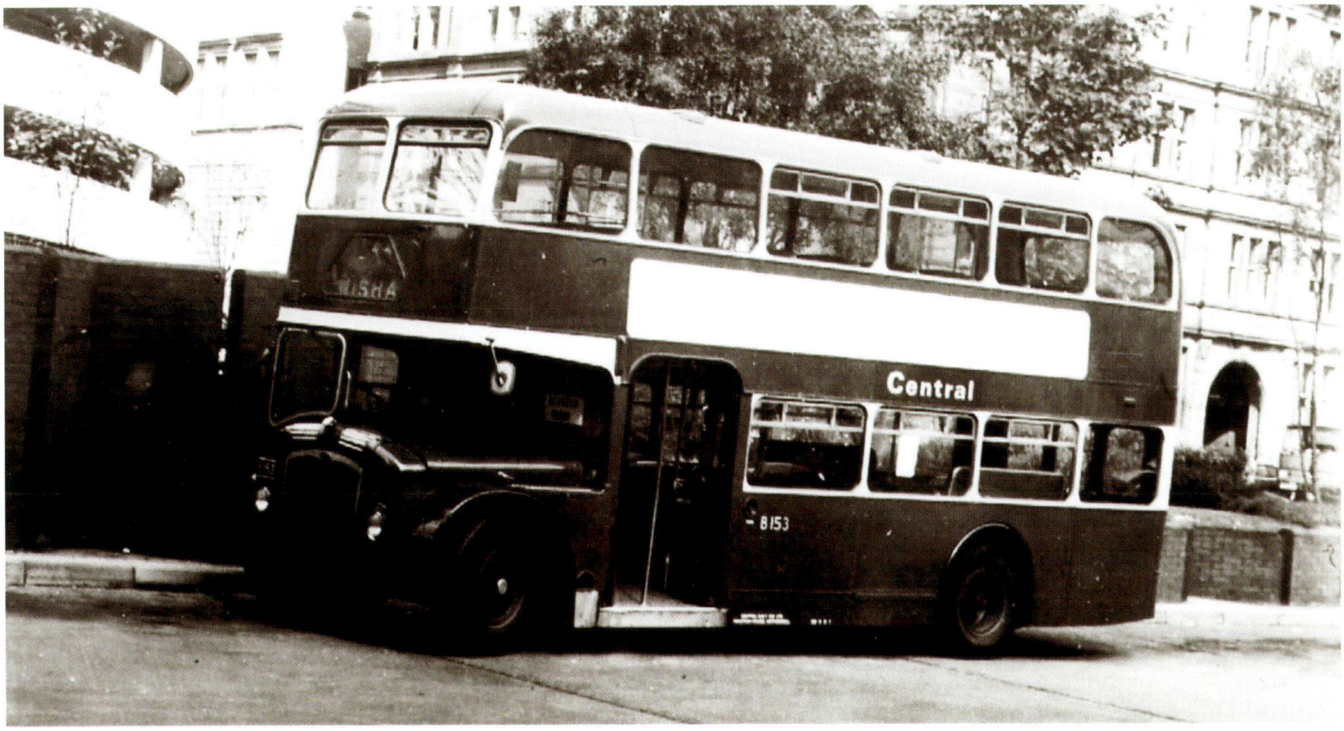

During April 1962 Central SMT received no less than fifteen FSF6Gs including B153 (DGM 453) working a journey for the Glasgow Show according to the front platform window. (Steve Kelly collection)

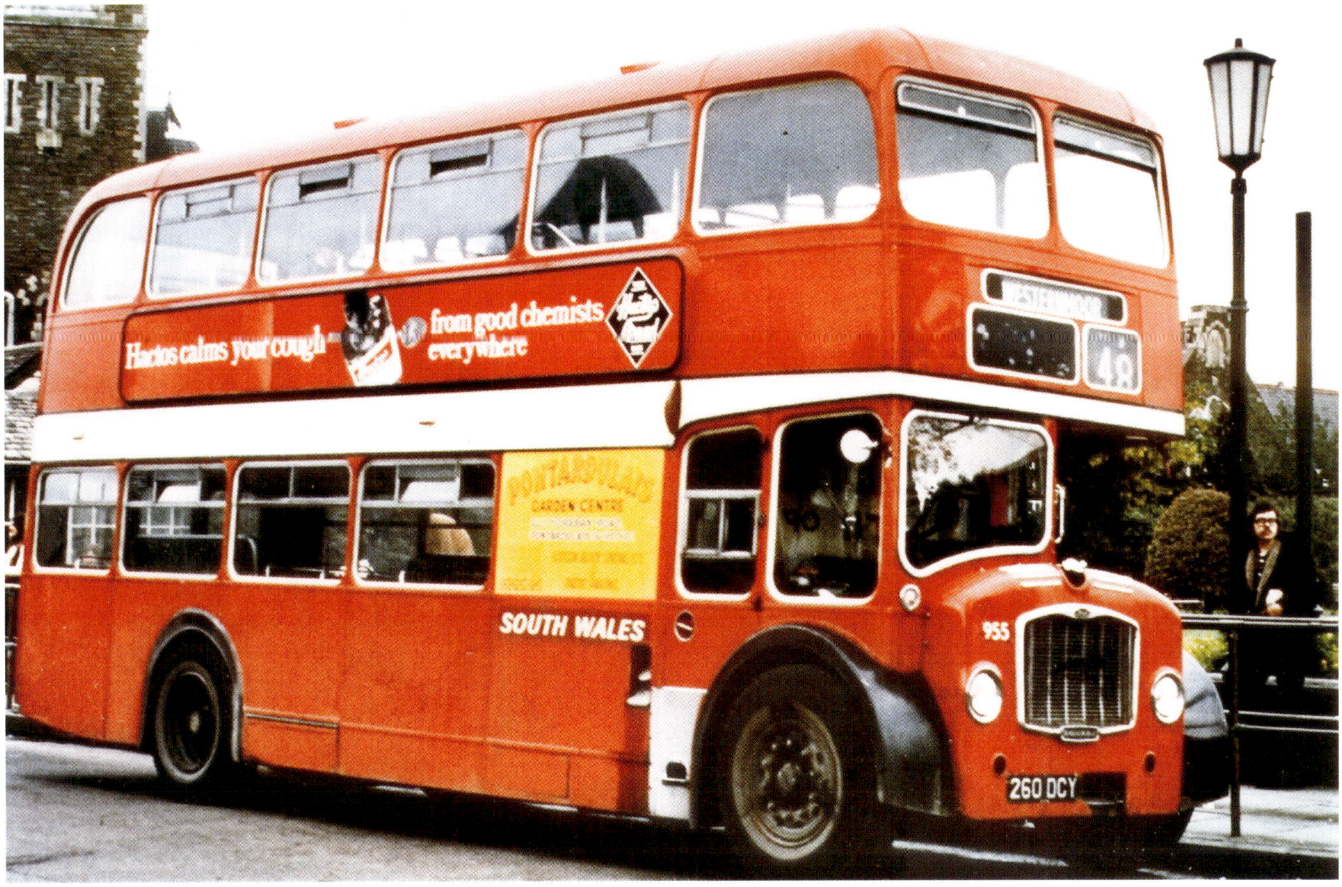

Another bus with temporary fleet names is South Wales 955 (260 DCY), new in 1962 to United Welsh. This FSF6G with illuminated advertisement and extra lower deck window ventilator is seen working to Westernmoor on Service 48. (Tony Robbins collection)

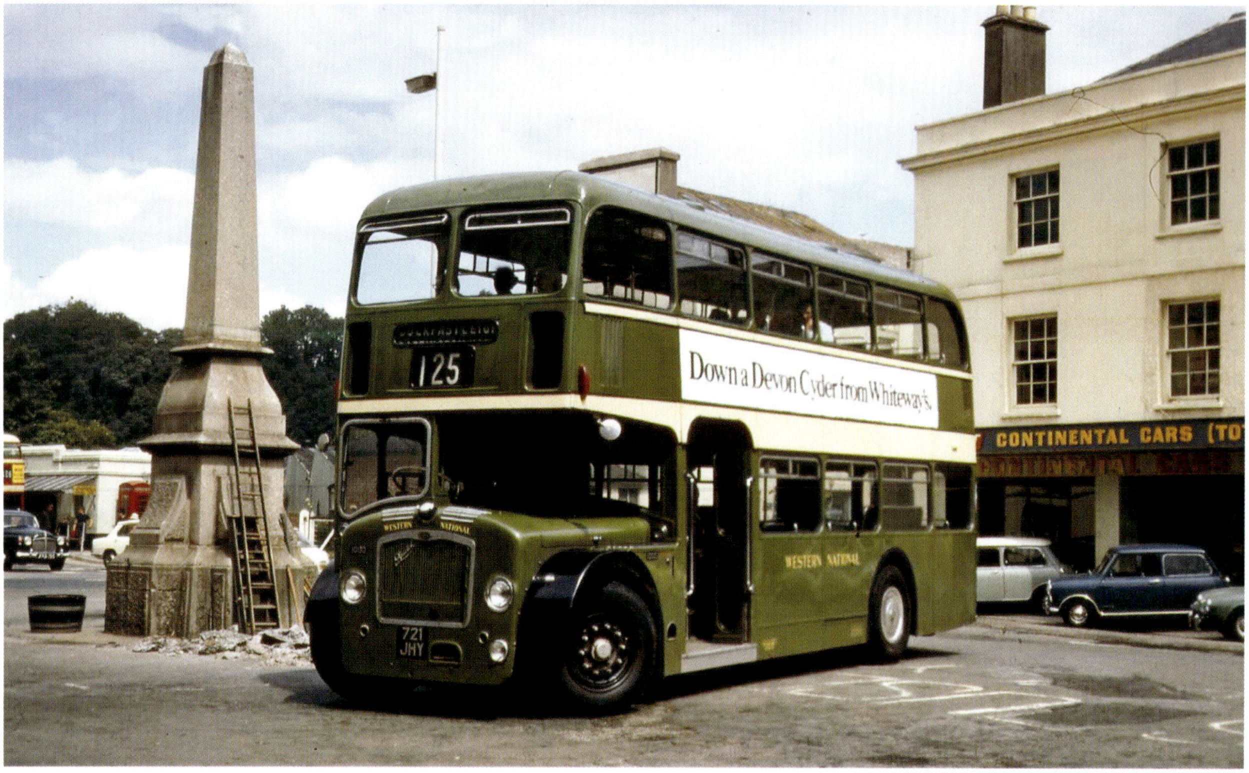

Totnes (The Plains) sees 1000 (721 JHY), previously 6022, an FSF6G that was new to Weston-super-Mare Depot in the Bristol Country fleet in 1961, waiting to depart for Buckfastleigh on 8th July 1969. This vehicle was transferred to Bath in 1966 until sold to Western National in August 1967 and numbered 1000 by the new owners. With the formation of the NBC on 1st January 1970 the bus returned to BOC with the transfer of services, vehicles and properties in the Trowbridge and Chippenham areas of Western National to Bristol Omnibus and was allocated to Bath, resuming its fleet number of 6022. (Colin Martin)

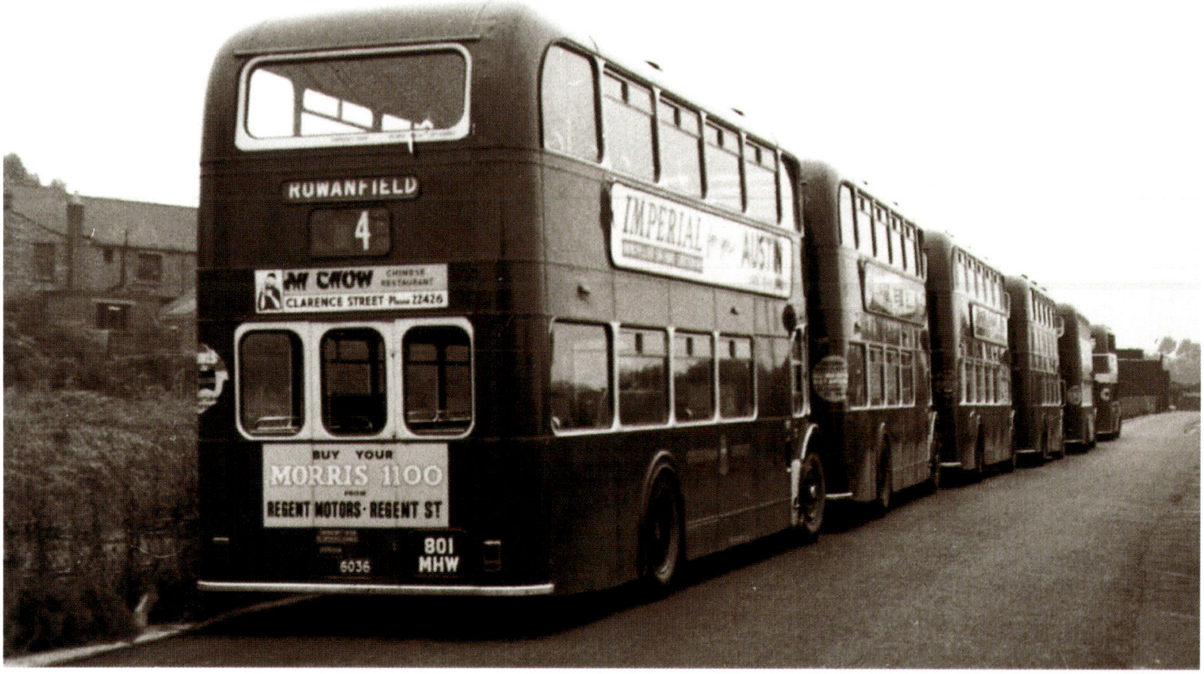

St. Mark's Depot at Cheltenham was situated next to the main Bristol to Birmingham railway line A rear view of Cheltenham District 6036 (801 MHW) with 6037 in front shows full use of the rear destination box and the offside illuminated advertisement panels on three FSFs in this line-up in late summer 1966. Buses were frequently parked on the approach road to the former tram depot on the side nearest the railway line but transferred to the opposite side after landslips. (Colin Martin)

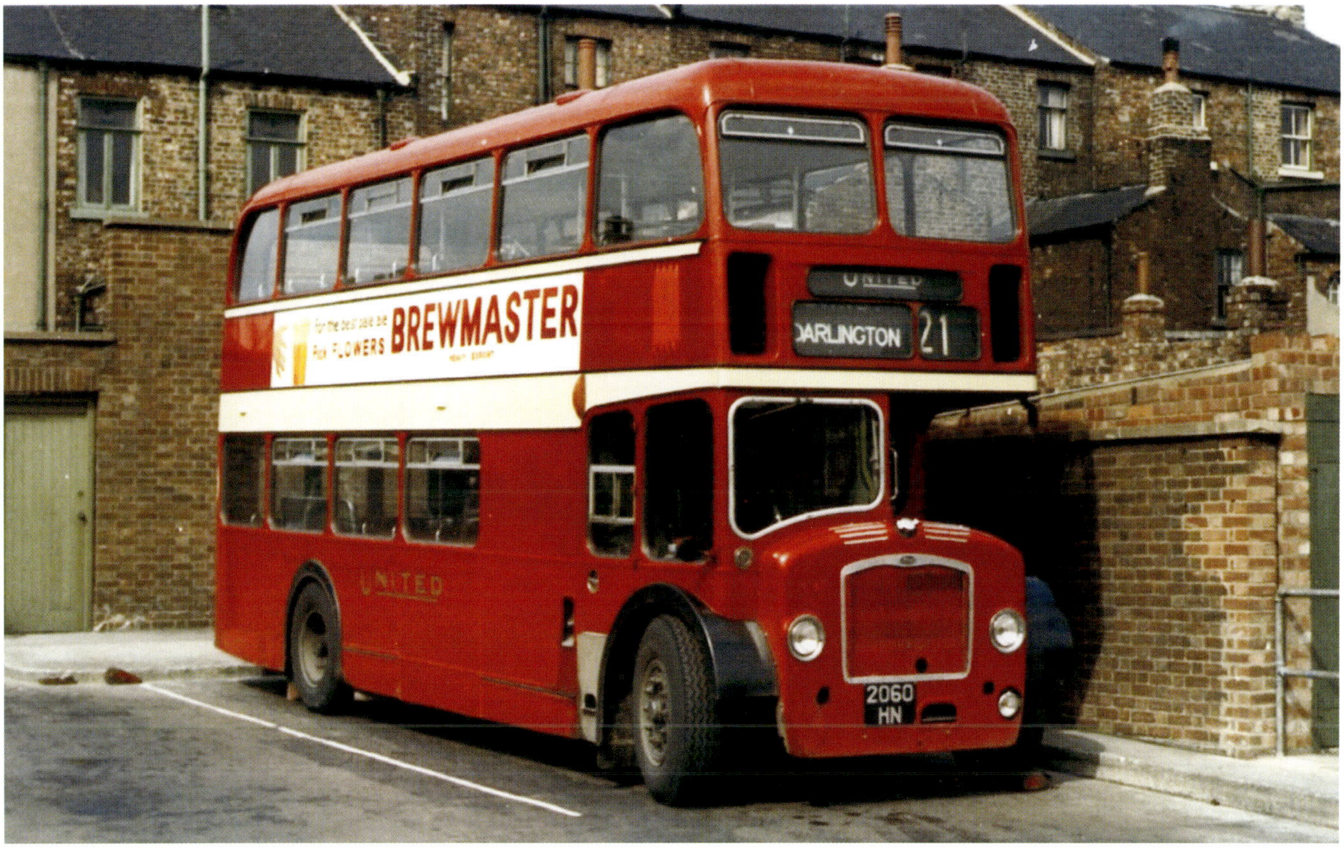

United BL60 (2060 HN) a 1960 FSF6B at Redcar Bus Station circa 1962 has already had its blinds set by the driver or conductor for its next departure for Darlington on a Service 21 journey. (Peter Horrex collection)

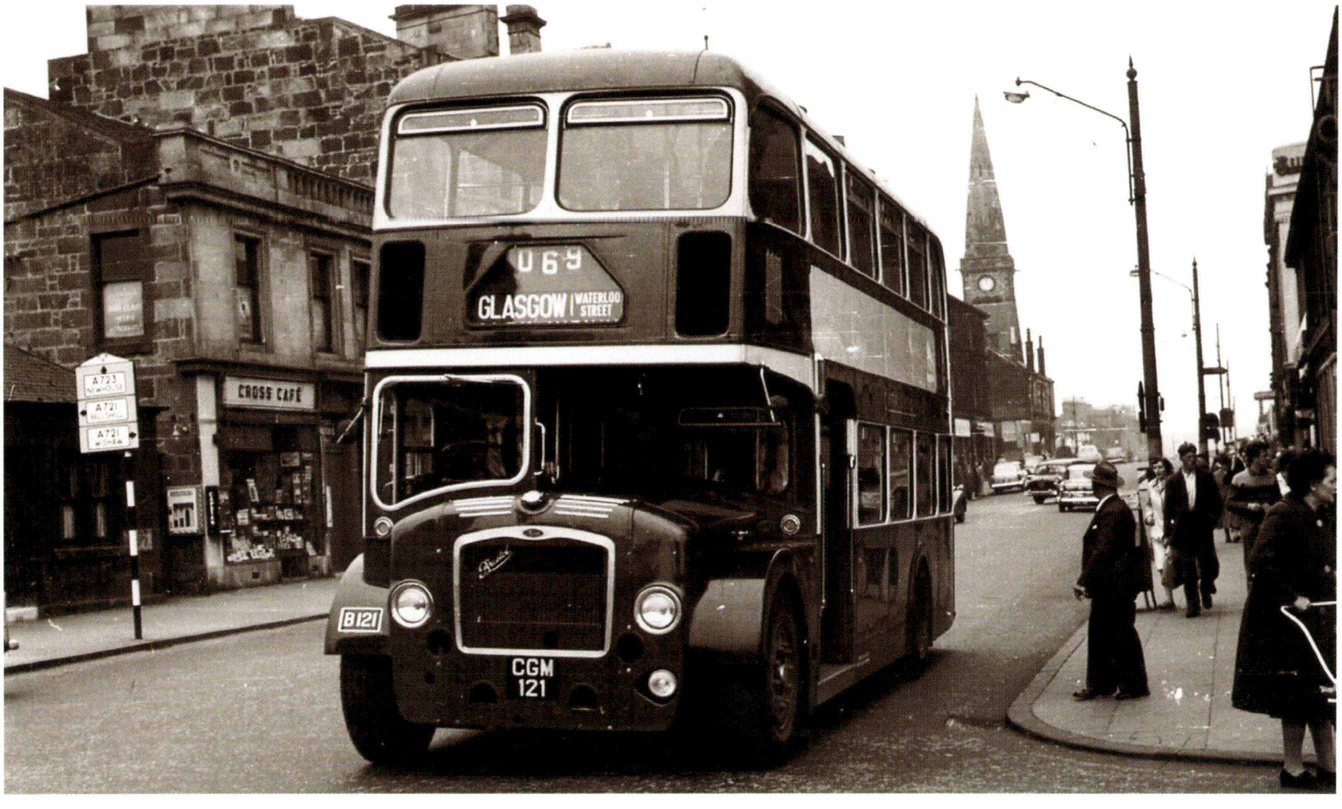

Typically 1960s scene with Central SMT B121 (CGM 121), a 1961 FSF6G from Wishaw Depot, on a Service 69 journey through Motherwell on its way to Glasgow (Waterloo Street) past period street furniture. (Tony Robbins collection)

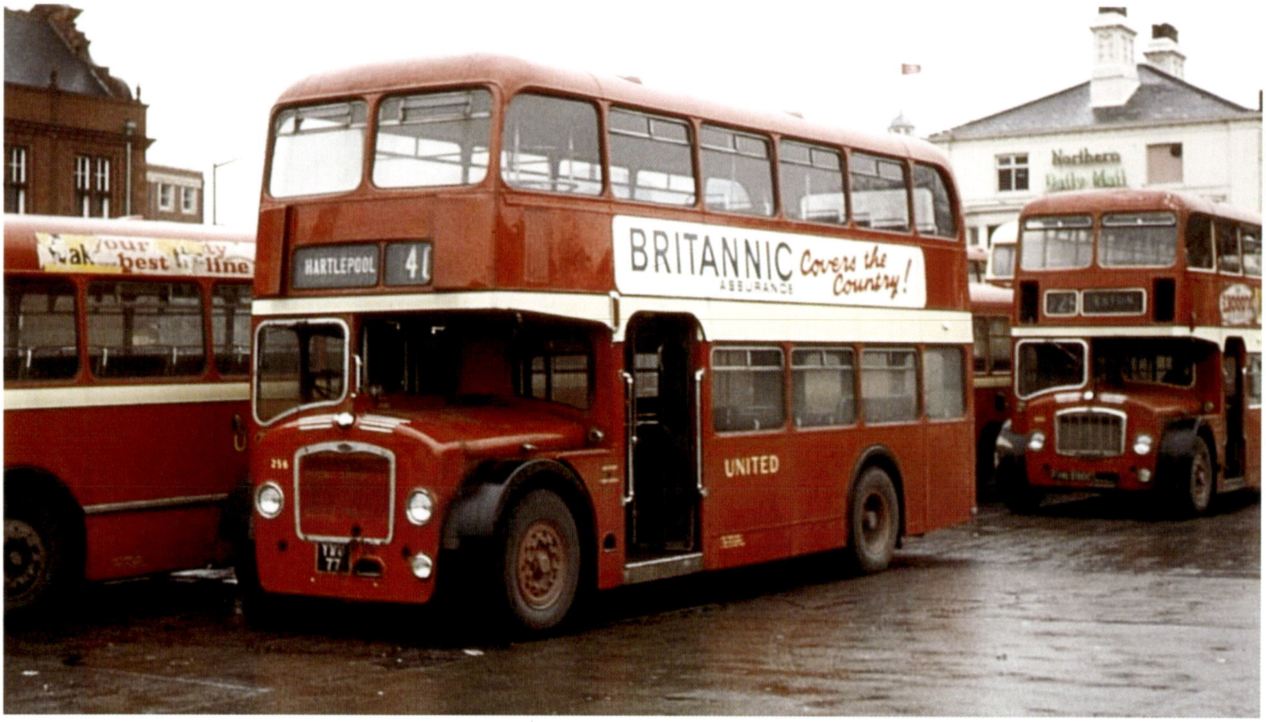

United 256 (YWW 77), the prototype 1960 Bristol FSF, was new to West Yorkshire as DX82 in May 1960 but proved to be extremely unpopular with drivers and conductors. As a result, in 1967, it was exchanged with L56 (456 LHN), a 1960 United rear entrance Lodekka. During the early 1970s L56 was renumbered 256 and modified with side by side destination indicators as seen in December 1971 at West Hartlepool Bus Station. (Donald Hudson)

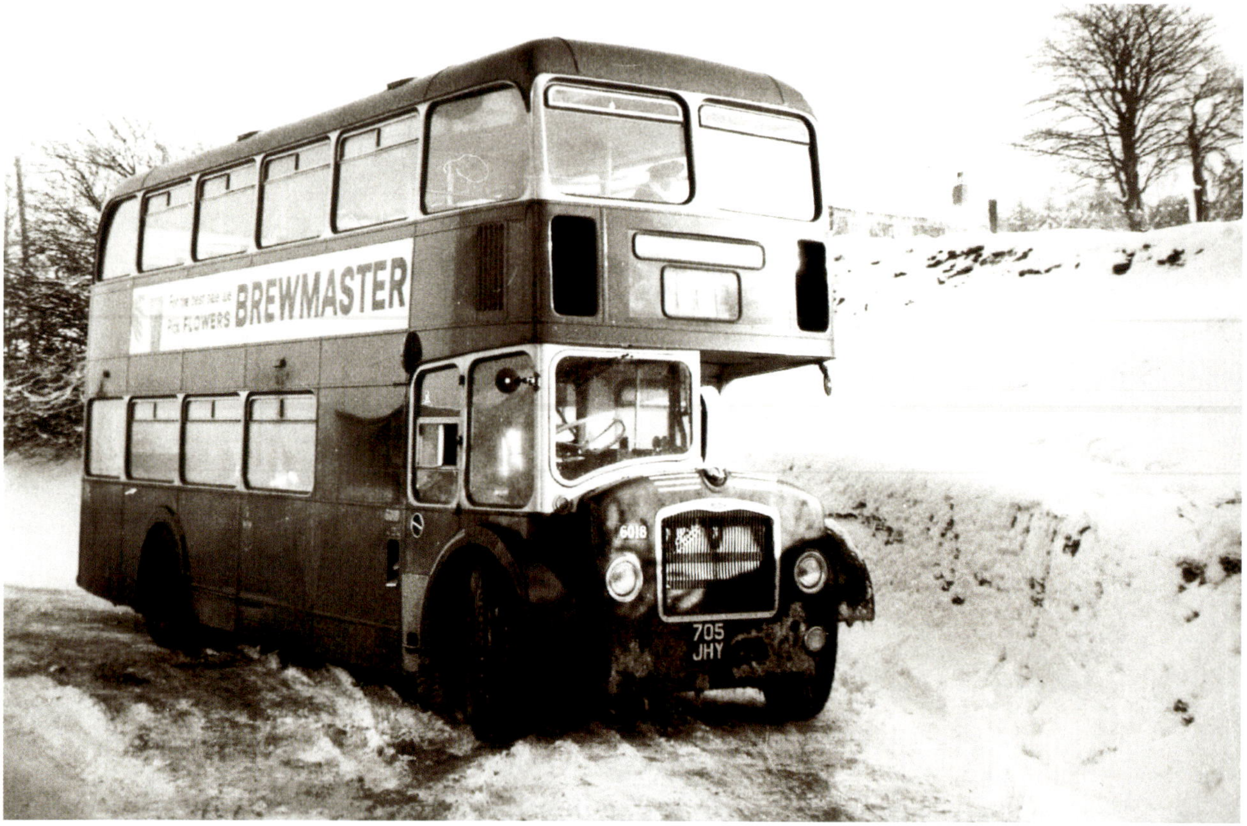

Decidedly bleak looking wintry conditions at Cleeve Hill Terminus has not prevented 6018 (705 JHY), delivered in November 1960 as L99 to Cheltenham District Traction Company, from achieving route success in December 1961. Driving in such conditions, especially buses, was definitely not for the faint hearted. (Colin Martin)

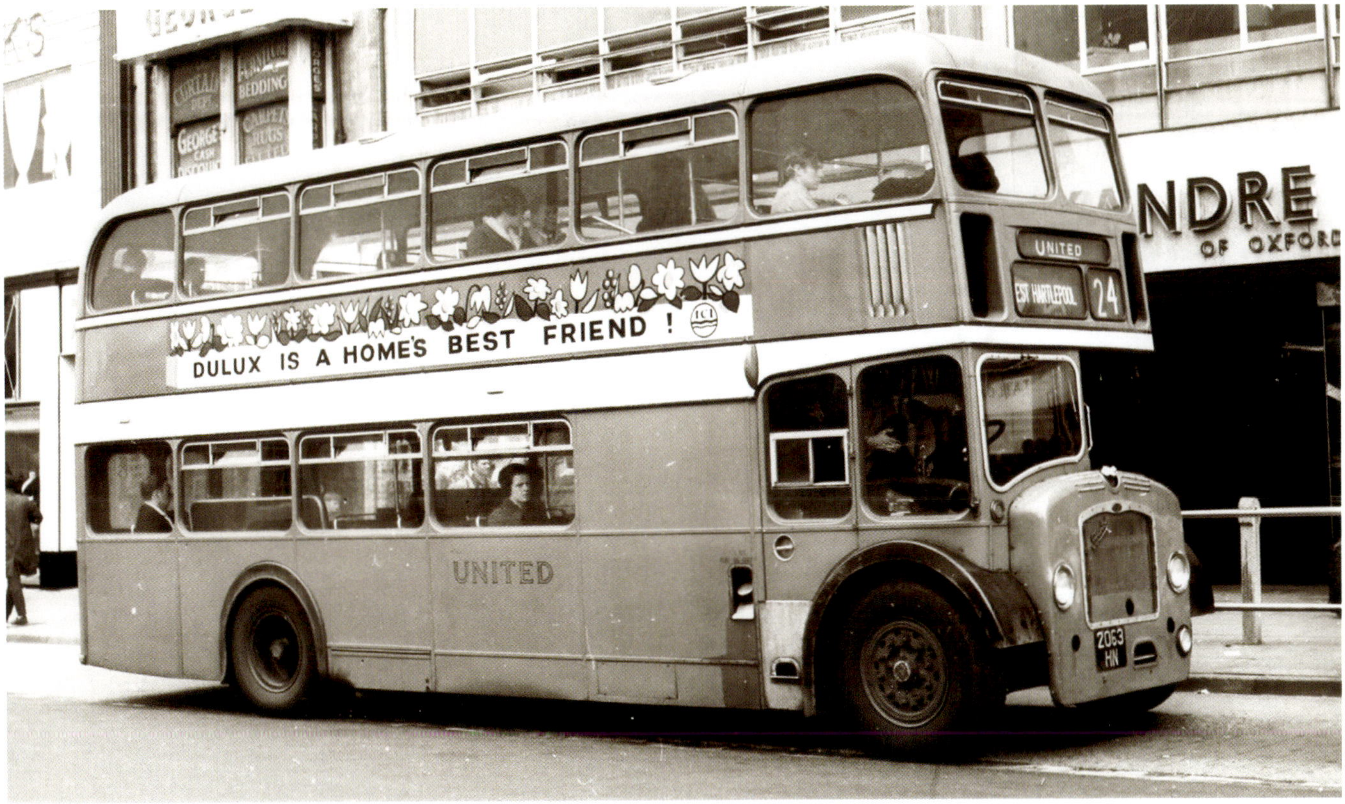

United BL63 (2063 HN), 1960 FSF6B, looks to be in its early years with the company complete with lined out livery and hand applied painted advertisement for ICI Dulux household paints and wallpapers. (Tony Robbins collection)

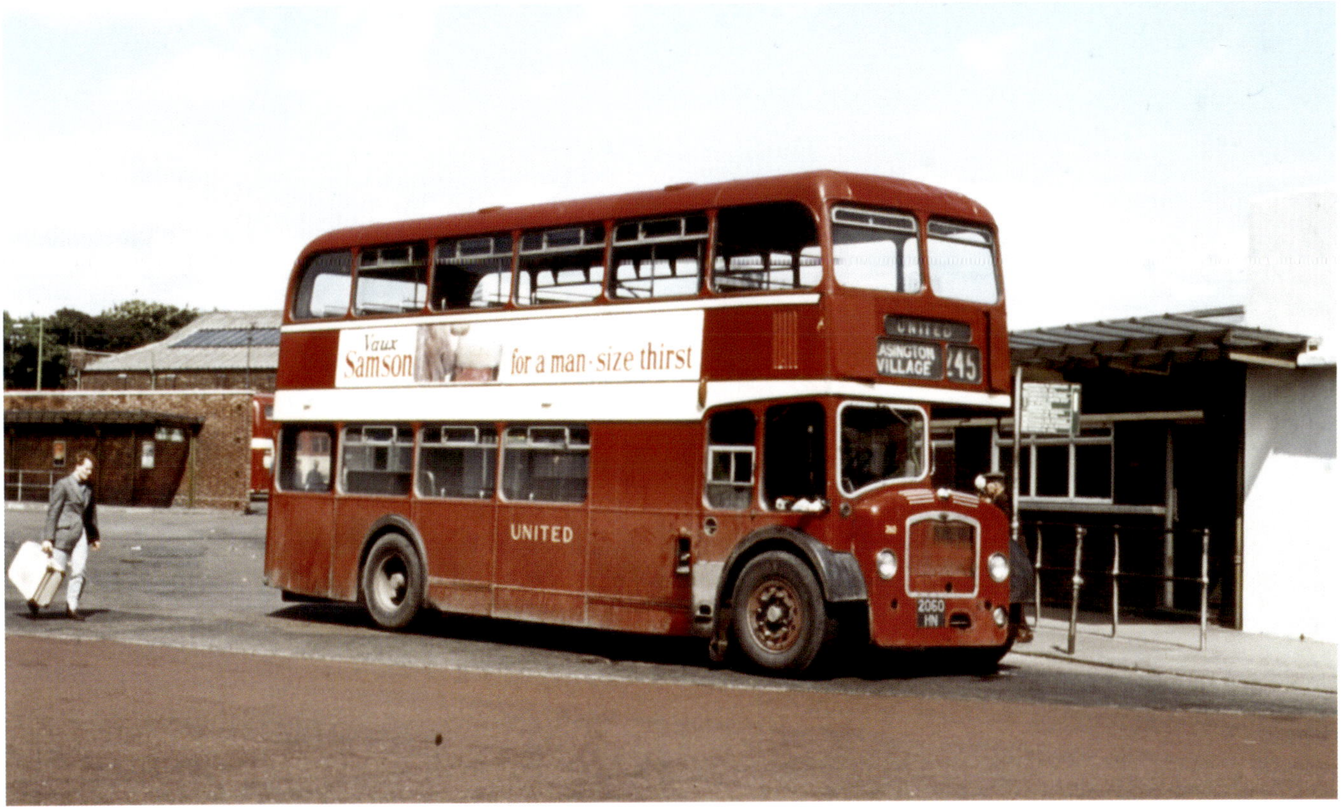

Waiting for passengers at West Hartlepool Bus Station in July 1971 United 260 (2060 HN) was new in December 1960 and was delivered with five other FSF6Bs during that month. All were scrapped without seeing further service with other operators after withdrawal from the United Automobile fleet. (Donald Hudson)

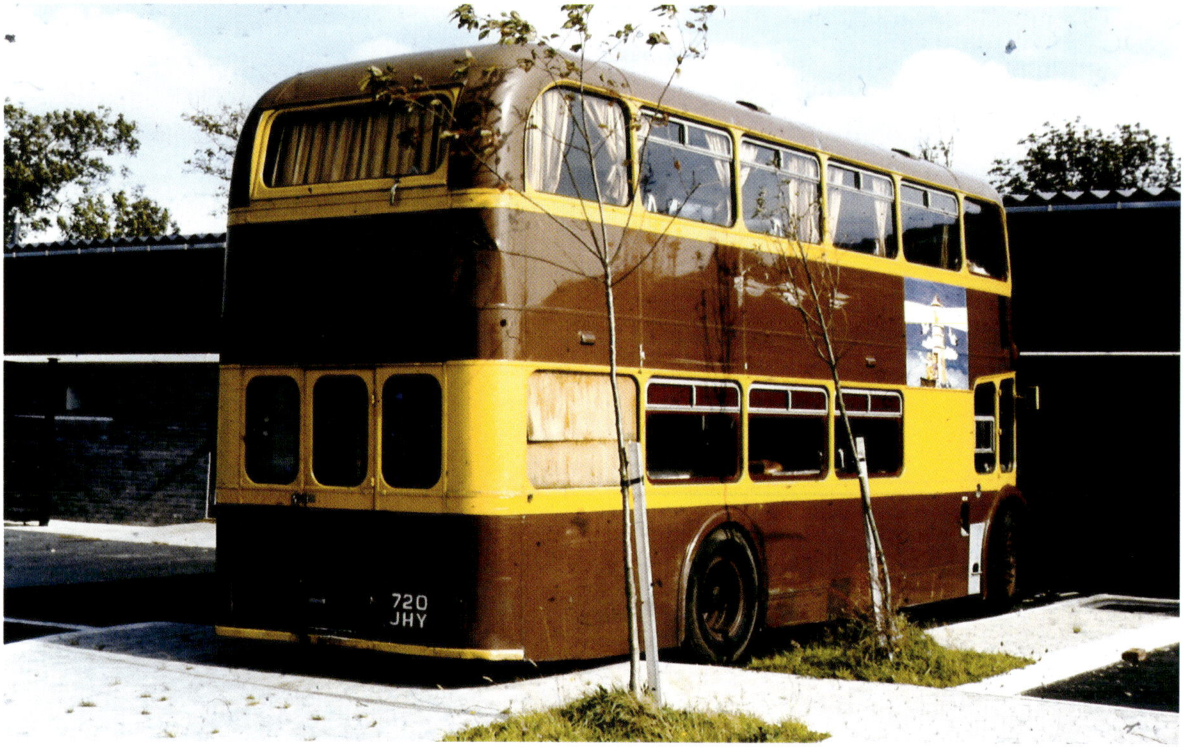

Originally at Weston-super-Mare in the Bristol Omnibus "country" fleet 6021 (720 JHY), a 1961 FSF6G, was transferred to Bath in February 1966 for only 18 months. In August 1967 it was bought by Southern National and allocated fleet number 1019 and retained that number when that fleet was absorbed by Western National in November 1969. After being withdrawn in August 1978 it was converted to a caravan and is seen in this condition at Caernarfon in September 1982. (Author's collection)

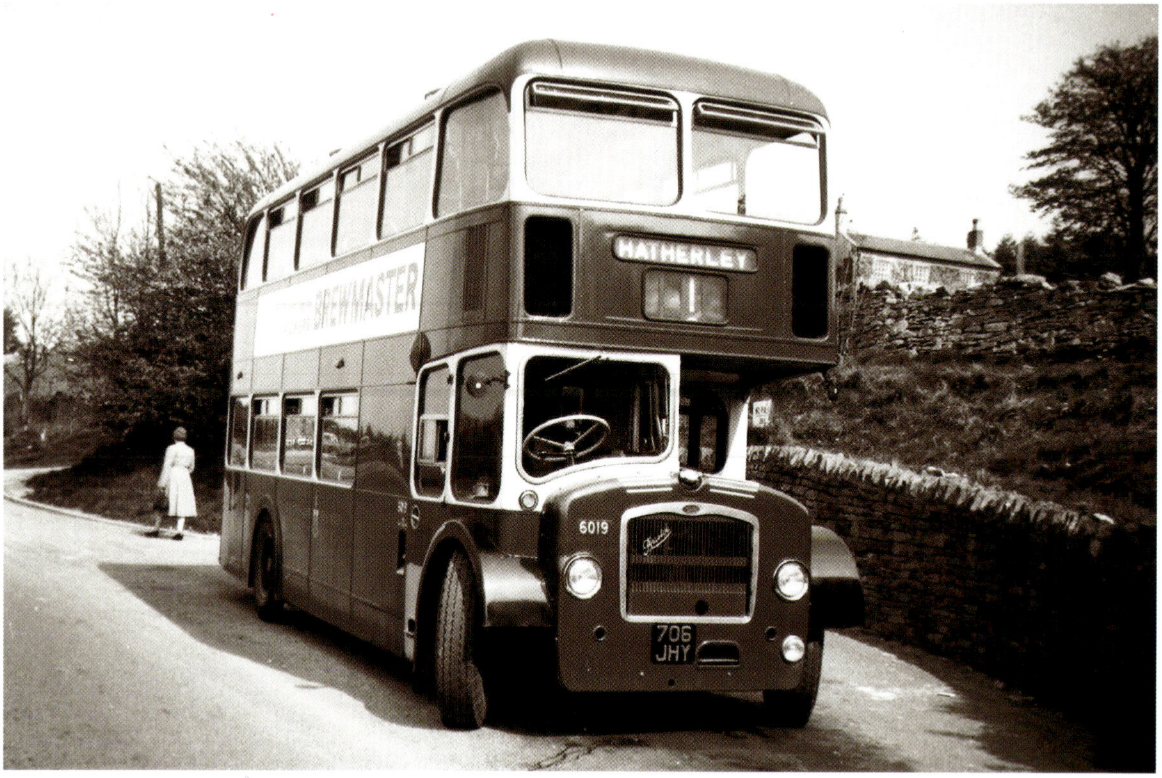

Caught at Cleeve Hill Terminus on a sunny Spring day in April 1961 6019 (706 JHY) was new to Cheltenham District Traction Company in November 1960. It carried fleet number L100, the highest CDT fleet number used, for only four months until renumbered as 6019 in March 1961. It was one of the FSF6Gs involved in the Western National purchase of Bristol Omnibus Company FSF6G vehicles and left Cheltenham in May 1967 becoming 1015 in the Southern National fleet. (Colin Martin)

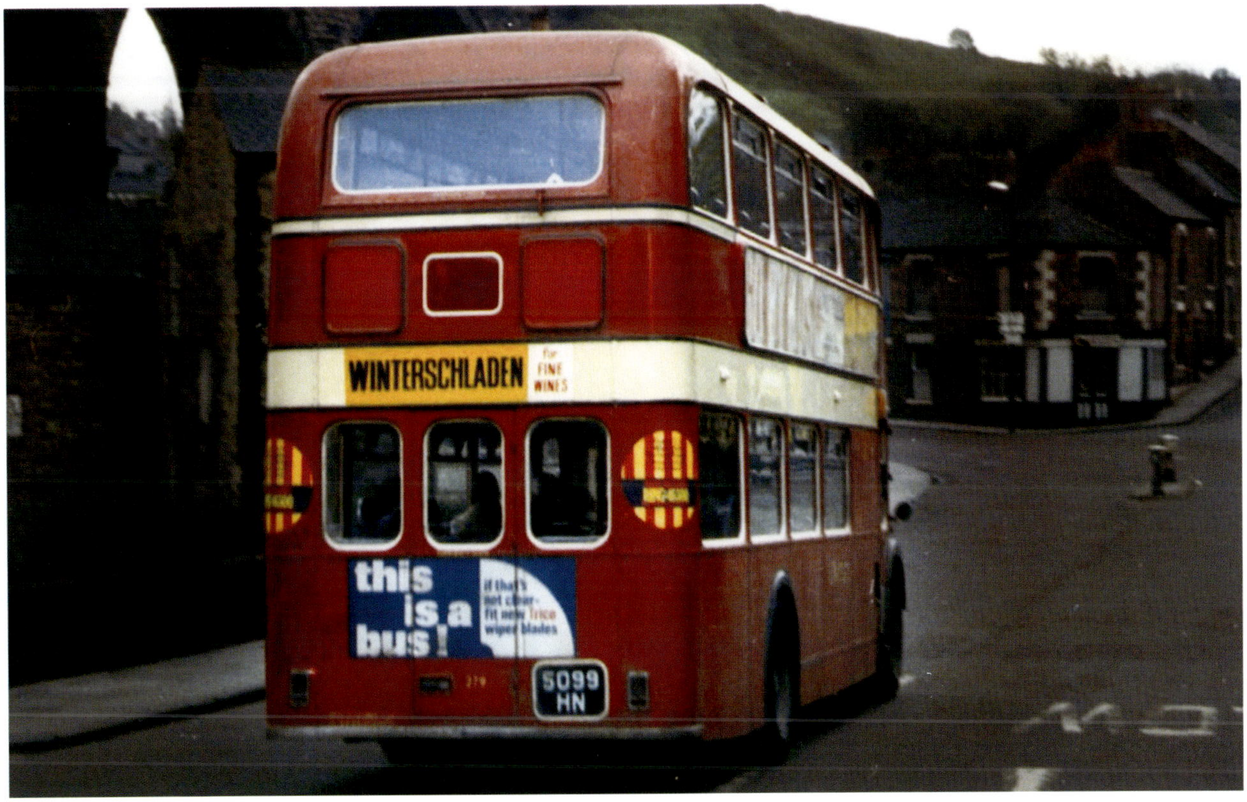

This rear view of United 279 (5099 HN), one of five FSFs received in November 1961, carries a rear advert that says it all! (Peter Horrex collection)

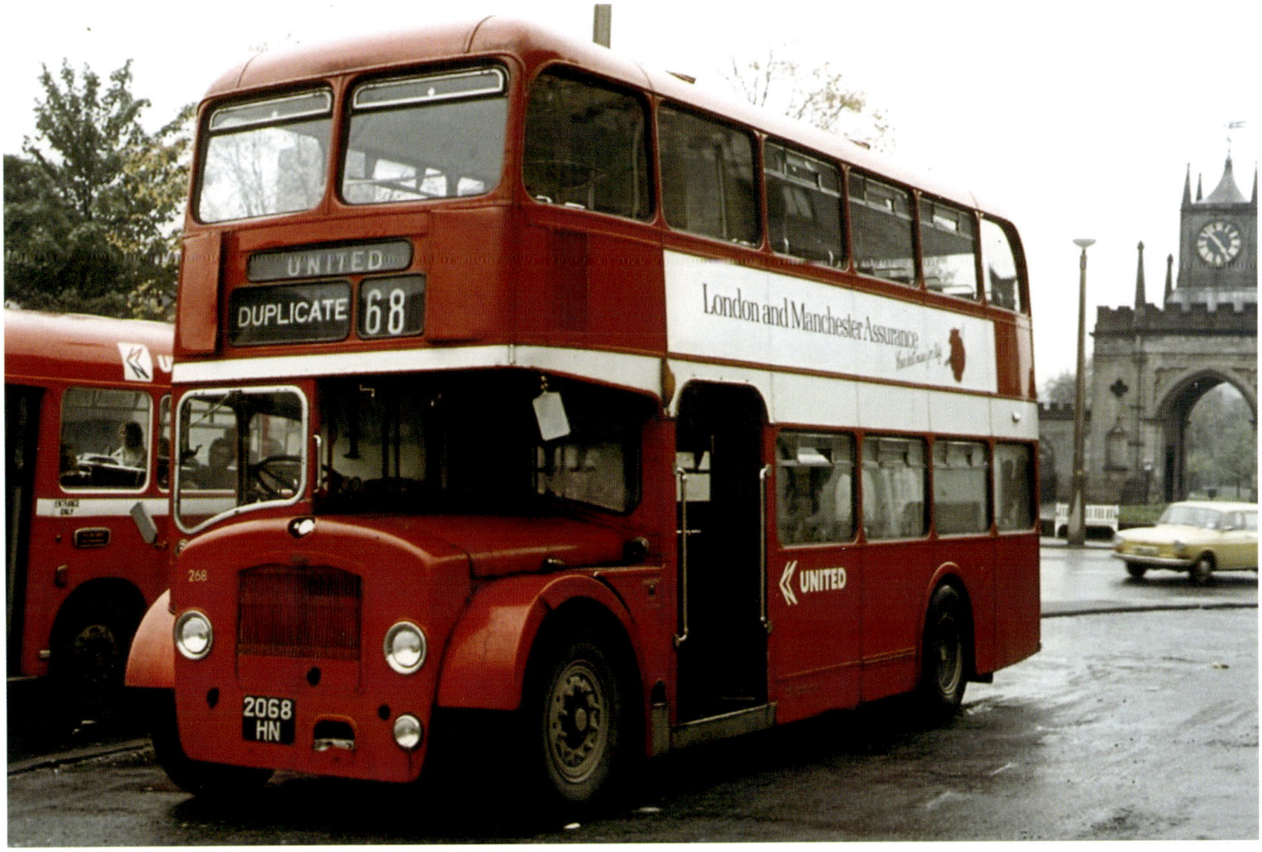

Bishop Auckland Bus Station is the setting for United 268 (2068 HN) waiting to operate a journey on Service 68 between Spennymoor and Byers Green in March 1977 the month that the bus was withdrawn from the fleet. (Peter Horrex collection)

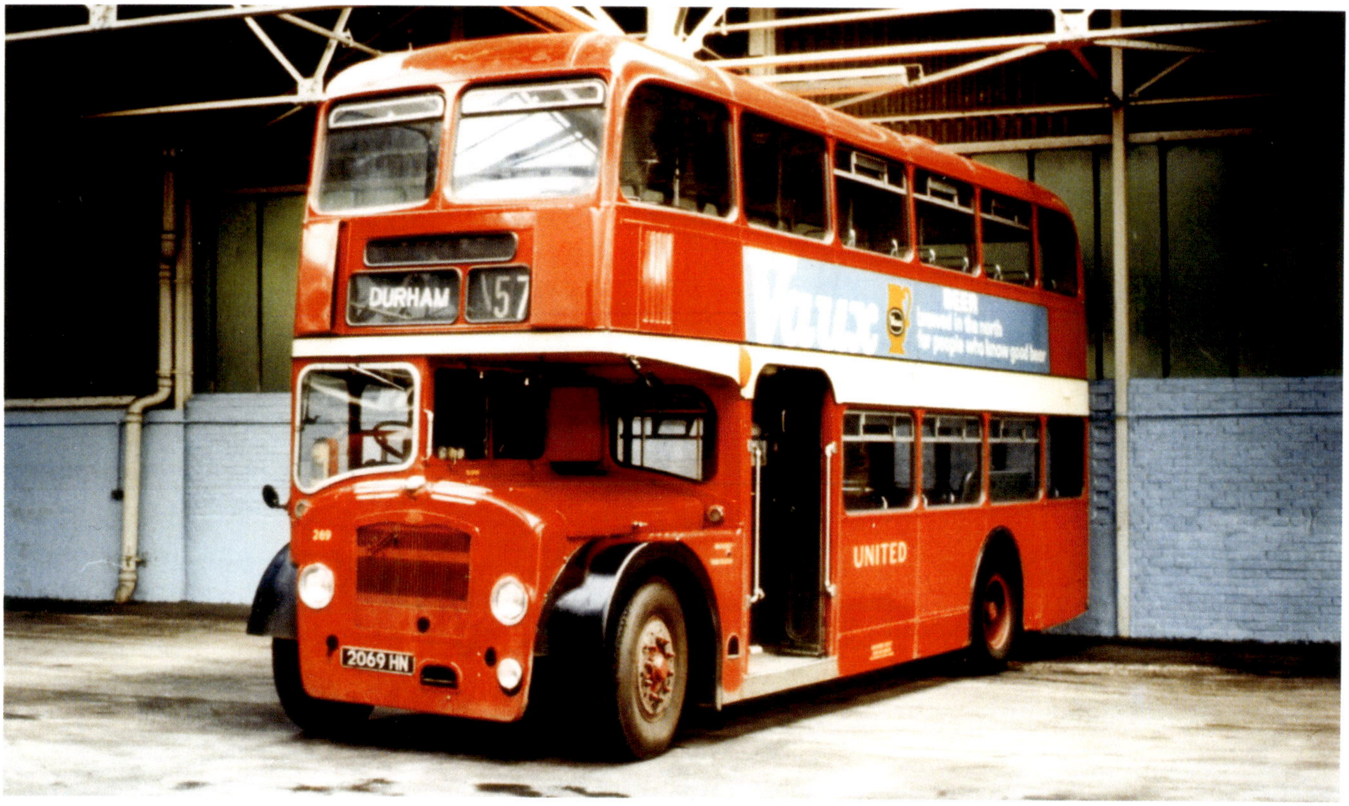

Carrying the unusual oblong front registration number plate United 269 (2069 HN) stands inside Durham Depot waiting to operate a duplicate journey on Service 57. At that time three operators were involved in working this timetable that ran half hourly from Sunderland Bus Station to Bishop Auckland Market Place daily with a two per hour short workings between Sunderland and Durham Bus Station on Mondays to Fridays and four per hour on Saturdays and Sundays. The other operators involved were Northern General and Sunderland District. (Phil Sposito collection)

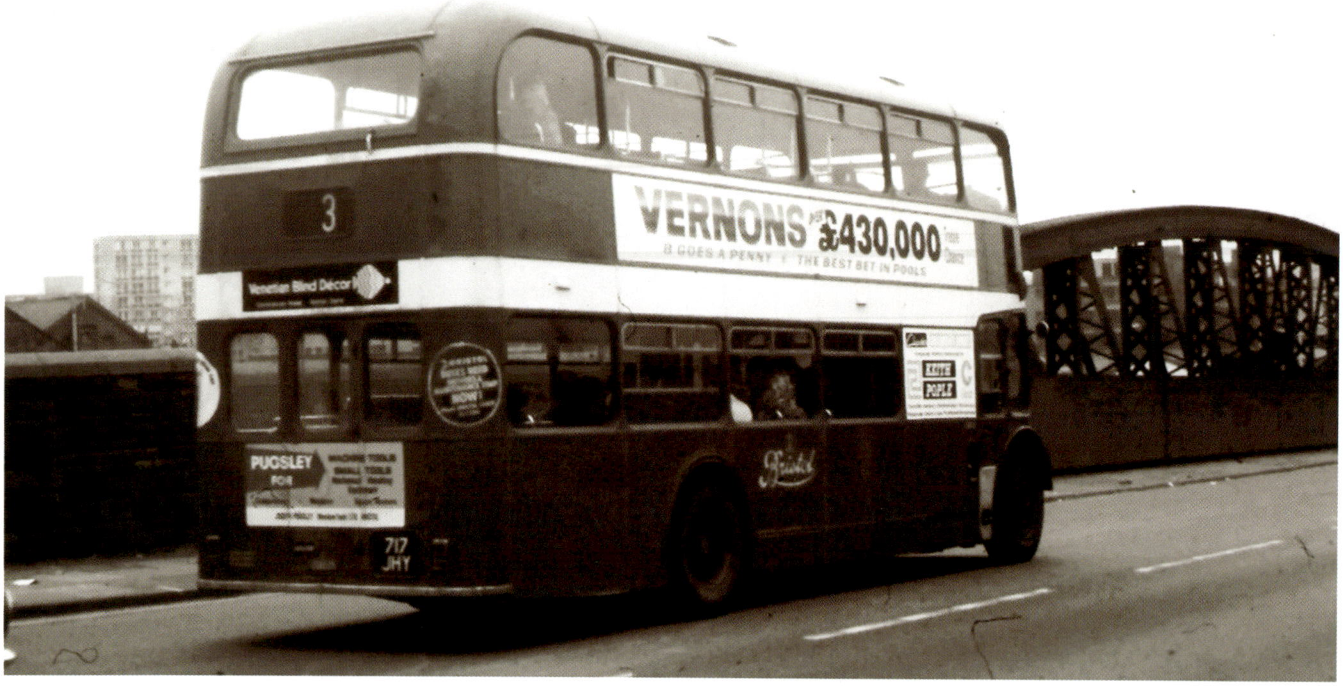

This rear offside view of C6025 (717 JHY) clearly shows the four track service number and letters only box fitted to all Bristol City FSFs and the clean rear end styling of the ECW bodies. Captured on film climbing up Bath Road heading towards Wells Road it is working on Service 3 to Whitchurch (Red Lion) on 13th May 1973. (Author's collection)

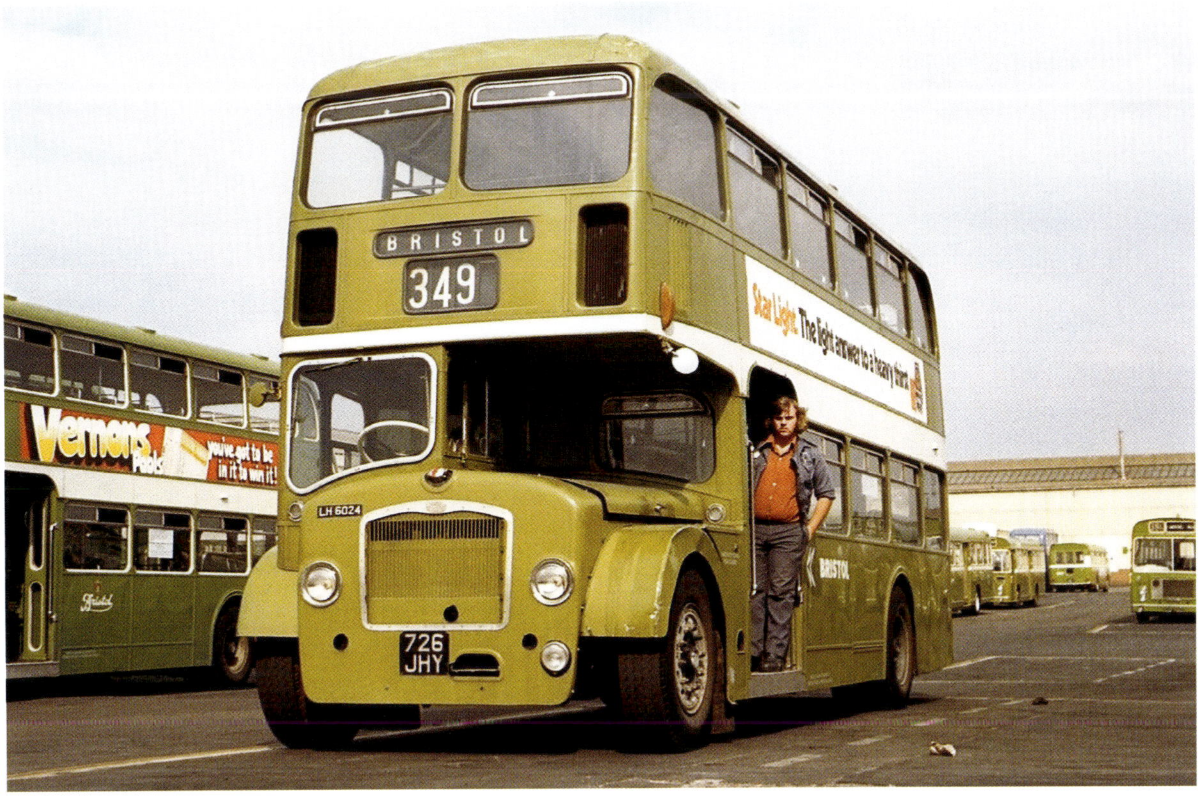

A few days before final withdrawal 6024 (723 JHY), a 1961 FSF6G, was one of those that were originally sold to Western National in 1967 but returned with the transfer of services in Chippenham and Trowbridge on 1st January 1970. It was pictured after transfer from Bath Depot and is seen in Lawrence Hill Depot on 27th August 1976. (Stephen Dowle)

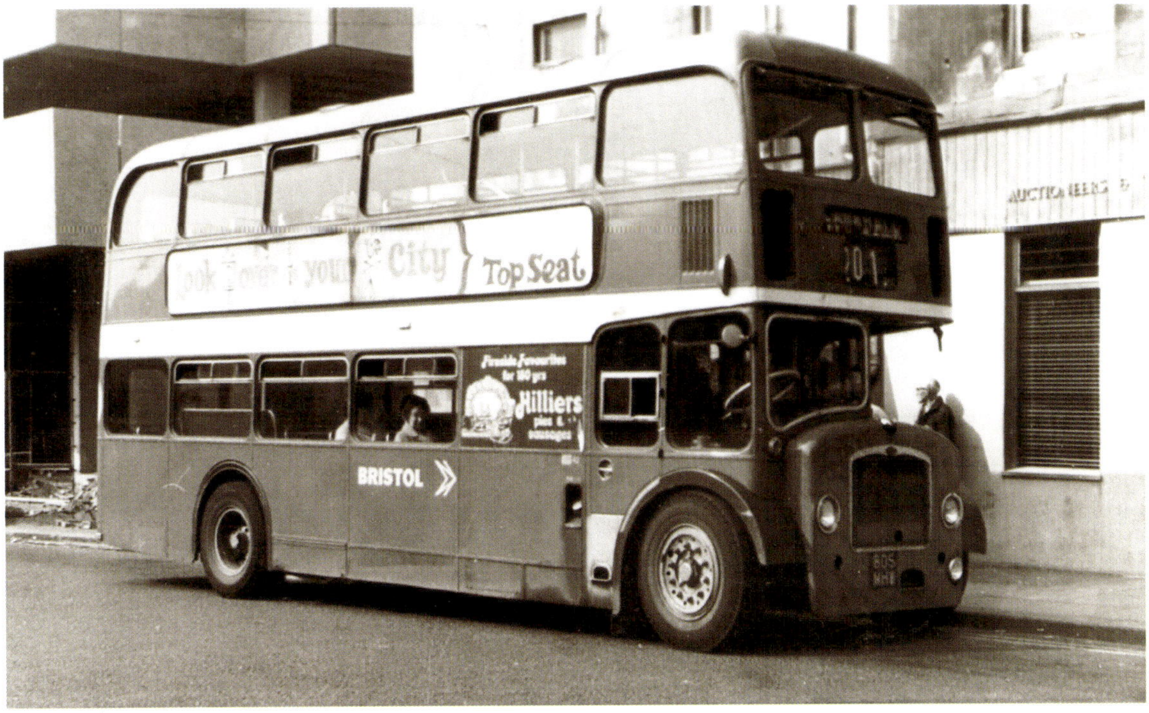

Transferred to Bath on 1st February 1971 6040, a 1961 former Gloucester FSF6G, stands in Railway Street in Bath on a City Service 201 between Odd Down and Larkhall (Square). The popularity of illuminated advertisements as a novel way to advertise businesses had waned by the time of this photograph. After withdrawal from the active fleet it was sold to dealer British Double Deckers of Wotton-under-Edge in Gloucestershire in August 1977 and exported to British Double Deckers in the United States of America the following month. (Tony Robbins collection)

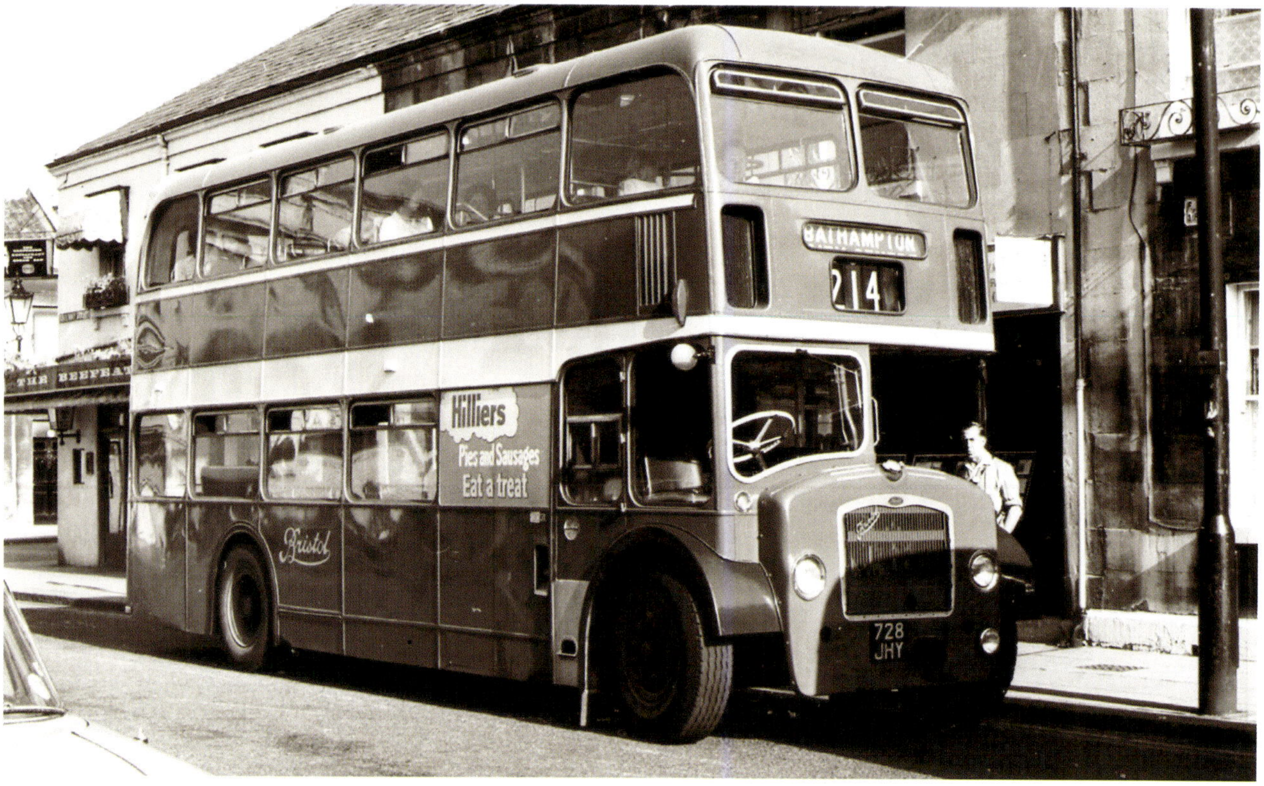

Bath based 6031 (728 JHY), a 1961 FSF6G, stands in Railway Street at the rear of Bath Bus Station waiting to depart for Bathampton on Service 214 from Moorlands Estate. This was one of the vehicles that went to Western National during April 1967 only to return to Bristol Omnibus on 1st January 1970 with the transfer of services operated in the West Wiltshire area. (Bristol Vintage Bus Group)

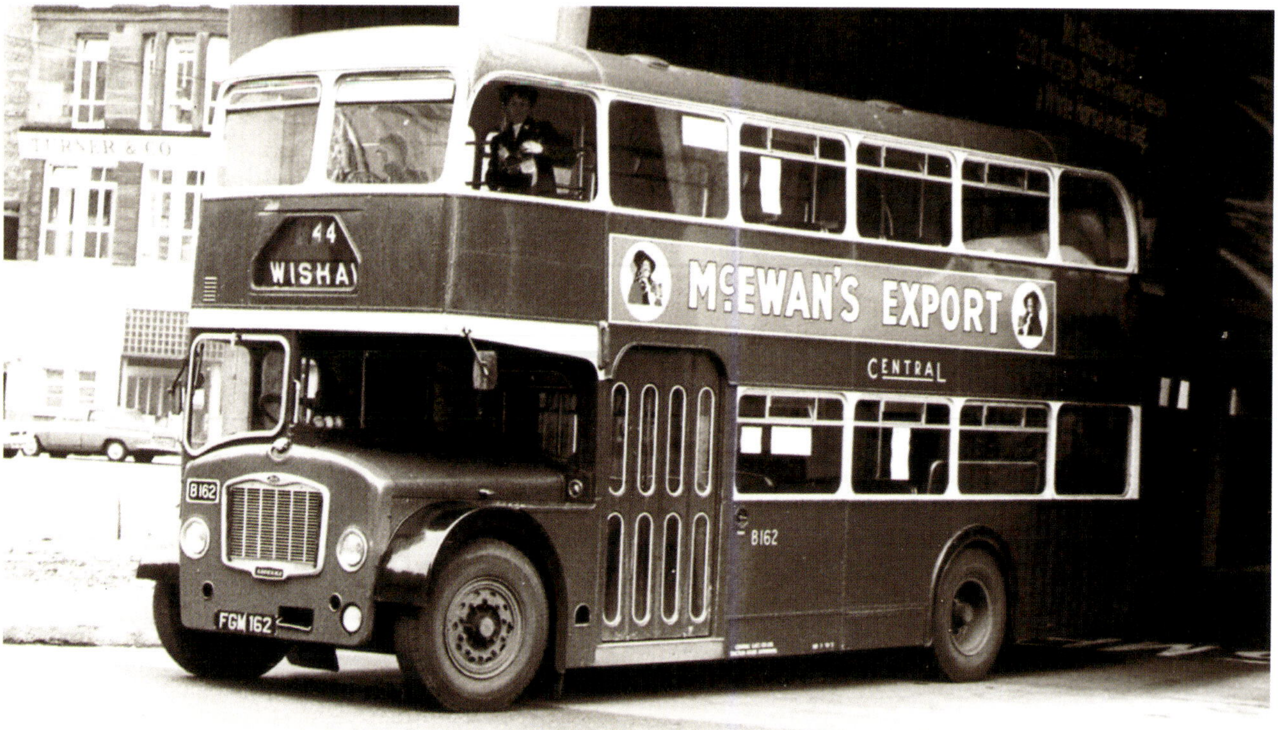

Seen departing Anderston Bus Station in Glasgow is Central SMT B162 (FGM 162) one of the final eleven FSFs built and delivered in September 1963 under Sanction 215. The previous FSF delivery was eight to United Welsh in November 1962 and the previous batch for Central SMT was 30 delivered in March and April 1962. B162 is working a quiet Service 44 journey to Wishaw. (Tony Robbins collection)

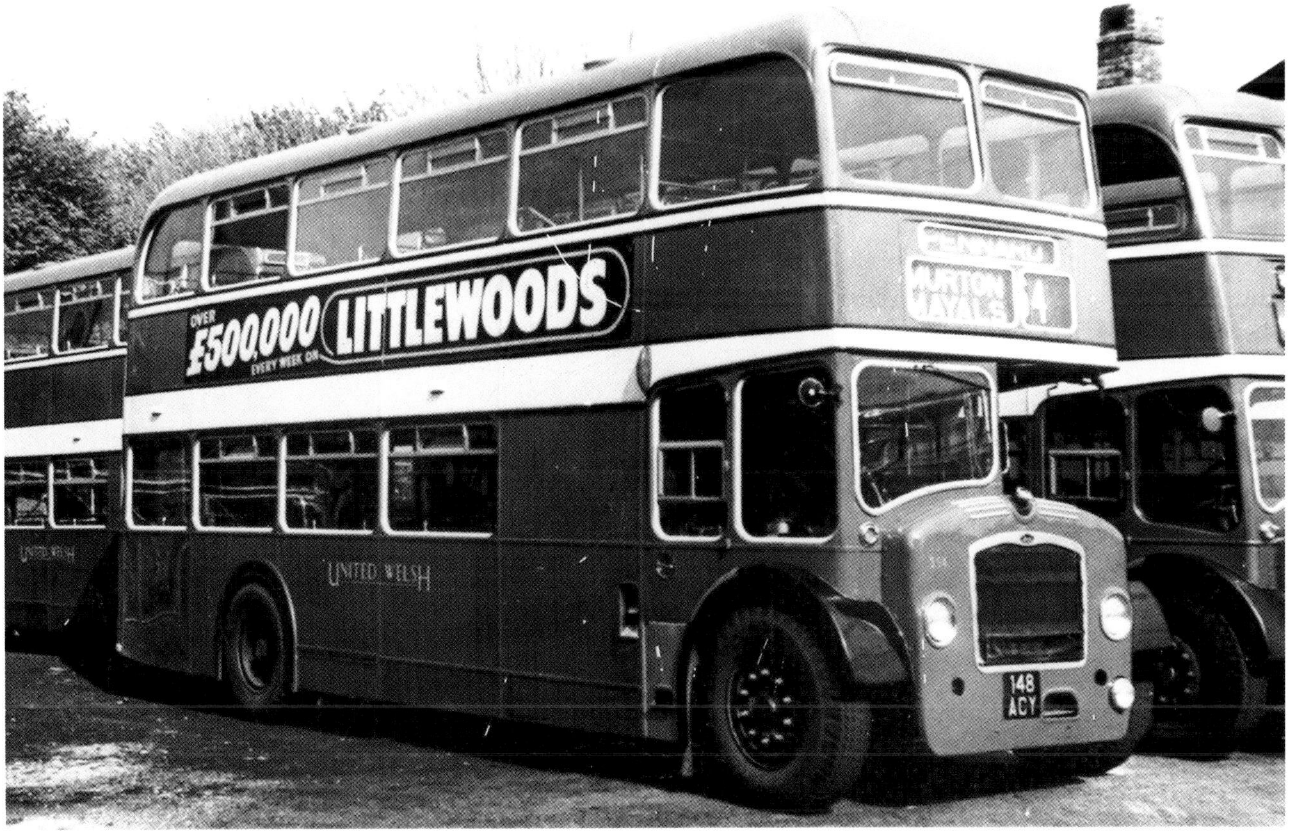

United Welsh 354 (148 ACY), 1961 FSF6G looking in excellent condition but does not have the additional lower deck ventilator in the rearmost window. It was only 360–376 (258 DCY–274 DCY), the November 1962 deliveries, that were fitted with these. (Robert F. Mack)

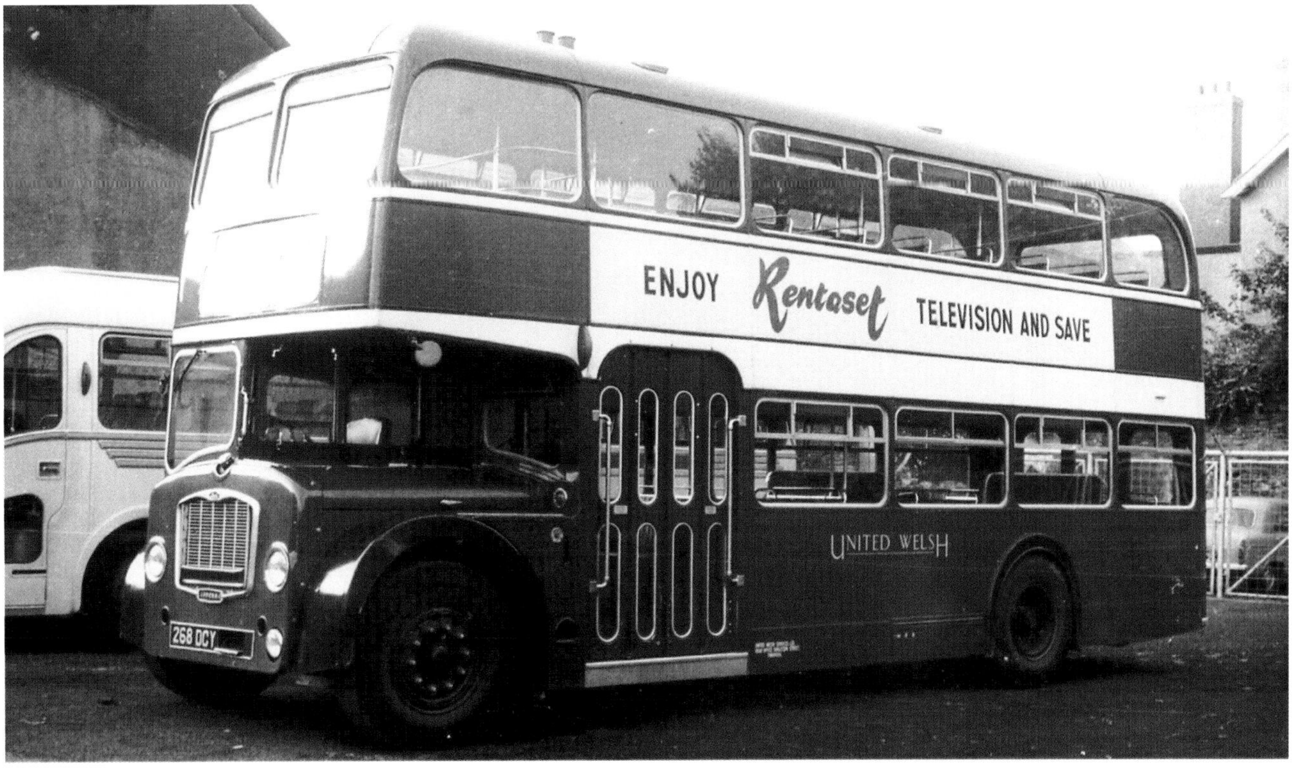

Who remembers Rentaset televisions advertised on the nearside of United Welsh 370 (268 DCY)? This 1962 FSF6G is seen when relatively new. (Tony Robbins collection)

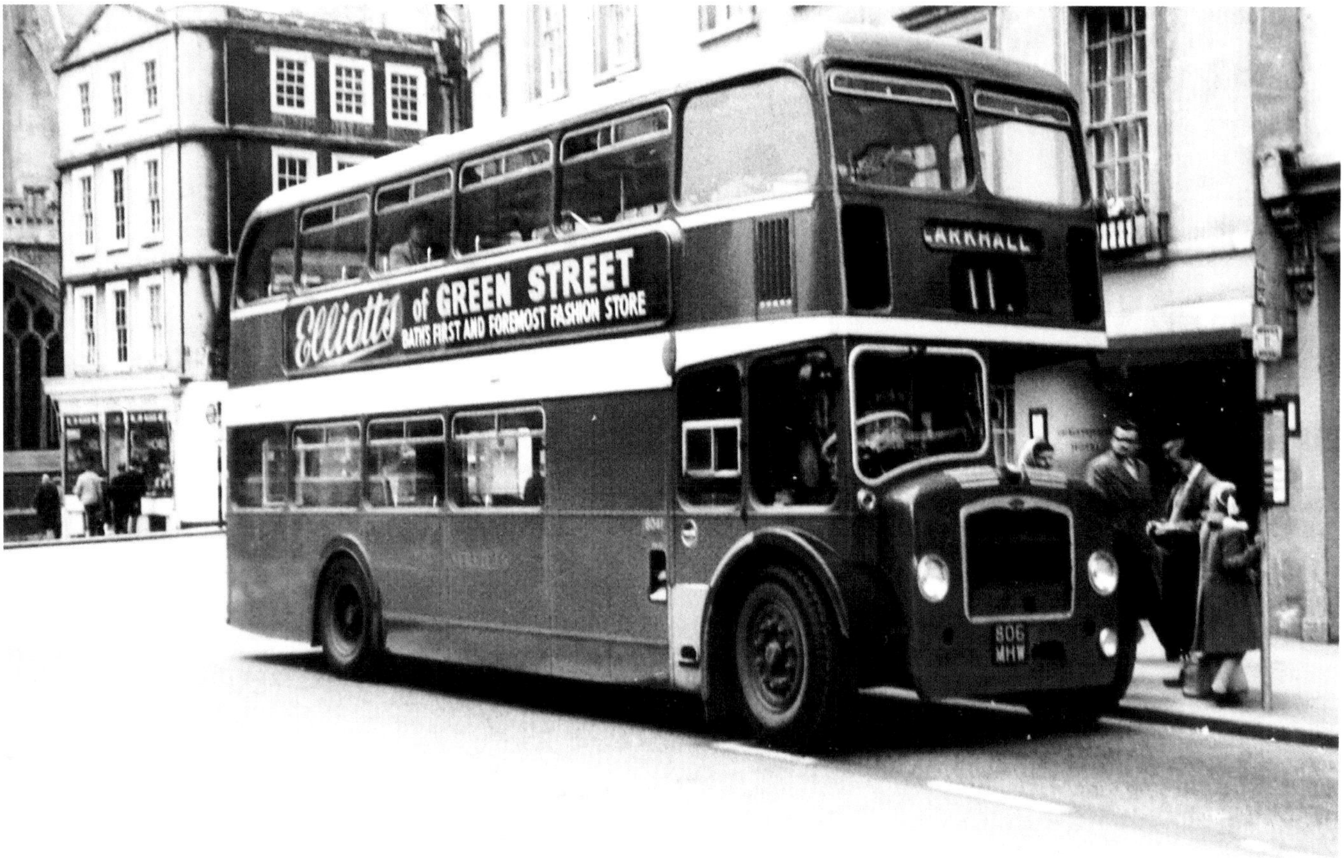

Elliott's was a regular local business to advertise on Bath buses as witnessed by Bath Services 6041 (806 MHW) with illuminated offside advertisement panel carrying their advert. This was the last FSF for any of the Bristol Omnibus fleets and is seen at the bus stop at Guildhall on High Street, Bath working a journey on Bath City Service 11 from Odd Down to Larkhall (Square) in April 1963. (Tony Robbins collection)

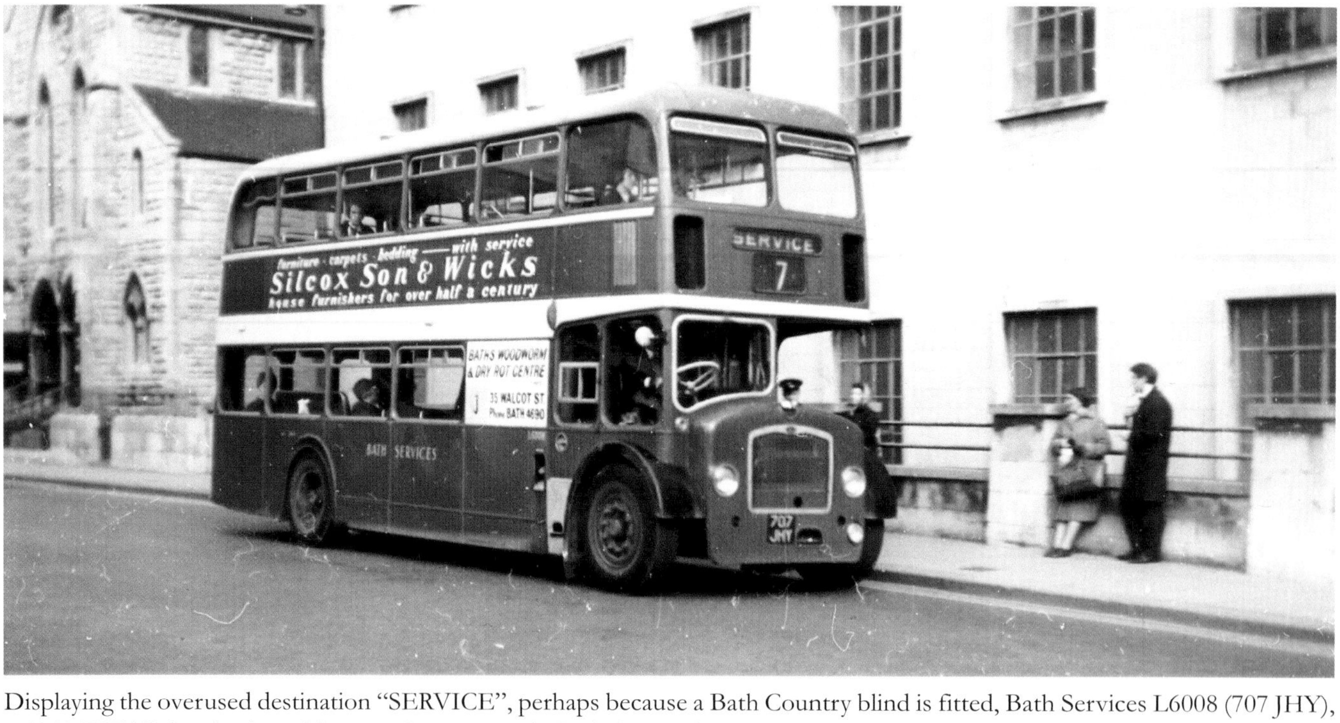

Displaying the overused destination "SERVICE", perhaps because a Bath Country blind is fitted, Bath Services L6008 (707 JHY), a 1960 FSF6G, heads along Manvers Street towards Bath Spa Railway Station on 16th March 1967 on a Bath City journey on Service 7 to Whiteway via Oldfield Park and The Hollow. (Allan Macfarlane)

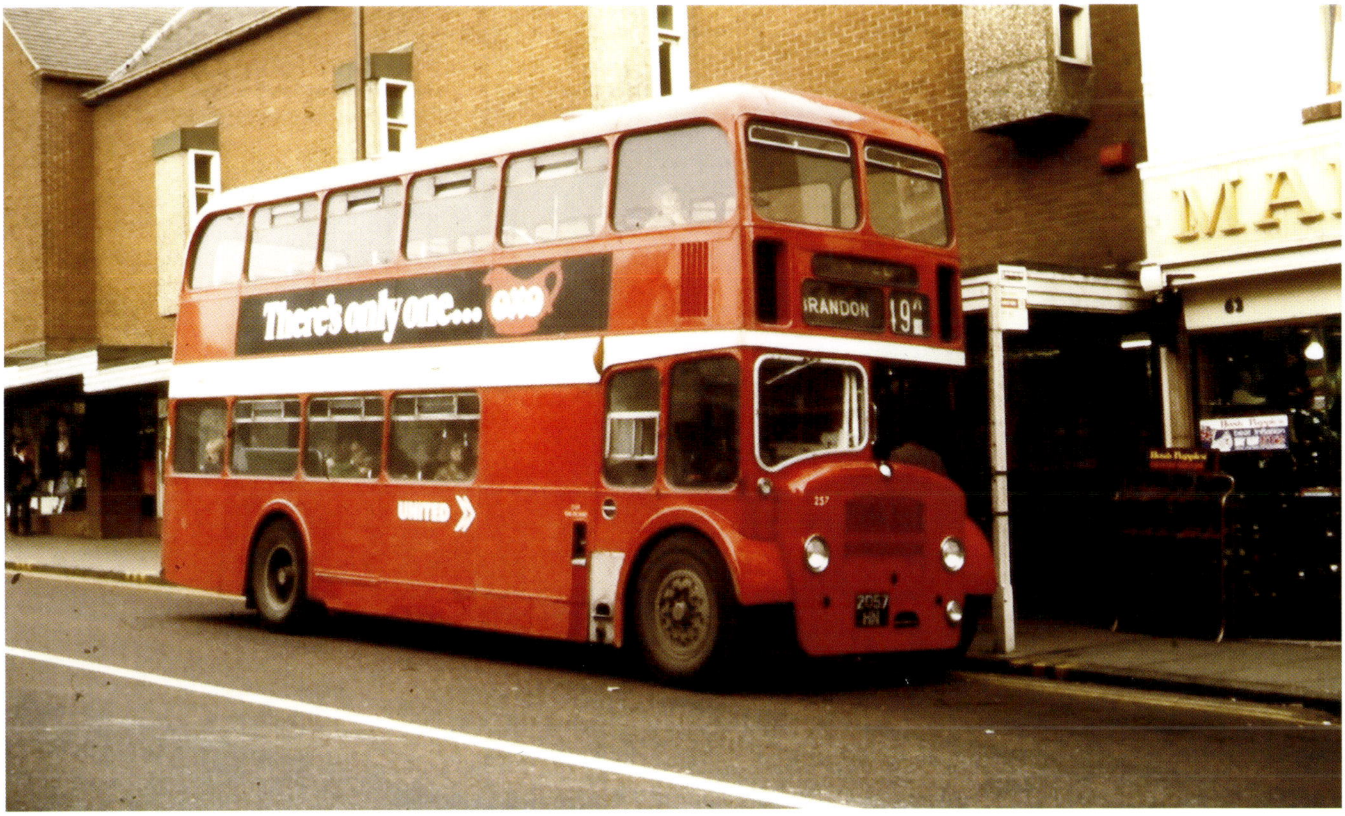

When the coal mines were a major employer, particularly in the north eastern area of England and South Wales, bus companies ran additional journeys to meet the needs of the collieries. In the 1960s United Automobile operated Service 49 between Durham (Bus Station) and Brandon Colliery every 15 minutes including Sundays. United 257 (2057 HN) was numerically the first FSF for the company received in November 1960 and scrapped after withdrawal from the fleet on an unknown date. (Chris Riley)

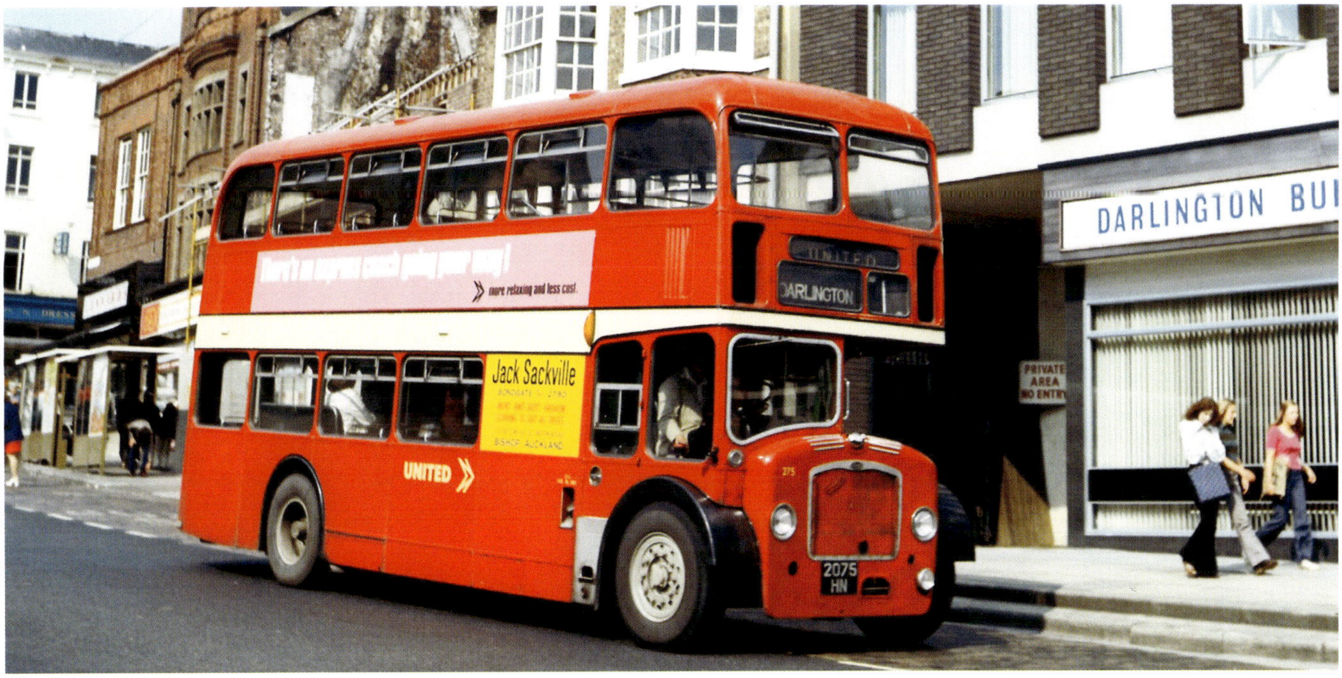

Almost arrived at Darlington (Leadyard) on a Service 1 journey from Bishop Auckland (Market Place) United Automobile 275 (2075 HN) has operated via Shildon, All Saints' and Heighington. According to the United Automobile Services Ltd. including Durham District Services Ltd. timetable for Durham, Tees-side and Yorkshire Area dated 1st June–30th September 1960 Heighington was described as typifying the "green village" for which County Durham is famous. It also has St. Michaels Church that dates back to the 13th century. (Author's collection)

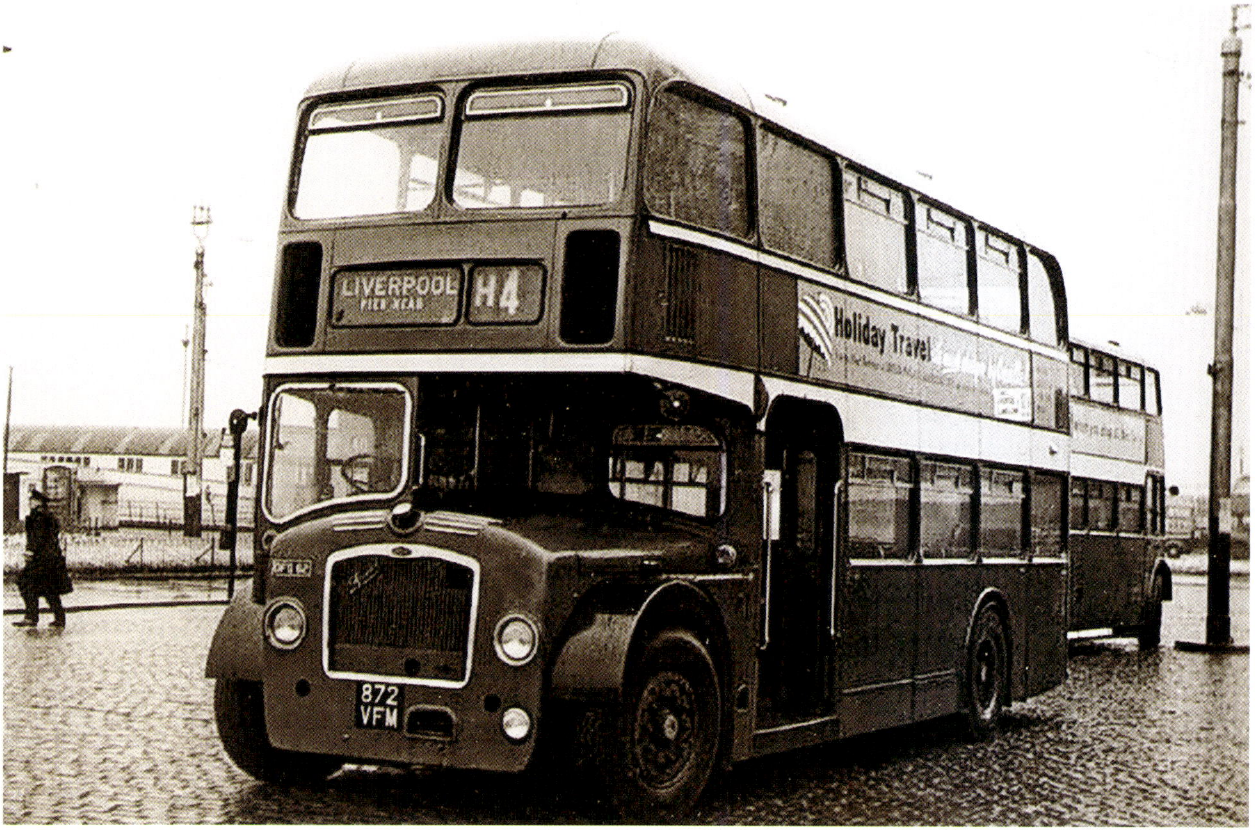

Pictured on the cobbles at Liverpool (Pier Head) in damp weather, Crosville DFG62 (872 VFM), a 1961 FSF6G, was damaged by fire at Wrexham in November 1980 and scrapped very soon afterwards. (Tony Robbins collection)

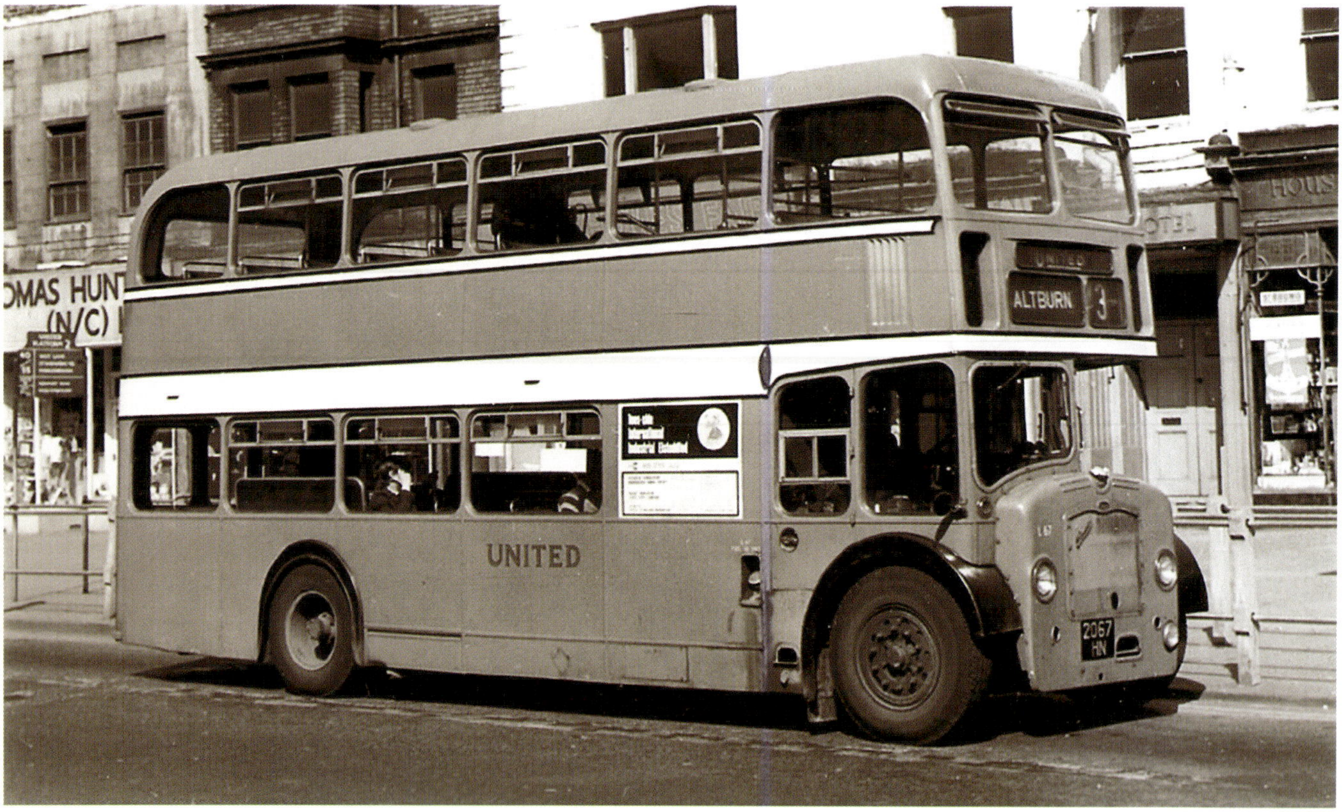

Waiting for intending passengers, United BL67 (2067 HN), a 1961 FSF6B, is seen at Stockton (High Street) on 15th May 1966 on a Service 73 through journey to Saltburn that generally operated every 30 minutes all week. (Gerry Mead)

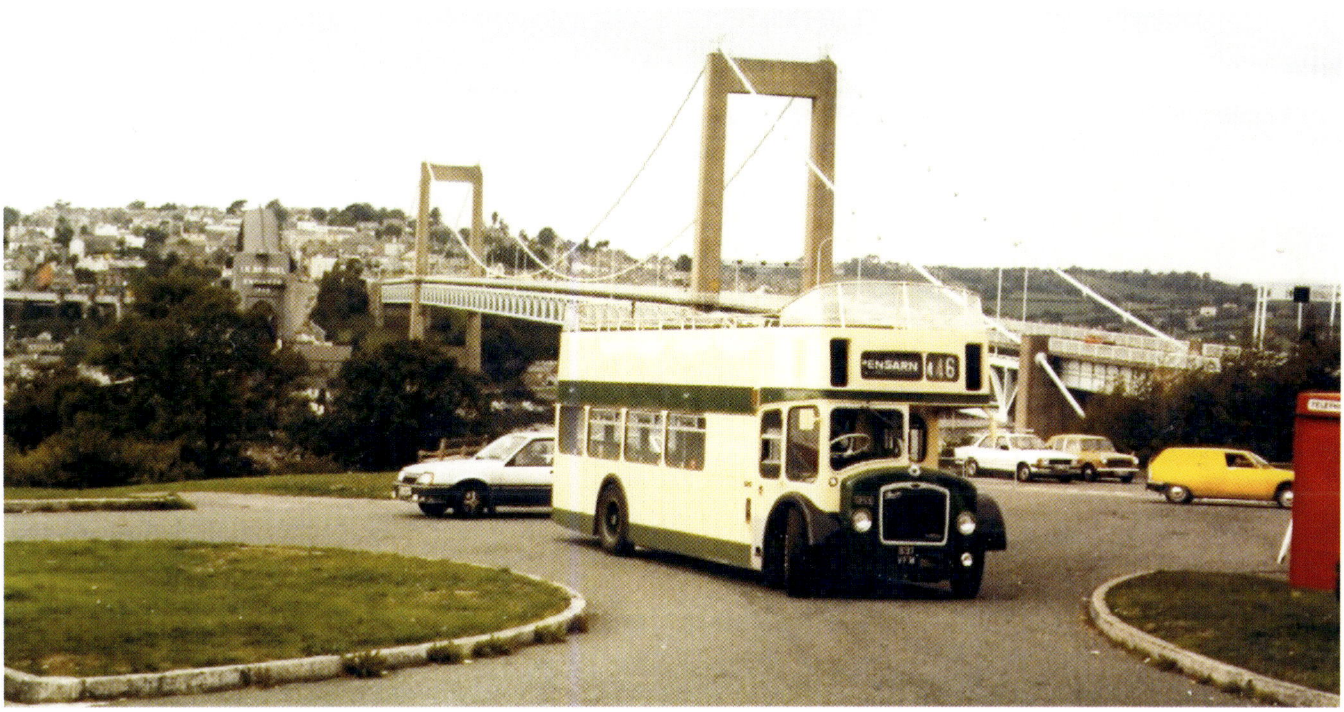

Preserved Crosville DFG81 (891 VFM), a 1962 FSF6G that was converted to open top in February 1977, is seen here on its way to or from a bus rally with Isambard Kingdom Brunel's Saltash Railway Bridge forming an impressive backdrop. (Stephen Kelly collection)

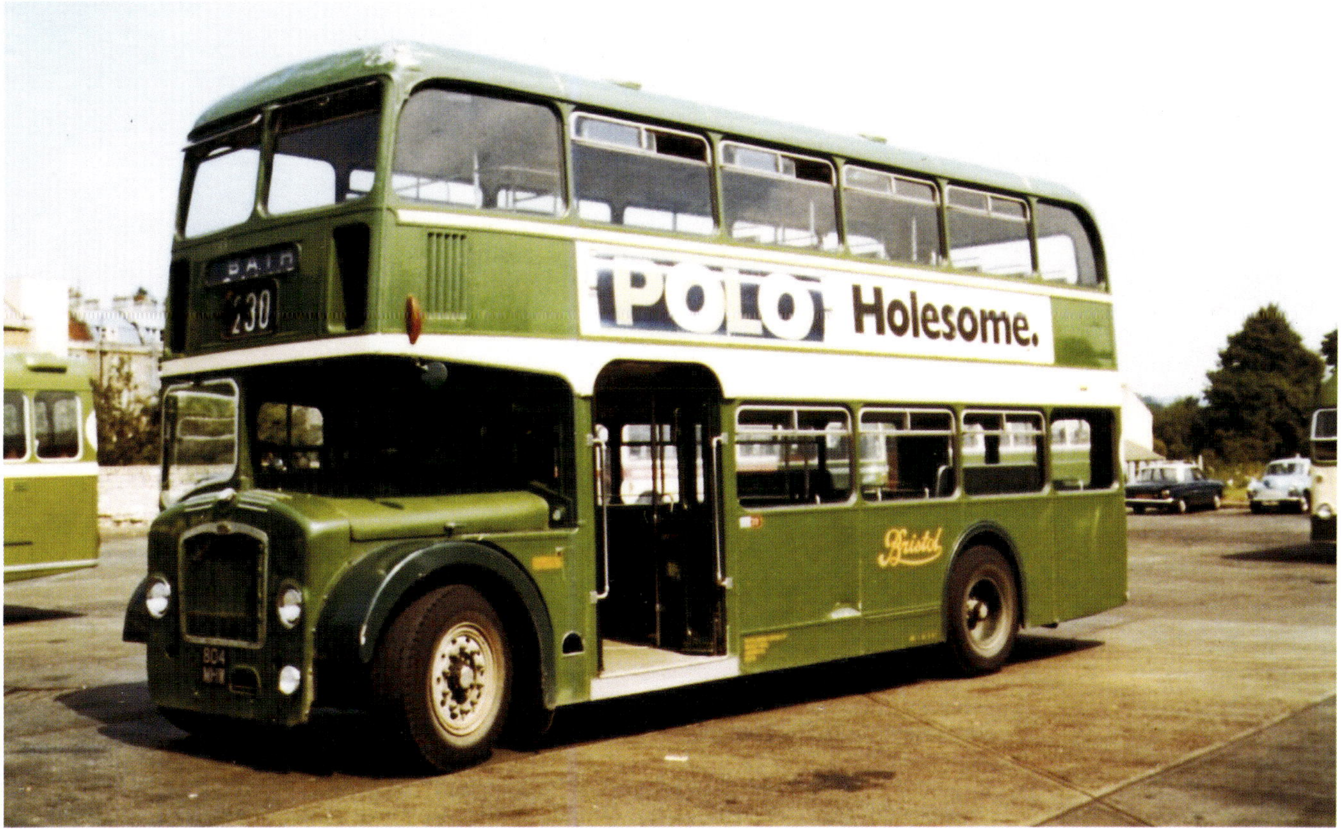

Standing in the open yard at Kensington Depot on London Road at Bath 6039 (804 MHW), a 1961 FSF6G, waits for its next turn of duty on 2nd August 1973. It was new to Gloucester City Services and originally numbered G6039 until renumbered when transferred to Bath with 6040 in June 1972. It was withdrawn from the operational fleet in 1976 and sold to Barnsley dealer Paul Sykes in January 1977 for scrap.

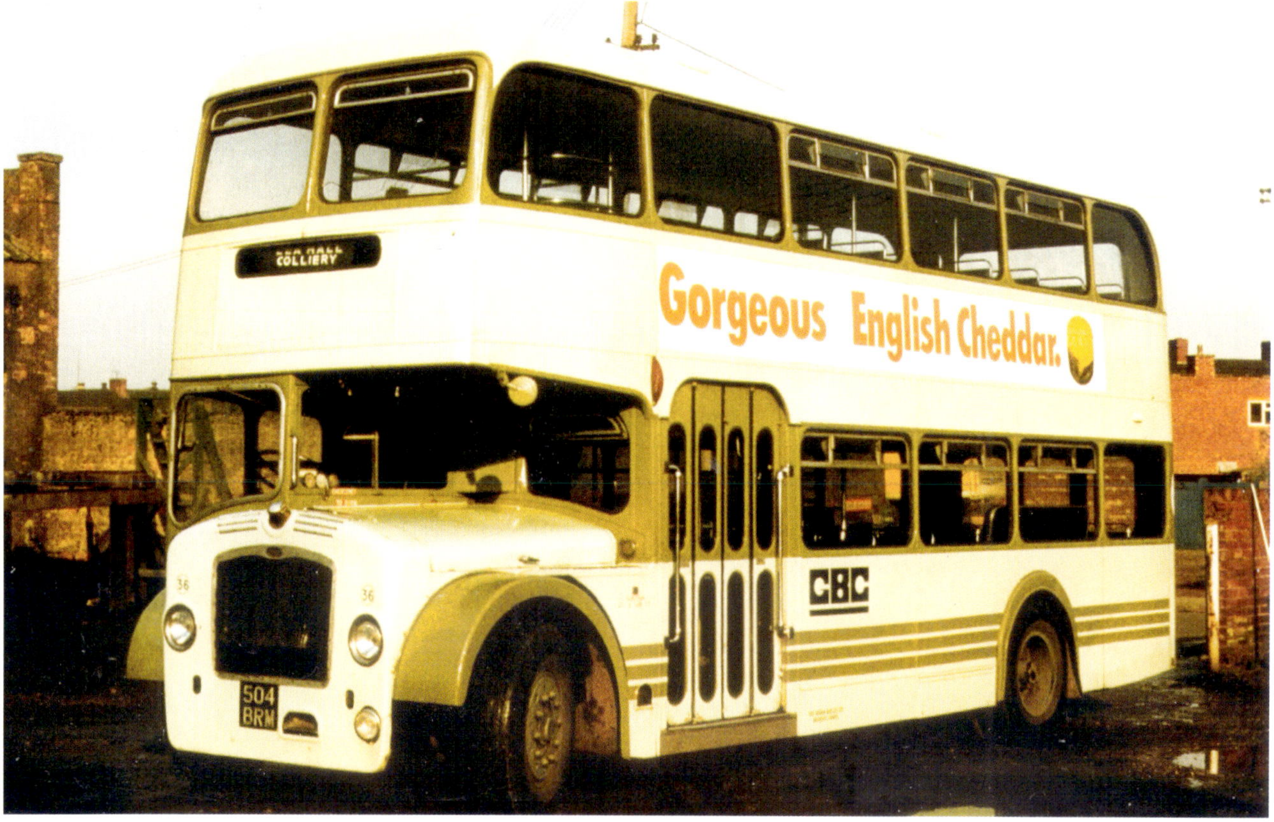

Green Bus Company (Rugeley) 36 (504 BRM), a 1960 ex Cumberland FSF6G, looks to be in good shape when caught on film at the company's depot but only operated with Green Bus Company from July to November 1973 when Midland Red took over the company and buses. Although the FSF was allocated fleet number 2175 it was never used by the new owners. (Tony Robbins collection)

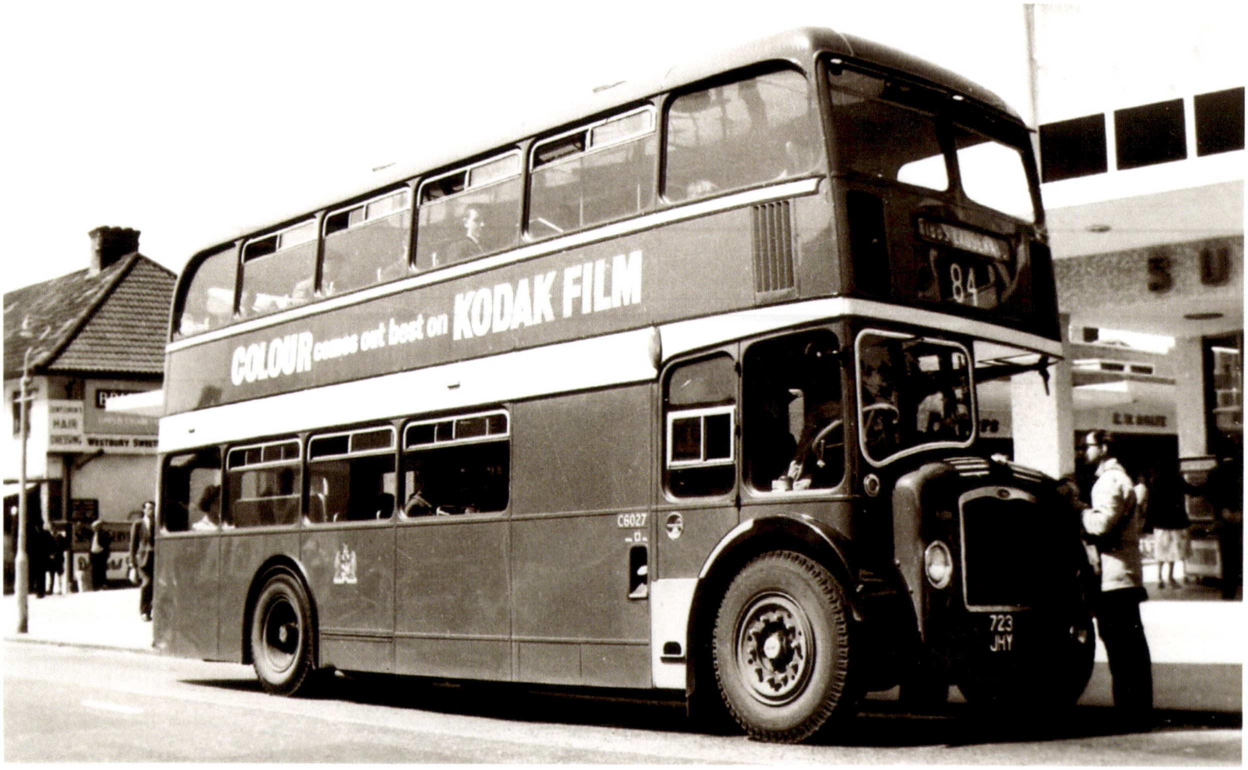

The conductor talks over the bonnet to the driver of C6027 (723 JHY), 1961 FSF6B, that only carries the Bristol coat of arms and looks pristine on Service 84 to Cribbs Causeway well before the M5 was built. (Allan Macfarlane)

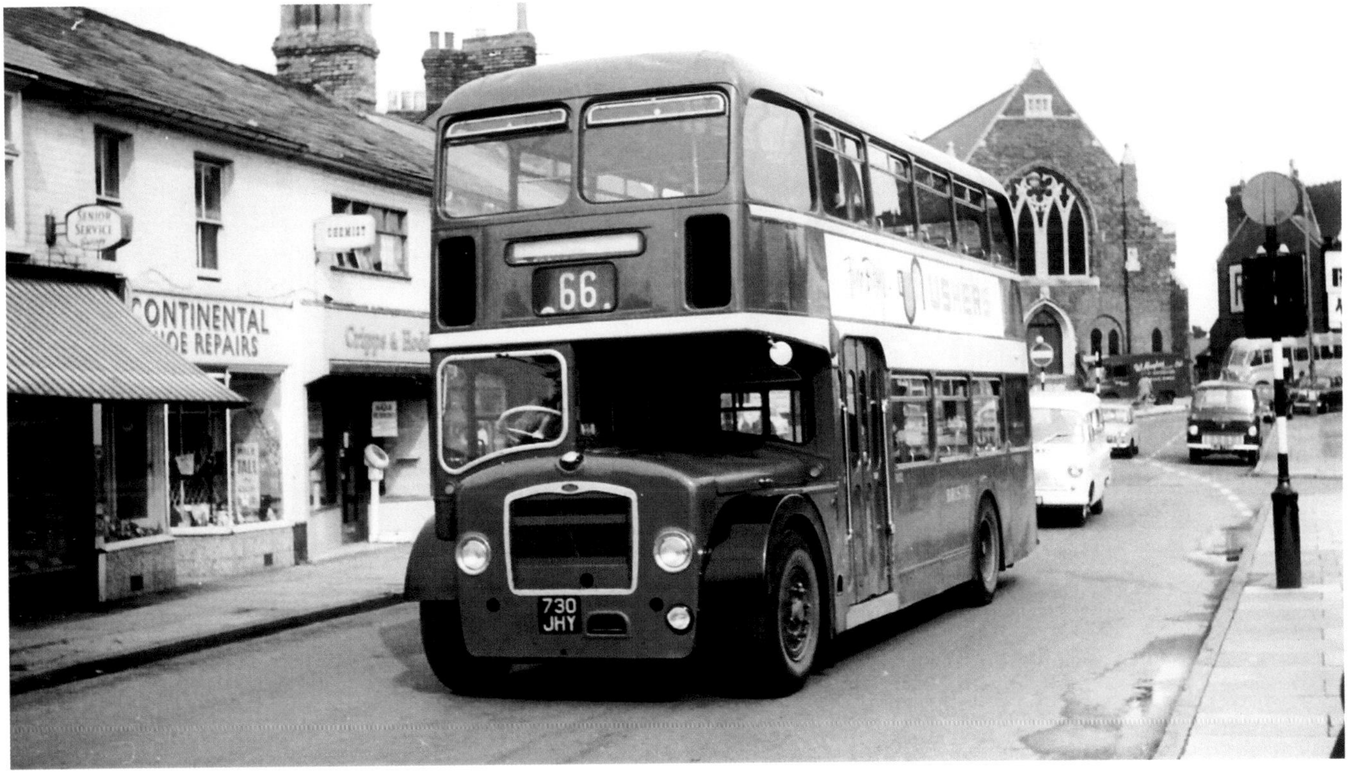

Swindon was the home depot for Bristol Country Area 6033 (730 JHY) seen here with gold block capital letter "Bristol" fleet name on a Service 66 journey to Purton Stoke on 23rd July 1965. It seemed, at the time, a common problem was that drivers and conductors just couldn't be bothered to find the correct destination on the blind and would wind it to show "SERVICE" or, as in this instance, a white blank. (A. J. Douglas)

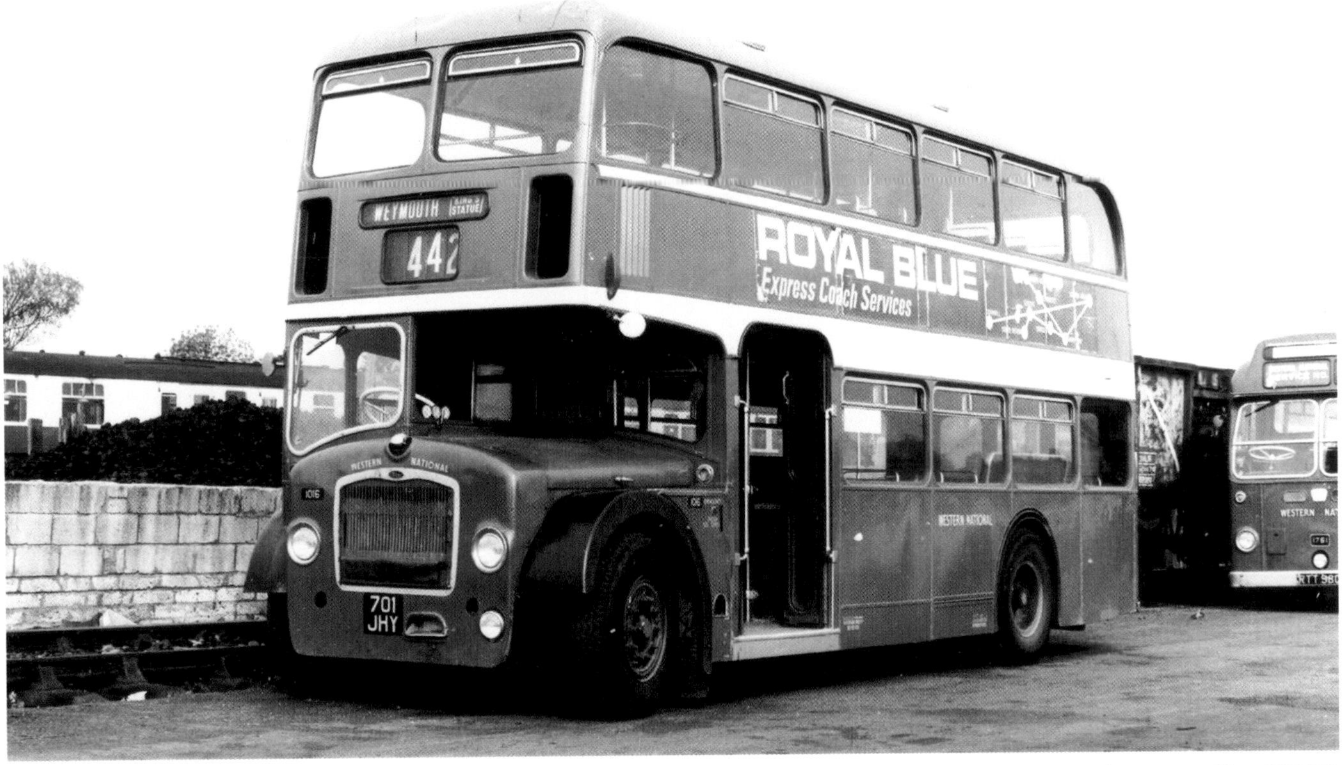

Carrying the small version of the pre-NBC fleet name Western National 1016 (701 JHY), a 1960 ex Gloucester City FSF6G, stands at the south coast resort of Weymouth. (Tony Robbins collection)

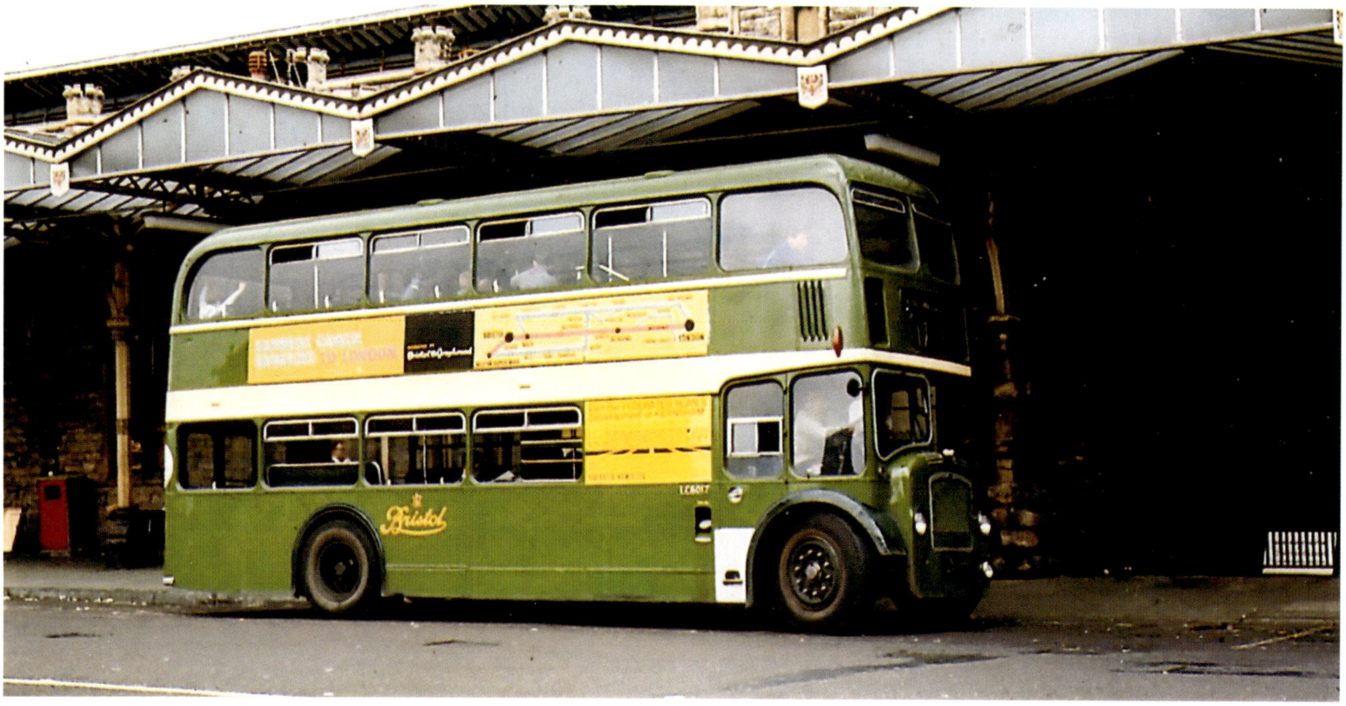

Bristol Omnibus LC6017 (716 JHY), a 1960 FSF6B at Temple Meads Railway Station, waits to depart for Clifton Zoo on Service 17. Delivered in November 1960 as LC8575 it was renumbered in January 1961 and again when it lost the L prefix between November 1967 and March 1968. It was down seated to 58 passengers in October 1965 when a lower deck double seat immediately behind the under stairs luggage compartment was removed to allow extra luggage capacity. (Adrian Hunt)

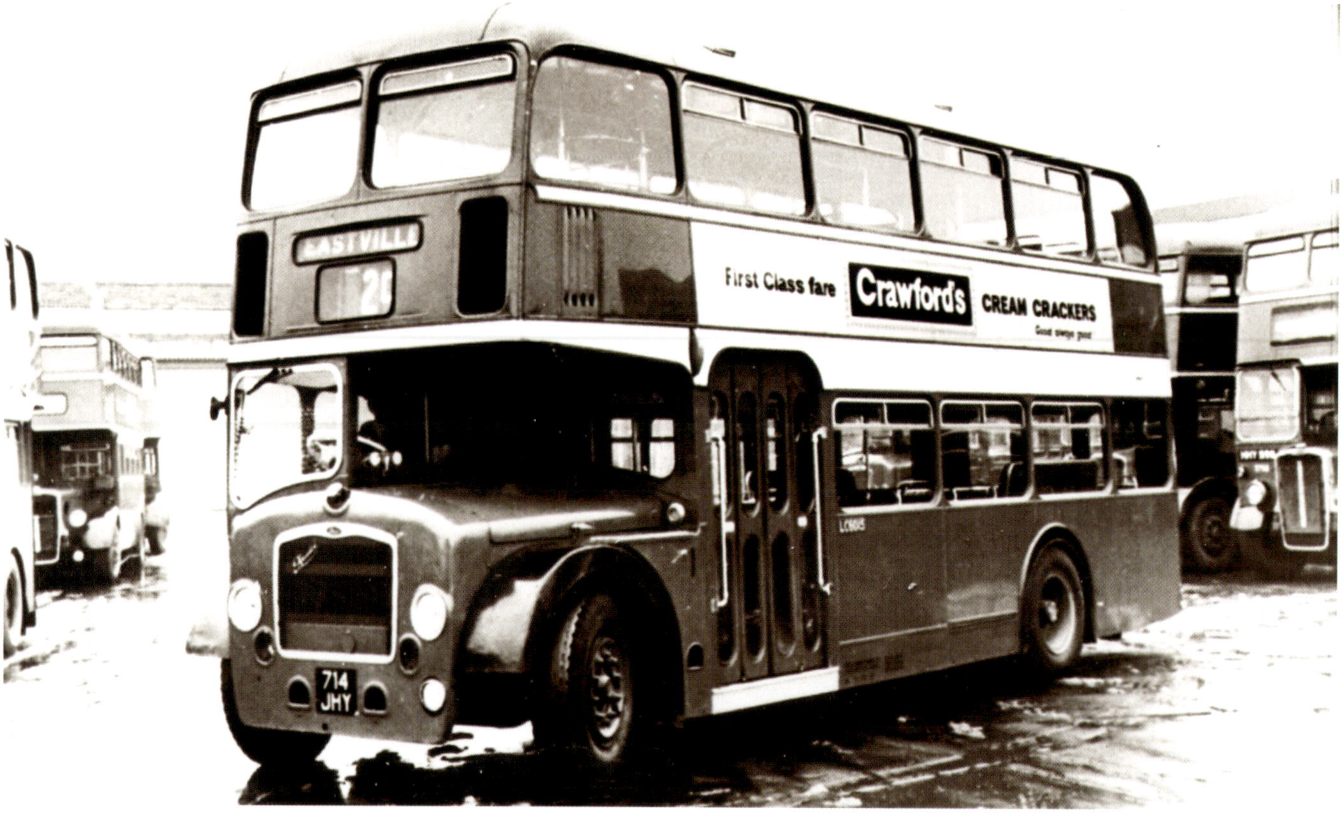

When new Bristol Omnibus Company C6015 (714 JHY), a 1960 FSF6B, was delivered as LC8573 in November 1960 and in 1965 was one of four Bristol Joint Services FSFs to be down seated to accommodate 58 plus eight standing passengers. The others similarly adapted to give the increased luggage space, particularly on Service 17 between Bristol Temple Meads Railway Station and Clifton Zoo were C6014, C6016 and C6017. (Bristol Vintage Bus Collection)

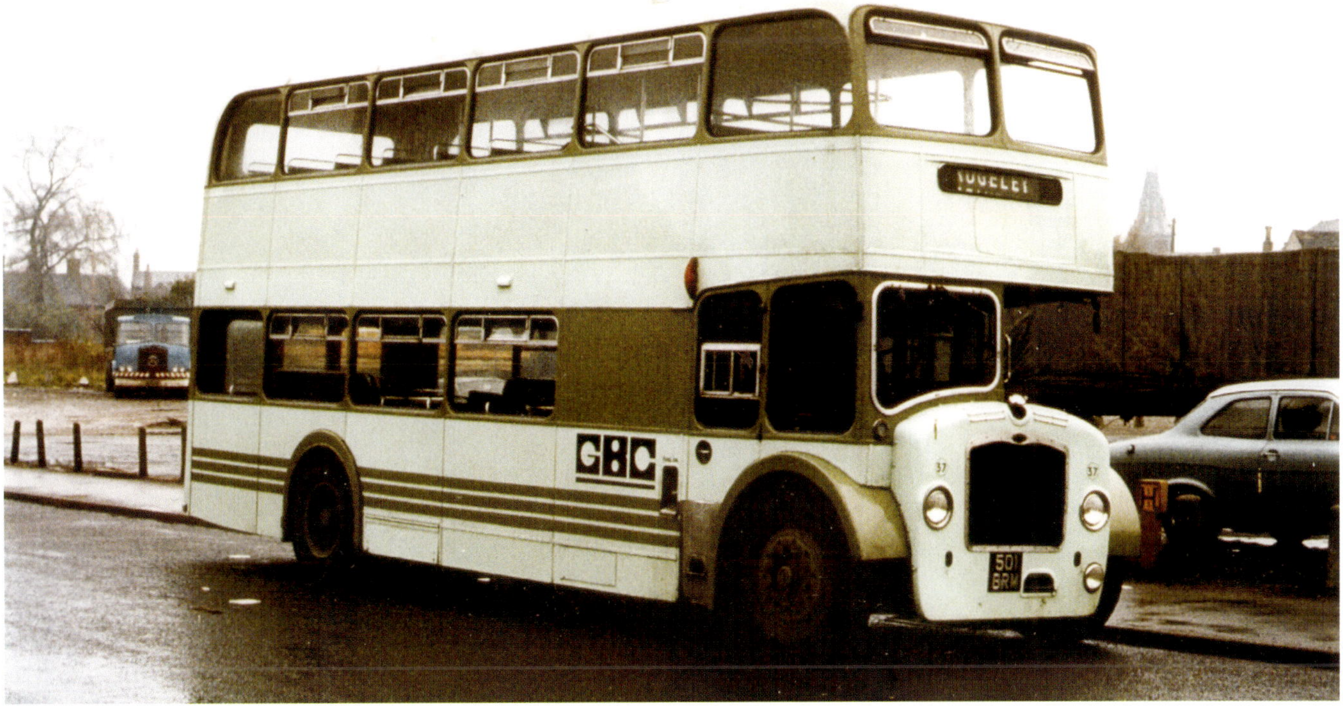

Amongst a number of Bristol double deck buses sourced from National Bus Companies Crosville and Cumberland was Green Bus Company (Rugeley) 37 (501 BRM). A 1960 former Cumberland FSF6G, it was received with fleet number C404 but this was later altered by Cumberland to 500. (Tony Robbins collection)

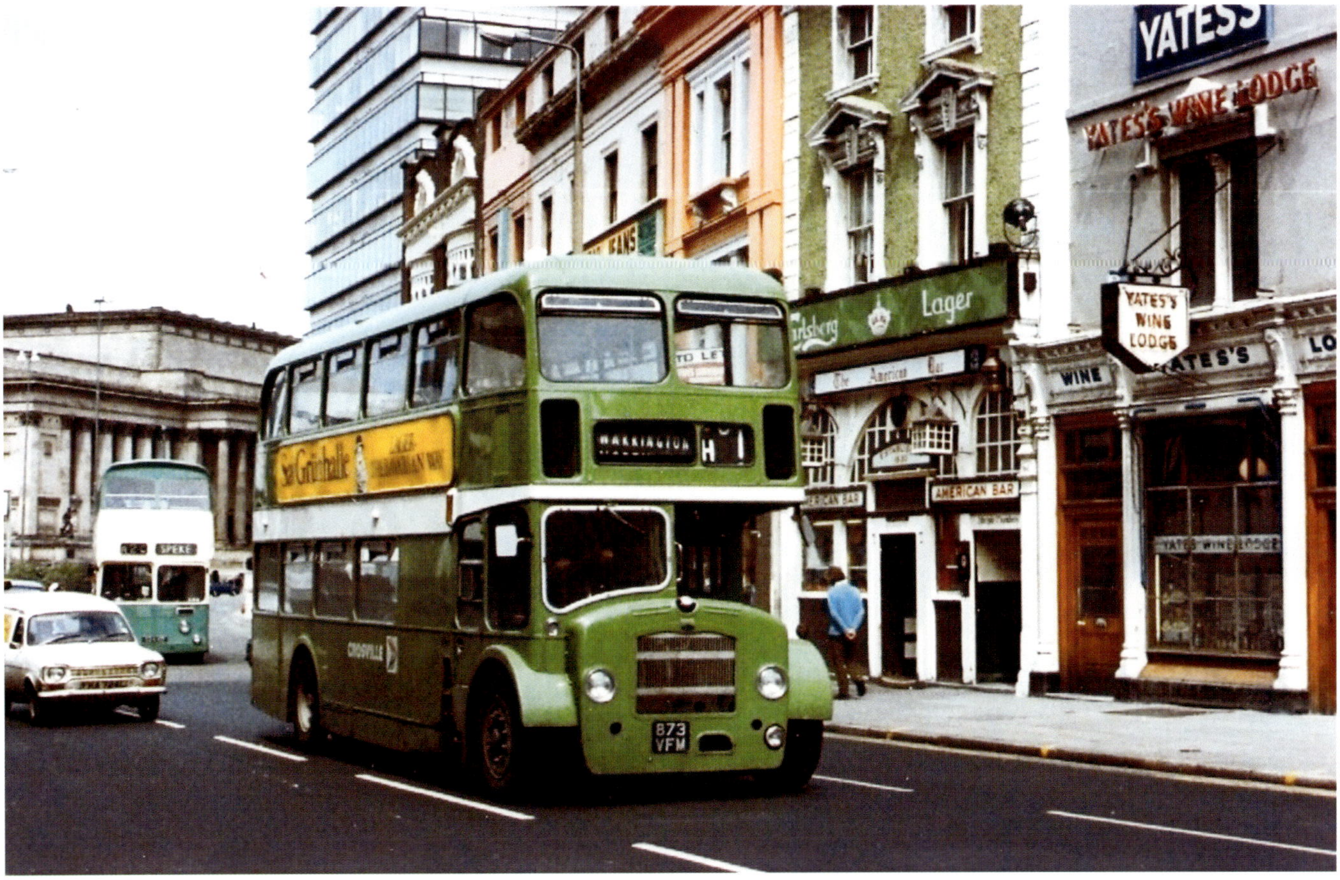

Crosville DFG83 (873 VFM), a 1962 FSF6G, leaves Liverpool on Service H1 to Warrington. (Steve Kelly collection)

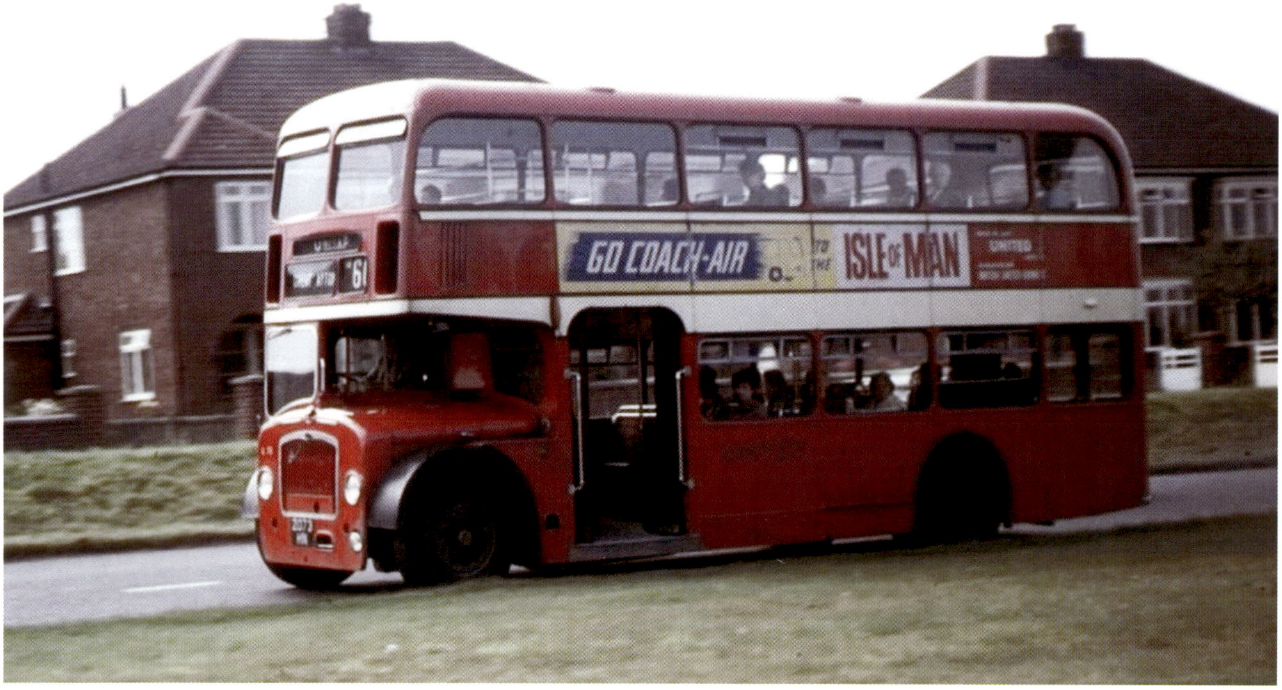

About to start up from Dixon's Bank from Stokesley Road in Marton during September 1967 is United L73 (2073 HN) a 1961 Bristol FSF6B carrying a reasonable number of passengers. (Donald Hudson)

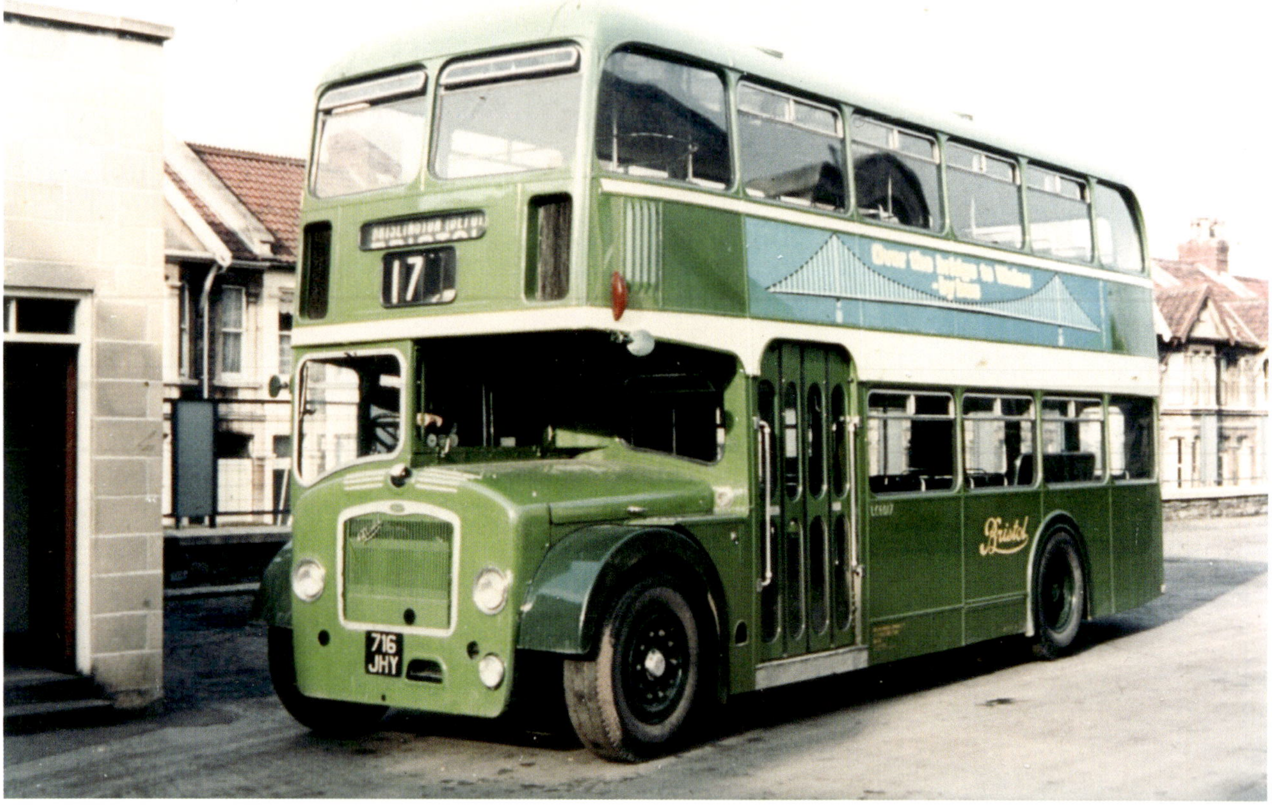

Originally Bristol City LC6017 (716 JHY) was numbered LC8575 and is here prepared to work on its usual route. Service 17 from Bristol Temple Meads to Clifton (Zoological Gardens) via Bristol Centre. The location is the open yard at Brislington Depot where tramcars and the early Bristol bus chassis were built and bodied. (Bristol Vintage Bus Group)

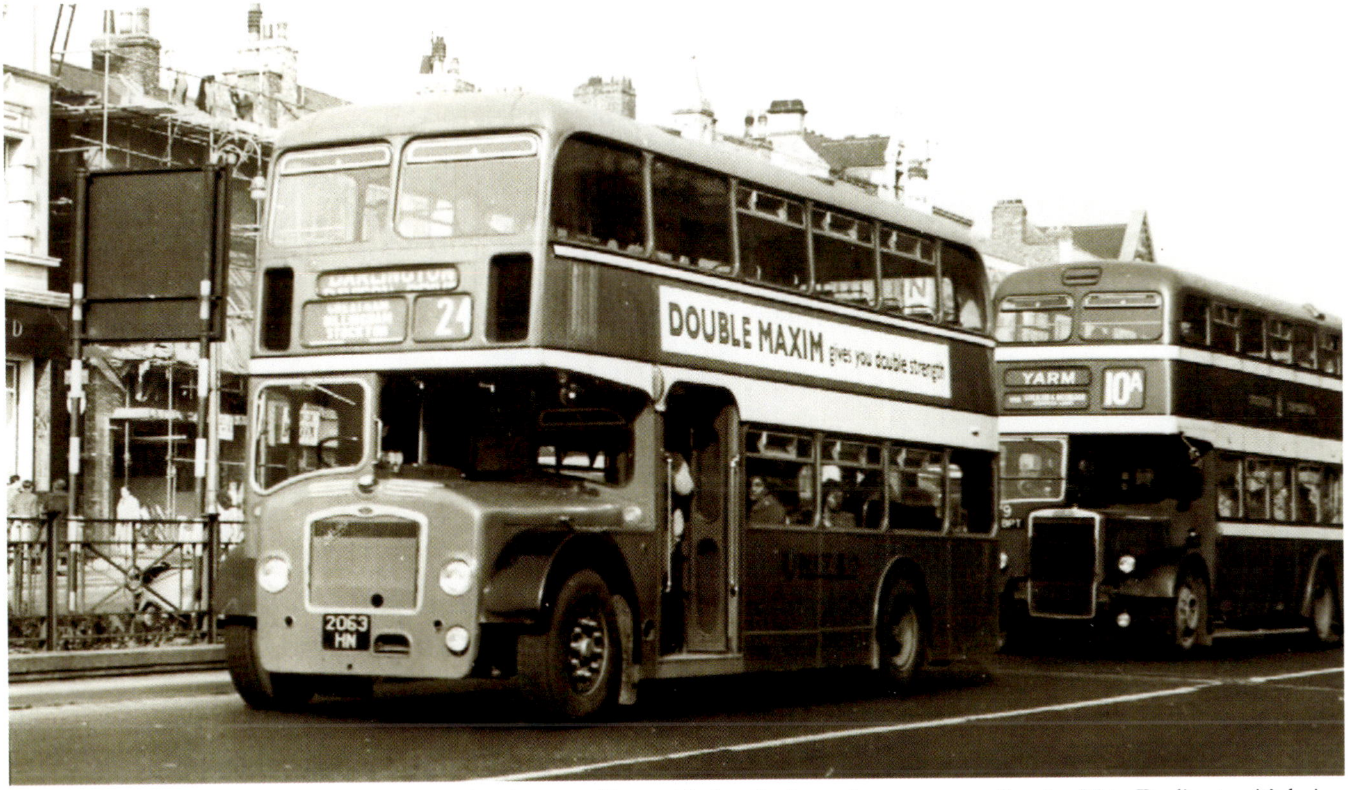

As United BL63 (2063 HN) passes through Stockton-on-Tees with the platform doors open on Service 24 to Darlington it's being pursued by Stockton Corporation 79 (205 BPT), a 1958 Leyland Titan PD2 with Weymann H35/28R body on Service 10A. (Steve Kelly collection)

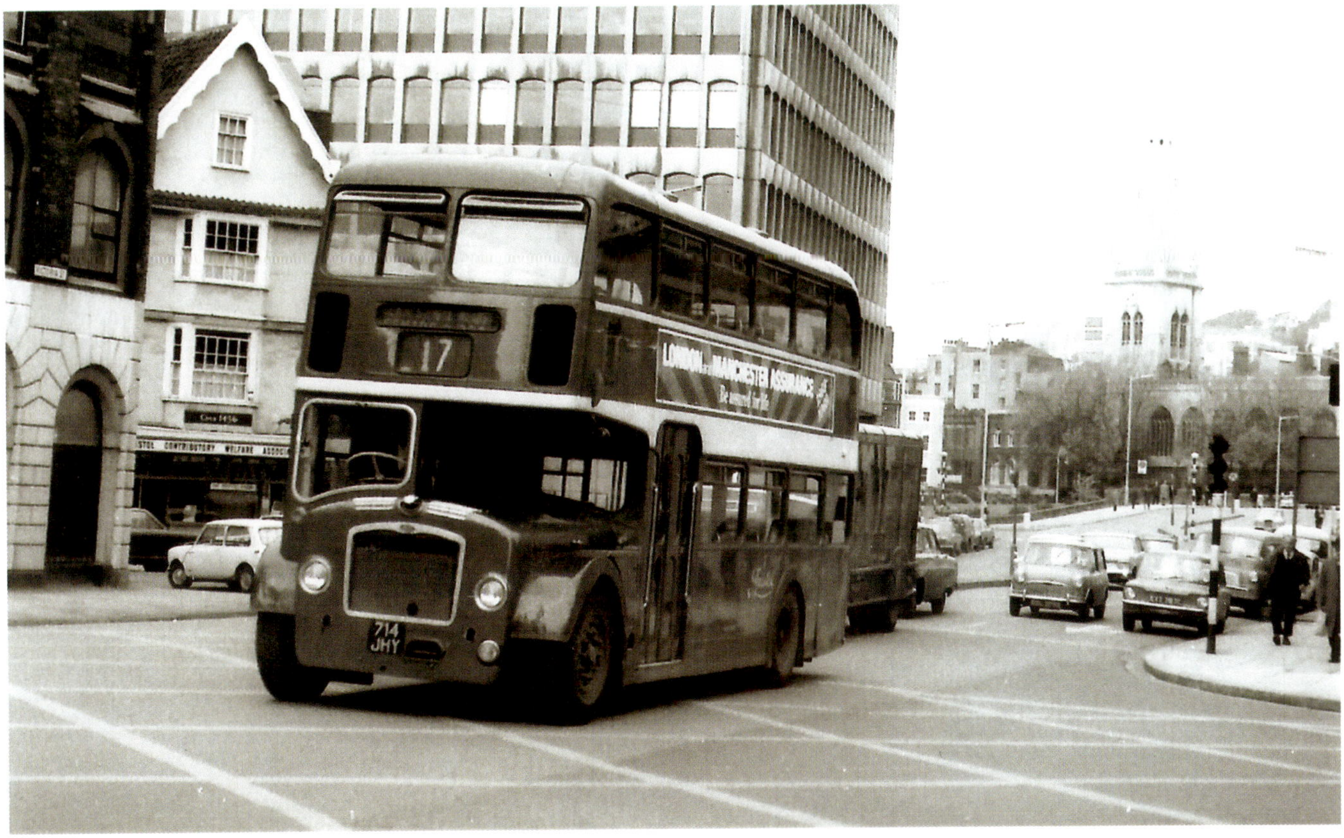

Crossing one of the many box junctions in the city Bristol Omnibus LC6015 (714 JHY) makes its way along Victoria Street heading towards Bristol Temple Meads Station on Service 17 from Clifton Zoo. (Phil Sposito collection)

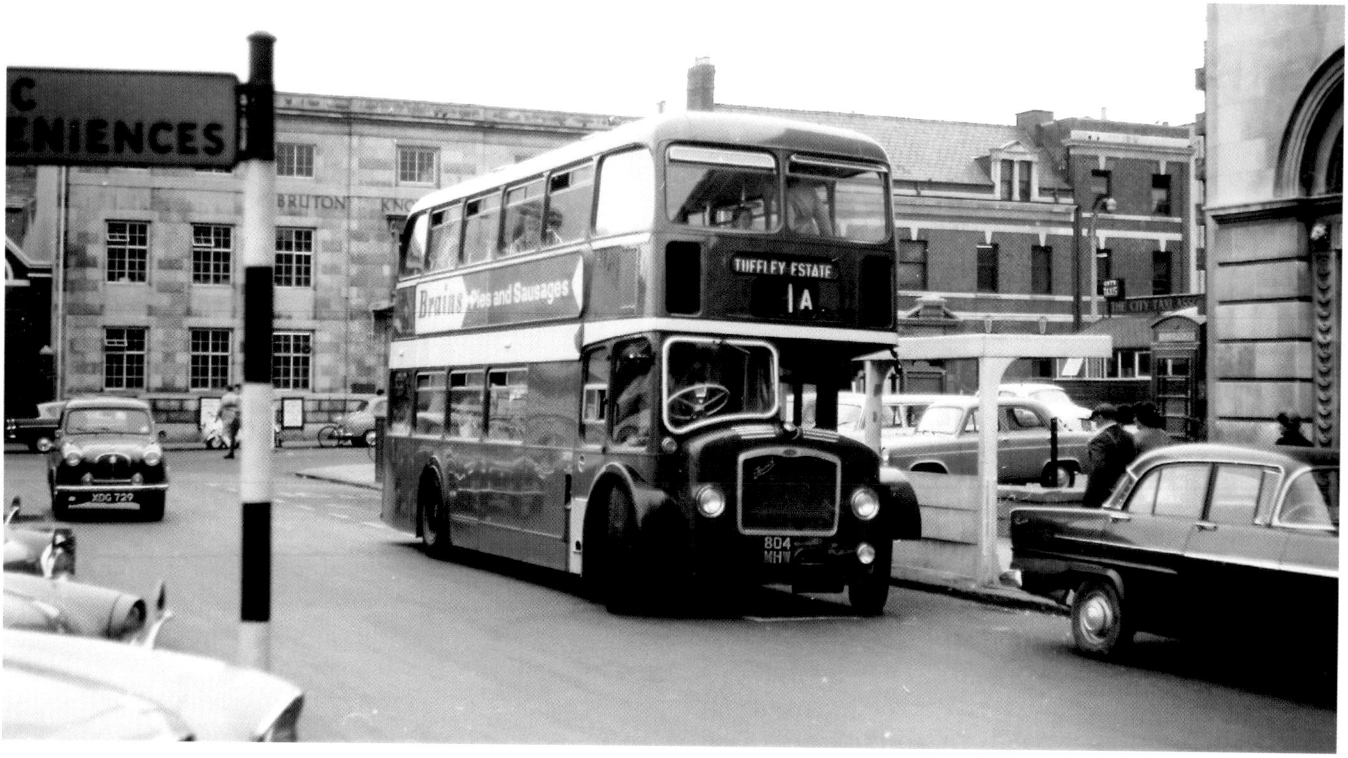

When Gloucester Depot received G6039 (804 MHW) during October 1961 illuminated advertisement panels were quite popular as can be seen by the Brains' Pies and Sausages advert in the photograph above. They lost their popularity quite rapidly and by 1965 very few buses were being built with exterior illuminated panels. G6039 is seen in central Gloucester on its way to Tuffley Estate on Service 1A. (A. J. Douglas)

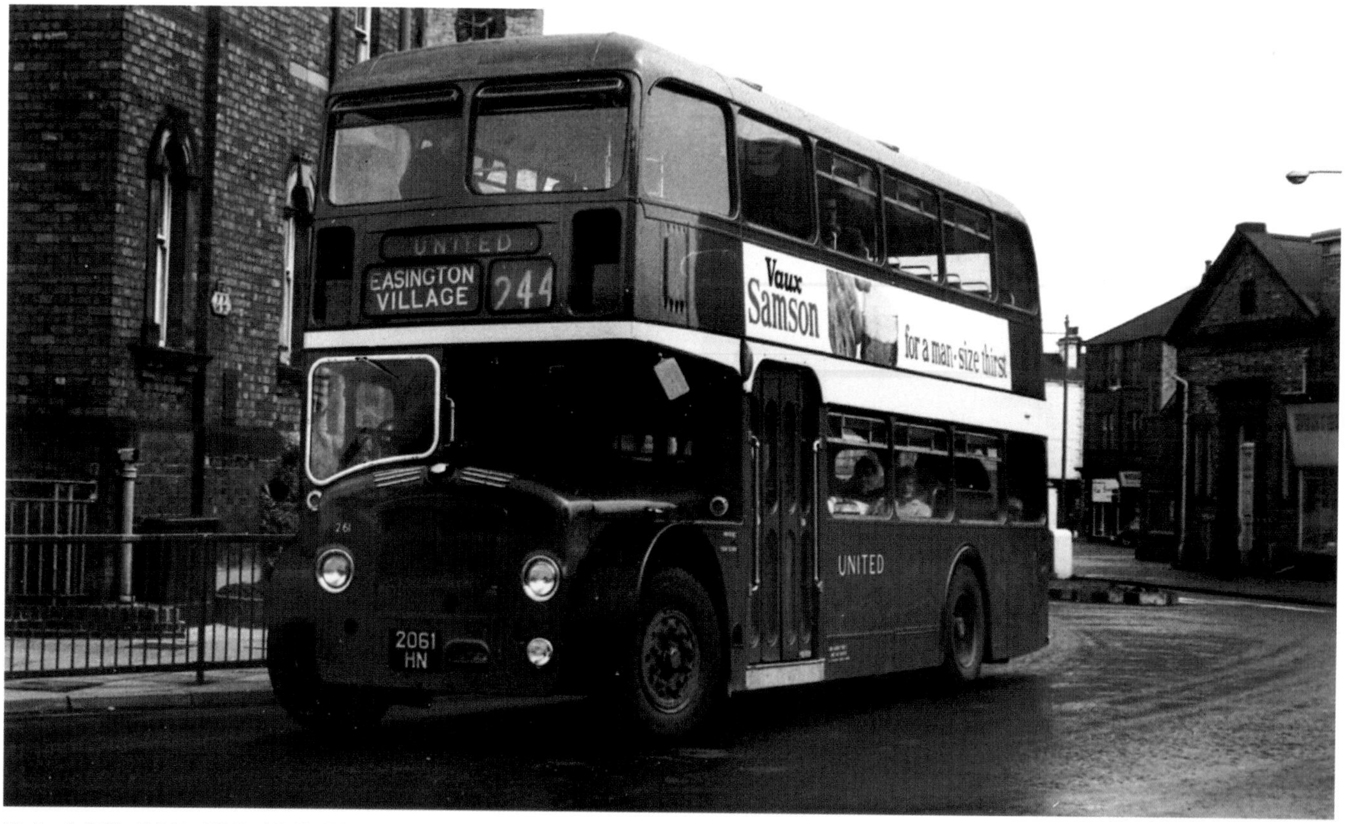

United 261 (2061 HN) 1960 FSF6B was originally BL61 when delivered and is pictured operating to Easington Village on Service 244. (Tony Robbins collection)

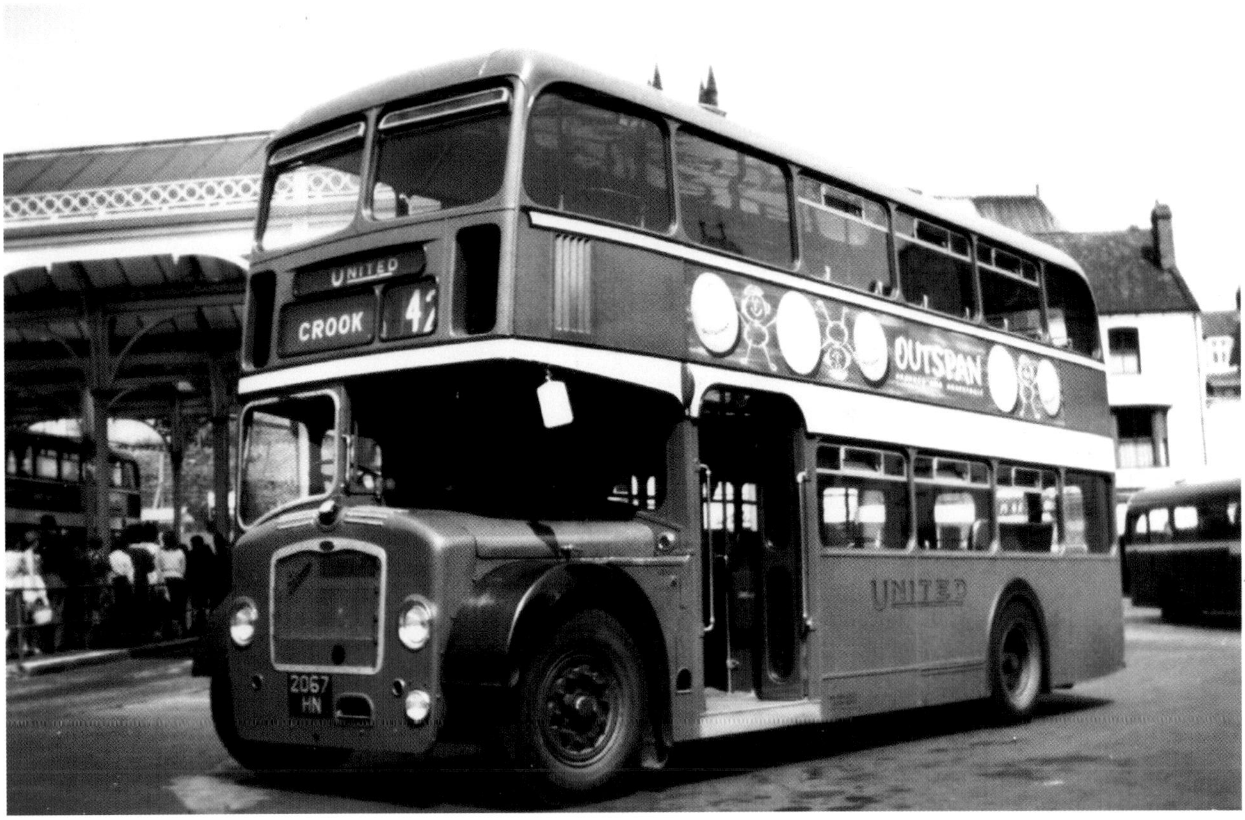

Looking exceptionally smart in lined out livery United Automobile BL67 (2067 HN) of 1961 awaits its driver and conductor for its departure time at Durham Bus Station to operate to Crook on Service 42. (Allan Macfarlane)

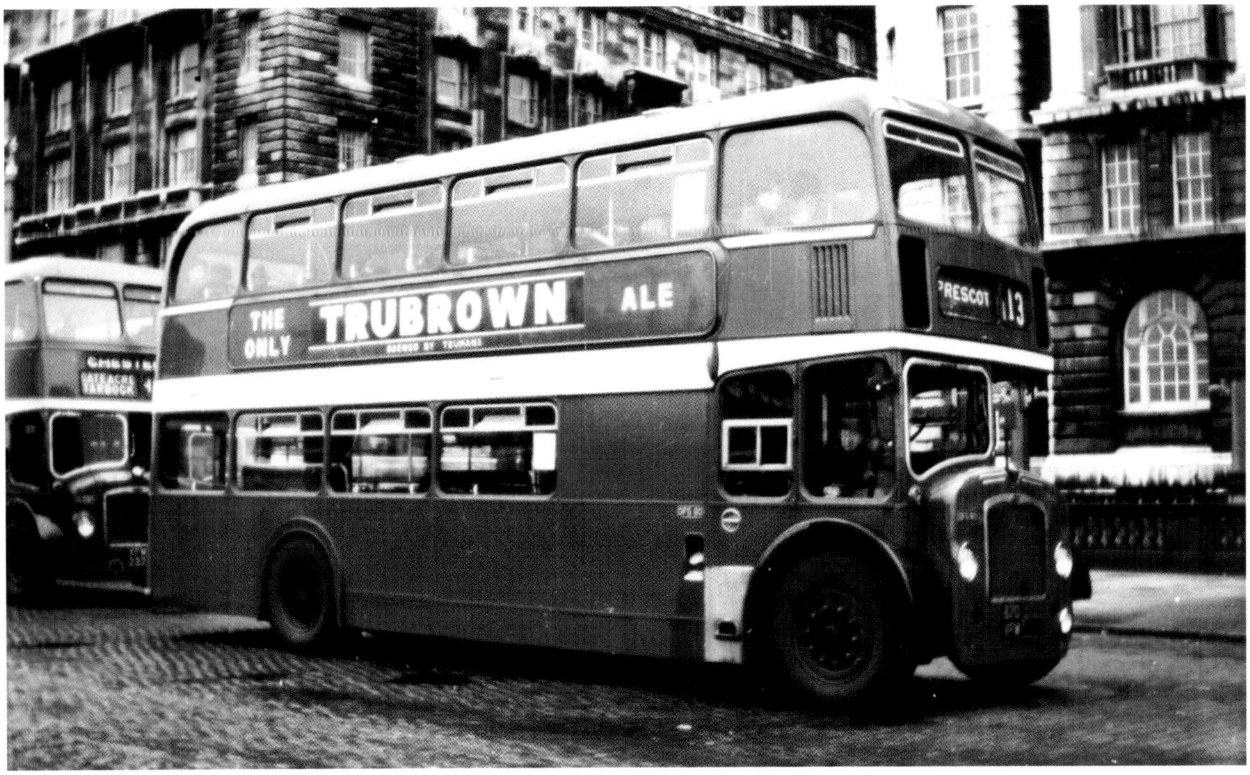

Standing on the cobbles at Liverpool (Pier Head) and looking impressive on 4th August 1962, Crosville DFG60 (870 VFM), one of the company's FSF6Gs, was delivered in November 1961 along with DFB56, DFG59 and DFG61–64. DFB56 (866VFM) was one of only five Bristol engine FSFs ordered by Crosville. (Allan Macfarlane)

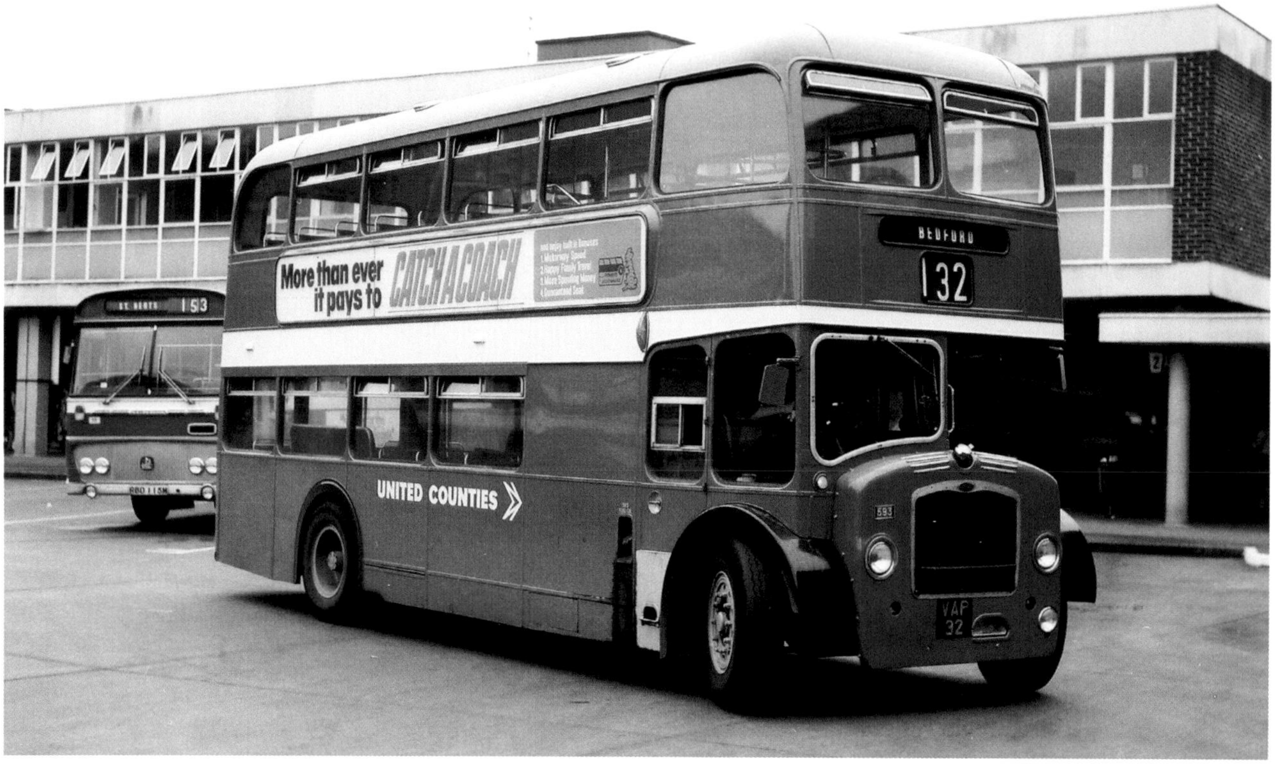

Bedford Bus Station has been visited by United Counties 593 (VAP 32), a 1961 ex Brighton Hove & District FSF6B with offside illuminated advert panel, purchased in December 1974. Two other former BH&D FSF6Bs, 597 and 598 (VAP 34/35), had been purchased in March 1973 with others being bought by Hants & Dorset. Both 597 and 598 were withdrawn from the fleet and scrapped in December 1976 but 593 remained operational until August 1977 when it too was scrapped. (Author's collection)

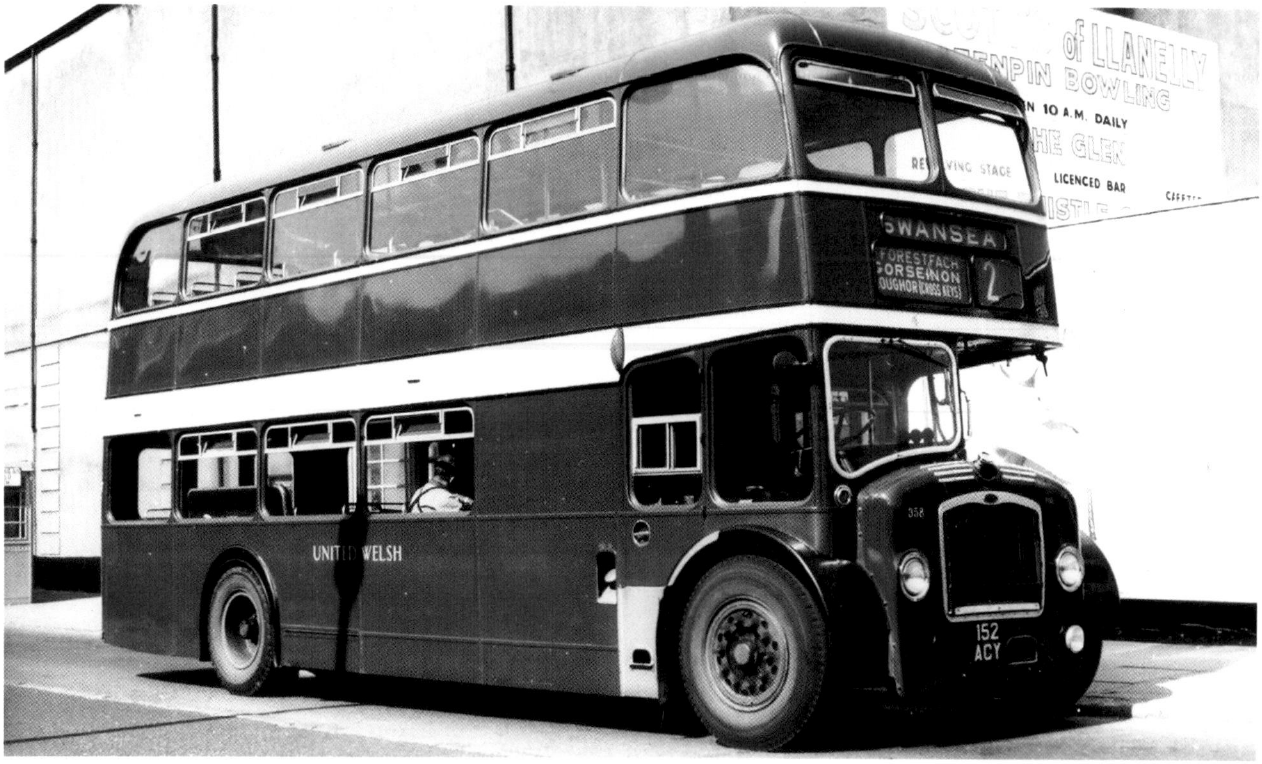

An absence of any advertisements on United Welsh 358 (152 ACY) would imply that this view in Llanelly was taken not long after delivery of this FSF6G in November 1961. It is prepared for a journey to Swansea via Fforestfach, Gorseinon and Loughor (Cross Keys) on Service 2. (Tony Robbins collection)

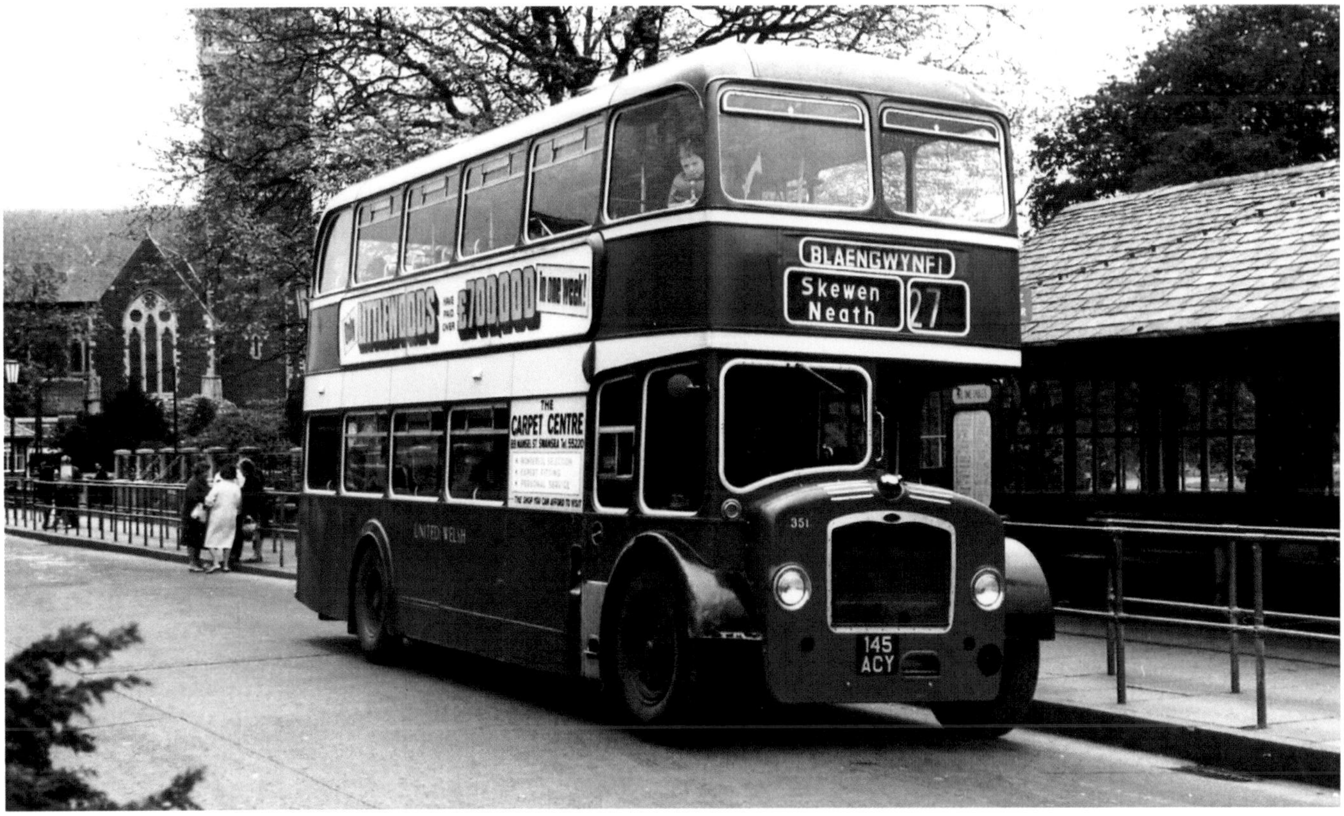

United Welsh 351 (145 ACY) 1961 FSF6G was in the first batch of FSFs received by the company numbered 349–355 (143–149 ACY) in October 1961. It was with all of the front destination apertures in full use on Service 27 to Blaengwynfi. (Tony Robbins collection)

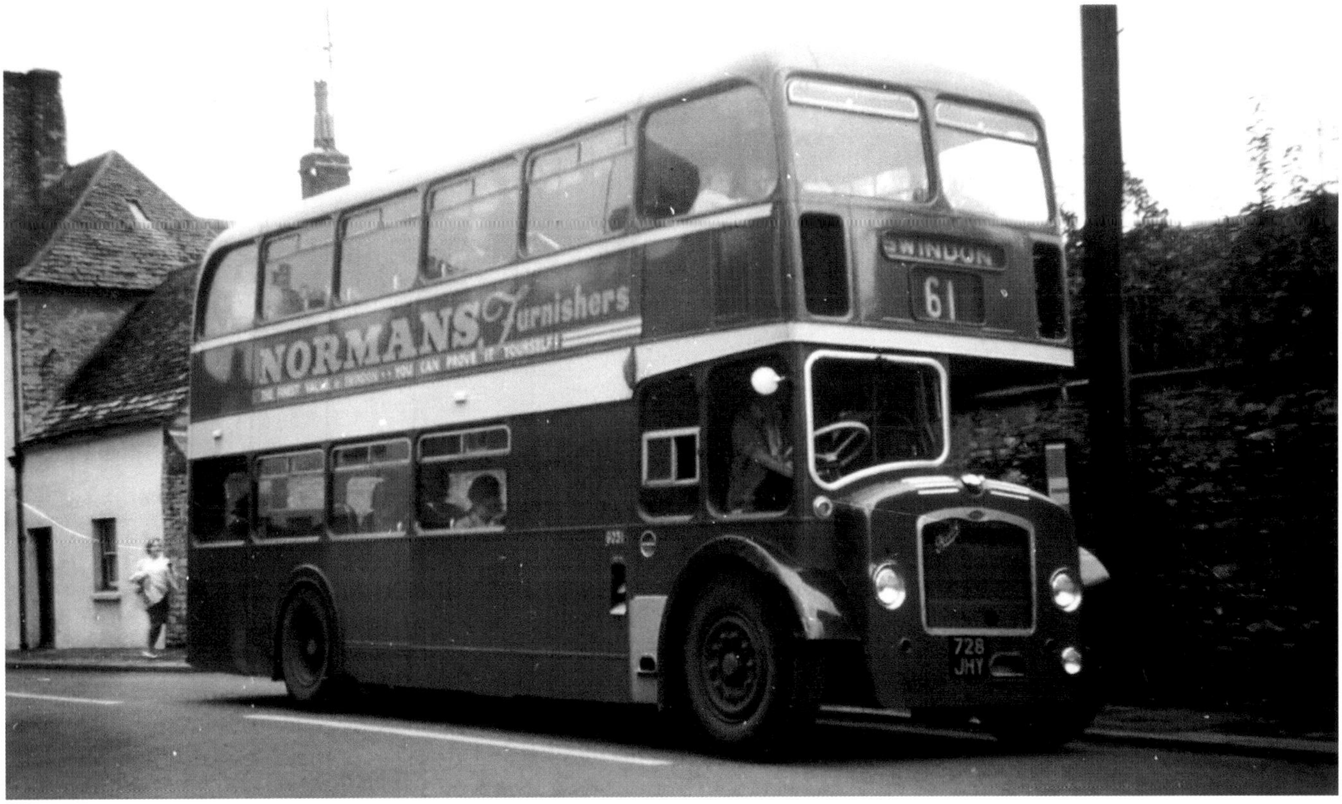

Bristol Omnibus Country Sector was allocated 6031 (728 JHY) in March 1961. The vehicle spent most of its time at Swindon and is seen here operating to its home town on Service 61 from Cheltenham. (Tony Robbins collection)

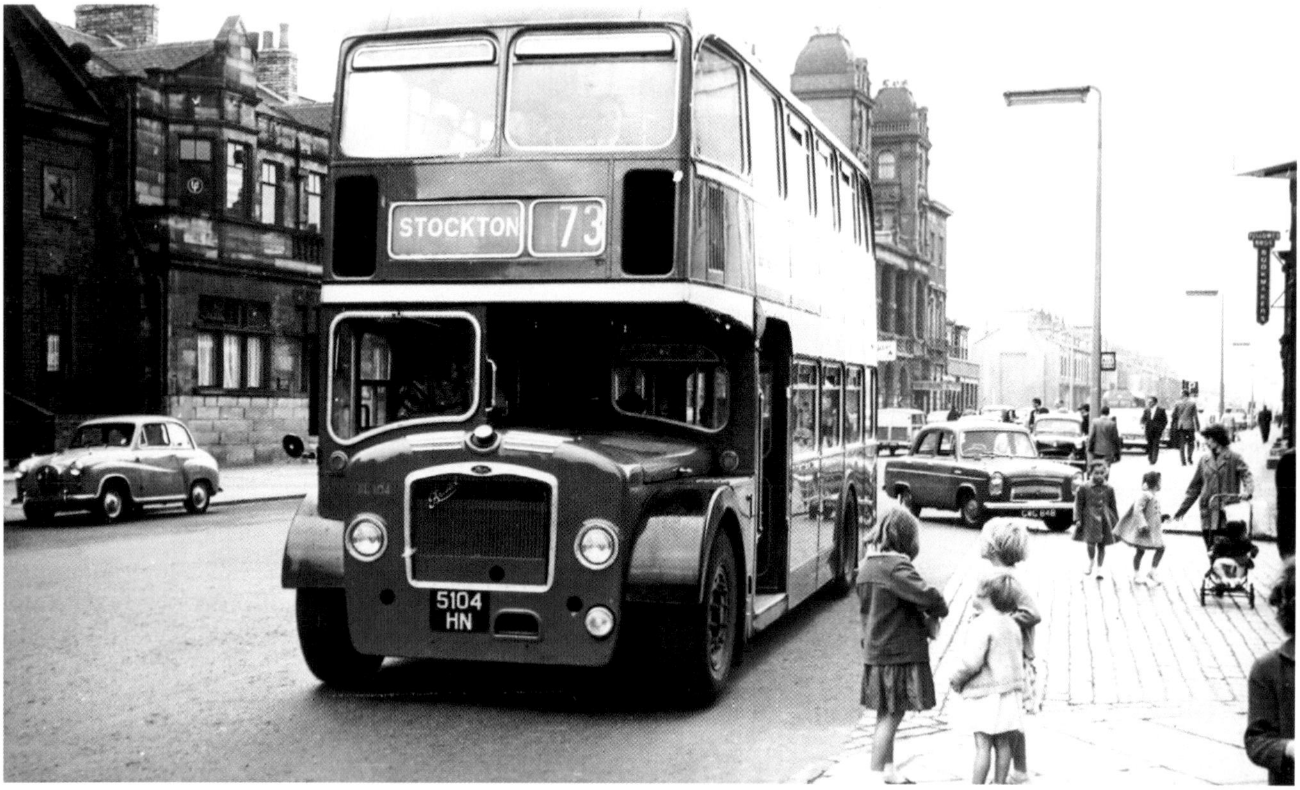

Children were considered to be safe so close to the kerb as United BL104 (5104 HN), received in November 1961, passes them on 8th September 1962 when operating on Service 73 to Stockton. Attitudes today would be very different. (Tony Robbins collection)

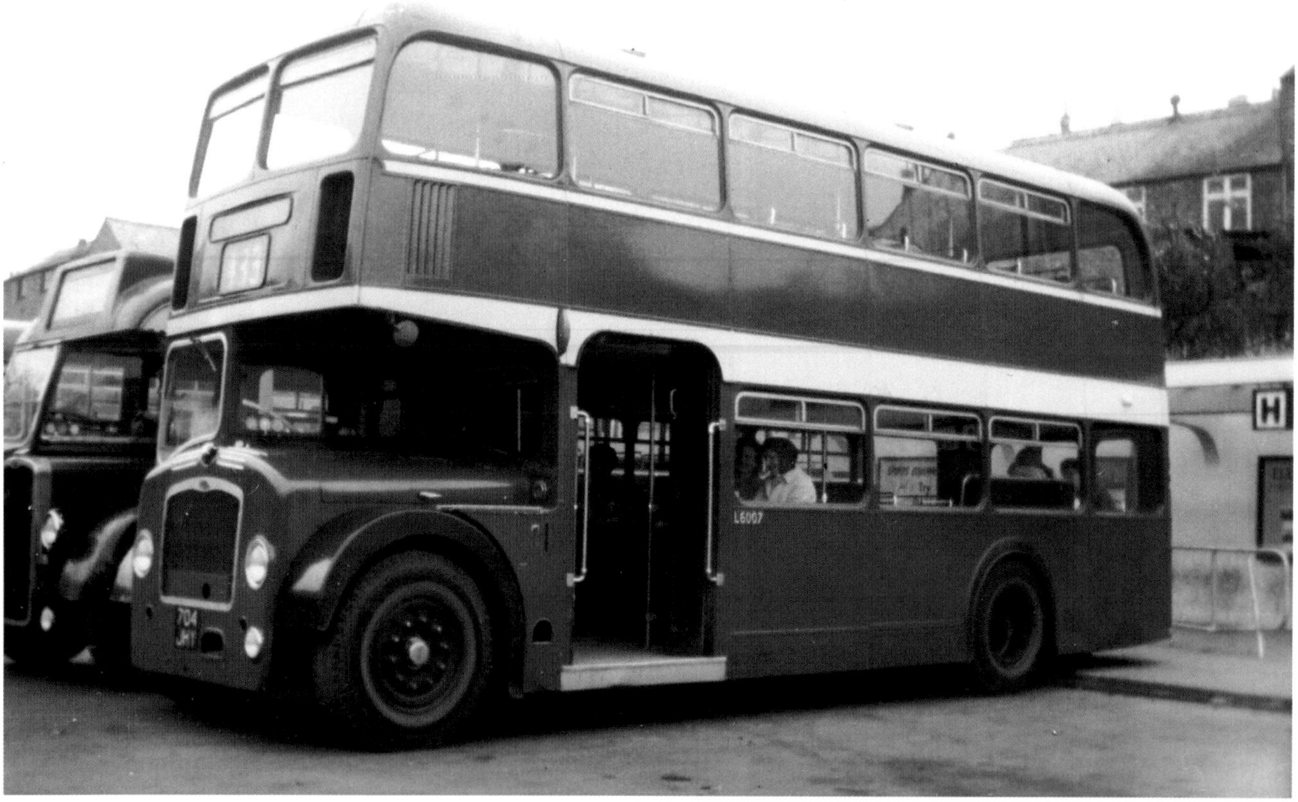

Stroud Bus Station is the setting for L6007 (704 JHY), a 1960 FSF6G, on 30th October 1963 waits for passengers to join the few already on board for stops on infrequent Service 433 to Stonehouse via Leonard Stanley. (Allan Macfarlane)

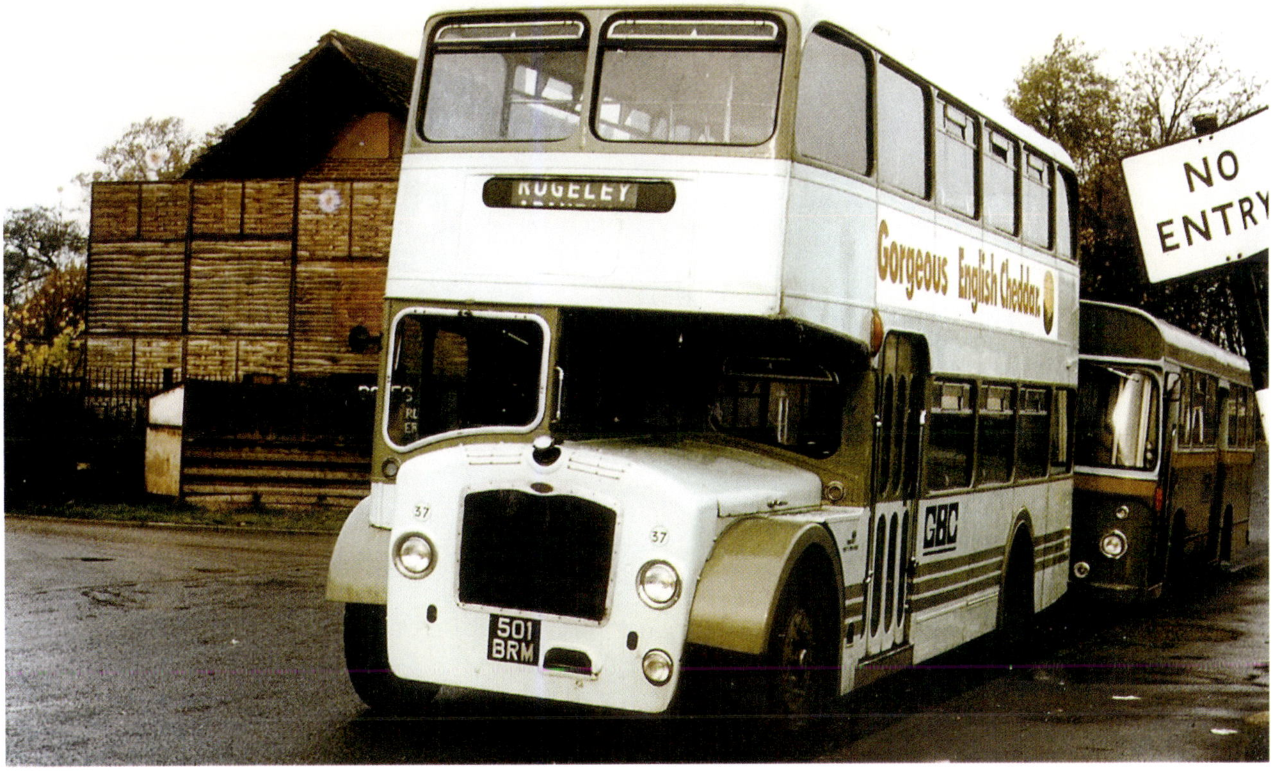

Green Bus Company 37 (501 BRM) was purchased in July 1973 together with 504 BRM. Both were ex Cumberland FSF6Gs. Seen here in Rugeley it is assumed that the no entry sign quite strategically placed refers to other vehicles rather than intending passengers even though the sign appears to be pointing towards the bus! (Tony Robbins collection)

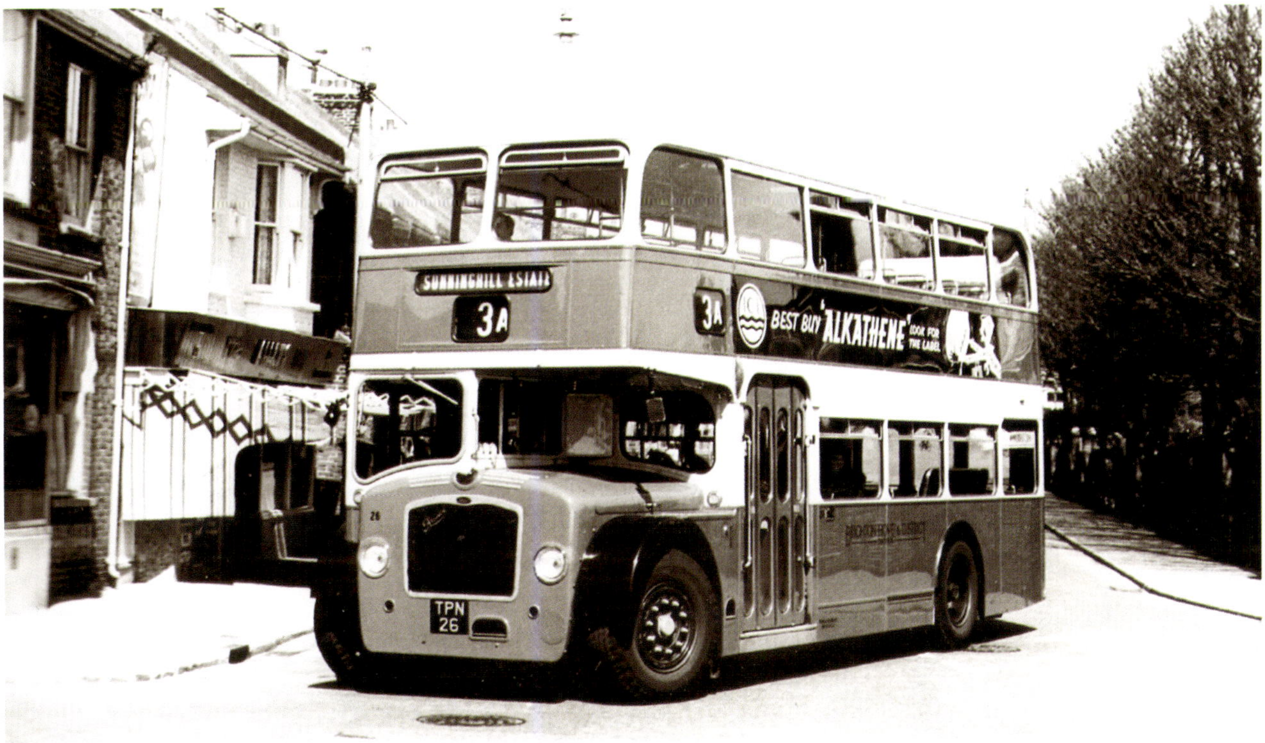

Sparkling with newness Brighton Hove & District 26 (TPN 26) looks extremely smart when working a journey to Whitehawk on Service 3A. The hand painted advert was for an ICI (Imperial Chemicals Industries) plastic called "Alkathene" that had been developed for use with foods with items such as lunch boxes. (Steve Kelly collection)

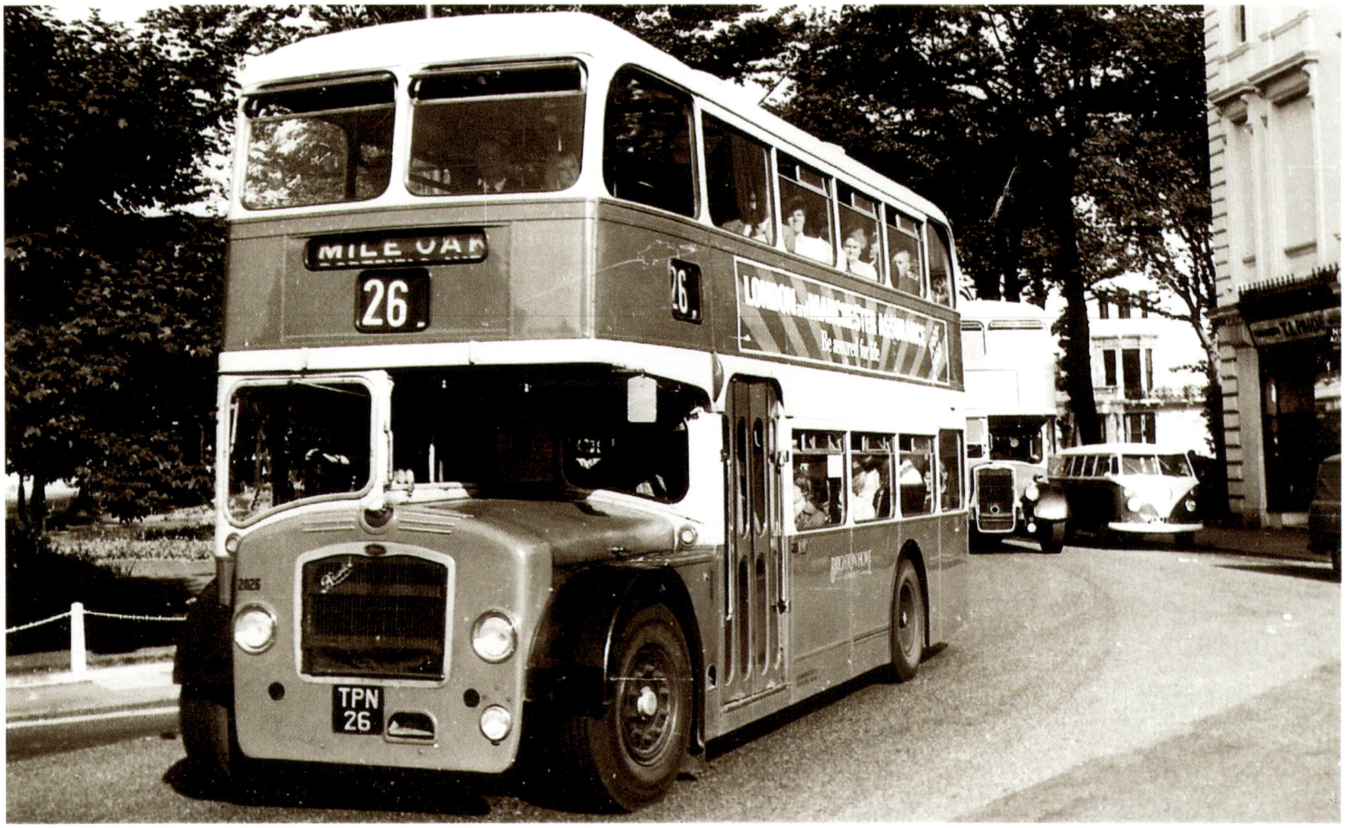

London and Manchester Assurance advertisements were to be found on buses throughout the United Kingdom in the 1960s, including Brighton Hove & District 2026 (TPN 26). Although in traditional livery it has been renumbered from 26 in preparation for absorption into the Southdown fleet as seen on Service 26 to Mile Oak in 1969. (Denis Clark)

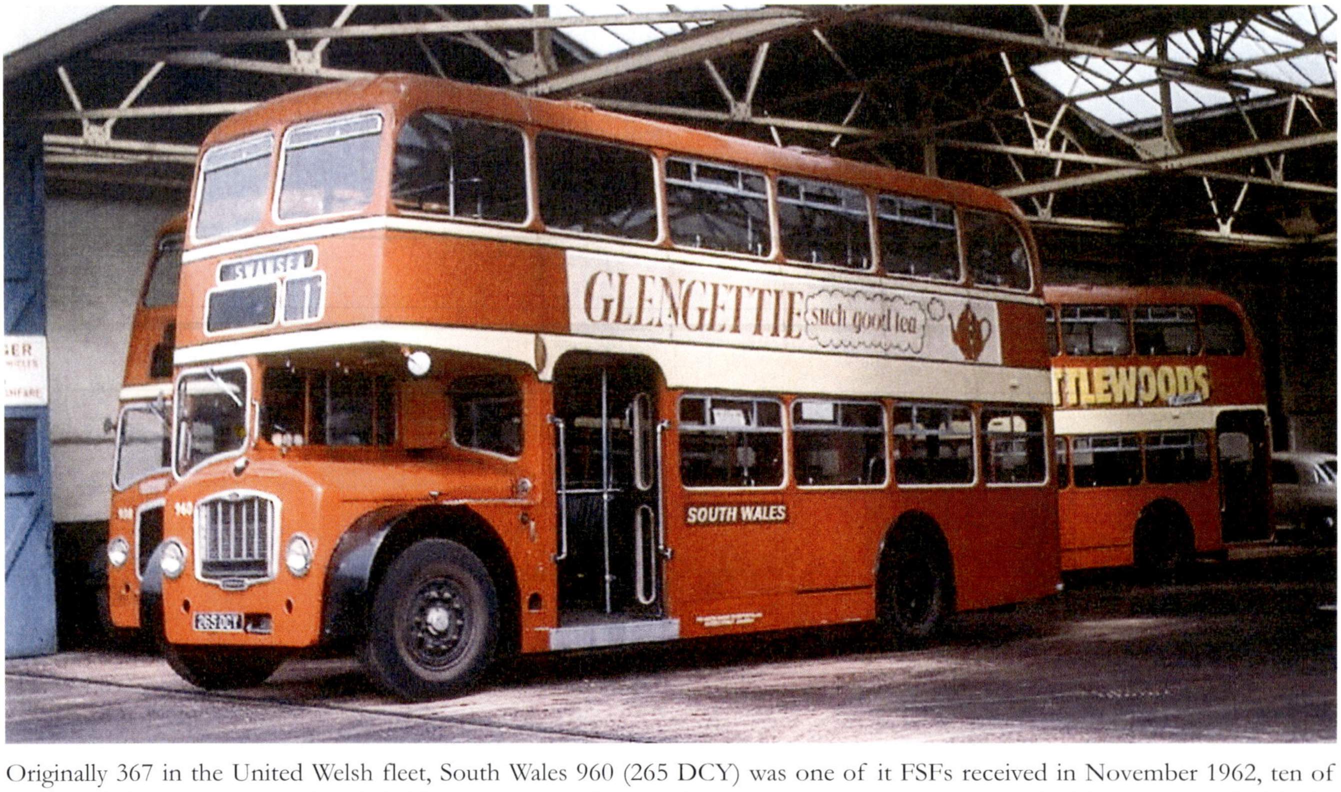

Originally 367 in the United Welsh fleet, South Wales 960 (265 DCY) was one of it FSFs received in November 1962, ten of which had Gardner engines like 960. The temporary adhesive fleet name vinyl is very apparent in this view taken inside the Swansea Depot premises. (Author's collection)

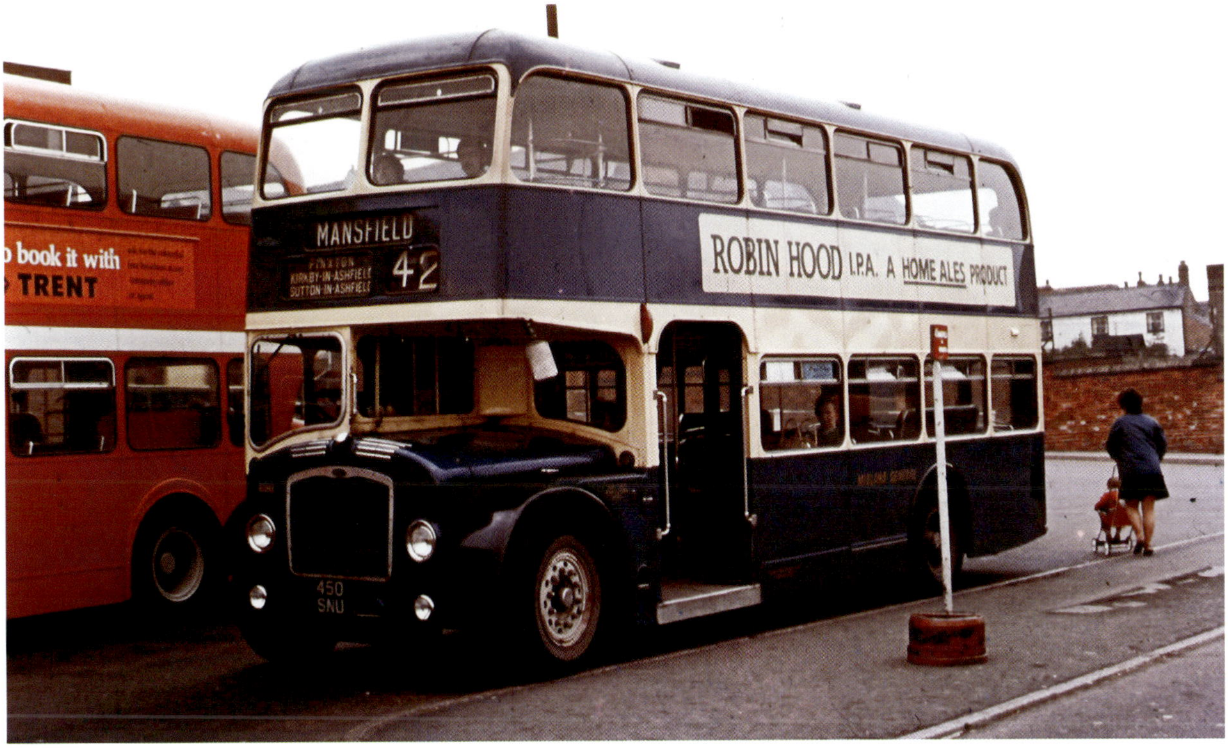

Midland General 686 (450 SNU) was the last FSF6G delivered to the company and was originally numbered 510 when received in June 1962. It is pictured here at Alfreton Bus Station ready to work a Service 42 journey via Flixton, Kirkby-in-Ashfield and Sutton-in-Ashfield to Mansfield. (Tony Robbins collection)

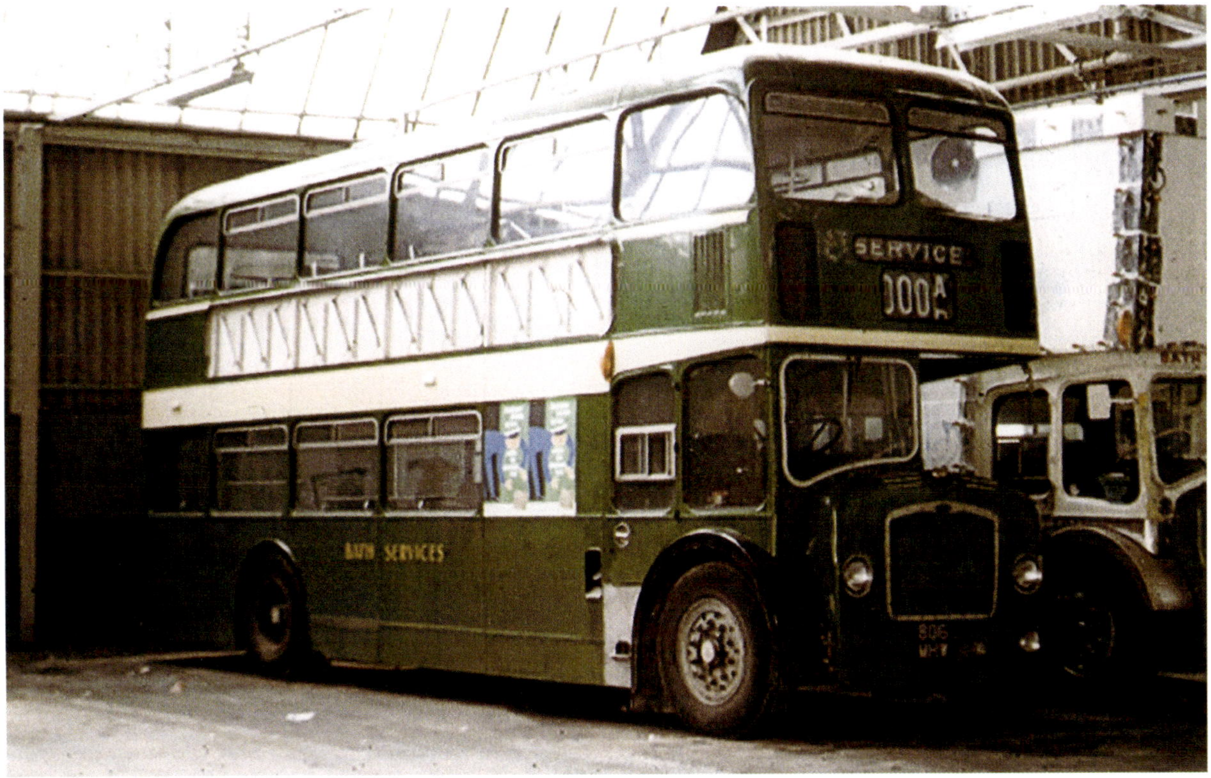

After the purchase from Western National former Bath Services 6041 (806 MHW) needed a number of projects completed to return it to its original state. Several items, mainly minor, were dealt with by Dave Bennett one of Bath Depot's mechanical engineers and his mates, a full repaint and refitting a four track numeral and destination box to the rear. The bus is seen here with the lighting tubes visible in the panel awaiting the fitting of a Pearl Assurance advert that was specially printed in Salisbury. (Clive A. Brown)

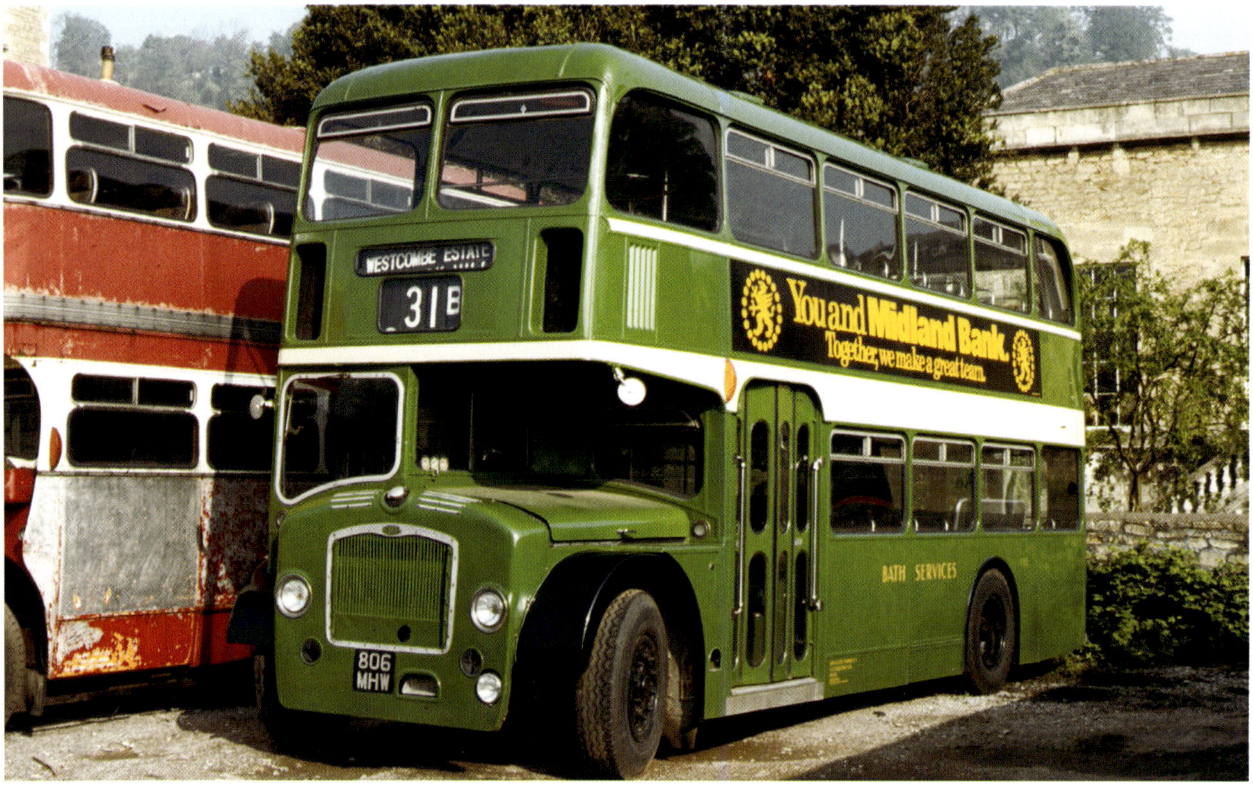

Bath Services 6041 (806 MHW), a 1961 FSF6G parked at the rear of York Villa that was positioned at the entrance to Kensington Depot on London Road, Bath. The house had been the Bath Tramways manager's house and latterly was the Bath Tramways Sports & Social Club as was the case when pictured on 19th May 1984. (Dave Mant)

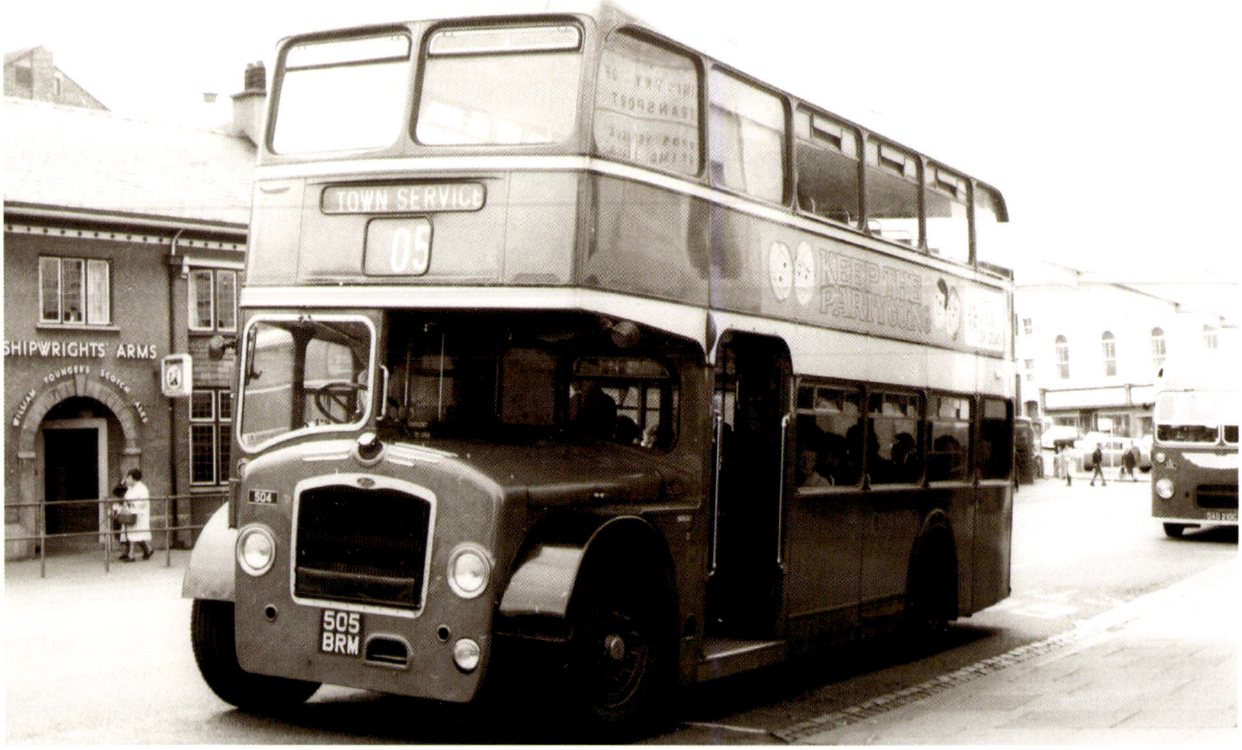

Followed by a Bristol, MW Cumberland 504 (505 BRM) has a decent passenger loading, on the lower deck at least, when working a journey on Whitehaven Town Service 05, a regular route operated by Bristol FSFs in the 1960s. (Tony Robbins collection)

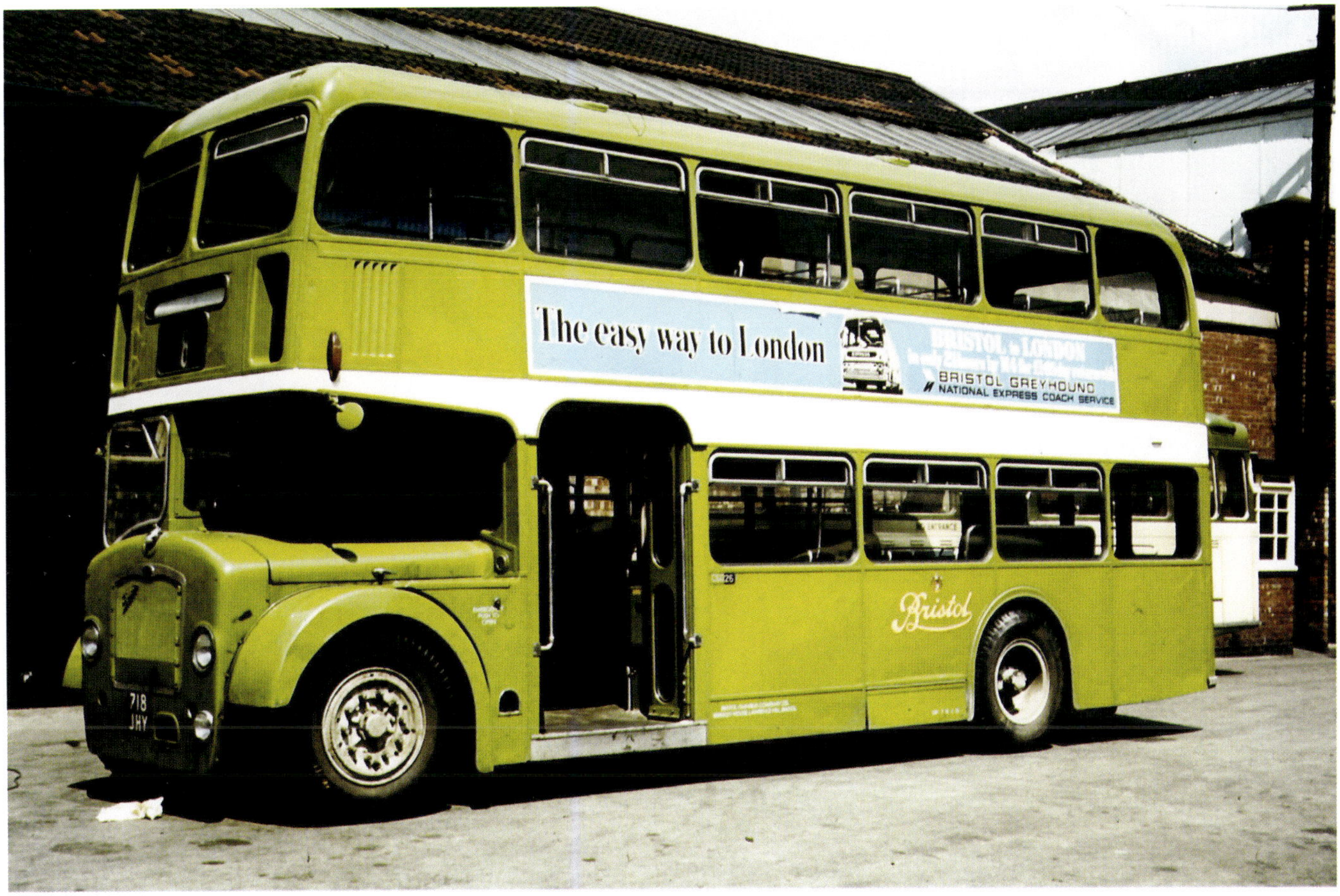

Glistening in the summer sun in the yard at Lawrence Hill Depot on 1st June 1973 Bristol Omnibus C6026 (718 JHY) clearly shows the Bristol scroll fleet name with city crest above used for all Bristol Joint Services vehicles. (Author's collection)

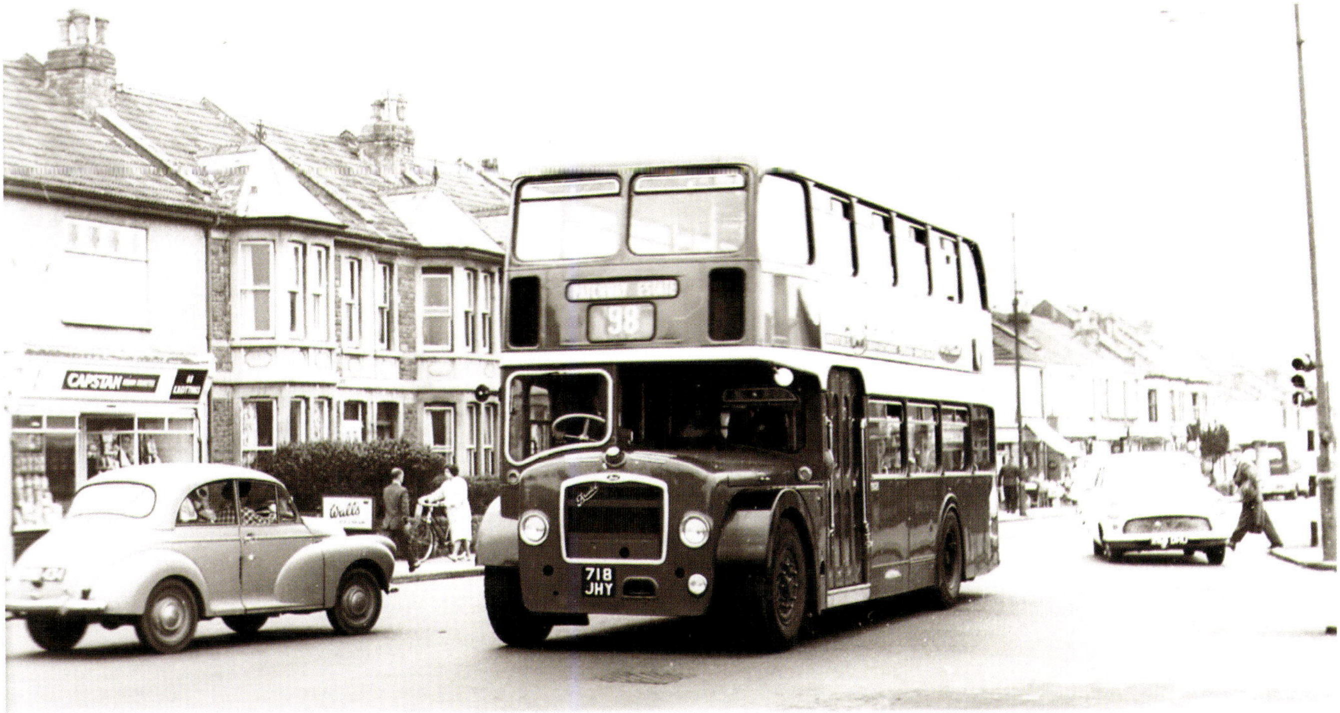

A very 1960s scene sees a Morris Minor, commonly referred to as the District Nurses' car, appearing to be aiming to ram Bristol Omnibus C6026 (718 JHY), a 1961 Bristol FSF6B. It is on a journey from Melvin Square to Patchway Estate on Service 98 that ran half hourly on weekdays and hourly on Sundays and was operated from Muller Road Depot. (Phil Sposito collection)

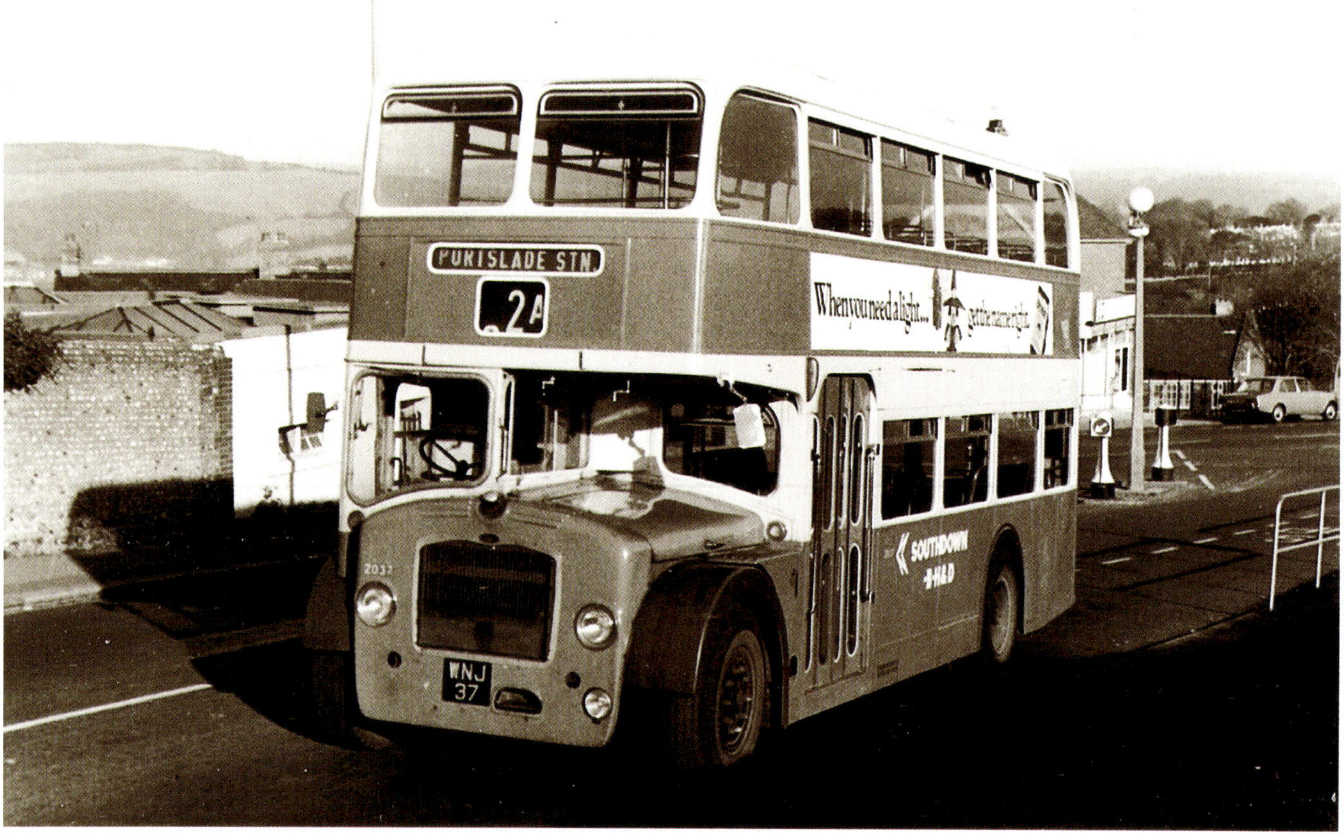

A picturesque and impressive countryside scene forms the backdrop for Southdown-BH&D 2037 (WNJ 37). This vehicle carries the traditional livery with NBC block fleet name and original double N logo but over-panelled canopy route number box as it waits in the sunshine on Service 2A. (Denis Clark)

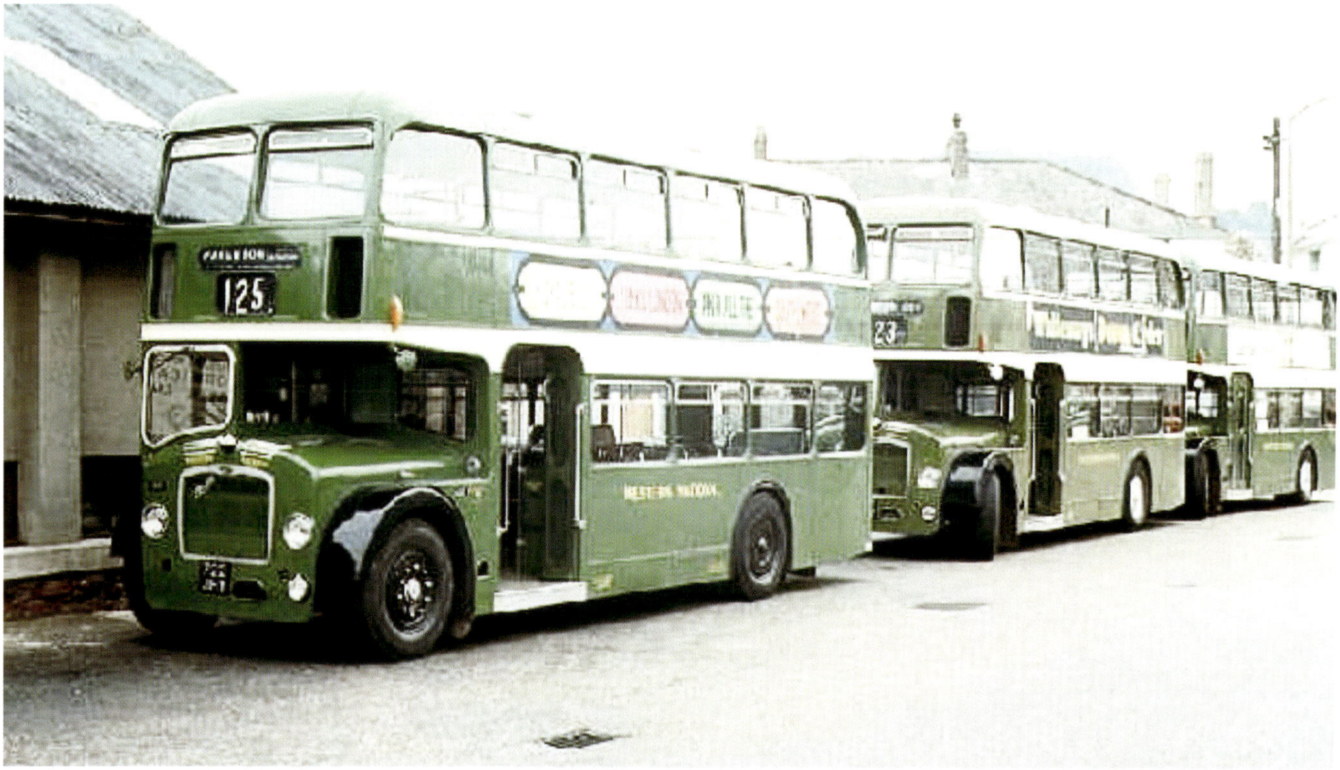

A trio of quality – Western National 1001 (722 JHY) heads a line of three ex Bristol Omnibus FSF6Gs at Paignton all awaiting their next crews and duties. (Cliff Essex)

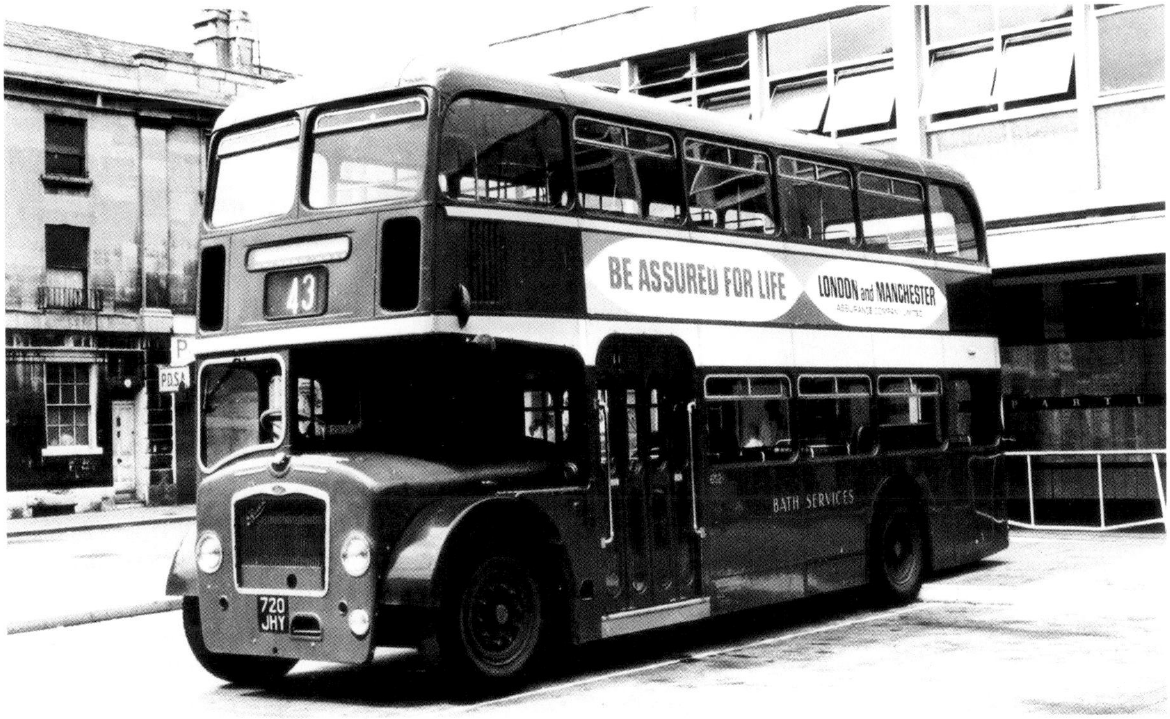

Former Weston super Mare based 6021 (720 JHY), a 1961 FSF6G, was transferred to Bath Electric Tramways in February 1966 and, as was the practice at the time because of the predominance of rear loading buses, stands reversed onto the platform at Bath Bus Station. After carrying Bath Services fleet names for barely 16 months it was acquired in August 1967 by Southern National and given fleet number 1019 until transferred to the main Western National fleet in November 1969. Finally withdrawn in August 1978 it was sold to North, vehicle dealer, of Sherburn-in-Elmet in Yorkshire and was last seen in use as a caravan in Caernarfon in September 1982. (Tony Robbins collection)

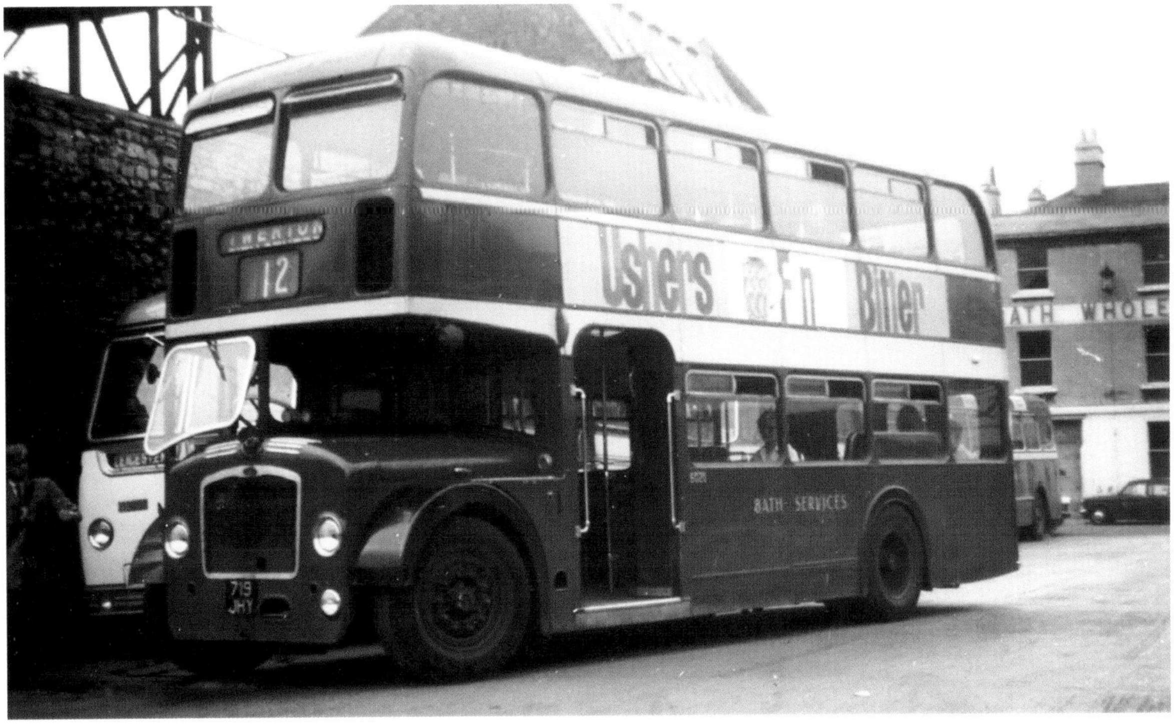

Receiving a water "top up" Bath Services 6020 (719 JHY) is pictured at Bath Bus Station when working to Twerton on Service 12. After further use with Southern National from May 1967 it was withdrawn in August 1978 and sold to dealer W North of Sherburn-in-Elmet, near Leeds. From there it was sold to Scaffolding (Great Britain) Ltd and was finally scrapped in 1984 having achieved a creditable service total of 23 years. (Tony Robbins collection)

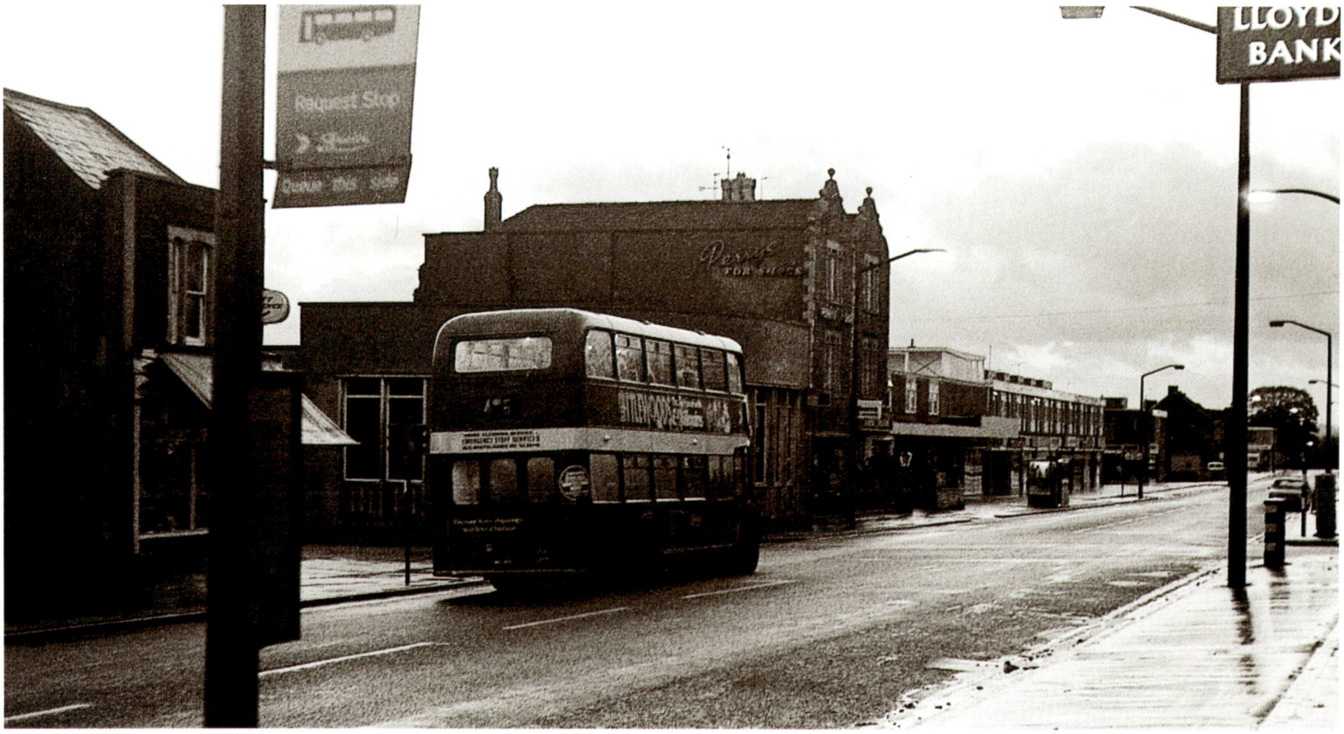

Bristol Omnibus C6015 (714 JHY) stands in the twilight of Broad Street, Staple Hill at 0630 as it works the 0550 Knowle West to Staple Hill Depot Service 45 journey on Saturday 7th September 1974. (Stephen Dowle)

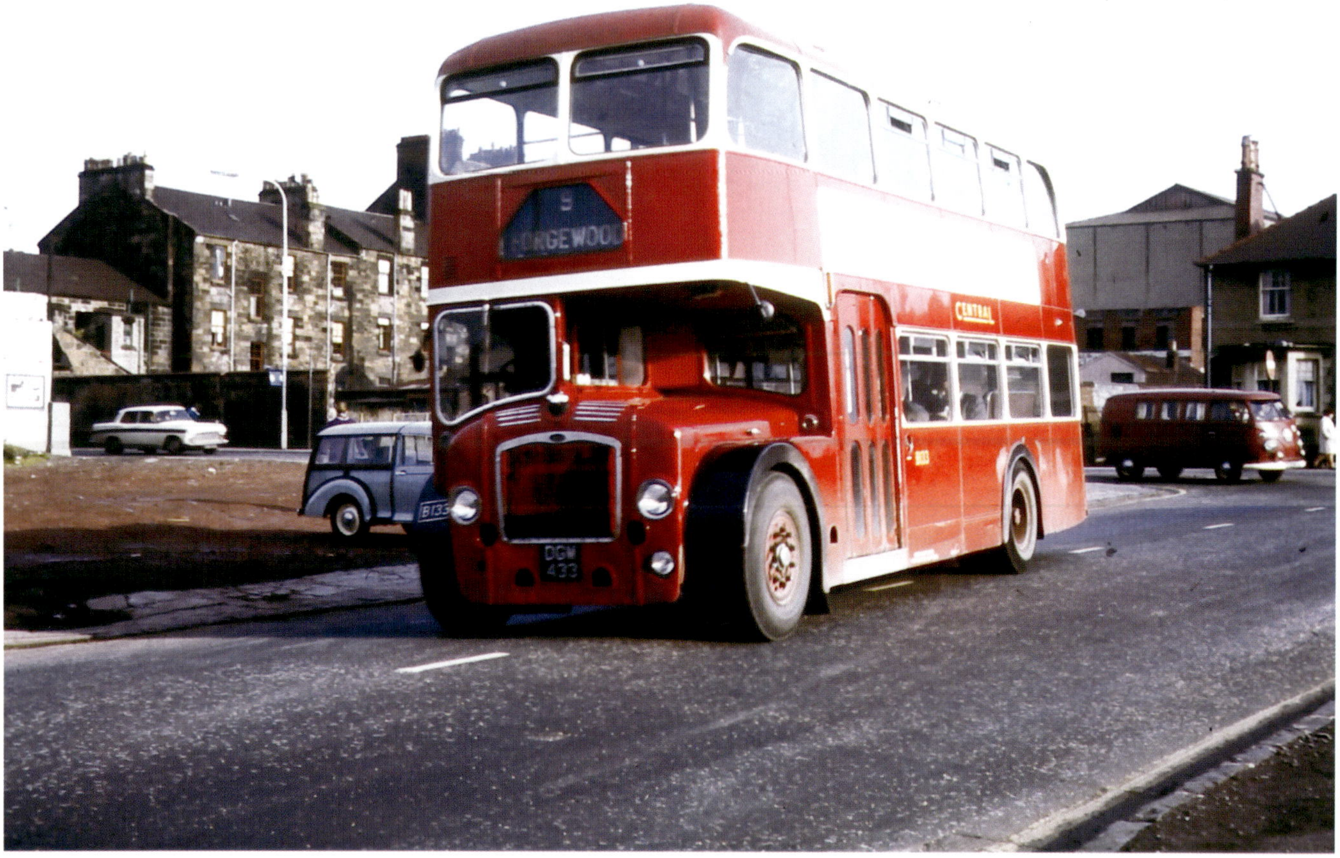

Considered now a classic vehicle; a VW "camper van" follows Central SMT B133 (DGM 433), a 1962 FSF6G, as it passes a Morris Minor Traveller with the once familiar wood trim as the bus works a journey in Motherwell on Service 9 to Forgewood. (Kevin Lane)

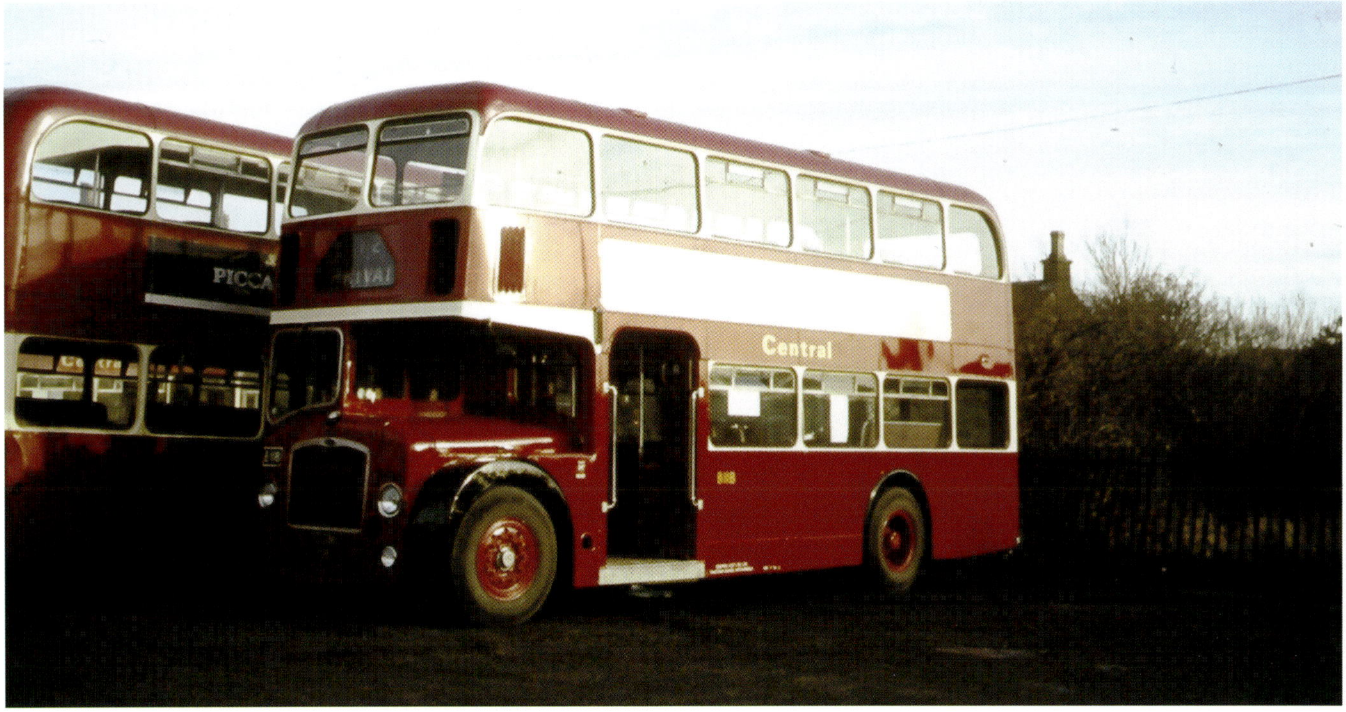

Appearing to be in particularly good condition despite fourteen years in service Central SMT B118 (CGM 118), a 1961 FSF6G with the expected ECW H34/26F bodywork, is found here at Motherwell in January 1975. (Kevin Lane)

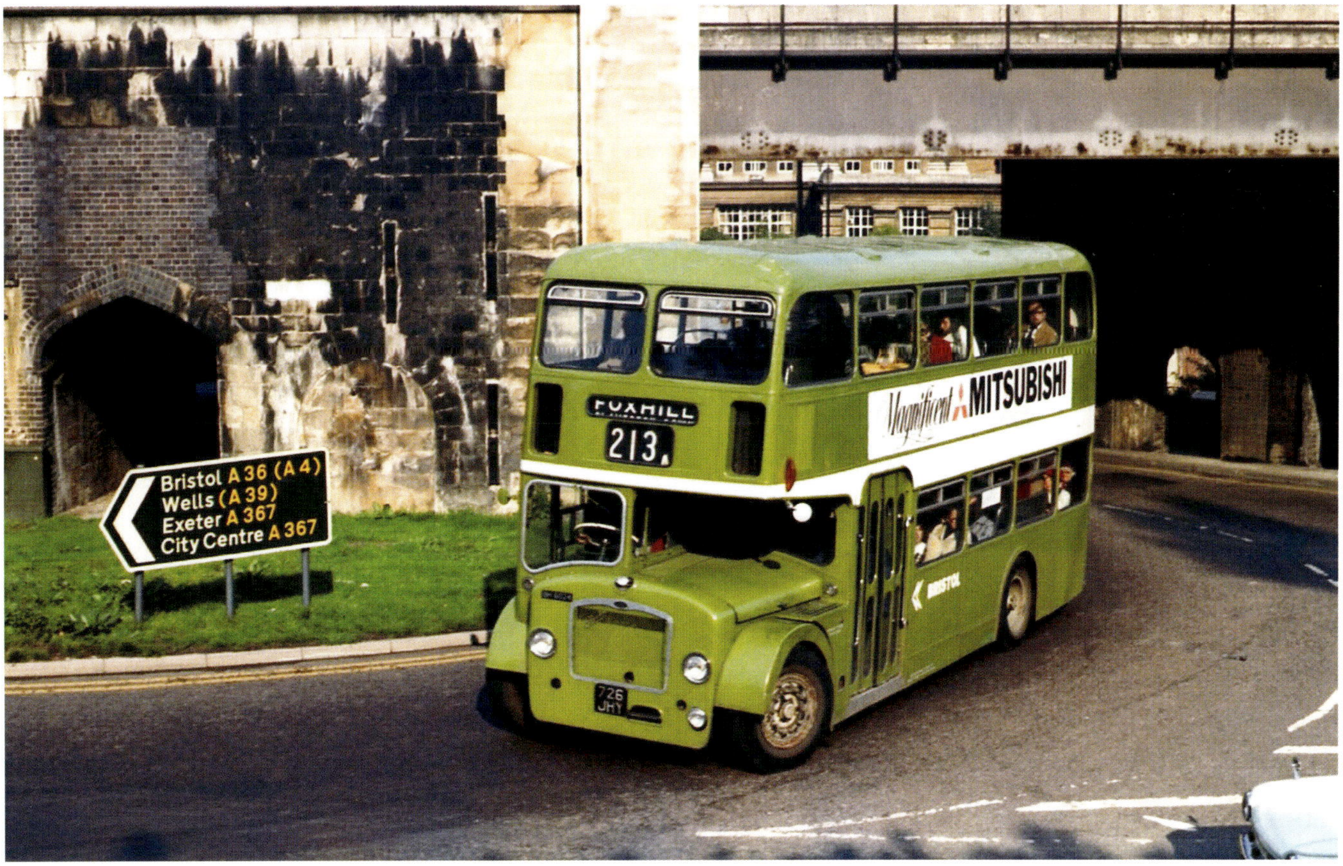

A marvellous view of Bath Depot's 6024 (726 JHY), a 1961 FSF6G returned to Bristol Omnibus with the transfer of West Wiltshire services and buses based at Chippenham and Trowbridge on 1st January 1970. Seen here on Thursday 16th October 1975 at Wells Road (Bottom) it looks to be in excellent condition as it passes under the "Great Western Railway" line just to the west of Bath Spa Station on a Service 213 journey between Elmhurst Estate and Foxhill Estate. (Stephen Dowle)

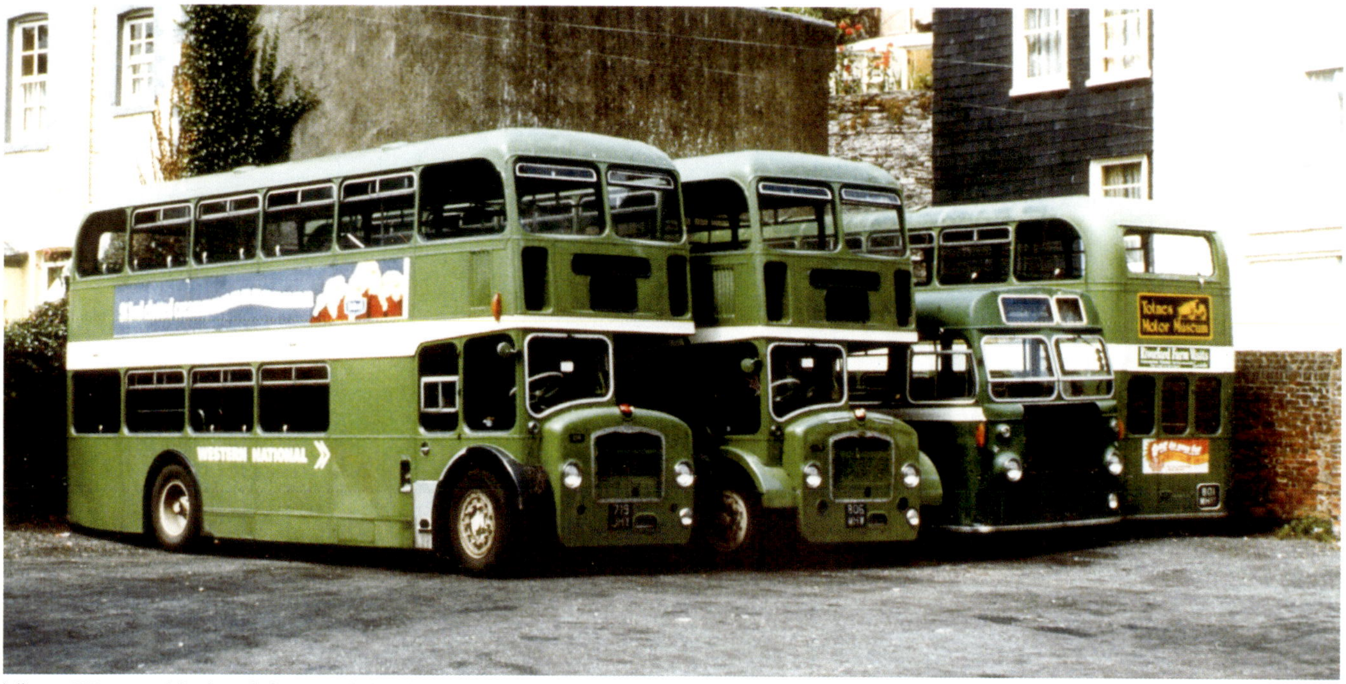

Three Western National former Bristol Omnibus FSFs 1018 (719 JHY), 1009 (806 MHW), 1010 (801 MHW) and a Bristol SU, all withdrawn from the operational fleet, stand at the rear of Totnes Depot in November 1978.

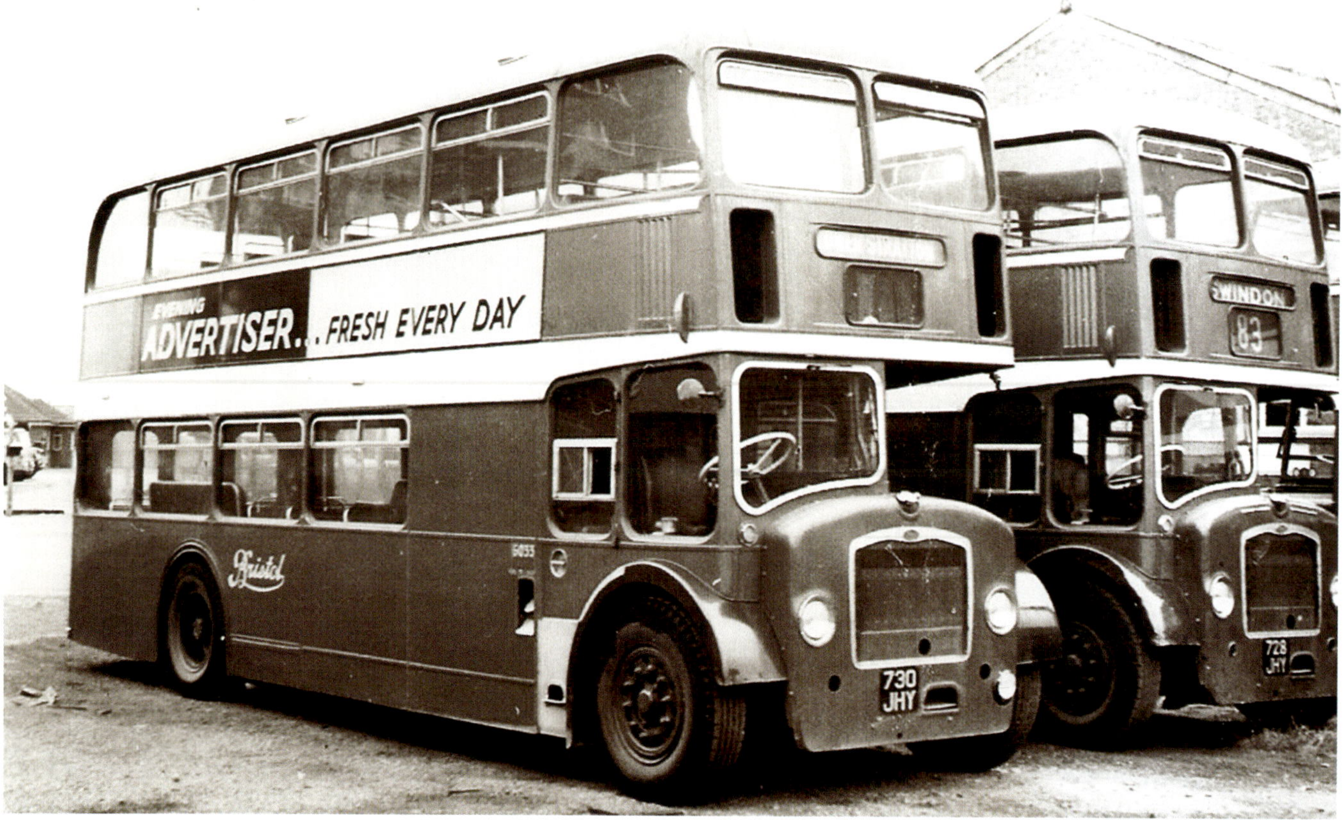

Swindon Depot sets the scene for 6033 (730 JHY) and 6031 (728 JHY), both received by Bristol Omnibus in March 1961 and both bought with other FSF6Gs by Western National in August 1967. They were numbered by their new owners 1006 and 1004 respectively in the usual random manner at that time. 1004 (728 JHY) returned to Bristol Omnibus on 1st January 1970 and resumed its original fleet number but 6033 remained with Western National until withdrawn in April 1978. (Bristol Vintage Bus Group)

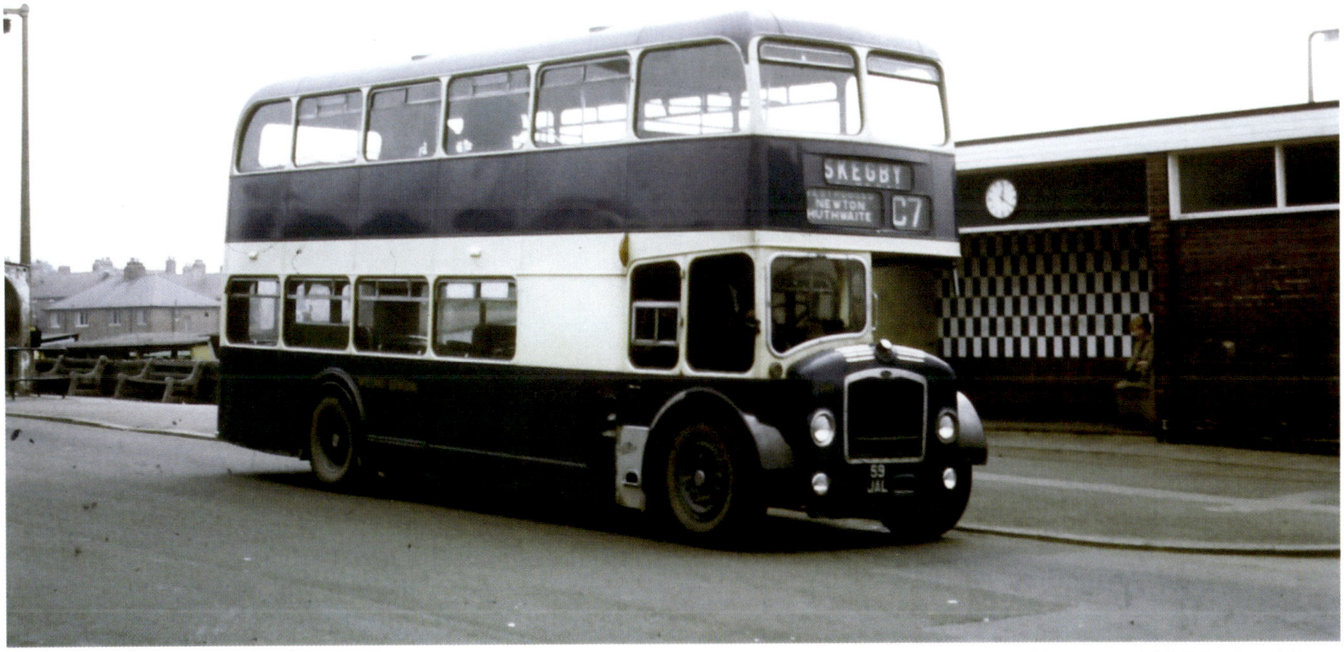

When new in June 1962, Midland General 543 (59 JAL) was one of the last three FSF6Gs received by Mansfield District. All ten vehicles were transferred to the main Midland fleet between May and August 1968 and 543 was renumbered 680 in October 1972. Seen here on 17th May 1970 at Alfreton it is operating a journey to Skegby (Healdswood Estate) on Service C7. (Author's collection)

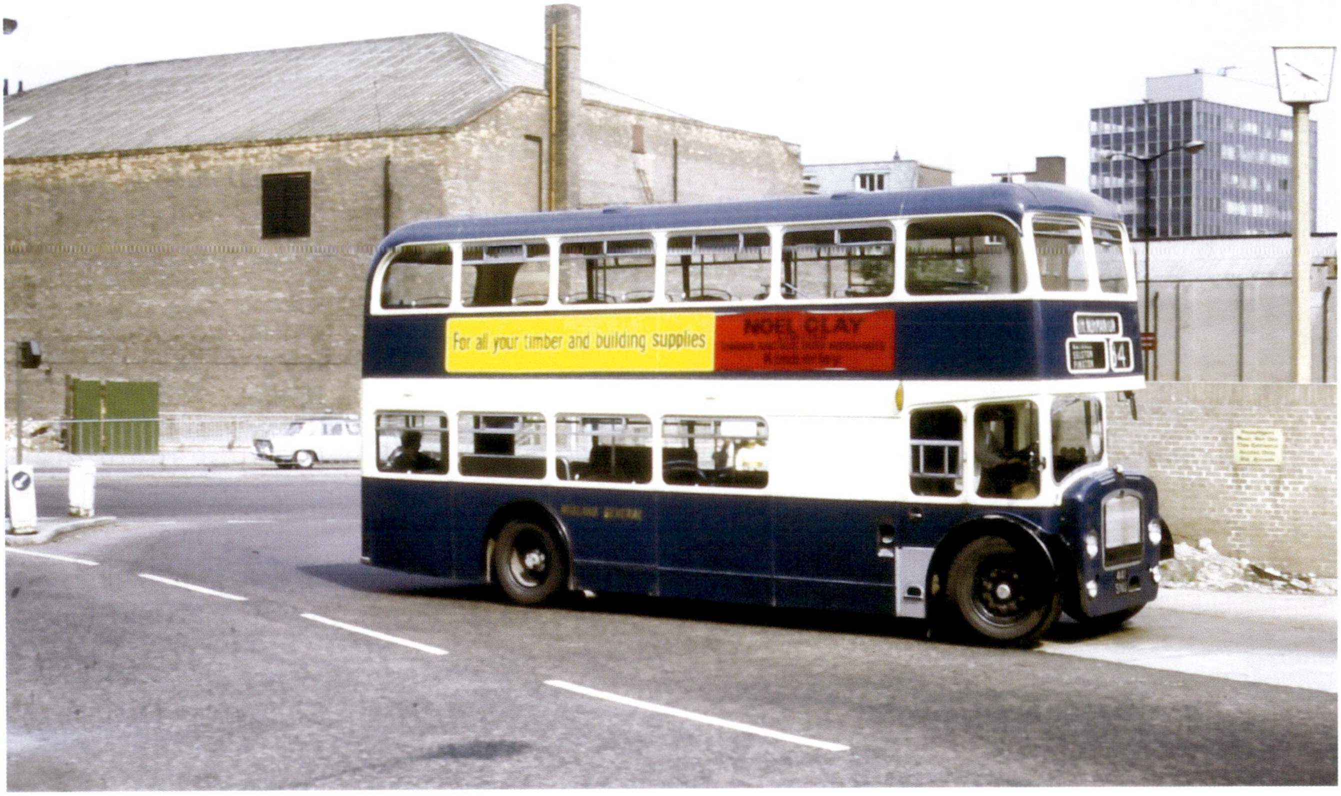

Delivered as 501 in November 1961, Midland General 601 (441 SNU) was renumbered 601 in 1968 and again to 671 in October 1972. It is seen here in July 1971 with destination set to work on Service B4 between Nottingham and South Normanton. (Author's collection)

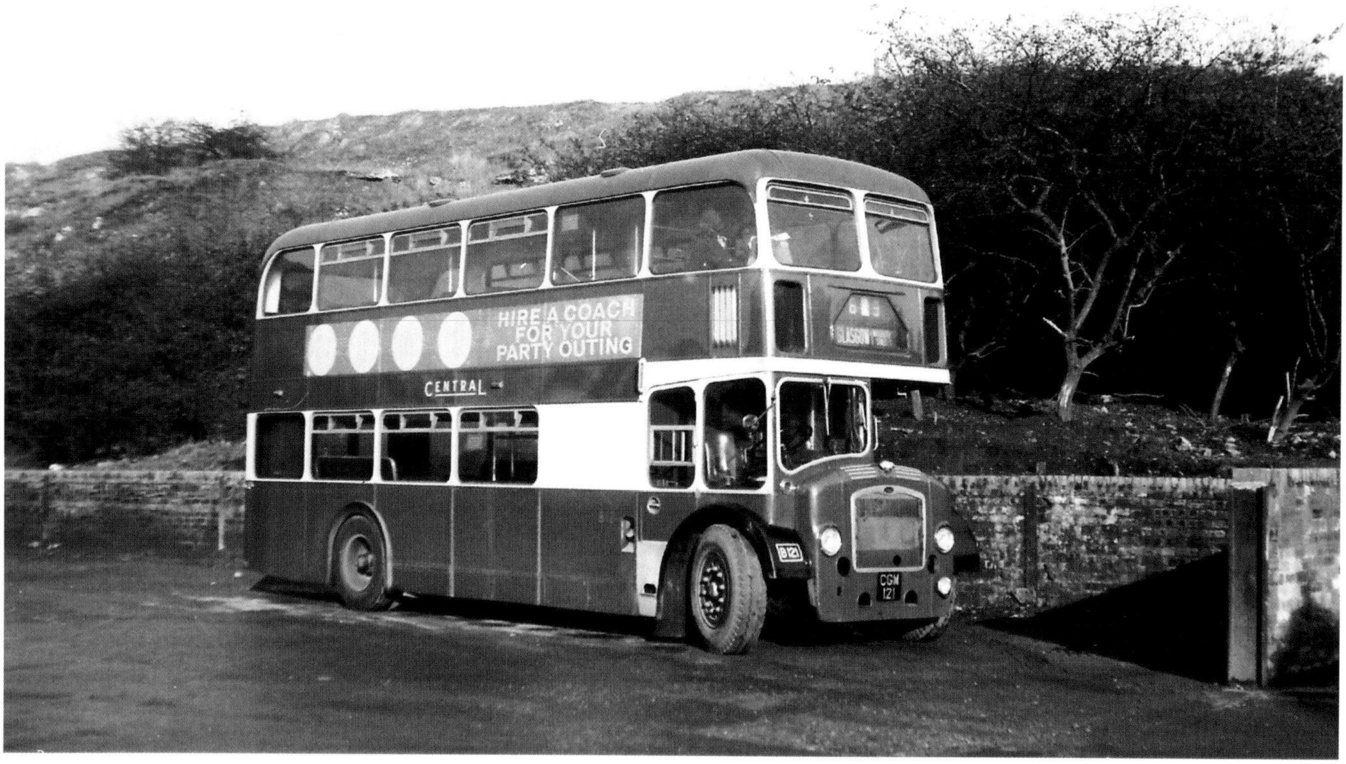

Received in March 1961 Central SMT B121 is pictured on 16th November 1963 on the site of the demolished Newmains Depot. This was one of the original seven FSFs delivered to Central SMT and is equipped with Cave-Browne-Cave radiators either side of the destination box. (A. J. Douglas)

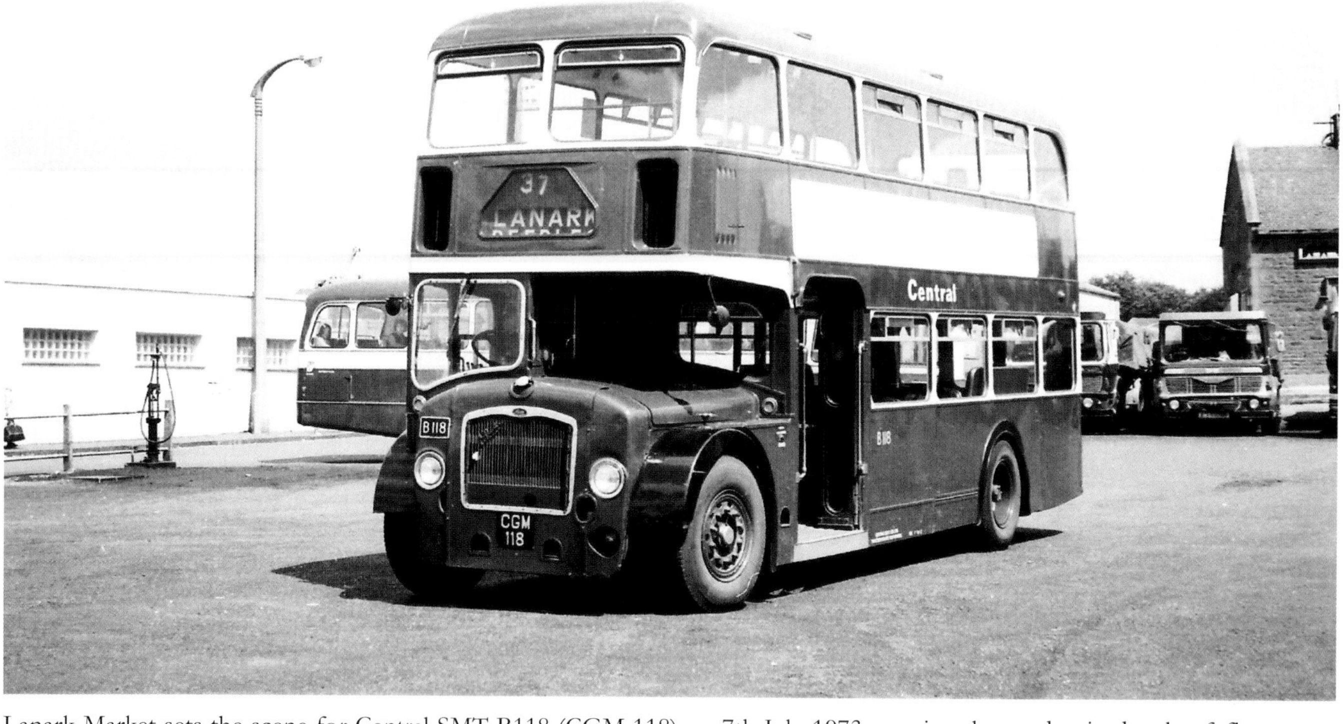

Lanark Market sets the scene for Central SMT B118 (CGM 118) on 7th July 1973 carrying the modernised style of fleet name after working a journey on Service 37. (A. J. Douglas)

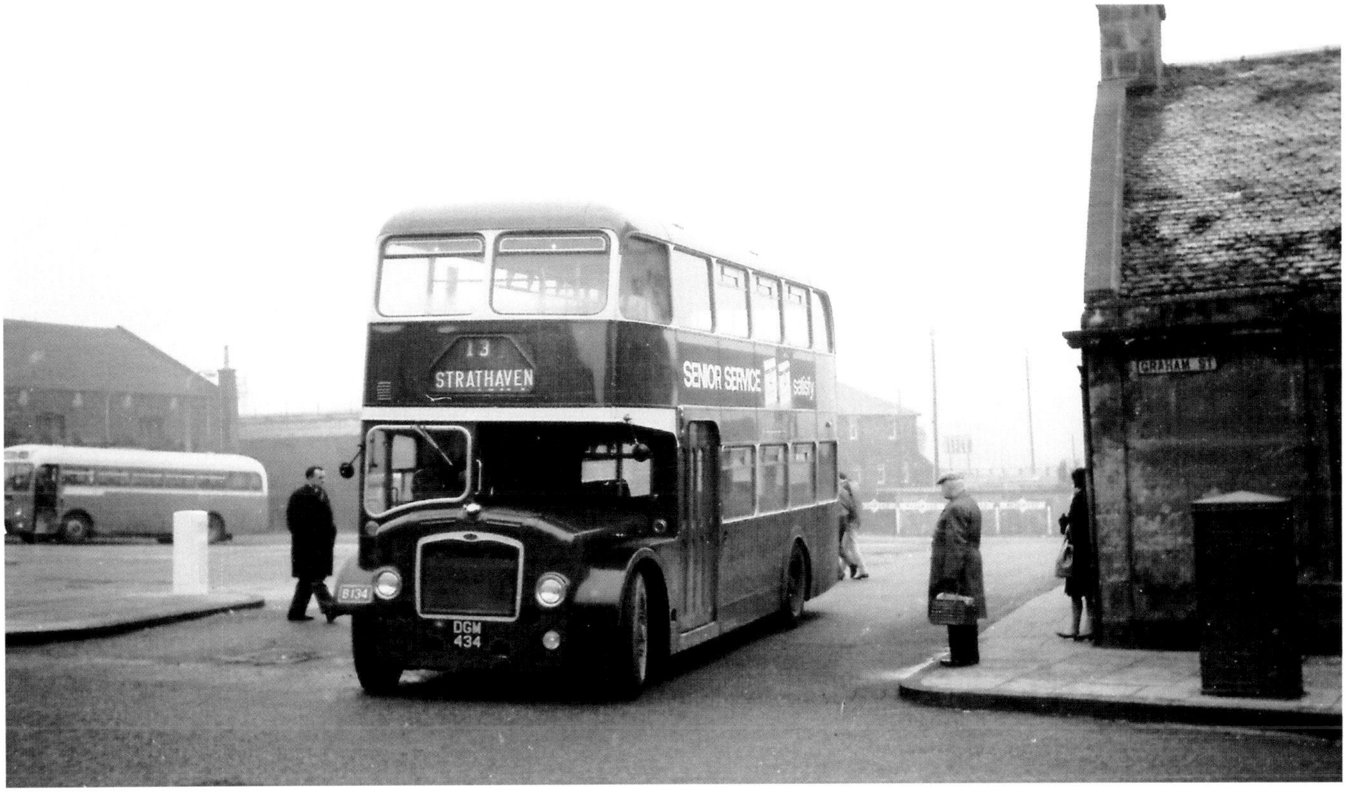

Departing Airdrie Bus Station on 4th January 1966 Central SMT B134 (DGM 434) heads for Strathaven on a Service 13 journey with few visible passengers. Hardly surprising in view of the unwelcoming damp and foggy weather! (A. J. Douglas)

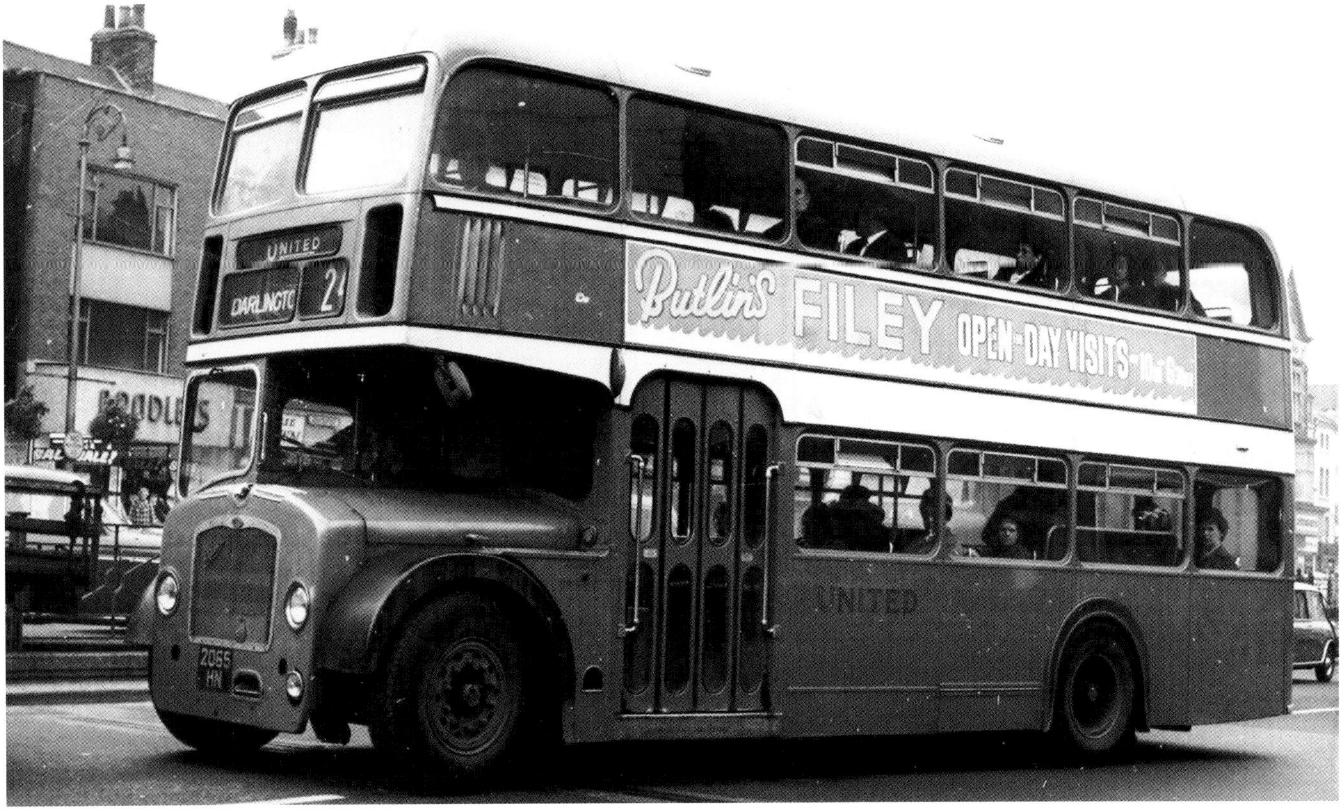

Seen when relatively new and looking smart in lined out livery BL65 (2065 HN), one of the 1960 deliveries of FSF6Bs, is heading to Darlington on Service 24. Who recalls Butlin's Day Visits advertised on the side of the bus, another leisure "product" of the 1960s? (Tony Robbins collection)

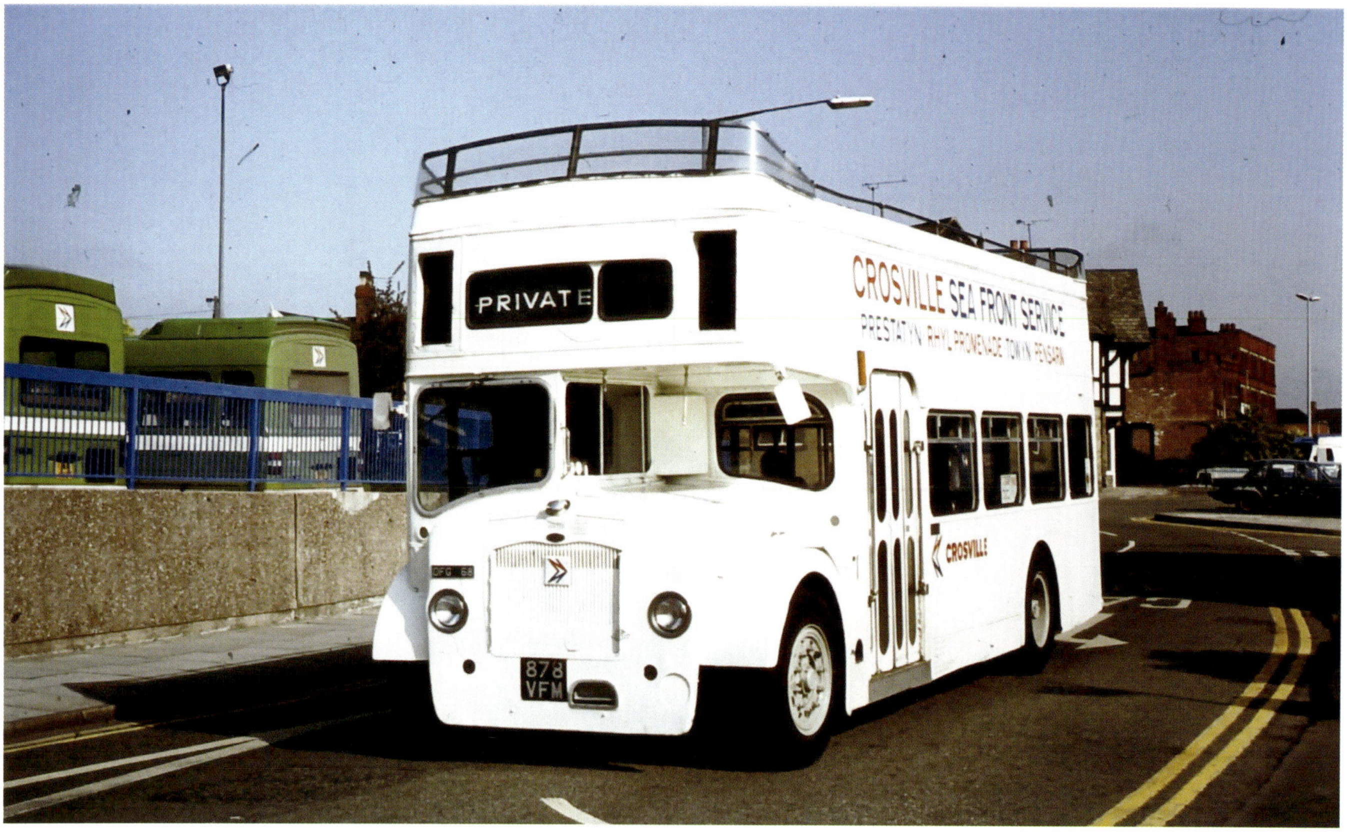

Crosville DFG68 (878 VFM) was rebuilt to permanent open top by the company in February 1977. It is seen at Chester on 31st May 1983 on what appears to be Private Hire work. (Geoff Gould)

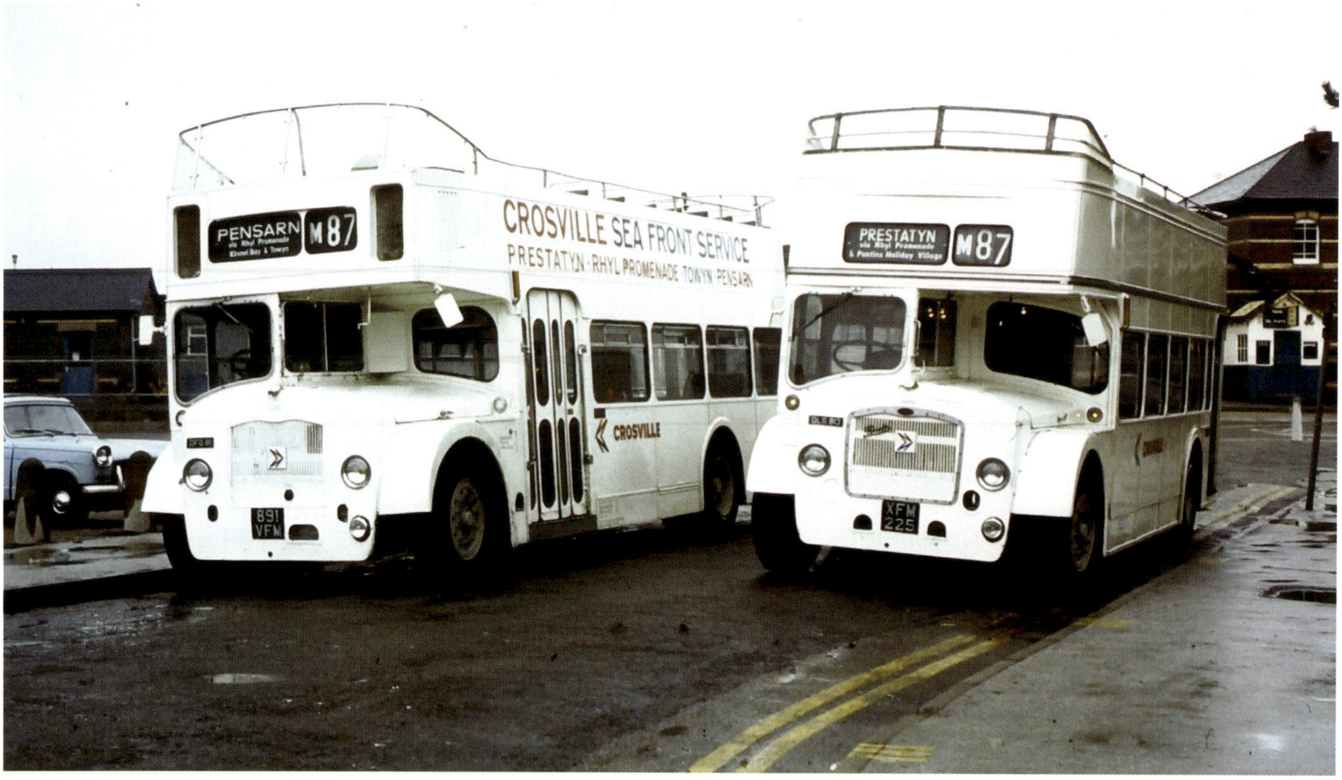

Waiting in Rhyl in the rain for passengers on Service M17 on 30th May 1983 is 1962 FSF6G DFG81 (891 VFM) that would see 21 years service the following month and DLG813 (XFM 225), a 1956 Bristol LD6G with ECW CO33+27RD bodywork that had been in service with Crosville exactly 27 years that month. (Geoff Gould)

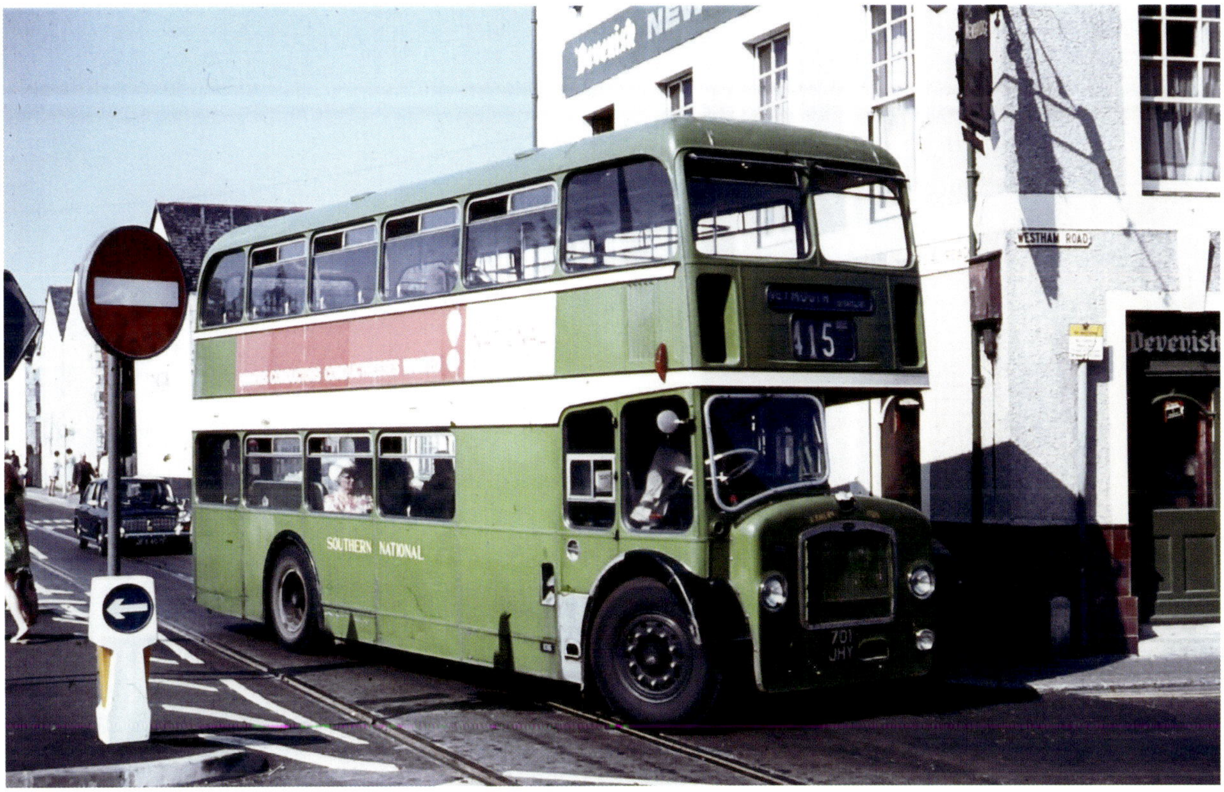

Southern National 1016 (701 JHY), a former Bath Tramways FSF6G, arrives in Weymouth and turns from Commercial Road into Westham Road on 6th August 1970 to reach King's Statue. (Author's collection)

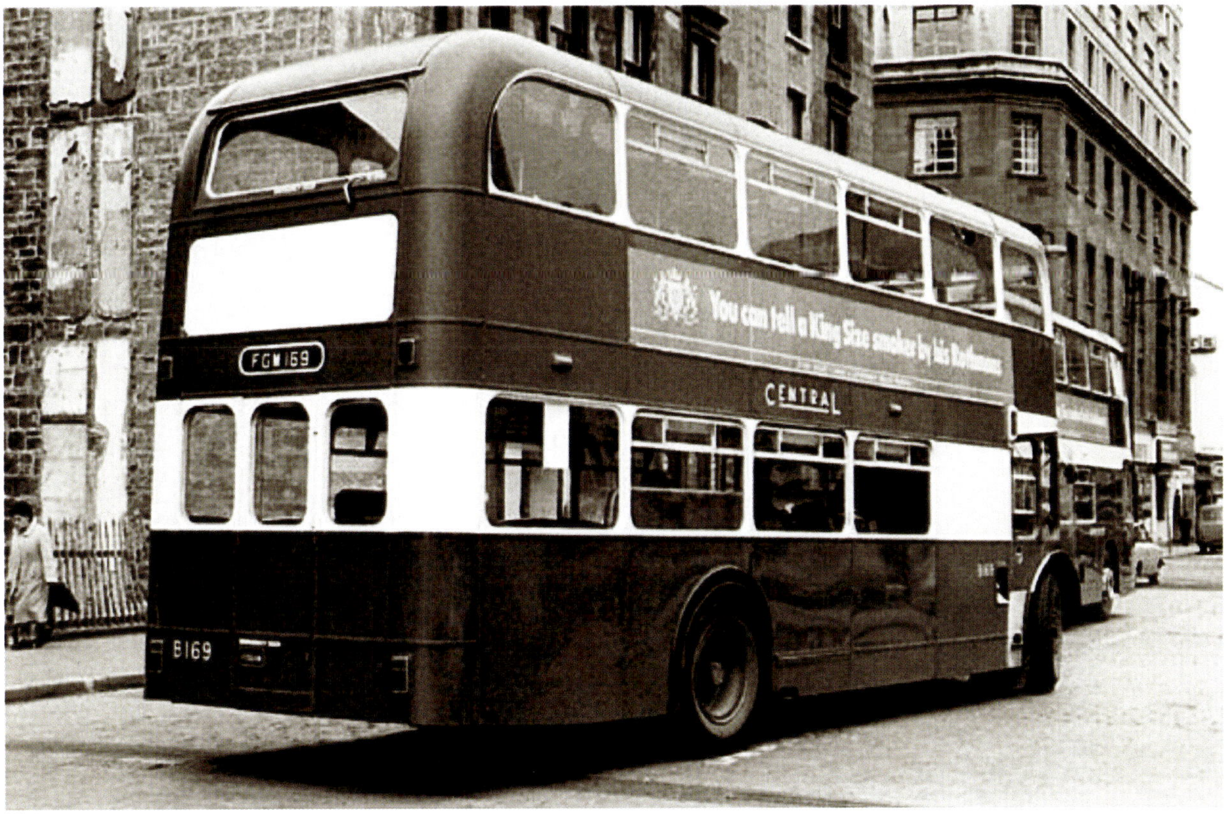

The rear end styling of the FSFs for Central SMT was significantly different to those for other operators as exemplified by this view of B169 (FGM 169) received by the company in September 1963. The most obvious differences includes no rear destination display or chrome finishing strip but additionally panel differences. (Bristol Vintage Bus Group)

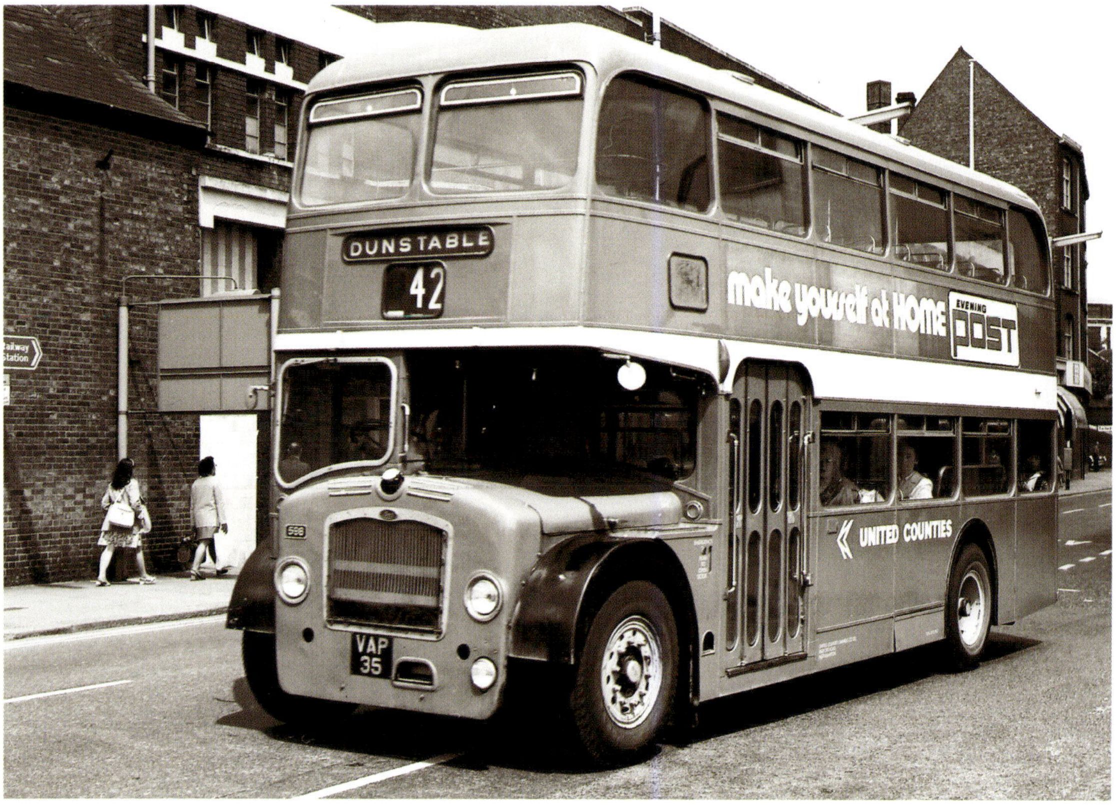

Carrying very few passengers to Dunstable on Service 42 United Counties 598 (VAP 35) was bought by United Counties from Southdown with 597 (VAP 34) in March 1973. These FSF6Bs were new to Brighton Hove & District in July 1961 and transferred into the parent Southdown fleet on 1st January 1969. Both were withdrawn from the operating fleet and scrapped in December 1976. (Author's collection)

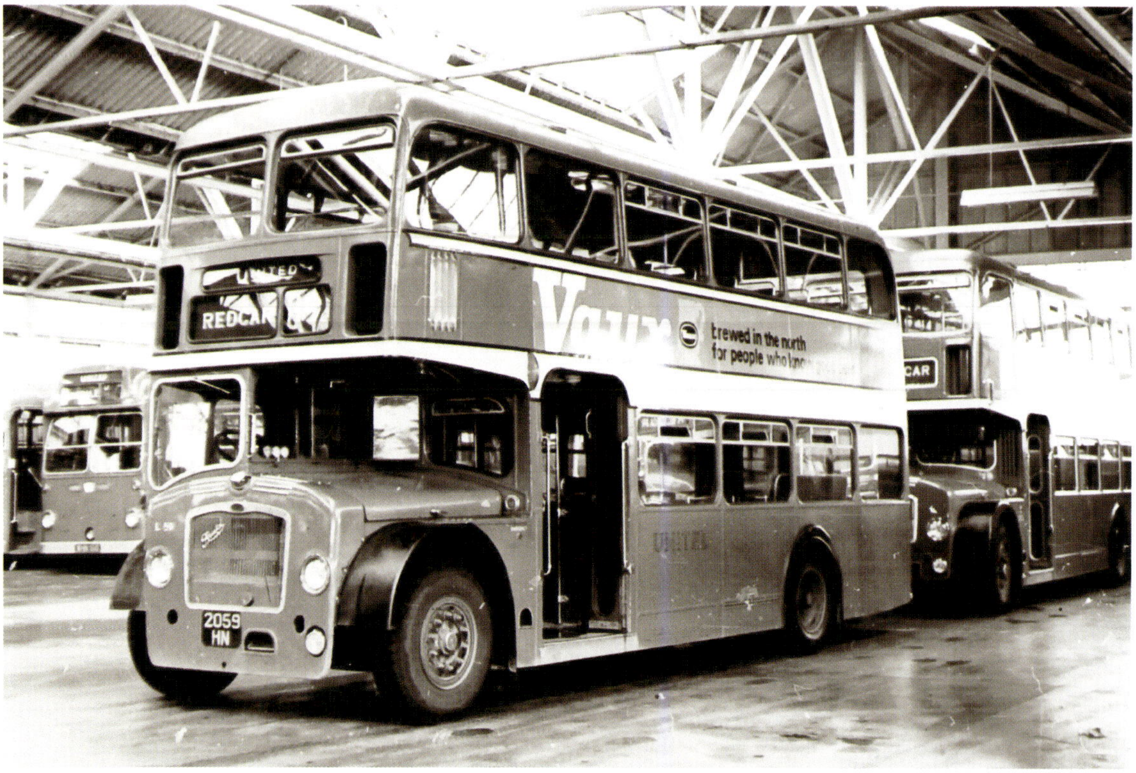

A classic view of United L59 (2059 HN) as it stands inside Redcar Depot finished in the standard but smart Tilling lined out red livery that was common in many areas of the country in the 1960s. (Phil Sposito collection)

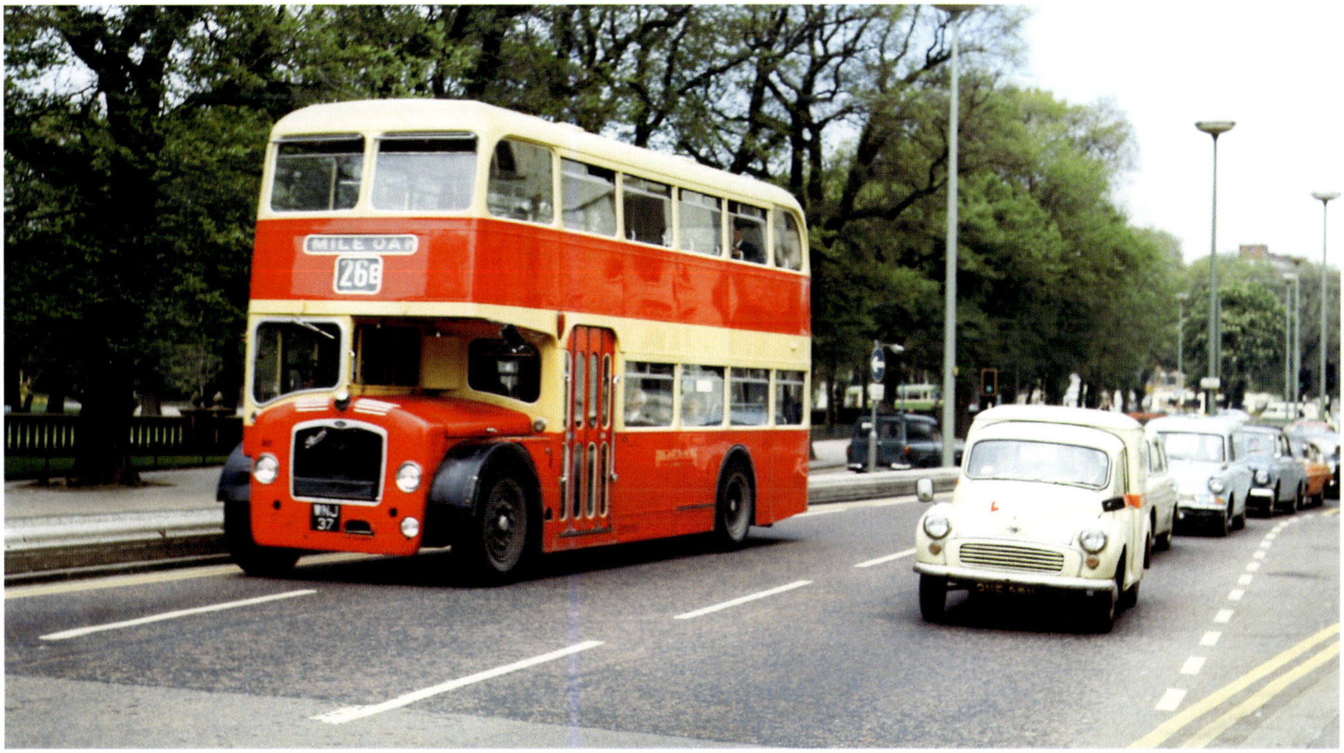

Driving licences were not a legal requirement until March 1934 and were introduced in 1935 along with L-plates and provisional licences. The style and size of L-plates has not changed over the years as seen on this Morris Minor van being passed by Brighton Hove & District 2037 (WNJ 37) in traditional red and cream livery but carrying its Southdown fleet number circa 1968. (Author's collection)

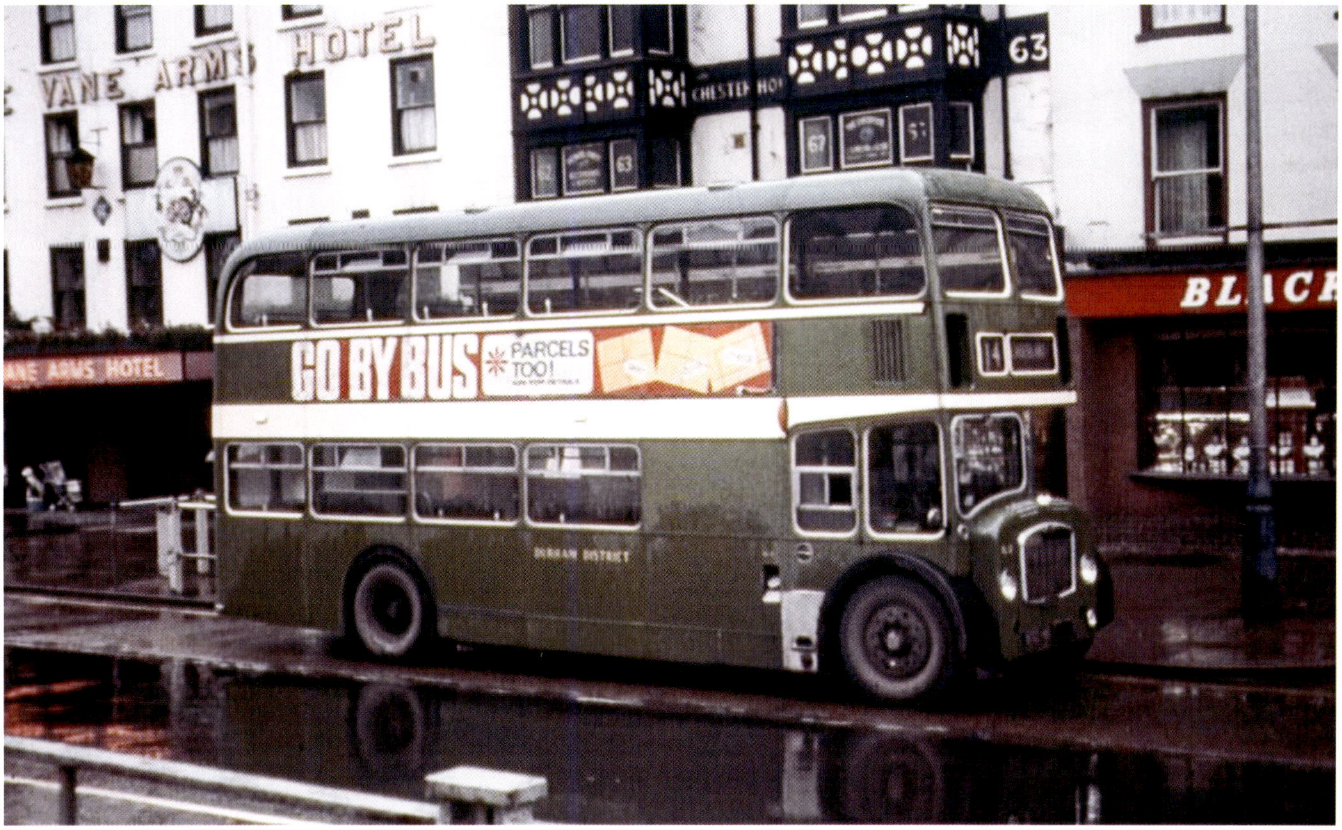

Looks like Durham District DL12 (8112 HN) is experiencing typical summer weather at High Street in Stockton when operating a service to Sunderland in July 1968. (Donald Hudson)

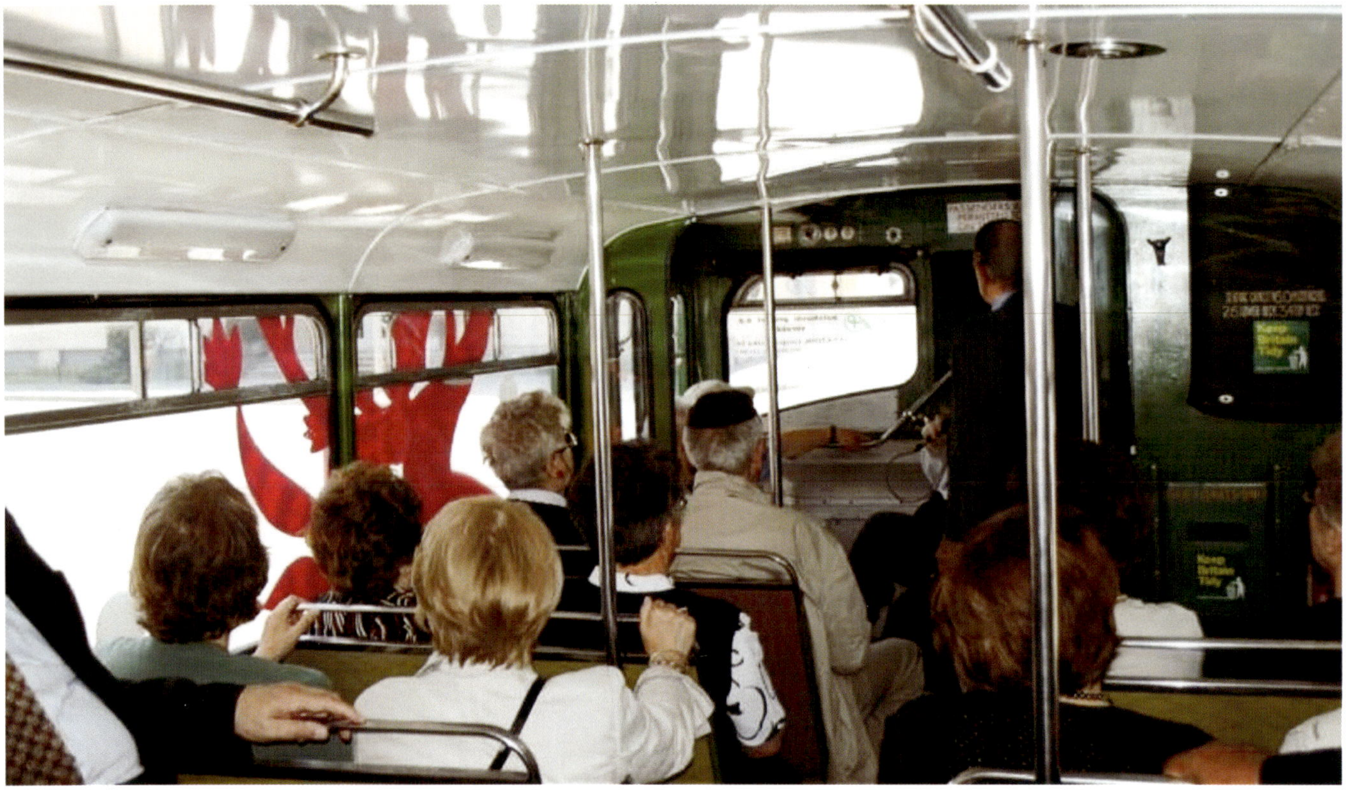

A forward looking view of the lower deck of ex Bath Electric Tramways 6041 (806 MHW) now with Varazdin Bus Company and registered as VZ 186-GH. As the tour guide sits on the lower steps leading to the upper deck there is a clear view of the bell pushes, grab rails and a "Keep Britain Tidy" vinyl stuck to the panel of the conductor's area and other original English notices. (Varazdin Bus Company)

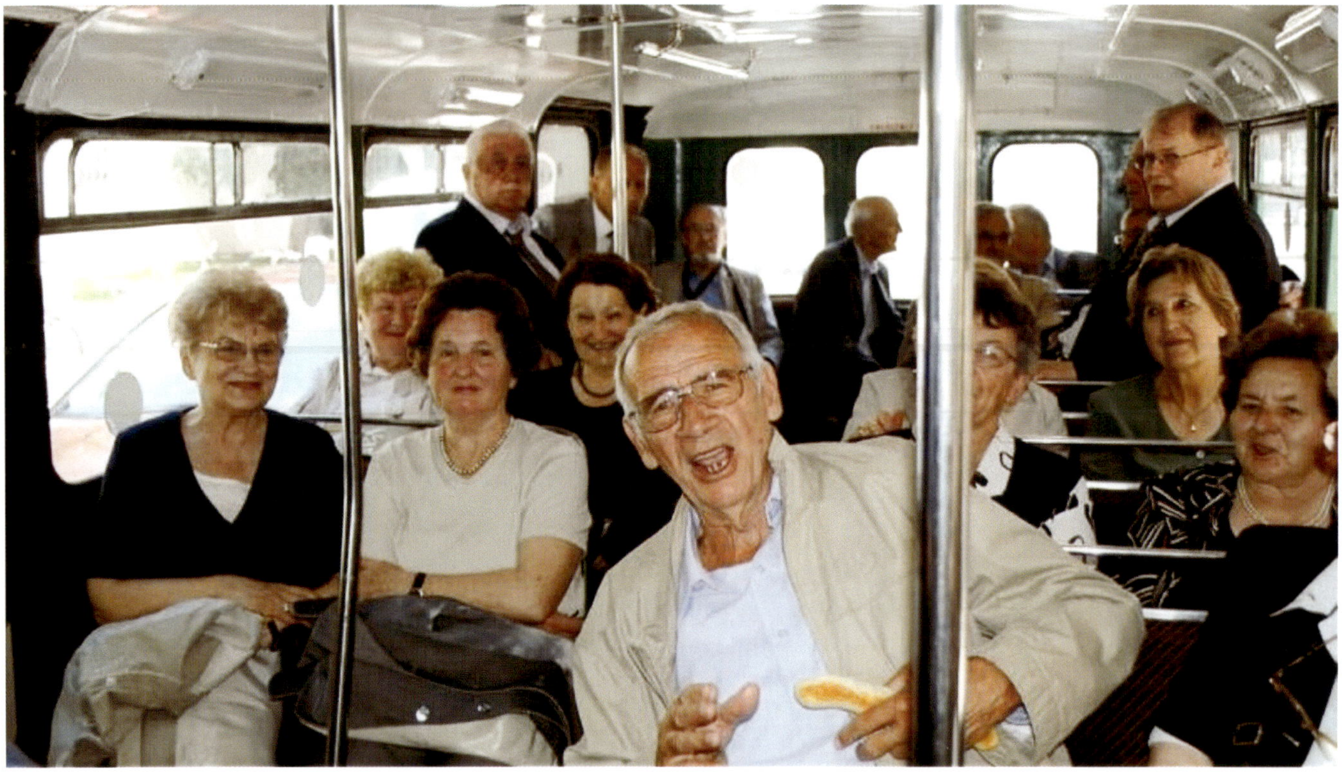

Looking towards the rear this view of the lower deck of VZ 186-GH shows the offside doors and the adaptation of the ceiling panels to accommodate these. The hatches on the rear curved ceiling panels give access to the winding gear for the rear destination box. (Varazdin Bus Company)

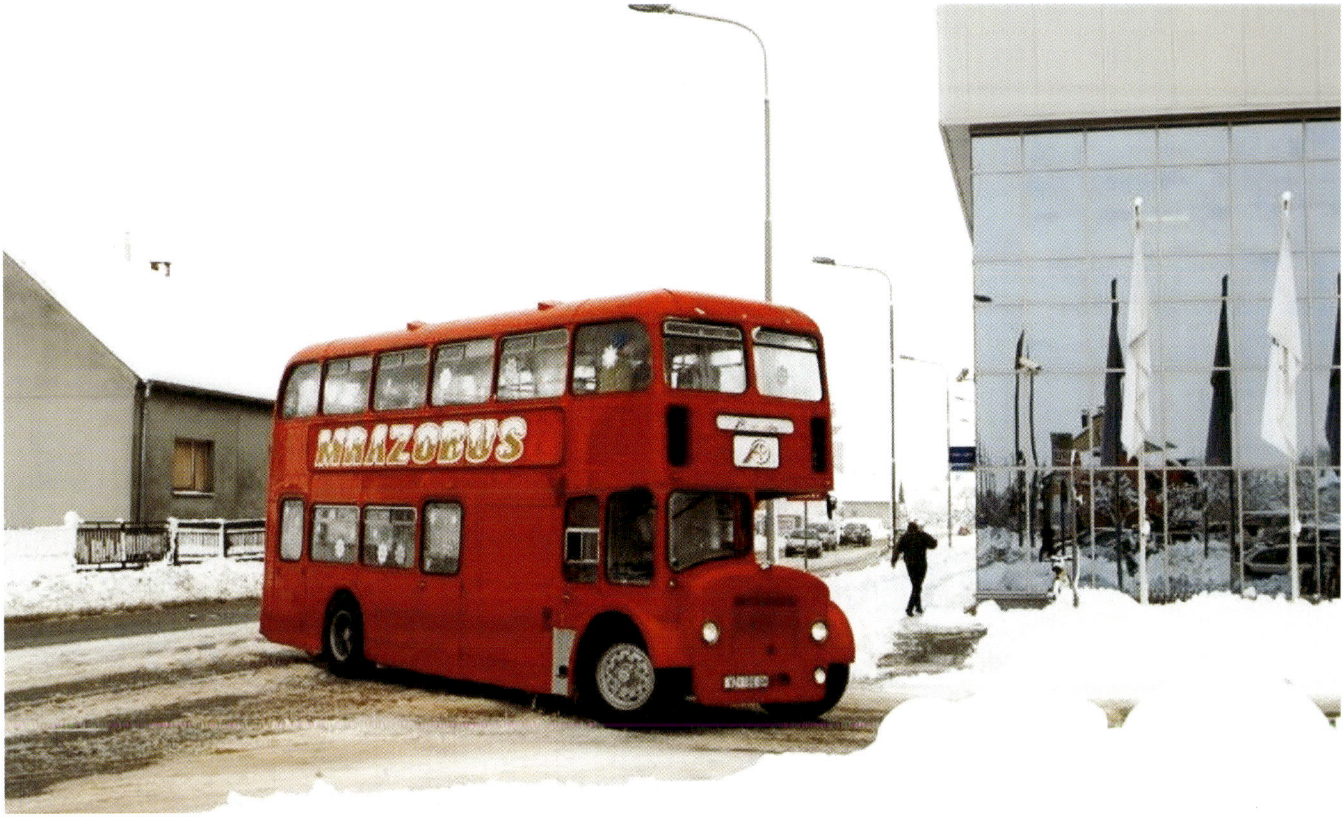

Treacherous looking road conditions in Varazdin find the bus, fitted with two offside doors for the safe loading of passengers, negotiating a slippery road junction. (Varazdin Bus Company)

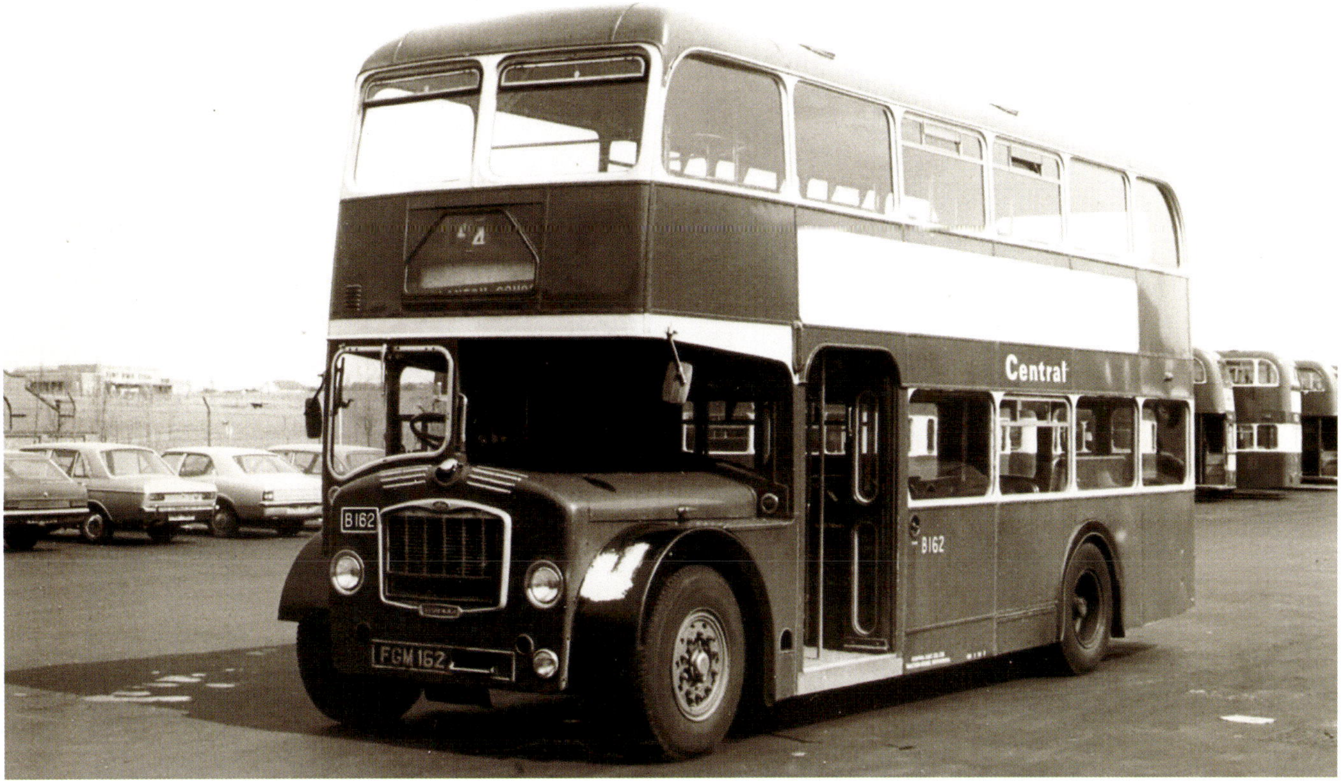

Window repairs have left Central SMT B162 (FGM 162) looking quite strange with an odd window layout as a result. This was one of the eleven final FSFs built under Sanction 215 and delivered in September 1963 fitted with Gardner engines. (Tony Robbins collection)

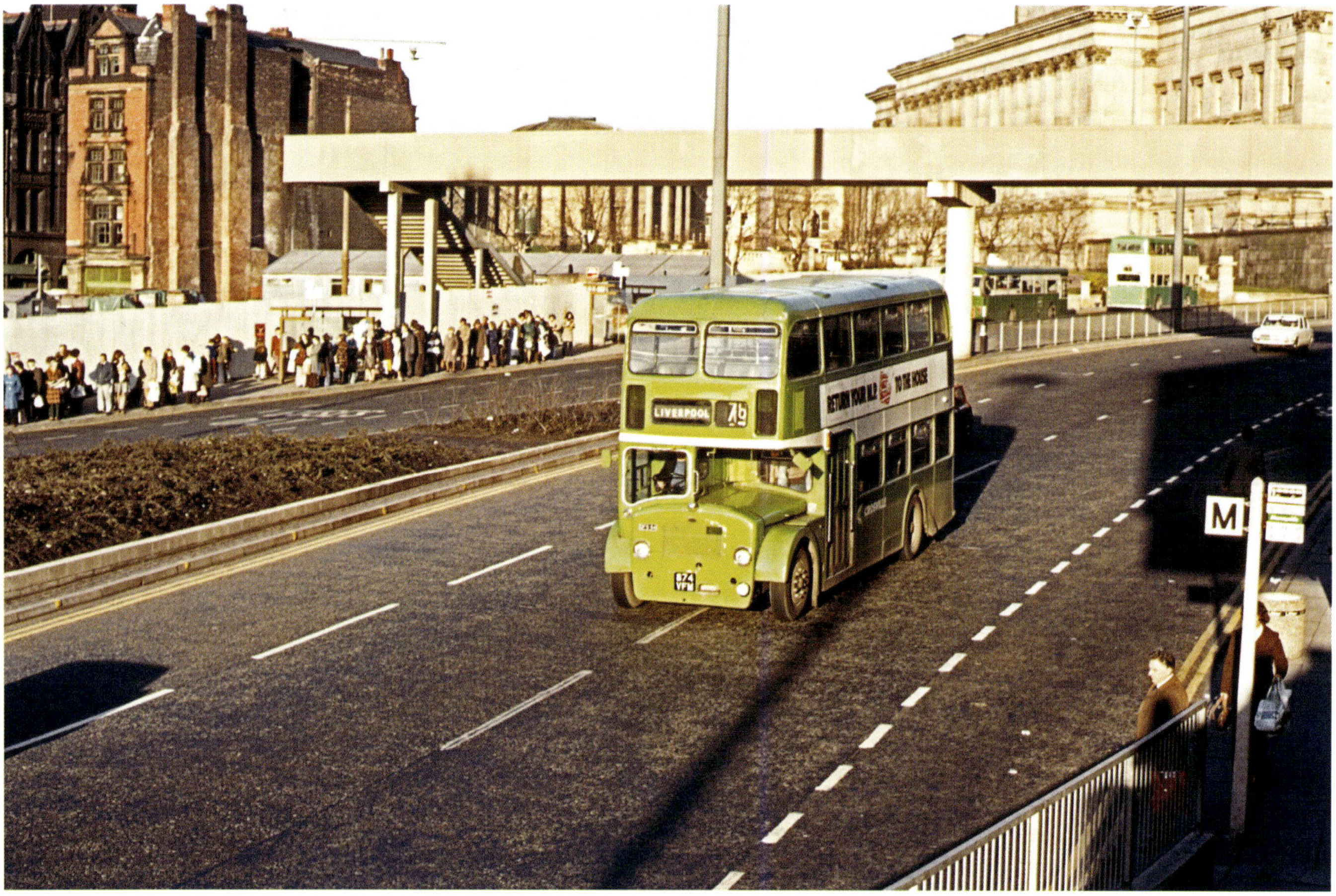

Pictured from an unusual aspect arriving in Liverpool on 10th November 1974, Crosville DFG64 (874 VFM) has completed a journey from Prescot on Service 76 with very few passengers remaining on board. (M. R. Hodges)

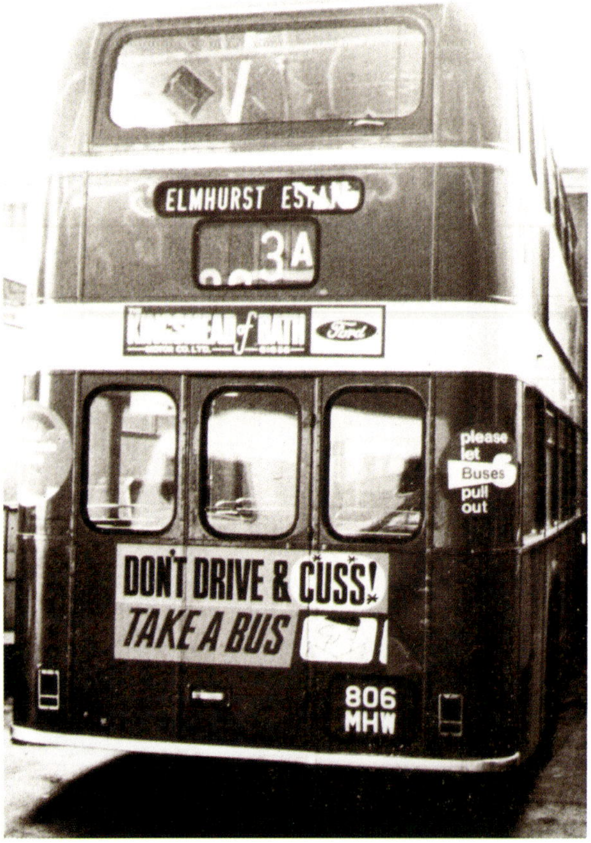

The most common sight that most people see of a bus is its rear and that's what sells advertising space. The rear of Bath Services 6041 (806 MHW), bought by the author of this book and Euel Lane a driver at Bath in November 1978, shows the sites that could be bought by advertisers with appropriate advertisements from the 1960s. Also clearly visible in Bath's Kensington Depot shed is the four track number display and destination layout. (Author's collection)

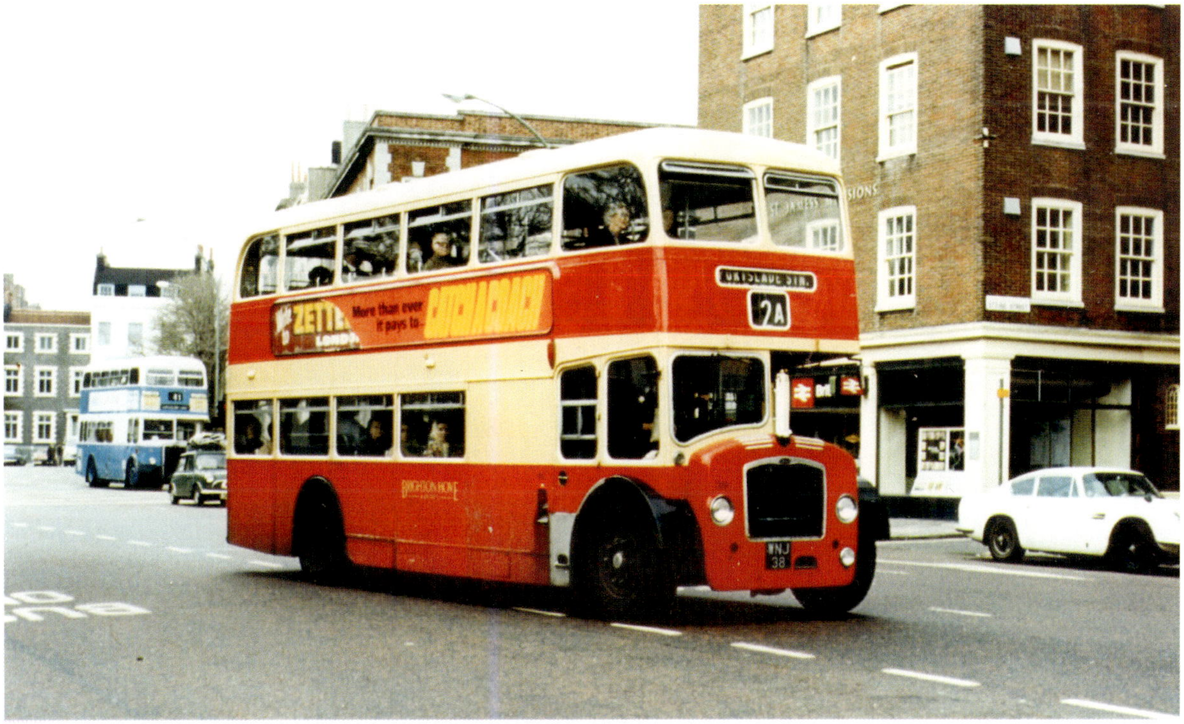

Not the best way to sell illuminated advertising is demonstrated on Brighton Hove & District 38 (WNJ 38), a 1962 FSF6B working a journey to Portslade Station on Service 2A. Most of the Zetters Football Pools advert has disappeared revealing the express coach services previously displayed. (Tony Robbins collection)

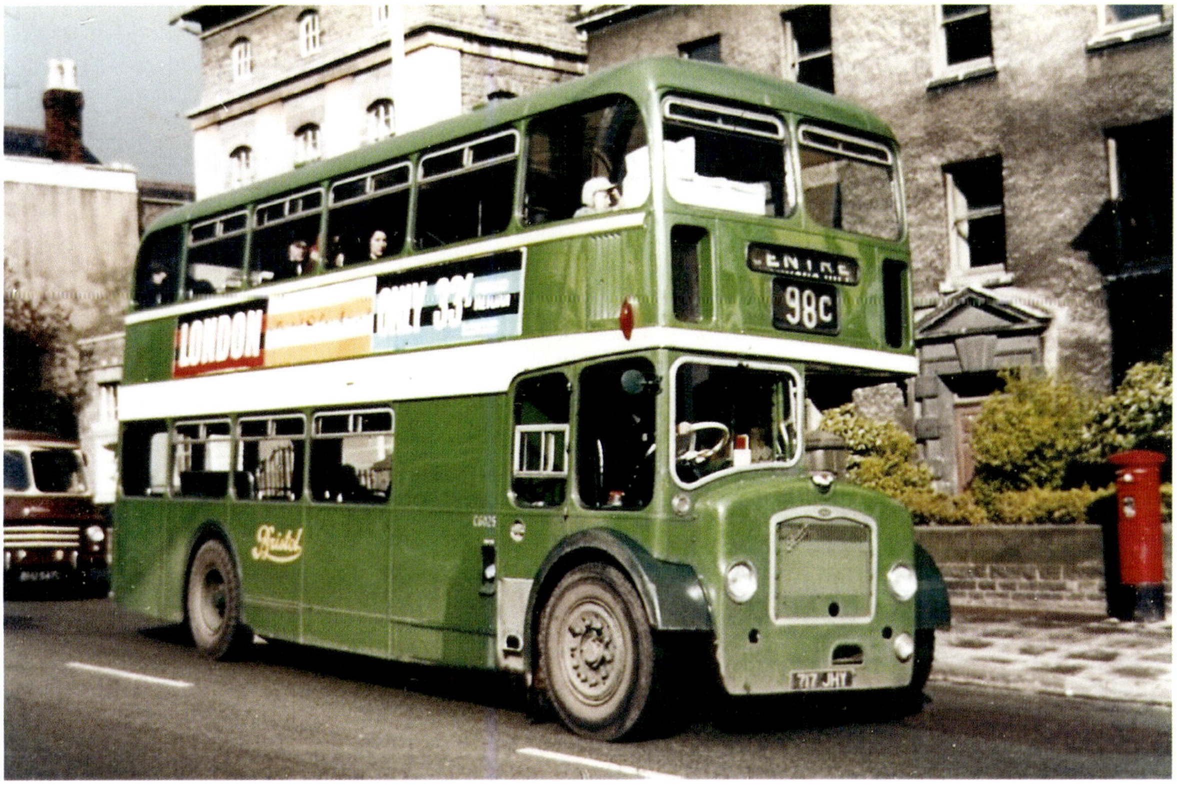

Only one FSF in the Bristol Omnibus group of companies carried an oblong front registration number plate as opposed to the regular square version. Bristol Joint Services C6025 (717 JHY) ably shows this on a journey to Centre, previously known as Tramways Centre until after the Second World War, on Service 98C that operated across the city between Rookery Farm Estate and Patchway. Cuts in Bristol City Services on 27th June 1976 made the bus redundant and it was sold to Barnsley dealer P Sykes and eventually scrapped. (Bristol Vintage Bus Group)

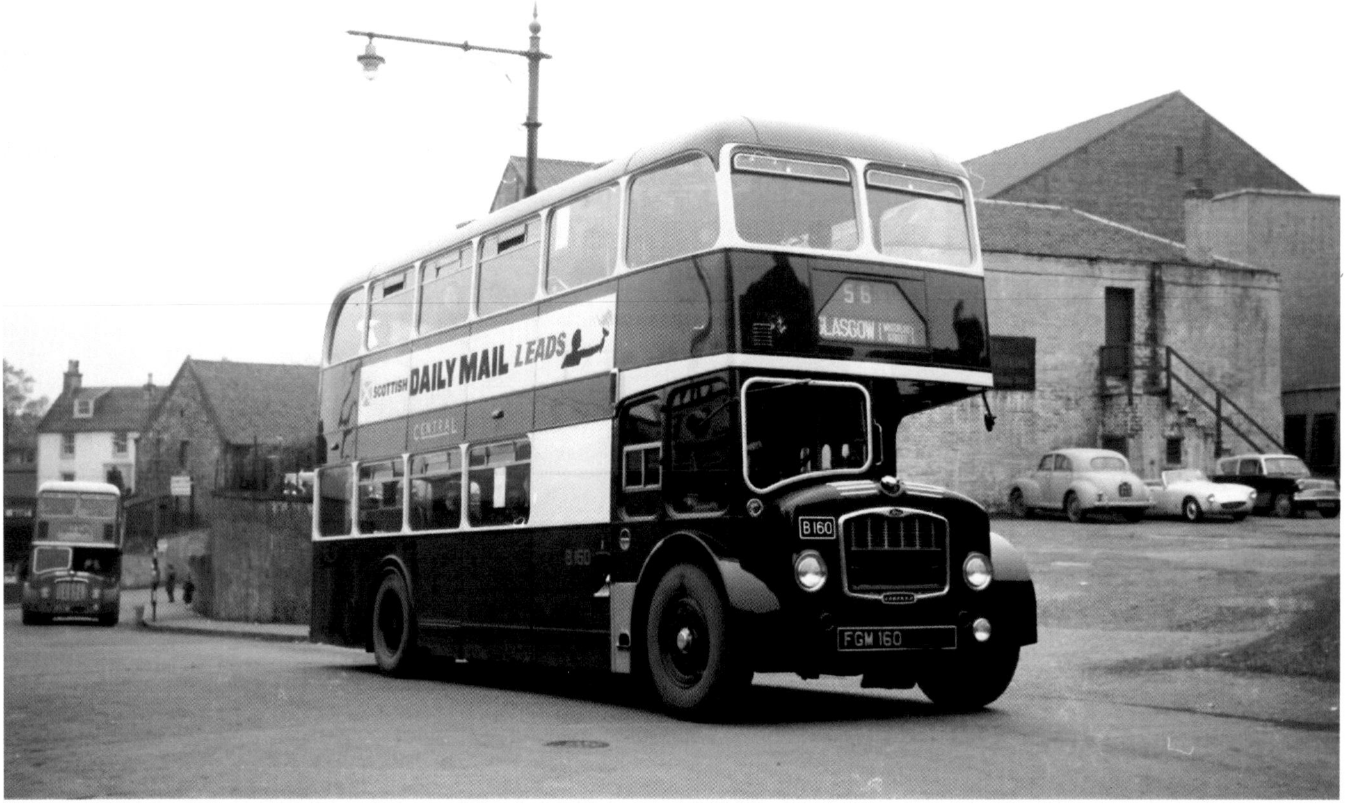

Central SMT B160 (FGM 160) was the first of the last batch of eleven FSFs that were built under Sanction 215 and delivered to the company in September 1963. It was withdrawn from the active fleet in January 1979 and scrapped. (A. J. Douglas)

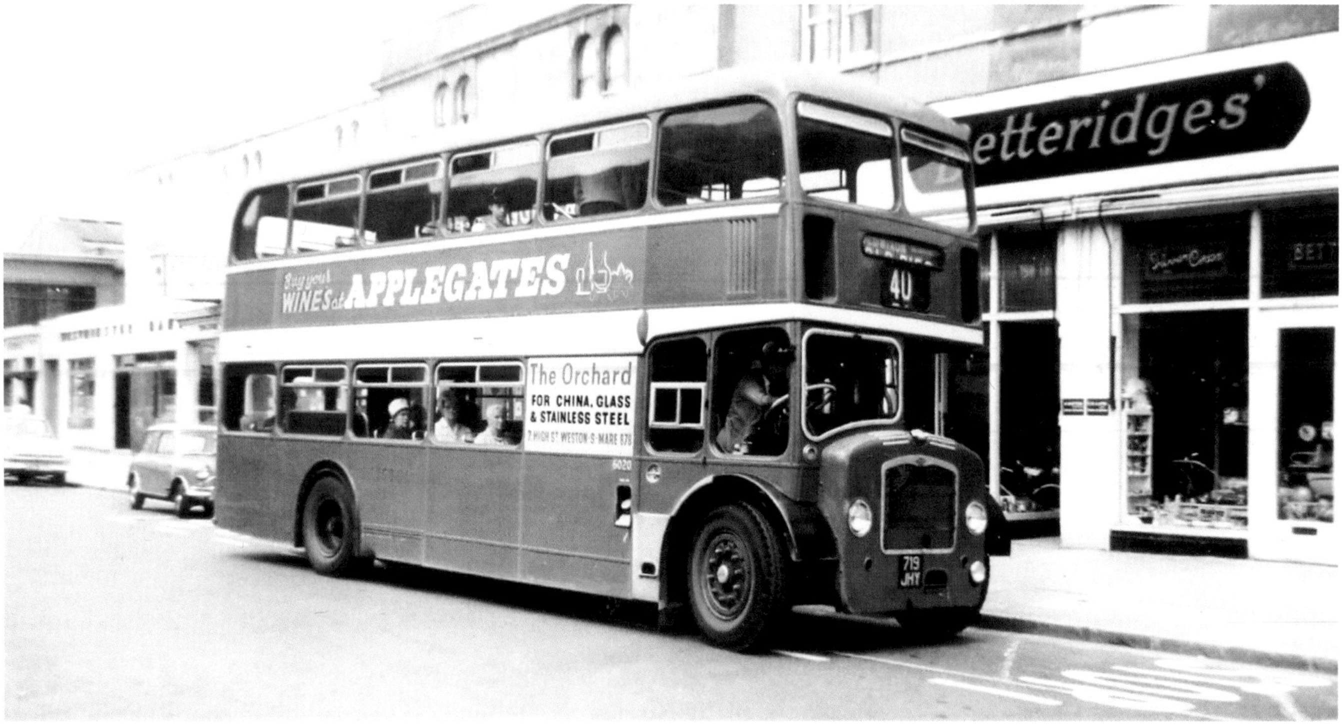

Waiting for passengers in Weston-super-Mare's Oxford Street on 22nd July 1965 is 6020 (719 JHY) that was new to the company in January 1961 and with similar 6021 and 6022 was allocated to Weston. All three were transferred to Bath in February 1966 and 6020 was sold to Southern National in May 1967 becoming their 1018. It was delicensed in August 1978 and purchased by Yorkshire dealer W North of Sherburn-in-Elmet who sold it on for further non PSV use and it was last seen at Bickenhill near Birmingham in 1984. (Author's collection)

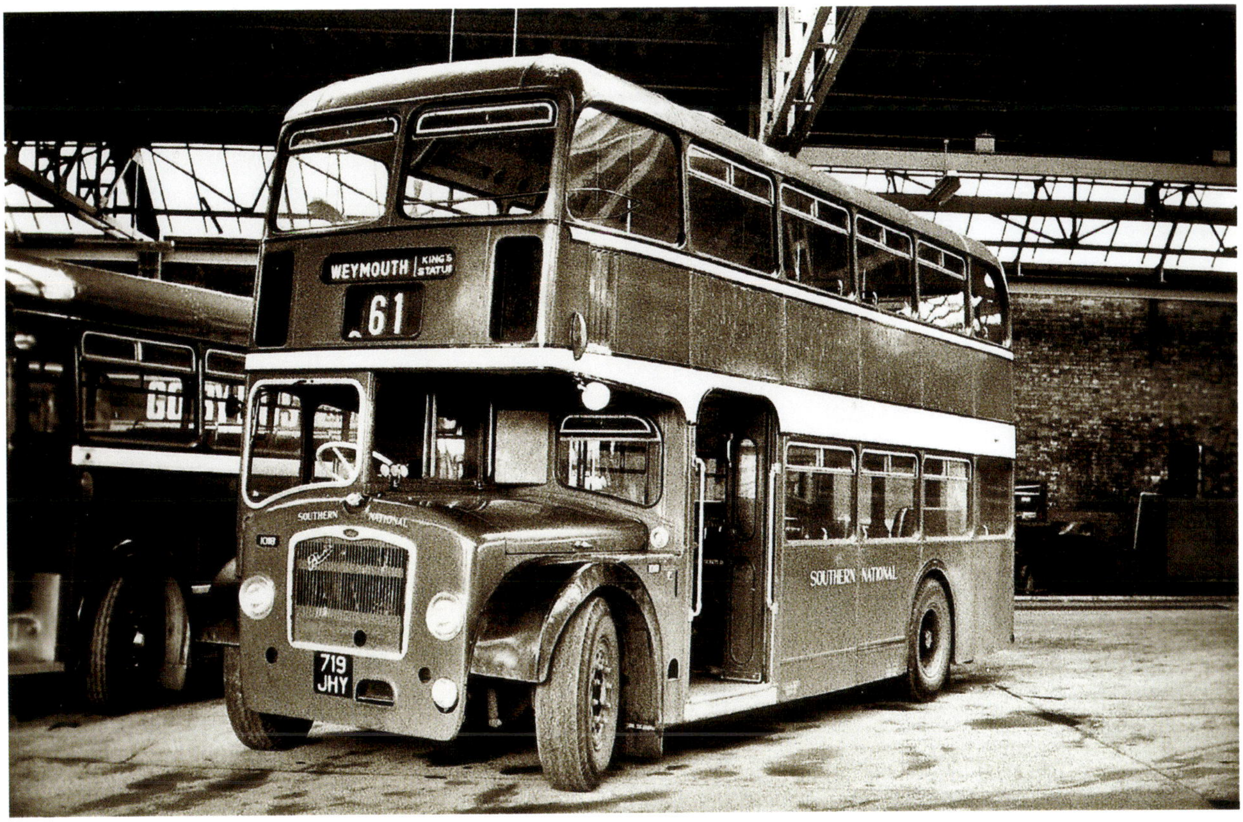

Safely parked away from the weather elements inside Weymouth Depot Southern National 1018 (719 JHY) was originally at Weston-super-Mare Depot but was allocated to Bath at the time that it was purchased from Bristol Omnibus Company. (Author's collection)

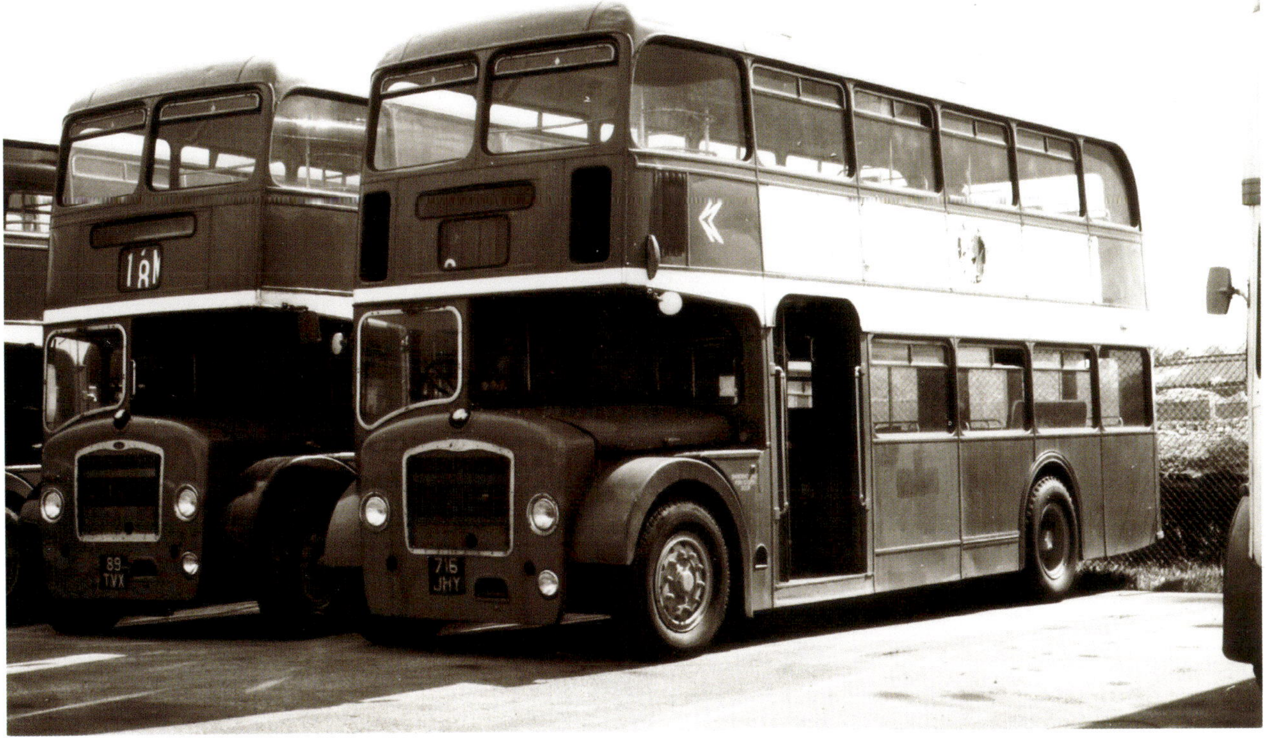

Former Bristol Joint Services C6017 (716 JHY) dating from November 1960 is seen in the yard of dealer and scrap merchant, Paul Sykes at Barnsley, in September 1976. Almost completing an impressive 16 years in service this compared very favourably with other buses available at that time that were usually withdrawn from fleets after twelve or thirteen years.

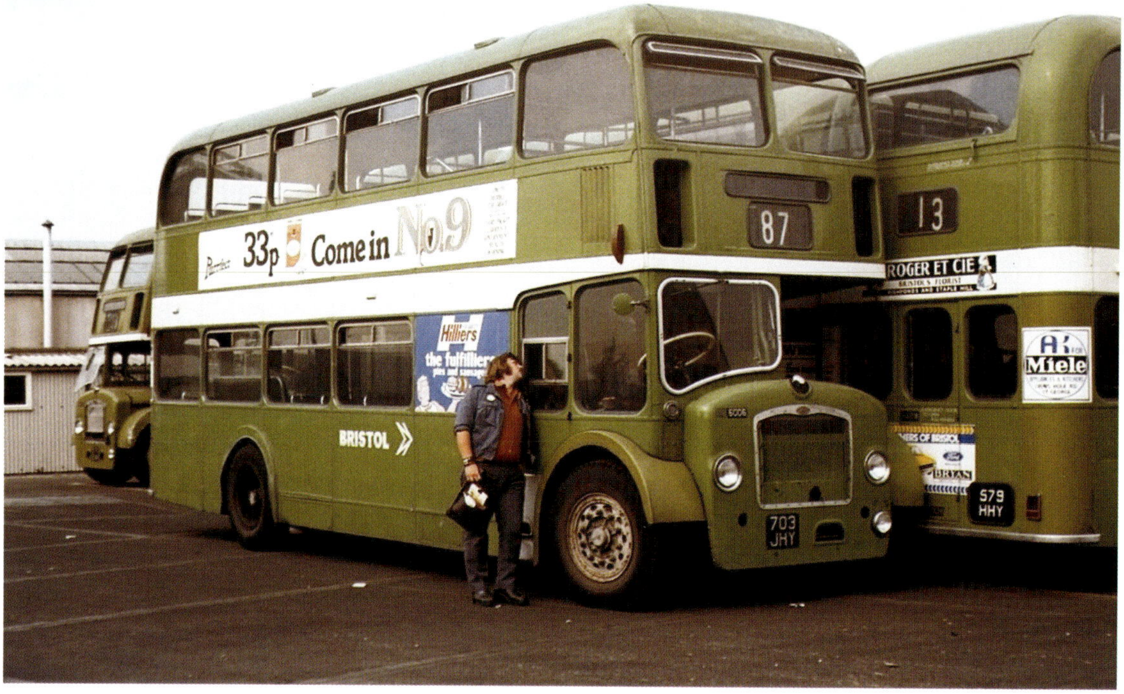

The severe Bristol City timetable service cuts made in June 1976 resulted in some withdrawn buses being reinstated for a few weeks from 1st July to cope with passenger loadings. Included in those chosen for such duties was 6006 (703 JHY) that had latterly been at Bath Depot but originally at Gloucester. It is seen here in withdrawn condition at Lawrence Hill Depot on Friday 27th August 1976 minus its destination blind which was a sure sign of the "death penalty". It was scrapped soon afterwards. Even in the mid 1970s smoking was acknowledged as harmful and the Black Cat No. 9 advert carries a government health warning. (Stephen Dowle)

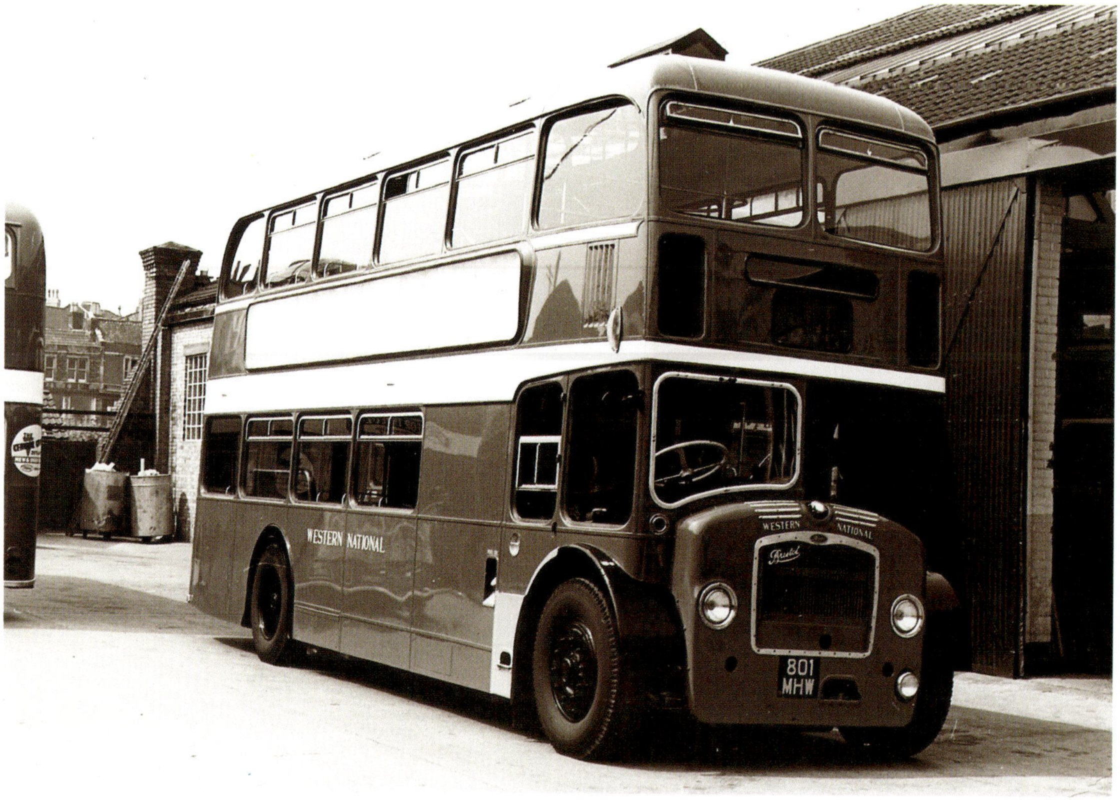

Looking as good as new with sparkling paintwork, Western National 1010 (801 MHW), ex Cheltenham District 6036, has yet to receive its new fleet number plates and is seen soon after repainting by Bristol Omnibus in June 1967. (Bristol Vintage Bus Group)

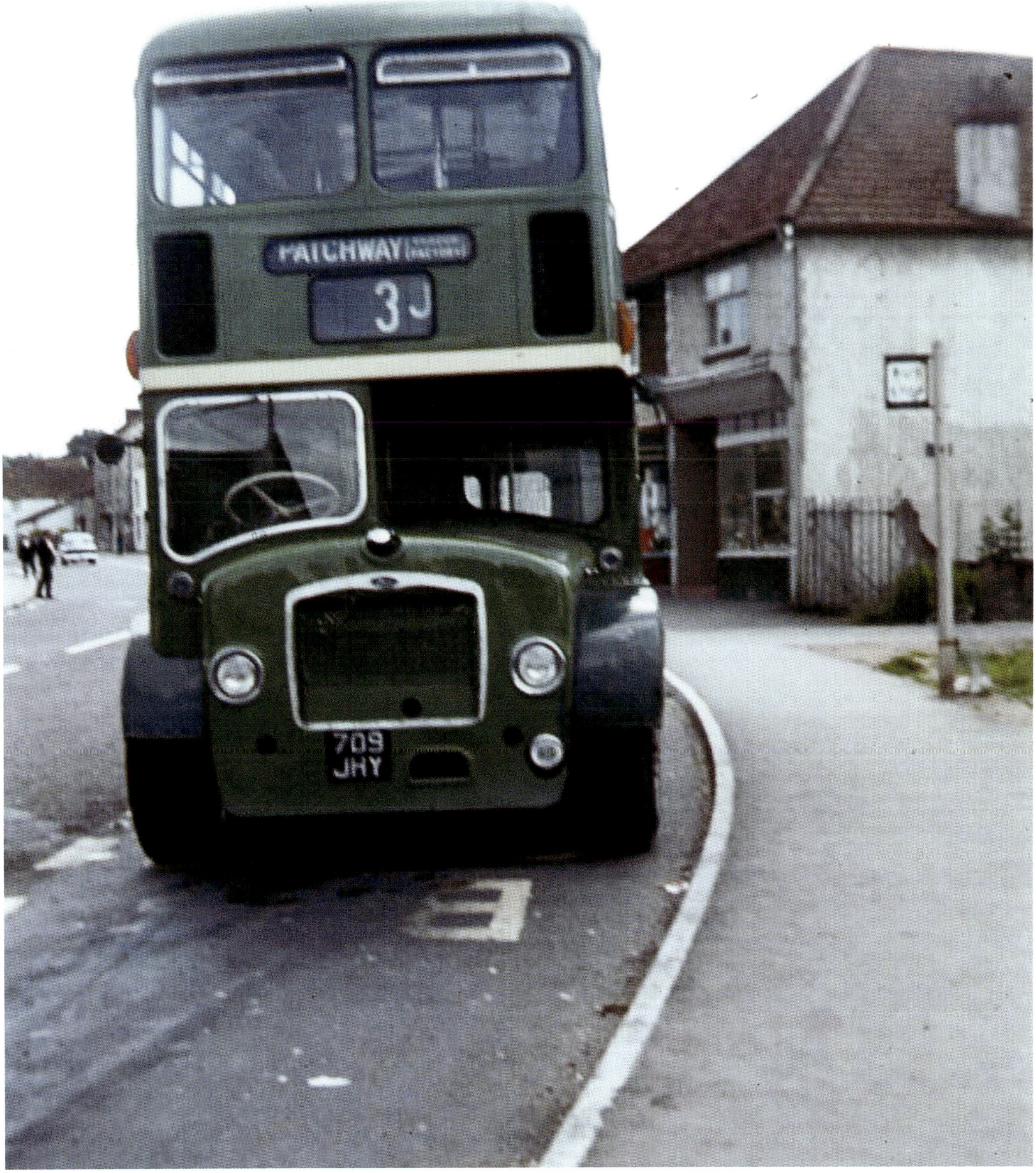

Whitchurch, just south of Bristol, is the location for C6010 (709 JHY) on 27th June 1971 prepared to operate an extended journey beyond the normal Service 3 terminus at Filton Church to Patchway (Shadow Factory) signified by the Service No. 3J. (Dr. Mike Walker)

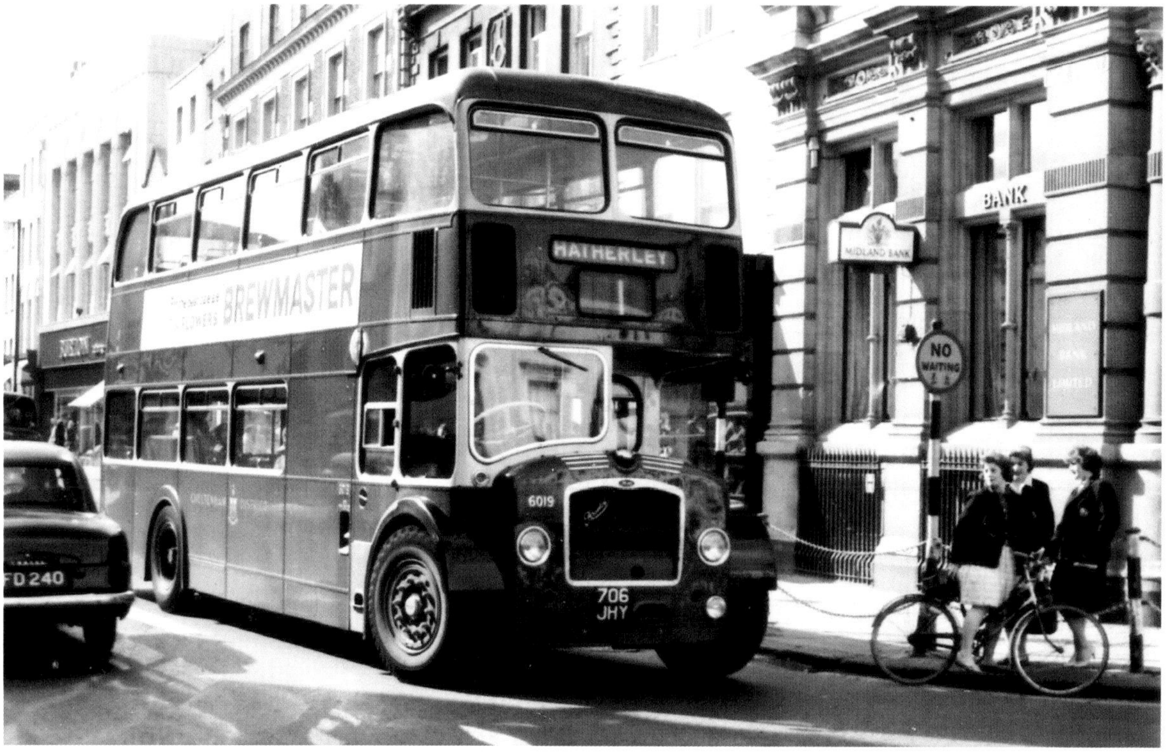

Clearly gaining the attention of some schoolgirls chatting outside the Midland Bank, now known as HSBC, Cheltenham District 6019 (706 JHY) turns off High Street when working a Service 1 journey to Hatherley. This bus was the highest numbered CDT vehicle when it was delivered as L100 in October 1960 but this fame was short-lived when it was renumbered into the main Bristol Omnibus fleet in March 1961. (Phil Sposito collection)

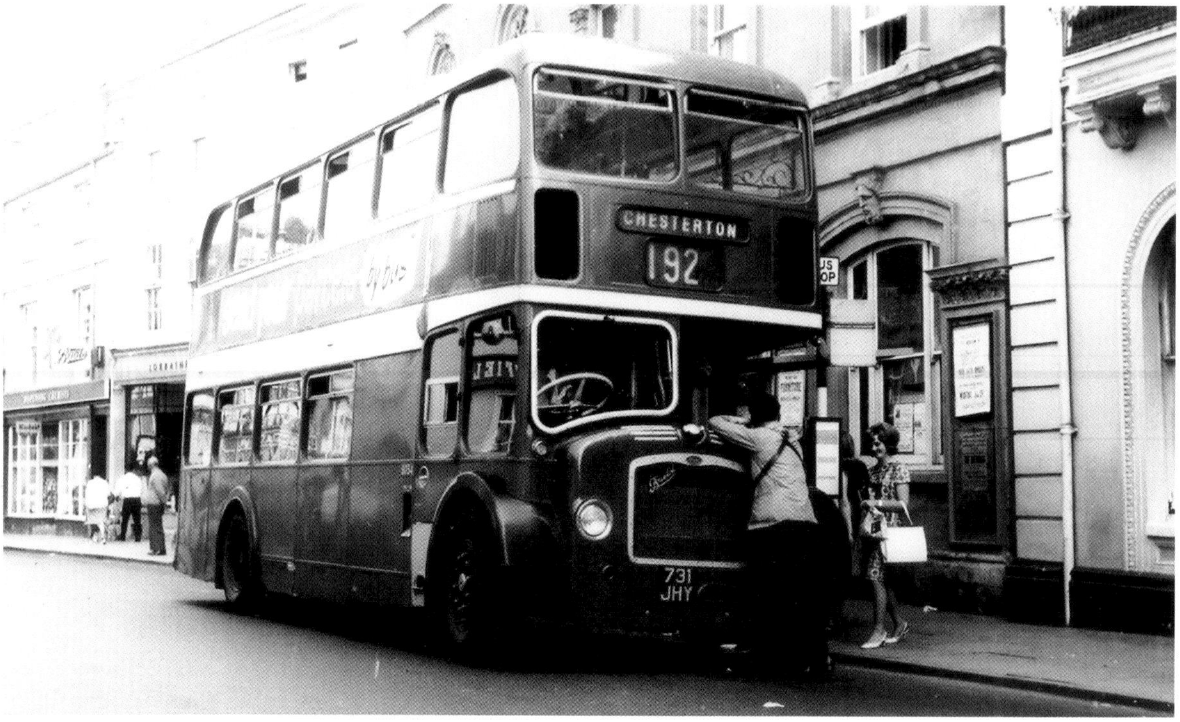

On 25th July 1964 the conductor of 6034 (731 JHY) chats to the driver over the bonnet of this 1961 FSF6G in Cirencester when it was working a journey to Chesterton on Service 192. This bus was one of a number sold by BOC to Western in August 1967 and worked for them until it was withdrawn from service in February 1978. It was then sold to the Royal Navy who re-registered it 21RN57 and it was used by them until it was again withdrawn in October 1982. It was known, however, to still be owned by the MOD in August 1983. (Robert F. Mack)

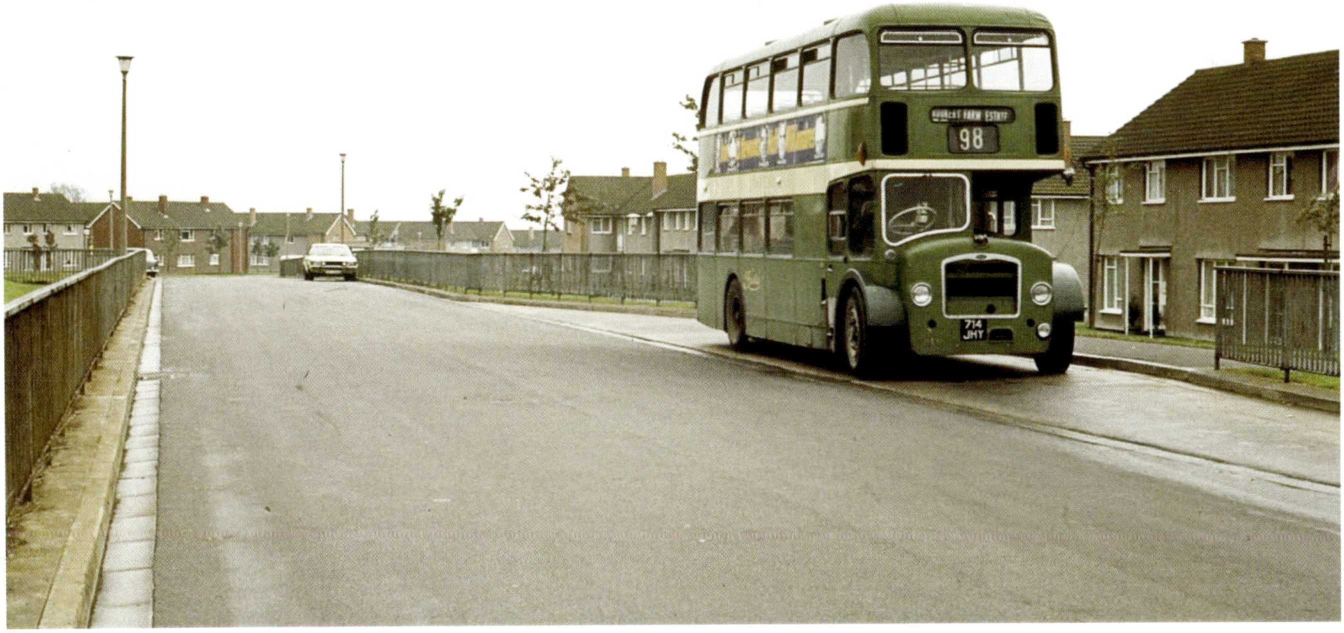

At Patchway Estate on a Service 98 journey to Rookery Farm Estate C6015 (714 JHY) waits in a bus lay-by at a quiet time of day judging by the volume of traffic on 6th October 1973. (Dr. Mike Walker)

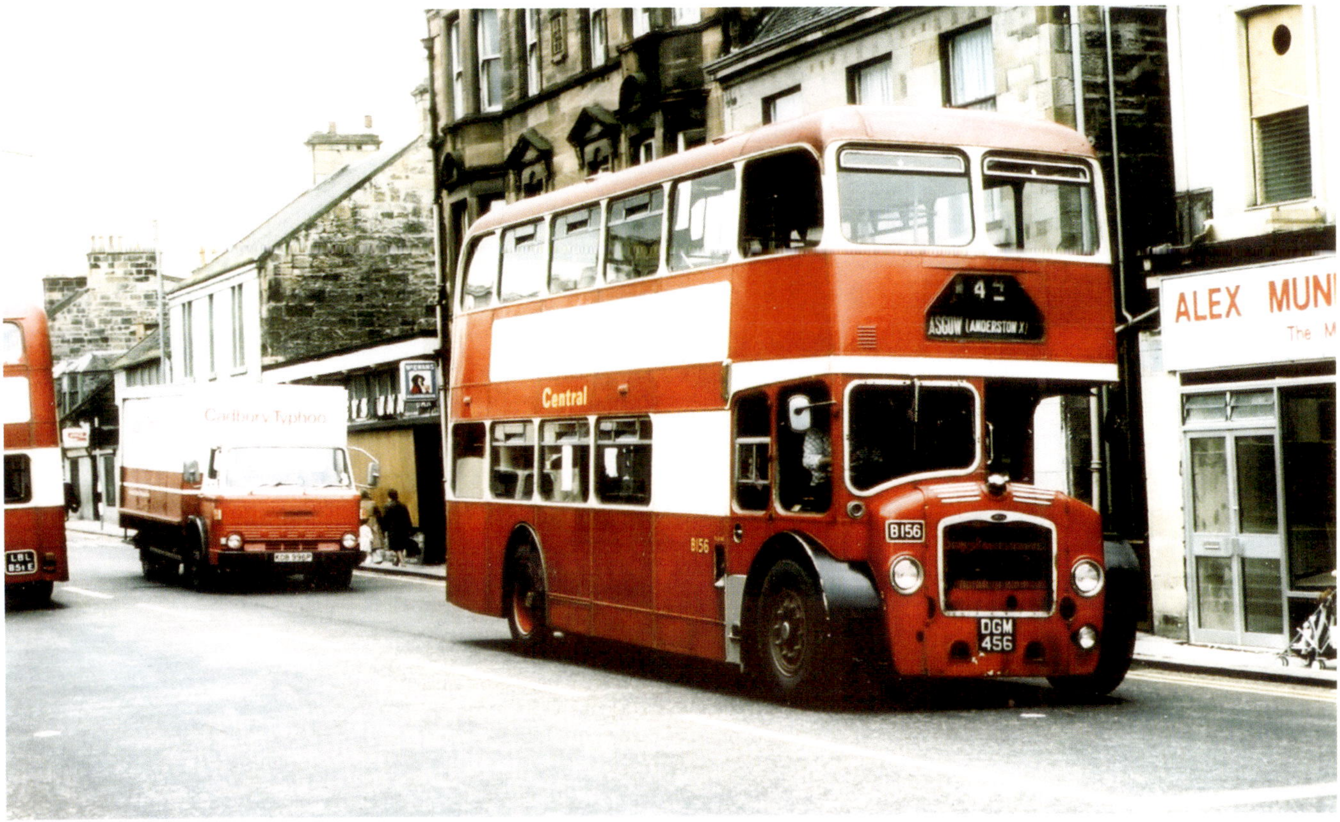

With the earlier radiator grille design Central SMT B156 (DGM 456) heads for Glasgow (Anderston Cross) on a Service 44 journey with a Cadbury Typhoo van in hot pursuit. (Tony Robbins collection)

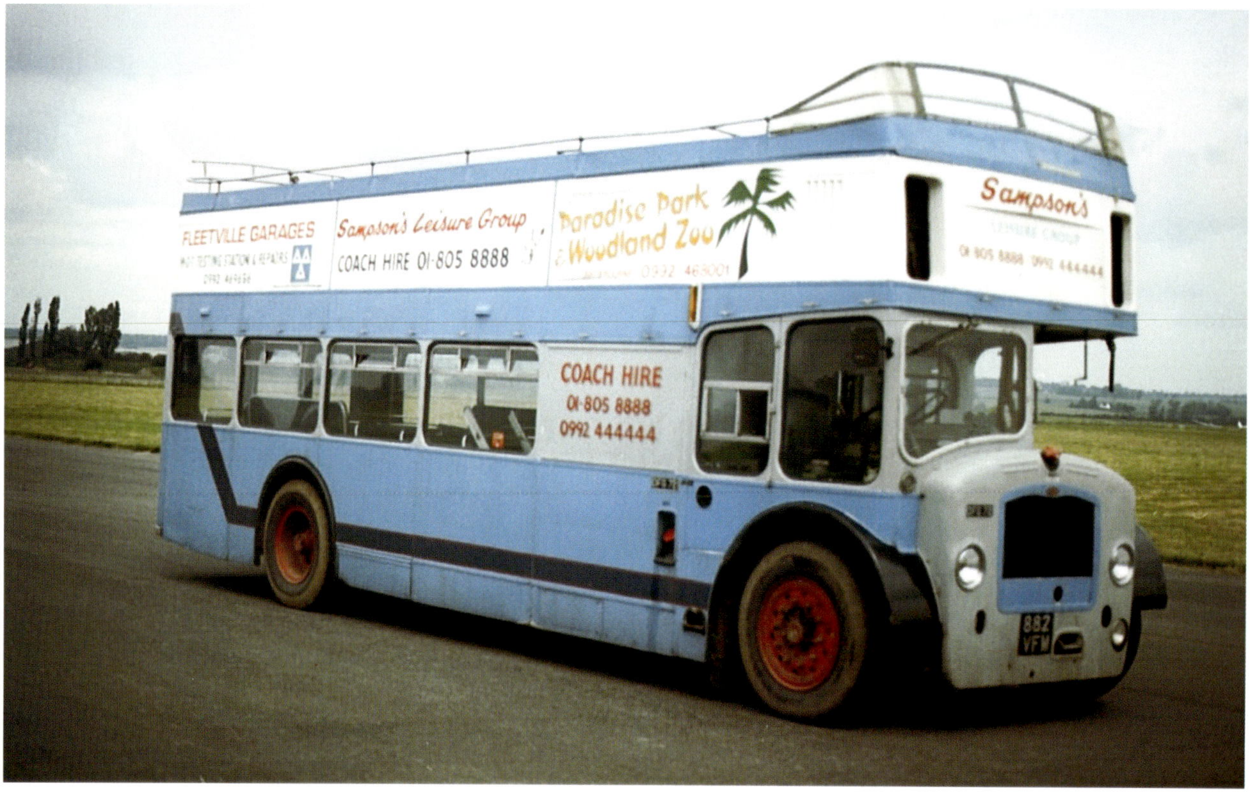

268 Sampsons 882 VFM carries evidence of its previous owner Crosville with the fleet number plate DFG72 still attached to the front at the North Weald Bus Rally on 28th June 1987. (Stephen Dowle)

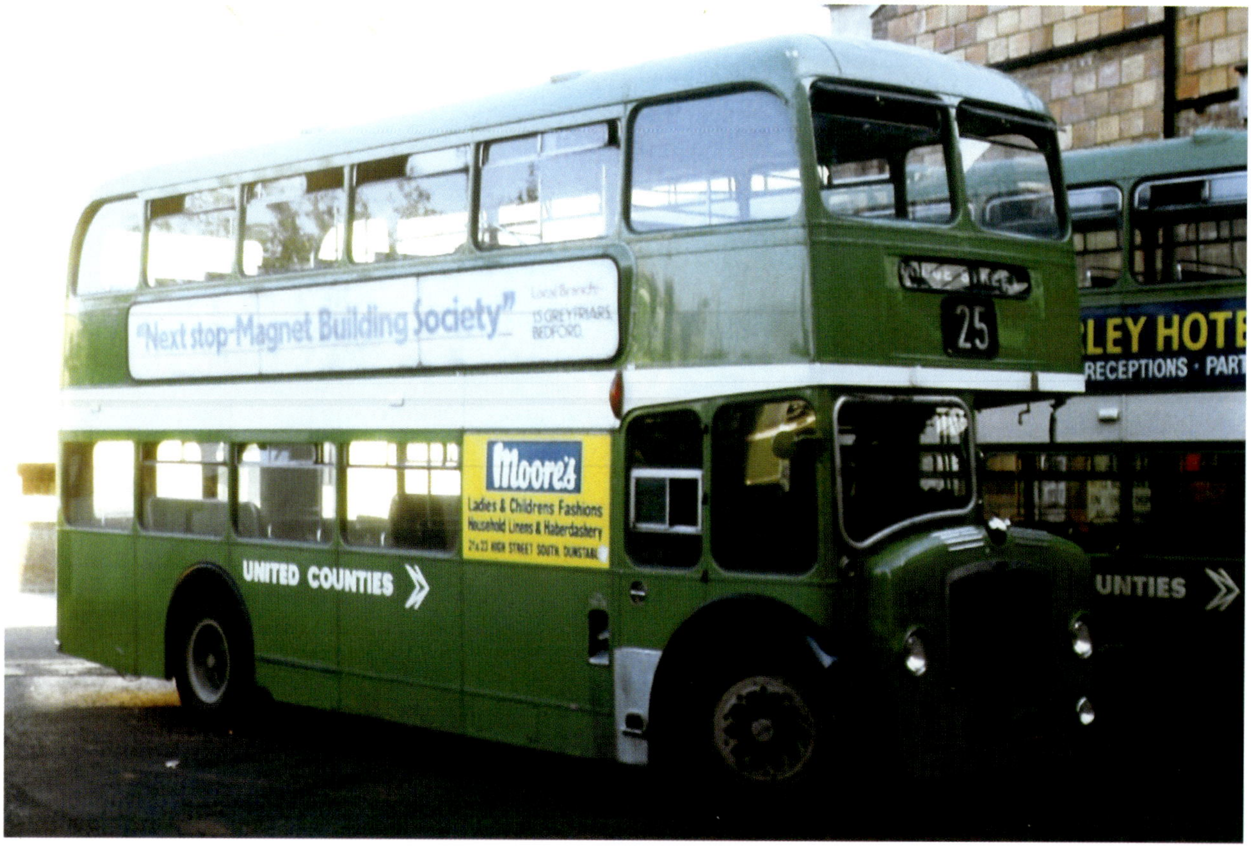

Looking good even in NBC livery, United Counties 593 (VAP 32) (one of three 1961 ex Southdown FSFs obtained), lasted the longest of them all, being purchased in December 1974 and withdrawn in August 1977 when it was scrapped. (Cliff Essex)

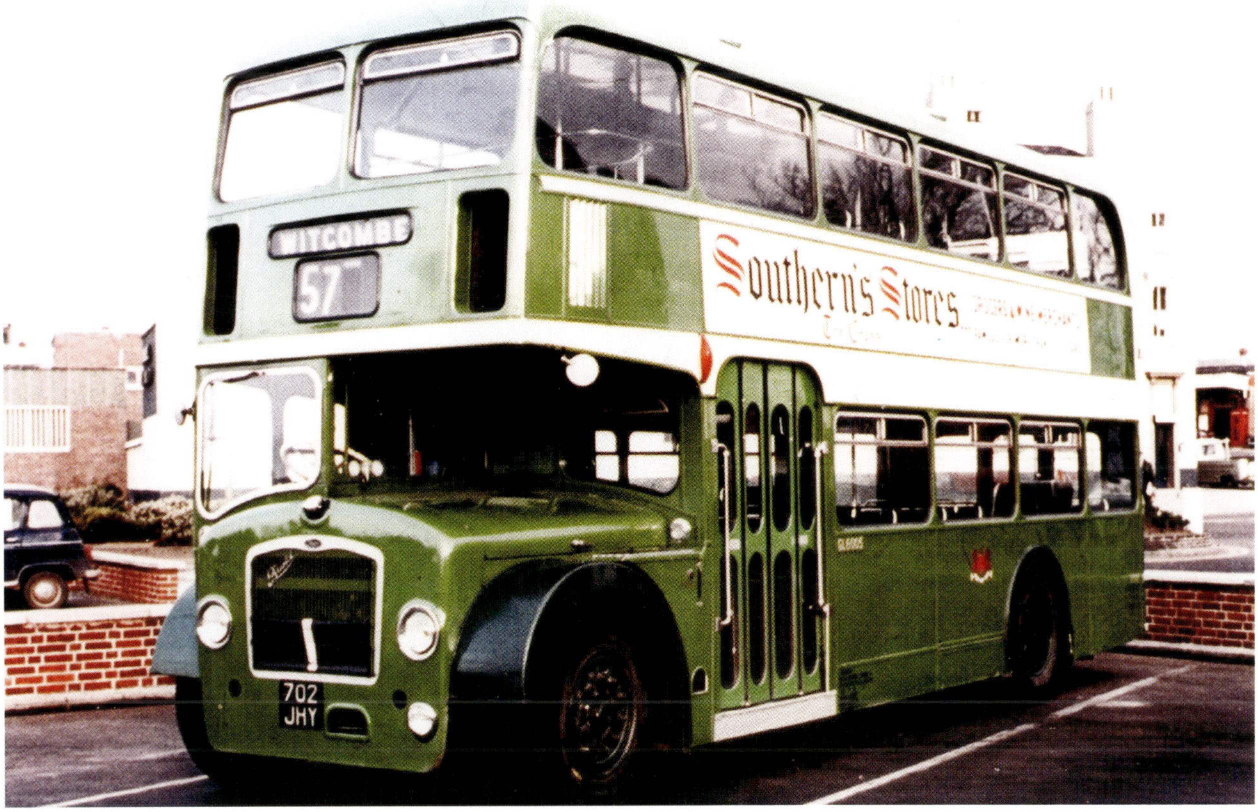

Occasionally Gloucester City buses were to be seen working on certain country journeys like GL6005 (702 JHY) waiting to operate to Witcombe on Service 57. (Bristol Vintage Bus Group)

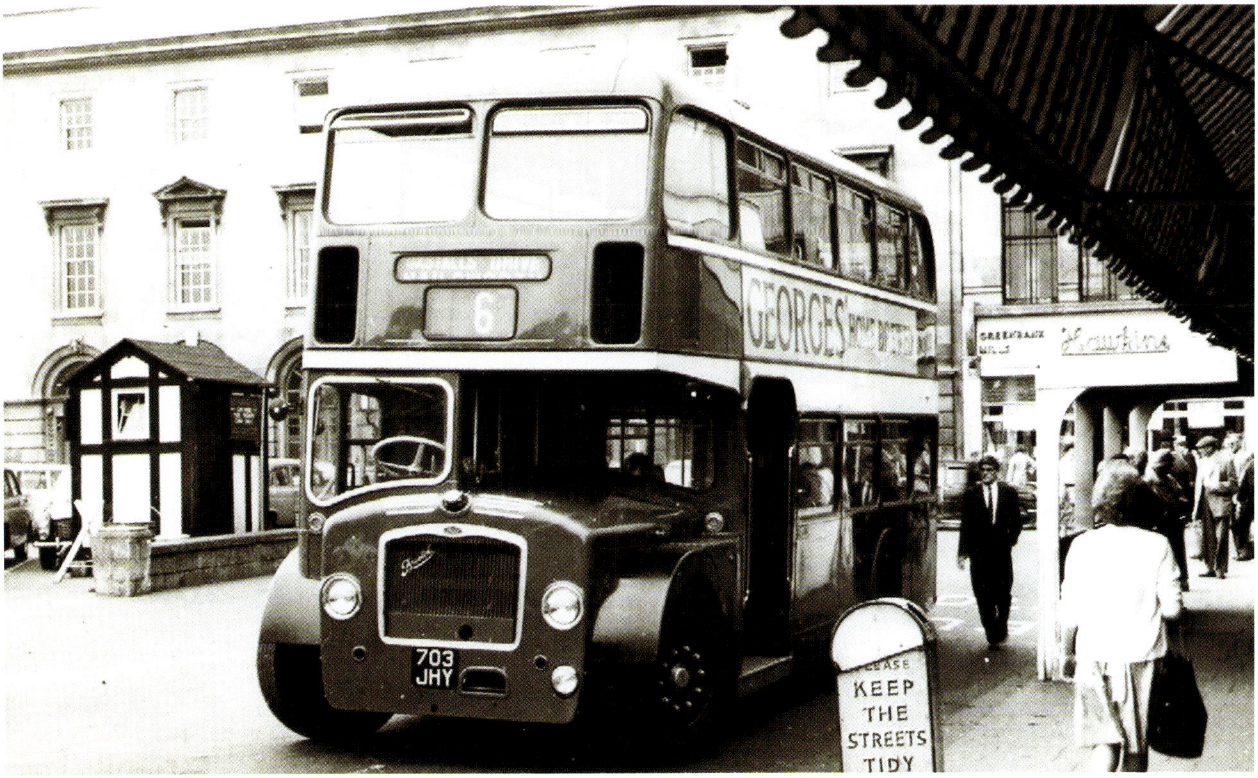

In a very 1960s period shot Gloucester GL8564 (703 JHY), an FSF6G, is seen soon after delivery in October 1960 working on Gloucester City Service 6 to Oxstalls Drive. It would be renumbered GL6006 in January 1961 and shows the high standard of skill required in producing good quality hand painted advertisements like Georges' Beers. (Steve Kelly)

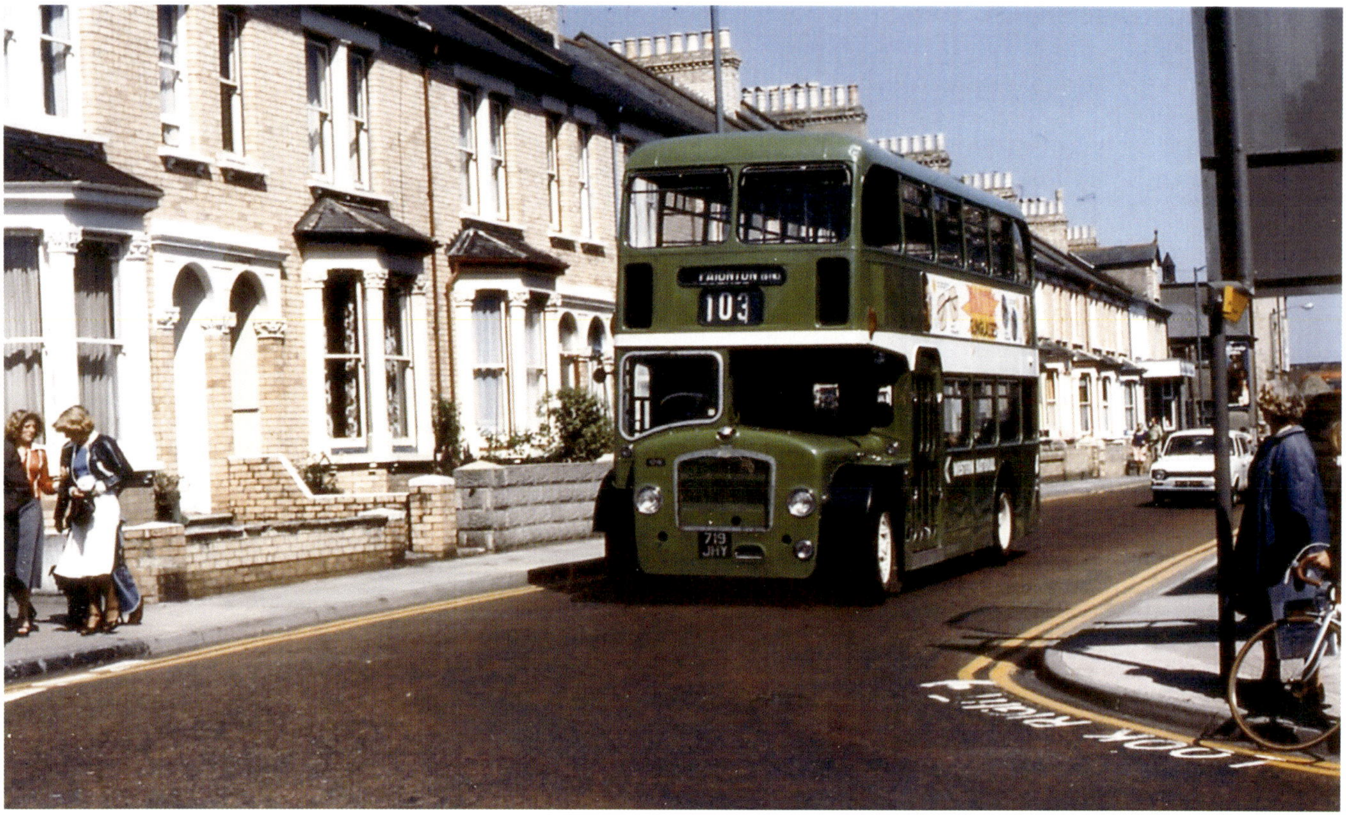

Making its way to Paignton Bus Station on Service 103, Western National 1018 (719 JHY) was new to Bristol Omnibus at Weston-super-Mare in February 1961 and was transferred to Bath Tramways Motor Company in February 1966. During August 1967 it was purchased by Southern National where it received fleet number 1018. It was transferred to the main Western National fleet in November 1969. (Author's collection)

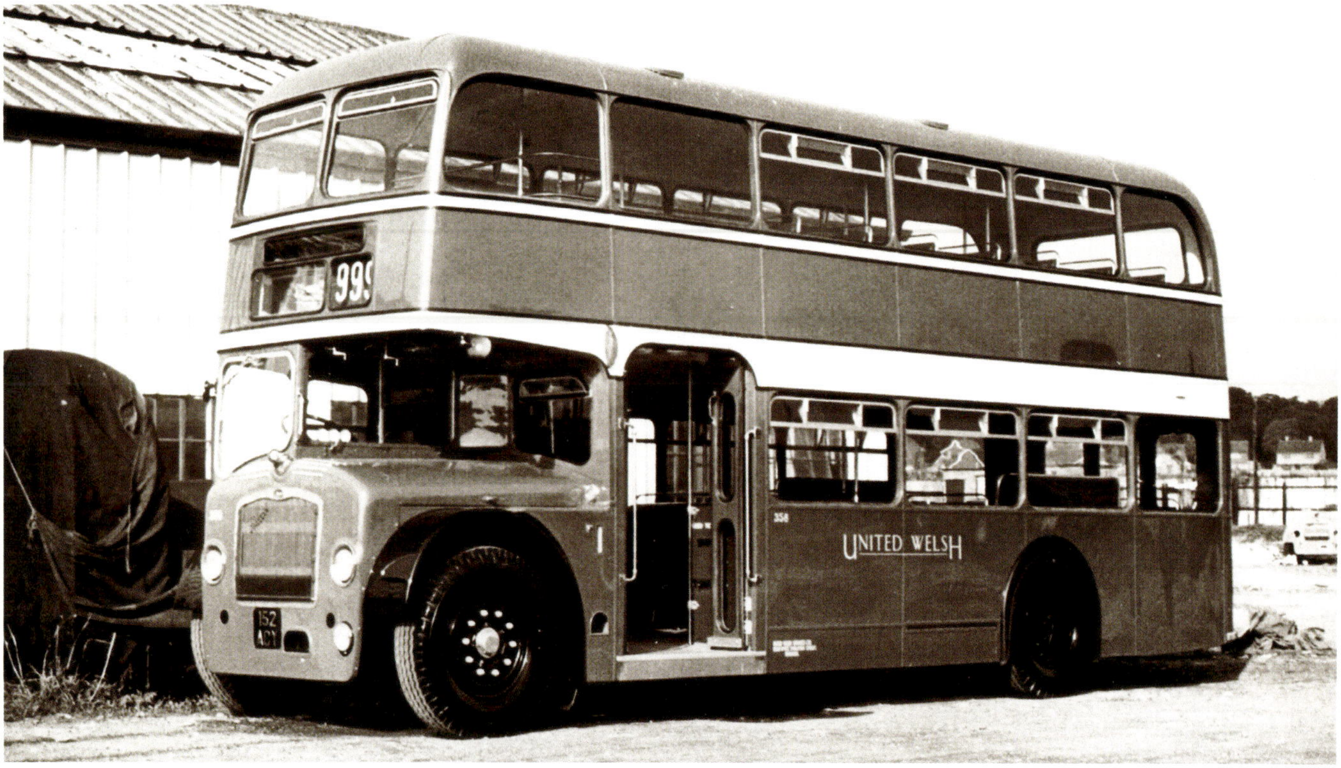

With glistening pristine bodywork and livery United Welsh 358 (152 ACY) is seen in November 1961 waiting for the fitting of destination blinds prior to entering revenue earning service with the company. (Robert F. Mack)

Operators

BATH SERVICES

As a born and bred "Bathonian" I am sure that readers will not mind me starting on "home ground" with the Bristol FSFs that carried Bath Services fleet names. Bath Electric Tramways Ltd. and Bath Tramways Motor Co Ltd. were both subsidiaries of Bristol Omnibus Co Ltd. but, generally, the vehicles owned by BET and BTM carried BATH SERVICES fleet names and staff could be easily identified by their Bath scroll uniform badges. There was a general pride in being considered as a separate entity from the main company and all vehicles based at Bath or Devizes were invariably well presented for duties. This extended to Trowbridge after the depot, bus station and services in West Wiltshire along with a number of vehicles, originally new to the Bristol companies, were taken over from Western National Omnibus Company Ltd. on 1st January 1970.

Bristol FSFs new to the Bath companies were:

Fleet No.	Registration No.	Date New	Additional Notes
L8566	707 JHY	November 1960 x	Renumbered L6008
L8567	708 JHY	November 1960 x	Renumbered L6009
6041	806 MHW	October 1961	

Transferred to Bath		Transfer Date	
6005	702 JHY	August 1971	from Gloucester
6006	703 JHY	April 1972	from Gloucester
6020	719 JHY	February 1966	from Weston-super-Mare
6021	720 JHY	February 1966	from Weston-super-Mare
6022	721 JHY	February 1966	from Weston-super-Mare*
6023	722 JHY	October 1973	from Towbridge
6024	726 JHY	January 1970 +	from Western National
6030	727 JHY	January 1970 +	from Western National
6031	728 JHY	January 1970 +	from Western National
6032	729 JHY	January 1970 +	from Western National
G6038	803 MHW	April 1972	from Gloucester as 6038
G6039	804 MHW	June 1972	from Gloucester as 6039
G6040	805 MHW	June 1972	from Gloucester as 6040

* Sold to Western National in 1967 but returned in 1970.

[X] Transferred to Bath Tramways Motor Company in December 1962.

The FSFs new to Bath were sold to Western National when that company wanted to order new FSFs for 1967 delivery. Bath vehicles were dispatched as follows:

L6008 in June 1967 became 1012 with Southern National but later repainted red and given Devon General fleet names in November 1976 and, it is believed, received internal blue painted panels in Devon General style.

L6009 in August 1967 became Southern National 1013 and later given livery treatment to DG style similar to L6008.

6041 in August 1967 becoming Western National 1009.

Other Bristol FSFs were transferred in at times to operate Bath based services from Weston-super-Mare or Gloucester. After the transfer of Western National vehicles to Bristol Omnibus in 1970 shown with '+' moved to Bath from Trowbridge between January 1971 and October 1973.

BRIGHTON HOVE & DISTRICT

All of the fifteen Bristol FSFs purchased by Brighton Hove & District were powered with Bristol rather than the more popular Gardner engines, fitted with distinctive Beetonson "Rapide Type W" ventilators and louvres that gave a square appearance to windows some of which had cream window rubbers.

Bristol FSFs new to the Brighton Hove & District company were:

Fleet No.	Registration No.	Date New	Additional Notes
26	TPN 26	January 1961	Became Southdown 2026
27	TPN 27	January 1961	Became Southdown 2027
28	UAP 28	February 1961	Became Southdown 2028
29	UAP 29	February 1961	Became Southdown 2029
30	UAP 30	February 1961	Became Southdown 2030
31	VAP 31	July 1961	Became Southdown 2031
32	VAP 32	July 1961	Became Southdown 2032
33	VAP 33	July 1961	Became Southdown 2033
34	VAP 34	July 1961	Became Southdown 2034
35	VAP 35	July 1961	Became Southdown 2035
36	WNJ 36	March 1962	Became Southdown 2036
37	WNJ 37	March 1962	Became Southdown 2037
38	WNJ 38	April 1962	Became Southdown 2038
39	WNJ 39	April 1962	Became Southdown 2039
40	WNJ 40	April 1962	Became Southdown 2040

All of these vehicles were transferred to Southdown Motor Services upon the creation of the National Bus Company on 1st January 1969 and the merger of Southdown Motor Services and Brighton Hove & District Omnibus Company. After almost 35 years the separate operation and identity of Brighton Hove & District ceased with all vehicles eventually receiving NBC logos on the leaf green livery and Southdown fleet names.

The company had been unique among Tilling transport companies being the only one to operate trolleybuses with a planned introduction on 1st May 1939 but these vehicles were stored for the duration of the war at the company's Whitehawk Depot and brought into service in 1945. Trolleybus and motorbus services in Brighton, Hove, Portslade, Rottingdean and Southwick formed a joint operating area from 1st April 1939 involving Brighton Corporation and Brighton Hove & District that also included Southdown Motor Services from 1st January 1961. From that date BH&D buses, including the FSFs, could be seen working "on hire" to Southdown. Trolleybus operation by BH&D ended on 24th March 1959, resulting in the company placing its first order for Bristol Lodekkas particularly as production of the Bristol KSW had now ceased.

BRISTOL OMNIBUS (BRISTOL JOINT SEVICES)

Between the implementation of the Bristol Transport Act 1937 and the ending of this agreement in July 1978 the Bristol City Services were operated by Bristol Omnibus Company in accordance with the terms and conditions of the Act. The Joint Transport Committee consisted of officials from both the bus company and Bristol Corporation with all Bristol Joint Services buses being equally owned by both parties with any profit or loss being shared by half the total. Vehicles operating under these arrangements were denoted by the letter "C" prefix being allocated to the fleet number.

All of the Bristol FSFs allocated to the City fleet were FSF6Bs as follows:

Fleet No.	Registration No.	Date New	Additional Notes
LC8568	709 JHY	November 1960	Renumbered LC6010*
LC8569	710 JHY	November 1960	Renumbered LC6011*
LC8570	711 JHY	November 1960	Renumbered LC6012*
LC8571	712 JHY	November 1960	Renumbered LC6013*
LC8572	713 JHY	November 1960	Renumbered LC6014*
LC8573	714 JHY	November 1960	Renumbered LC6015*
LC8574	715 JHY	November 1960	Renumbered LC6016*
LC8575	716 JHY	November 1960	Renumbered LC6017*
C6025	717 JHY	February 1961	
C6026	718 JHY	February 1961	
C6027	723 JHY	February 1961	
C6028	724 JHY	February 1961	
C6029	725 JHY	February 1961	

* Renumbered in January 1961 and again losing the L prefix between November 1967 and March 1968 to become C6010 to C6017.

Nos. C6014–C6017 (713 JHY–716 JHY) were standard H34/26F but in 1965 equipped with additional luggage space in the lower deck immediately behind the luggage space under the stairs especially for the Bristol Temple Meads to Clifton Zoo services. This resulted in the loss of two seats.

Bristol FSFs were to be found at all Bristol City depots at times including Hanham where there was a mix of City and Country services work. Only a four track service number box was carried on the rear of these buses but a standard "T type" destination box was carried at the front. In order that passengers could identify "short workings" on routes a series of letters were used to identify these.

In the Bristol City Services timetable dated 14th January 1967 until further notice the following was included after the list of services:

1. Cross City Routes with journeys terminating in the Central Area.
The service number is followed by the letter "C" if the journey terminates in the Central Area (Centre, Horsefair or Old Market) on what is normally a cross-city route.

2. Regular Short Workings were listed as:

Service	Journey	Letter
3	New Fosseway Road from Filton	A
4 & 4A	Staple Hill from Knowle West	B
7	Southmead (Lanercost Road) from Hartcliffe	B
9	Ashton Gate from Hanham	A
11	Fishponds from Hengrove or East Dundry Road	A
11	Hengrove from Oldbury Court or Fishponds	B
15	Westbury from Hotwells	A
19	Glenside Hospital from Ashton Vale	A
21	Melvin Square from Lockleaze or Ashley Down	A
21	Ashley Down rom Knowle West	A
36	Knowle (Red Lion) from Patchway	A

3. Extensions to B.A.C Factories beyond Filton on Services 3, 5, 6, 12, 16, 89, 90 carry the following letter after the service number:

Rodney Works	F
Patchway Bus Park	H
Patchway Shadow Factory	J

4. Extensions to Chittening Trading Estate beyond Avonmouth on Services 28, 28B, 99 will show the following:

Smelting Works via Sea Mills	28F
Smelting Works via Coombe Dale	28H
Severn Road via Sea Mills	28J
Severn Road via Coombe Dale	28K
Smelting Works via Old Market and Centre	99F
Severn Road via Old Market and Centre	99J

Journeys operating beyond Avonmouth on Services 27 and 94 carry the following letters after the service number:

Smelting Works	F
Severn Road	J

5. Extension to Brislington Trading Estate on Service 16 will operate as 16A.

6. Other Short Workings.
Buses operating other short journeys other than to points specified above will carry the letter "L" after the service number to indicate they are of a local nature. Conductors on such journeys will give every assistance in calling out the destination.

BRISTOL OMNIBUS (BRISTOL COUNTRY)

Other than Bath City, Cheltenham Town, Gloucester City and Bristol City services all other routes were operated as "country area" services. This arrangement included Weston-super-Mare Town, Swindon Local or services operated jointly with Swindon Corporation, Stroud and Cirencester Town services.

When Western National and Southern National required front entrance 60 seat double deckers with Gardner engines they were informed by Bristol Commercial Vehicles that the FSF model had been withdrawn from those available to operators. It was Bristol Omnibus Company that answered their request by offering all "country area" FSFs. All of the Bristol FSFs allocated to the Bristol City fleet were jointly owned with Bristol Corporation and were equipped with Bristol engines anyway. Gloucester City Services were operated jointly by Gloucester Corporation and Bristol Omnibus with joint ownership of buses carrying the "G" prefix to fleet numbers. The timetables that were operated by Cheltenham District as Cheltenham Town Services were not subject to any joint operation agreements and were the sole responsibility of Bristol Omnibus Company even though the buses operating these services were finished in a completely different livery.

The depots involved in the transfer of vehicles from the Bristol Omnibus constituent companies were the "country" sector garages including Bath, Cheltenham, Gloucester, Stroud, Bristol (Marlborough Street), Swindon and Hanham although Hanham operated both city and country services.

During the 1960s when the Bristol FSF buses entered service there was strict accounting of service buses from one fleet being used by another to operate services. Mileage and associated costs were allocated from one company to another with accuracy being essential. This even occurred when a bus allocated to Bath Electric Tramways Limited was used on a Bath Tramways Motor Company service or a Bristol Omnibus "general" fleet vehicle worked any journey on Bristol City services governed by the Bristol Joint Services agreement.

When the Bristol Joint Services agreement was terminated in July 1978 and Bristol Omnibus Company then became the sole owner of all buses in the fleet the practice of transferring mileage and other costs was no longer necessary. Former BJS vehicles could then be found operating country area services and likewise "country" buses were to be found operating on Bristol City services.

CENTRAL SMT

Central SMT was the only Scottish Bus Group company to order Bristol FSFs and these were delivered between February 1961 and September 1963 and notably included the last FSF built. With a total of 48 vehicles this was the highest number of FSFs ordered by any individual bus company and all were fitted with Gardner engines.

Fleet No.	Registration No.	Date New	Additional Notes
B116	CGM 116	February 1961	
B117	CGM 117	March 1961	
B118	CGM 118	February 1961	
B119	CGM 119	March 1961	
B120	CGM 120	March 1961	
B121	CGM 121	March 1961	
B122	CGM 122	March 1961	
B130	DGM 430	March 1962	To Eastern Scottish July 1977*
B131	DGM 431	March 1962	
B132	DGM 432	March 1962	
B133	DGM 433	March 1962	
B134	DGM 434	March 1962	
B135	DGM 435	March 1962	
B136	DGM 436	March 1962	
B137	DGM 437	March 1962	To Eastern Scottish July 1977*
B138	DGM 438	March 1962	To Eastern Scottish July 1977*
B139	DGM 439	March 1962	
B140	DGM 440	March 1962	
B141	DGM 441	March 1962	To Eastern Scottish July 1977*
B142	DGM 442	March 1962	
B143	DGM 443	March 1962	
B144	DGM 444	March 1962	To Eastern Scottish July 1977*
B145	DGM 445	April 1962	
B146	DGM 446	April 1962	
B147	DGM 447	April 1962	
B148	DGM 448	April 1962	To Eastern Scottish July 1977*
B149	DGM 449	April 1962	
B150	DGM 450	April 1962	
B151	DGM 451	April 1962	
B152	DGM 452	April 1962	
B153	DGM 453	April 1962	

* Numbered AA430–AA438 respectively and withdrawn from service in February 1979 (AA441); March 1979 (AA430); July 1979 (AA448); October 1978 (AA437 and AA438) and October 1979 (AA444).

CENTRAL SMT

Fleet No.	Registration No.	Date New	Additional Notes
B154	DGM 454	April 1962	
B155	DGM 455	April 1962	
B156	DGM 456	April 1962	
B157	DGM 457	April 1962	
B158	DGM 458	April 1962	
B159	DGM 459	April 1962	
B160	FGM 160	September 1963	
B161	FGM 161	September 1963	
B162	FGM 162	September 1963	
B163	FGM 163	September 1963	
B164	FGM 164	September 1963	
B165	FGM 165	September 1963	
B166	FGM 166	September 1963	
B167	FGM 167	September 1963	
B168	FGM 168	September 1963	
B169	FGM 169	September 1963	
B170	FGM 170	September 1963	
B157	DGM 457	April 1962	
B158	DGM 458	April 1962	
B159	DGM 459	April 1962	
B160	FGM 160	September 1963	
B161	FGM 161	September 1963	
B162	FGM 162	September 1963	
B163	FGM 163	September 1963	
B164	FGM 164	September 1963	
B165	FGM 165	September 1963	
B166	FGM 166	September 1963	
B167	FGM 167	September 1963	
B168	FGM 168	September 1963	
B169	FGM 169	September 1963	
B170	FGM 170	September 1963	

CHELTENHAM DISTRICT TRACTION COMPANY

All other subsidiary companies in the Bristol Omnibus group carried the Tilling green and cream livery but Cheltenham District vehicles intended to operate the Cheltenham Town Services were painted maroon and cream. This distinction continued into the National Bus Company era with CDT vehicles painted in NBC poppy red and white whilst the remainder of the Bristol Omnibus Company fleet were painted in the NBC leaf green and white livery.

Four FSF6G buses were added to the Cheltenham District fleet as listed below:

Fleet No.	Registration No.	Date New	Additional Notes
L99	705 JHY	November 1960	Renumbered 6018
L100	706 JHY	November 1960	Renumbered 6019
6036	801 MHW	October 1961	Offside illuminated advert
6037	802 MHW	October 1961	Offside illuminated advert

L99 was renumbered on 26th March 1961.

L100 was the highest fleet number allocated in the Cheltenham District numbering series before all vehicles were renumbered into the main Bristol Omnibus fleet numbering scheme.

6018 and 6019 were sold to Southern National in May 1967 with 6036 and 6037 going to Western National in June 1967 after the delivery of the first Bristol RELL6Ls allocated to Cheltenham depot 1000–1003 (KHW 306E–KHW 309E). The RELL single deckers arrived in Cheltenham in June 1967 and were initially operated on the Cheltenham Town Services network as crew vehicles with conductors. The RELLs seated 53 passengers – only seven passengers less than the FSF double deckers that they were replacing.

The FSFs were numbered 1014, 1015, 1010 and 1011 respectively by Southern and Western National. Initially retaining their full rear destination display equipment the destination aperture invariably merely showed "WESTERN NATIONAL", "SOUTHERN NATIONAL" or "SERVICE NO." after being fitted with the via blind transferred from other vehicles.

CROSVILLE MOTOR SERVICES

A total of 30 Bristol FSFs were delivered to Crosville Motor Services Ltd between October 1961 and June 1962 and were powered by both Bristol and Gardner engines.

Deliveries of new Bristol FSFs to Crosville identified as DFB for those with Bristol engines and DFG for those equipped with Gardner engines were:

Fleet No.	Registration No.	Date New	Additional Notes
DFB54	864 VFM	October 1961	
DFB55	865 VFM	October 1961	
DFB56	866 VFM	November 1961	
DFB57	867 VFM	May 1962	
DFB58	868 VFM	May 1962	
DFG59	869 VFM	November 1961	
DFG60	870 VFM	November 1961	
DFG61	871 VFM	November 1961	
DFG62	872 VFM	November 1961	
DFG63	873 VFM	November 1961	
DFG64	874 VFM	November 1961	
DFG65	875 VFM	January 1962	
DFG66	876 VFM	January 1962	
DFG67	877 VFM	January 1962	
DFG68	878 VFM	February 1962	Converted to open top
DFG69	879 VFM	March 1962	
DFG70	880 VFM	March 1962	
DFG71	881 VFM	March 1962	
DFG72	882 VFM	March 1962	Converted to open top
DFG73	883 VFM	April 1962	
DFG74	884 VFM	April 1962	
DFG75	885 VFM	June 1962	
DFG76	886 VFM	June 1962	
DFG77	887 VFM	June 1962	
DFG78	888 VFM	June 1962	
DFG79	889 VFM	June 1962	
DFG80	890 VFM	June 1962	
DFG81	891 VFM	June 1962	Converted to open top
DFG82	892 VFM	June 1962	
DFG83	893 VFM	June 1962	

A number of these vehicles, indicated above, were converted to operate as permanent open top buses. DFG68 and DFG81 were rebuilt in February 1977 with DFG72 dealt with in April 1979 and painted white with red NBC style CROSVILLE fleet names for numerous seafront services.

CUMBERLAND MOTOR SERVICES

Registered in 1921 Cumberland Motor Services Ltd was a major operator providing bus services in the former Cumberland region of north-west England that now forms part of today's Cumbria. Initially the fleet was dominated by Leyland vehicles and it was only when the Lodekka was introduced in the mid-1950s that Bristol buses first appeared in the Cumberland Motor Services fleet. Just five Bristol FSFs were delivered to the company and were all supplied with Bristol engines. These were to be seen working on most of the services operated by double deckers and more often than not on the Whitehaven Town Services. Below is the list of buses built for the company with their delivery dates.

Fleet No.	Registration No.	Date New	Additional Notes
C404	501 BRM	October 1960	Renumbered 500
C405	502 BRM	October 1960	Renumbered 501
C406	503 BRM	October 1960	Renumbered 502
407	504 BRM	November 1960	Renumbered 503
408	505 BRM	November 1960	Renumbered 504

The C prefix indicated indicates allocation to Carlisle City services.

DURHAM DISTRICT SERVICES

Using operating depots at Durham, Darlington, Sunderland, Barnard Castle, Ferryhill, Sedgefield and also using the United Automobile Services Depot in Middlesbrough Durham District Services Ltd. was formed in August 1950 by amalgamating Express Omnibus Company (Durham) Ltd.; Gilesgate Moor Garage of Durham; Darlington Triumph Services Ltd. and ABC Motors of Ferryhill. The company was controlled by the management team of United Auto and an extremely varied fleet was inherited including Leyland, Dennis, AEC and Guy vehicles. Two fleet names were in use throughout the existence of the company with either Durham District or Durham District Services being the alternatives. The five Bristol FSFs with Bristol engines were delivered in 1962 and were all transferred to the main United fleet in August 1968 with the merger of the two companies.

Fleet No.	Registration No.	Date New	Additional Notes*
DBL9	8109 HN	September 1962	289
DBL10	8110 HN	September 1962	290
DB11	8111 HN	September 1962	291
DBL12	8112 HN	October 1962	292
DBL13	8113 HN	October 1962	293

* Fleet numbers as at January 1969 with United.

Letter B for Bristol chassis removed from November 1964.

GLOUCESTER CITY SERVICES

Between the opening of the 9 ¾ mile electric tramway system on 7th May 1904 and its closure on 12th January 1933 the replacement bus services were the sole responsibility of Gloucester Corporation. On 12th June 1936, however, all vehicles in the Corporation fleet were transferred to the Bristol Tramways & Carriage Company and from that date all services were leased by Gloucester Corporation to the company. Responsibility for vehicles and its crews was also transferred to the company on that date but the routes followed by those services and timetables operated in agreement by the company and members of the transport committee of Gloucester Corporation. The buses that were used to operate the Gloucester City Services continued to carry the city crest and were identified by the prefix letter "G" allocated before the fleet number from 1959.

A total of six FSF6G buses were new to the Gloucester City fleet as listed below:

Fleet No.	Registration No.	Date New	Additional Notes
GL8562	701 JHY	October 1960	Renumbered GL6004
GL8563	702 JHY	October 1960	Renumbered GL6005
GL8564	703 JHY	October 1960	Renumbered GL6006
G6038	803 MHW	October 1961	Offside illuminated advert
G6039	804 MHW	October 1961	Offside illuminated advert
G6040	805 MHW	October 1961	Offside illuminated advert

GL8562–GL8564 were renumbered in January 1961.

GL6004 was sold to Southern National in August 1967 taking fleet number 1016.

In March 1968 GL6005 and GL6006 were renumbered G6005 and G6006 and then lost the G prefixes in January 1971 when transferred to the Bristol Country sector. 6005 and 6006 were sold to Paul Sykes, a Barnsley dealer, in August and October 1976 with 6005 passing to Wiltshire Area Health Authority for use on the staff and patient service operated daily, including Christmas Day, between Salisbury Infirmary at Fisherton Street and Odstock Hospital. GL6004 went to Yorkshire dealer, W North at Sherburn-in-Elmet, in August 1978.

G6038 lost the G prefix in April 1972 when it was transferred to Bath with G6039 and G6040 following in June 1972. 6039 was withdrawn in 1976 and sold to Paul Sykes in January 1977 for scrap. Both 6038 and 6040 were also sold to Paul Sykes in August 1977 quickly passing to British Double Deckers, a dealer based in Wotton-under-Edge in August 1977. These vehicles were exported to the British Double Deckers operating company based in Denver, Colorado in the United States of America during the following month. Former 6038 was later seen working in October 1985 at Atlanta in Georgia.

MANSFIELD DISTRICT TRACTION COMPANY

With a total of ten Bristol FSFs delivered new to the company these represented a significant proportion of the Mansfield District fleet. The fleets of Mansfield District, Midland General Omnibus Company Ltd. and the buses operated by Nottinghamshire & Derbyshire Traction Company were run as separate entities but were treated as a single company in certain ways that included a common fleet numbering system from the mid 1960s. The depot for Mansfield District vehicles was situated at Sutton Road in Mansfield and buses wore a livery of green and white.

Fleet No.	Registration No.	Date New	Additional Notes
535	51 JAL	February 1962	To Midland General in May 1968 and with Trent as 667 October 1976–October 1979
536	52 JAL	February 1962	To Midland General in May 1968 and with Trent as 668 October 1976–December 1977
537	53 JAL	February 1962	To Midland General in May 1968 and with Trent as 669 October 1976–December 1977
538	54 JAL	February 1962	To Midland General in May 1968 and with Trent as 670 October 1976–July 1977
539	55 JAL	March 1962	To Midland General in May 1968 and with Trent as 676 October 1976–July 1977
540	56 JAL	March 1962	To Midland General in May 1968 and with Trent as 667 October 1976–October 1977
541	57 JAL	March 1962	To Midland General in May 1968 and with Trent as 678 October 1976–July 1977
542	58 JAL	June 1962	To Midland General in August 1968 and with Trent as 679 October 1976–December 1977
543	59 JAL	June 1962	To Midland General in August 1968 and with Trent as 680 October 1976–December 1977
544	60 JAL	June 1962	To Midland General in August 1968 and with Trent as 681 October 1976–December 1977

All of these vehicles were renumbered from 5XX to 6XX by Midland General in October 1972 before they were transferred to Trent Motor Traction Company.

MIDLAND GENERAL OMNIBUS COMPANY LIMITED

Formed in 1920 as a subsidiary of the Nottinghamshire & Derbyshire Tramway Company, more commonly known as "Notts & Derby", Midland General began operating bus services two years later. Within seven years it had developed into the largest operator within the Midland General group of companies. Owned by Balfour Beatty that was, at that time, an important electricity supply company in addition to owning Notts & Derby, and Midland General it also owned Mansfield District. Both Notts & Derby and Midland General carried very smart blue and cream livery liveries. When the electricity industry in 1948 was mostly nationalised, Balfour Beatty sold its bus operating businesses to the British Transport Commission and they were allocated to the Tilling Group. After the formation of the National Bus Company in 1968 the group was split between Trent Motor Services who took over Notts & Derby and East Midland Motor Services who took over Mansfield District. A total of ten Bristol FSFs were added new to the Midland General fleet as listed below. A further ten Bristol FSF6Gs from Mansfield District were transferred from Mansfield District in May and August 1968. Both Mansfield District and Midland General fleets carried a recognisable common fleet numbering scheme during the 1960s. A total of ten Bristol FSFs, all with Gardner engines, were received in 1961 and 1962.

Fleet No.	Registration No.	Date New	Additional Notes
501	441 SNU	November 1961	
502	442 SNU	November 1961	
503	443 SNU	November 1961	
504	444 SNU	November 1961	
505	445 SNU	November 1961	
506	446 SNU	February 1962	
507	447 SNU	February 1962	
508	448 SNU	February 1962	
509	449 SNU	June 1962	
510	450 SNU	June 1962	

UNITED AUTOMOBILE SERVICES LIMITED

A strange but true fact is that United Auto was first registered in April 1912 with a head office at Lowestoft in Suffolk and commenced operating bus services between Lowestoft and Southwold far from where United Automobile is normally associated with today. There was a rapid development of operations, not only in Suffolk but further afield in County Durham, and after the First World War new services were a regular occurrence in Northumberland, South Durham, North Yorkshire and within its origin county of Suffolk. In 1926 the company moved its head office to York and again in 1932 to Darlington since which time the company has been more associated with the north east of England.

A total of 28 FSFs all fitted with Bristol engines were delivered new with the addition of the sole FSF6B of West Yorkshire to the United Auto fleet in April 1967.

Fleet No.	Registration No.	Date New	Additional Notes*
BL57	2057 HN	November 1960	257
BL58	2058 HN	November 1960	258
BL59	2059 HN	November 1960	259
BL60	2060 HN	December 1960	260
BL61	2061 HN	December 1960	261
BL62	2062 HN	December 1960	262
BL63	2063 HN	December 1960	263
BL64	2064 HN	December 1960	264
BL65	2065 HN	December 1960	265
BL66	2066 HN	March 1961	266
BL67	2067 HN	March 1961	267
BL68	2068 HN	March 1961	268
BL69	2069 HN	March 1961	269
BL70	2070 HN	March 1961	270
BL71	2071 HN	March 1961	271
BL72	2072 HN	March 1961	272
BL73	2073 HN	March 1961	273
BL74	2074 HN	March 1961	274
BL75	2075 HN	April 1961	275
BL76	2076 HN	May 1961	276
BL99	5099 HN	November 1961	279
BL100	5100 HN	October 1961	280
BL101	5101 HN	October 1961	281
BL102	5102 HN	October 1961	282
BL103	5103 HN	November 1961	283
BL104	5104 HN	November 1961	284
BL105	5105 HN	November 1961	285
Bl106	5106 HN	November 1961	286
Acquired from West Yorkshire Road Car			
L56	YWW 77	May 1960	Transferred in April 1967

All were renumbered in November 1964 when the BL prefix was changed to L.
* Final fleet numbers used from 1st January 1969.

UNITED WELSH SERVICES LIMITED

Formed in 1938 to amalgamate and consolidate a number of bus operators in the Swansea area United Welsh was itself a subsidiary of Red & White Services Ltd. Garages were opened by United Welsh and operated in Swansea, Neath, Gorseinon, Clydach and Stoutall with the main engineering works based at Neath Abbey.

A total of 28 FSFs were delivered new to the company of which seven were fitted with Bristol engines. All vehicles were transferred to South Wales Transport when United Welsh passed to that company in January 1971.

Fleet No.	Registration No.	Date New	Additional Notes
349	143 ACY	October 1961	
350	144 ACY	October 1961	
351	145 ACY	October 1961	
352	146 ACY	October 1961	
353	147 ACY	October 1961	
354	148 ACY	October 1961	
355	149 ACY	October 1961	
356	150 ACY	November 1961	
357	151 ACY	November 1961	
358	152 ACY	November 1961	
359	153 ACY	November 1961	
360	258 DCY	November 1962	Bristol engine
361	259 DCY	November 1962	Bristol engine
362	260 DCY	November 1962	
363	261 DCY	November 1962	
364	262 DCY	November 1962	
365	263 DCY	November 1962	
366	264 DCY	November 1962	
367	265 DCY	November 1962	
368	266 DCY	November 1962	
369	267 DCY	November 1962	
370	268 DCY	November 1962	
371	269 DCY	November 1962	
372	270 DCY	November 1962	Bristol engine
373	271 DCY	November 1962	Bristol engine
374	272 DCY	November 1962	Bristol engine
375	273 DCY	November 1962	Bristol engine
376	274 DCY	November 1962	Bristol engine

WEST YORKSHIRE ROAD CAR COMPANY

The first Bristol FSF produced was the only front entrance Lodekka ever owned and operated by West Yorkshire Road Car Company Limited. When received in May 1960 it carried the standard Eastern Coach Works style H34/26F bodywork but like the first Bristol FLF was fitted with a sliding passenger door that was later replaced by a standard four-leaf folding door. It was fitted with the Bristol option of engine and was exchanged in 1967 for a standard rear entrance Bristol LD6B from United Automobile Services Ltd.

Fleet No.	Registraton No.	Date New	Additional Notes
DX82	YWW77	May 1960	Transferred to United Auto in 1967

WEST YORKSHIRE ROAD CAR AREA

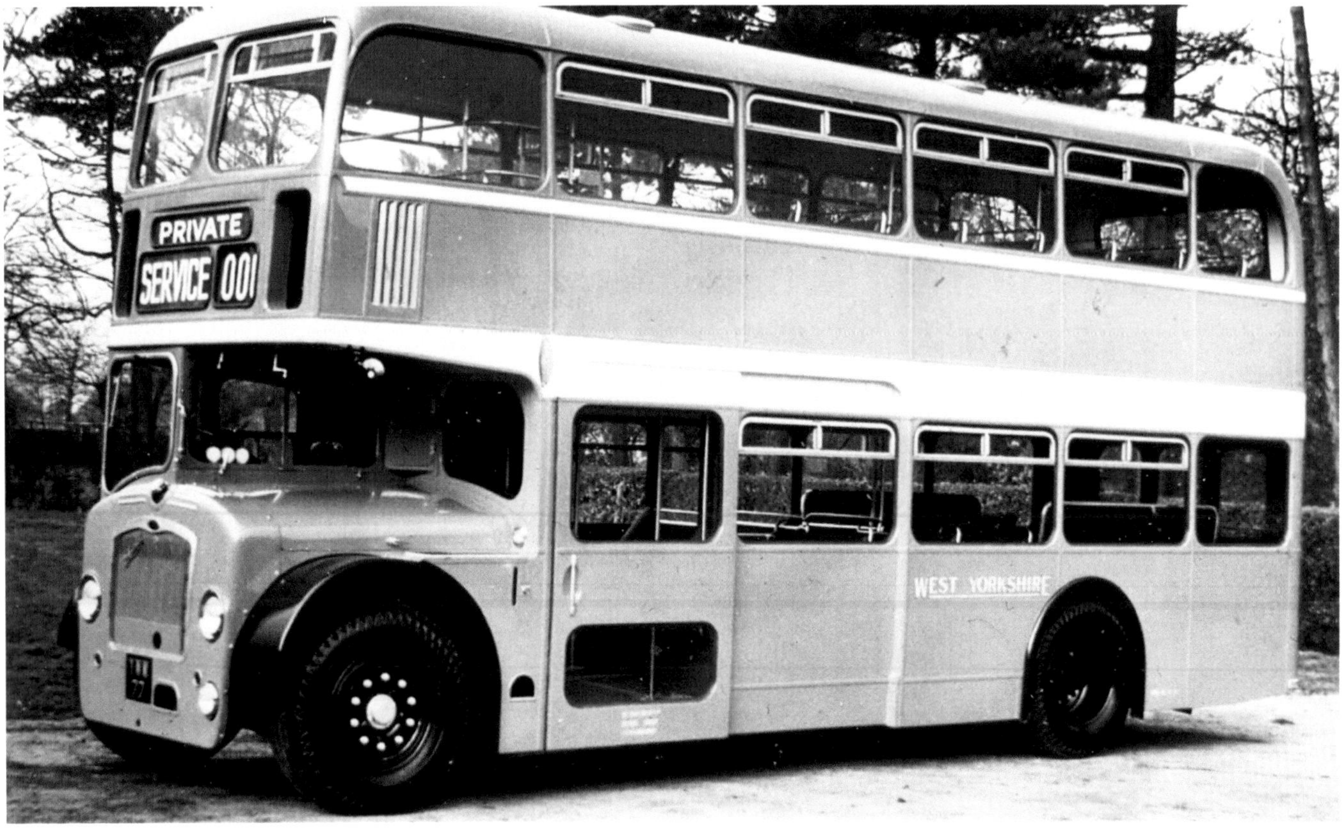

An official pre-delivery photograph of West Yorkshire DX82 (YWW 77), the "prototype" Bristol FSF with the original three panel destination layout, gives a general sense of quality that is also pleasing to look at. The vehicle was equipped with a driver controlled sliding door that was subsequently rebuilt with the standard four-leaf electric folding door that became the recognised standard fitted to ECW bodied front entrance buses right up until the last Bristol VRT was produced in 1981. Even the general body styling of windows, domes and curves was retained until the last VRT body was assembled at Lowestoft. (Eastern Coach Works)

PILGRIM'S PROGRESS – STILL AT WORK IN CROATIA AFTER 50 YEARS

When Bath Electric Tramways 6041 was sold in 1995 to a buyer in Croatia it was assumed that the bus would never be seen again, particularly with the conflicts that were occurring at that time in a number of the former Eastern Bloc countries. As this book was being prepared for printing "out of the blue" came an email from Rob Sly with the subject heading of "You're not going to believe what has just popped into my inbox, Steve you're going to have to rewrite your book..." with an attachment of several photographs. My favourite FSF was still active after almost 50 years, a fact that, as Dr Mike Walker states in his foreword to this book, highlights the renowned rugged reliability of the "Bristol" range of buses. In June 2011 it remains as an active vehicle in the Varazdin Bus Company fleet in Varazdin, North West Croatia mainly as a tourist sightseeing bus during most of the year and as an eye catching mode of transport for Santa Claus at Christmas!

Many of its original features including the original folding platform doors, offside illuminated advertisement panel, staircase and even a "Keep Britain Tidy" sticker on the stair panel remain. What of the future? It would be great to think that, just maybe, the bus can be purchased and brought back to where it belongs...

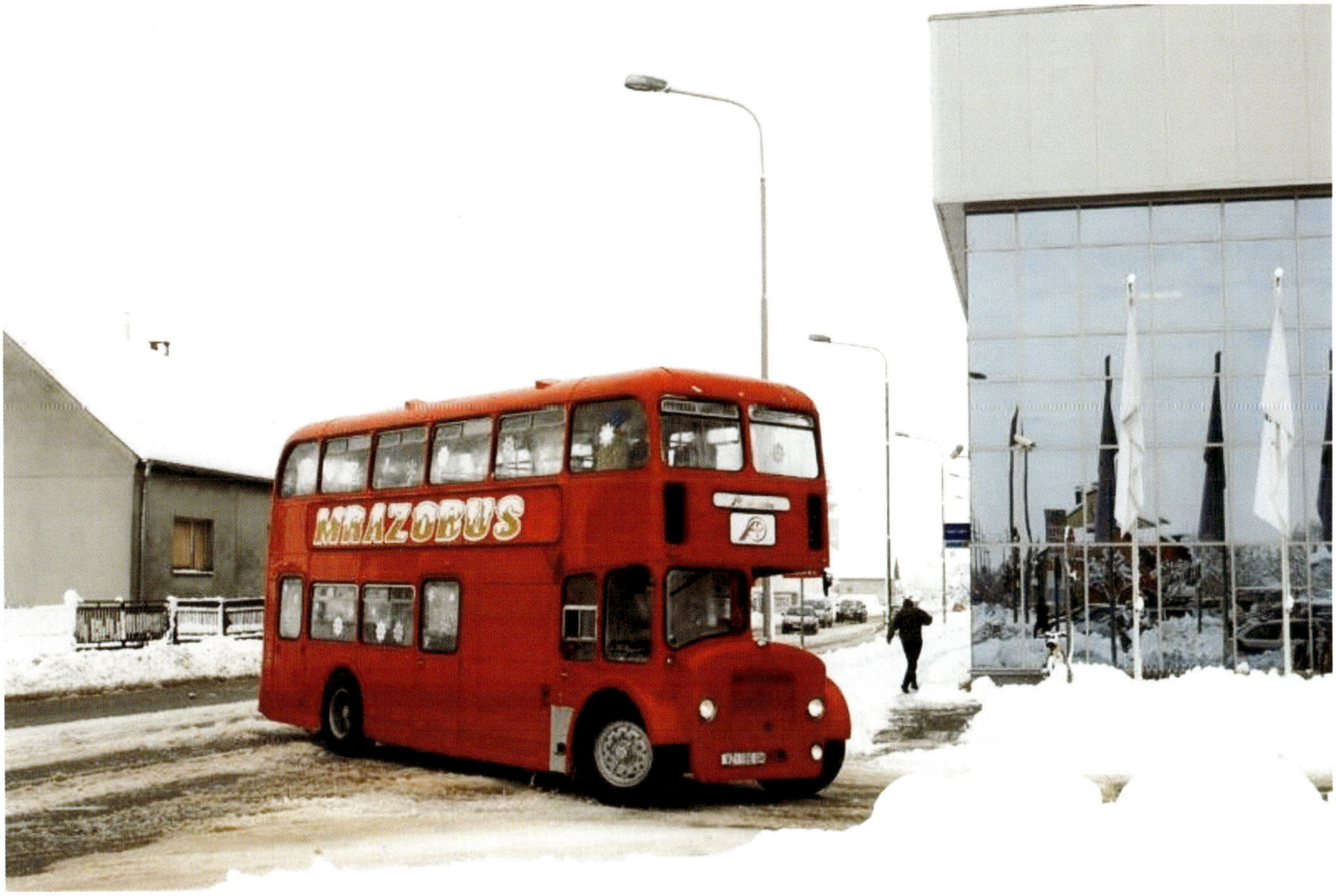

Well kept and looking particularly impressive Varazdin Bus Company ex Bath Electric Tramways 6041 now carrying registration number VZ 186-GH decorated for its Christmas duties. (Varazdin Bus Company)

LIST OF BRISTOL FSF BUILDS BY DATE

The list below is the order in which Bristol FSFs were built and the Sanction numbers applying to these. All vehicles were scrapped unless indicated.

Month/Year New	Registration	Company & Original Fleet No.	Chassis No.	Body No.
1960				
Sanction 156				
May	YWW 77	West Yorkshire DX82	156002	11093
November	707 JHY	Bath Tramways Motor L8566	156015	11543
November	708 JHY	Bath Tramways Motor L8567	156016	11544
November	705 JHY	Cheltenham District L99	156017	11541
November	706 JHY	Cheltenham District L100	156018	11542
October	701 JHY	Bristol Omnibus GL8562	156019	11538
October	702 JHY	Bristol Omnibus L8563	156020	11539
1960				
Sanction 167				
October	703 JHY	Bristol Omnibus GL8564	167001	11540
October	704 JHY	Bristol Omnibus GL8565	167002	11526
November	501 BRM	Cumberland C404	167003	11545
November	502 BRM	Cumberland C405	167004	11546
November	503 BRM	Cumberland C406	167005	11547
November	2057 HN	United Automobile BL57	167006	11550
November	2058 HN	United Automobile BL58	167007	11551
November	2059 HN	United Automobile BL59	167008	11552
November	709 JHY	Bristol Omnibus LC8568	167009	11513
November	710 JHY	Bristol Omnibus LC8569	167010	11514
November	711 JHY	Bristol Omnibus LC8570	167011	11515
November	712 JHY	Bristol Omnibus LC8571*	167012	11516
		*Last seen in Italy in July 1978		
November	713 JHY	Bristol Omnibus LC8572	167013	11517
November	714 JHY	Bristol Omnibus LC8573	167014	11518
November	715 JHY	Bristol Omnibus LC8574	167015	11519
November	716 JHY	Bristol Omnibus LC8575	167016	11520
November	504 BRM	Cumberland 407*	167017	11548
		*Last seen in Holland in October 2002		
November	505 BRM	Cumberland 408	167018	11549
December	2060 HN	United Automobile BL60	167019	11553
December	2061 HN	United Automobile BL61	167020	11554
December	2062 HN	United Automobile BL62	167021	11555
December	2063 HN	United Automobile BL63	167022	11556
December	2064 HN	United Automobile BL64	167023	11557
December	2065 HN	United Automobile BL65	167024	11558
1961				
January	TPN 26	Brighton Hove & District 26	167025	11508
January	TPN 27	Brighton Hove & District 27	167026	11509
March	2066 HN	United Automobile BL66	167027	11559
March	2067 HN	United Automobile BL67	167028	11560

Month/Year New	Registration	Company & Original Fleet No.	Chassis No.	Body No.
1961				
Sanction 167 continued				
March	2068 HN	United Automobile BL68	167029	11561
February	719 JHY	Bristol Omnibus 6020	167030	11527
February	720 JHY	Bristol Omnibus 6021	167031	11528
February	721 JHY	Bristol Omnibus 6022	167032	11529
February	722 JHY	Bristol Omnibus 6023	167033	11530
February	726 JHY	Bristol Omnibus 6024	167034	11531
March	2069 HN	United Automobile BL69	167035	11562
March	2070 HN	United Automobile BL70	167036	11563
February	717 JHY	Bristol Omnibus C6025	167037	11521
February	718 JHY	Bristol Omnibus C6026	167038	11522
February	723 JHY	Bristol Omnibus C6027	167039	11523
February	724 JHY	Bristol Omnibus C6028	167040	11524
February	725 JHY	Bristol Omnibus C6029	167041	11525
February	727 JHY	Bristol Omnibus 6030	167042	11532
March	728 JHY	Bristol Omnibus 6031*	167043	11533
		*Last seen in Holland in September 1977		
March	729 JHY	Bristol Omnibus 6032	167044	11534
March	730 JHY	Bristol Omnibus 6033	167045	11535
March	731 JHY	Bristol Omnibus 6034	167046	11536
March	732 JHY	Bristol Omnibus 6035	167047	11537
February	UAP 28	Brighton Hove & District 28	167048	11510
February	UAP 29	Brighton Hove & District 29	167049	11511
February	UAP 30	Brighton Hove & District 30	167050	11512
March	2071 HN	United Automobile BL71	167051	11564
March	2072 HN	United Automobile BL72	167052	11565
February	CGM 116	Central SMT B116	167053	12260
March	CGM 117	Central SMT B117	167054	12261
February	CGM 118	Central SMT B118	167055	12262
March	CGM 119	Central SMT B119	167056	12263
March	CGM 120	Central SMT B120	167057	12264
March	CGM 121	Central SMT B121	167058	12265
March	CGM 122	Central SMT B122	167059	12266
March	2073 HN	United Automobile BL73	167060	11566
March	2074 HN	United Automobile BL74	167061	11567
April	2075 HN	United Automobile BL75	167062	11568
May	2076 HN	United Automobile BL76	167063	11569
October	143 ACY	United Welsh 349	167064	12381
October	144 ACY	United Welsh 350	167065	12382
October	145 ACY	United Welsh 351	167066	12383
October	146 ACY	United Welsh 352	167067	12384
October	864 VFM	Crosville DFB54	167068	12303
November	5099 HN	United Automobile BL99	167069	12358
October	5100 HN	United Automobile BL100	167070	12359

Month/Year New	Registration	Company & Original Fleet No.	Chassis No.	Body No.
1961				
Sanction 179				
July	VAP 31	Brighton Hove & District 31	179001	12267
July	VAP 32	Brighton Hove & District 32	179002	12268
July	VAP 33	Brighton Hove & District 33	179003	12269
November	441 SNU	Midland General 501	179004	12348
November	442 SNU	Midland General 502	179005	12349
1962				
February	51 JAL	Mansfield District 535*	179006	12338
		*Last seen in the USA in March 2010		
February	52 JAL	Mansfield District 536	179007	12339
1961				
October	865 VFM	Crosville DFB55	179008	12304
October	147 ACY	United Welsh 353	179009	12385
October	148 ACY	United Welsh 354	179010	12386
October	149 ACY	United Welsh 355	179011	12387
July	VAP 34	Brighton Hove & District 34	179012	12270
July	VAP 35	Brighton Hove & District 35	179013	12271
October	5101 HN	United Automobile BL101	179014	12360
October	5102 HN	United Automobile BL102	179015	12361
November	5103 HN	United Automobile BL103	179016	12362
November	5104 HN	United Automobile BL104	179017	12363
November	5105 HN	United Automobile BL105	179018	12364
November	869 VFM	Crosville DFG59	179019	12306
November	870 VFM	Crosville DFG60	179020	12307
October	806 MHW	Bath Electric Tramways 6041*	179021	12290
		*Last seen in Varazdin, Croatia in June 2011		
October	801 MHW	Cheltenham District 6036	179022	12284
October	802 MHW	Cheltenham District 6037*	179023	12285
		*Last seen at Wythall Transport Museum, Birmingham in 2011		
October	803 MHW	Bristol Omnibus G6038	179024	12301
November	871 VFM	Crosville DFG61	179025	12308
November	872 VFM	Crosville DFG62	179026	12309
November	873 VFM	Crosville DFG63	179027	12310
November	874 VFM	Crosville DFG64	179028	12311
November	443 SNU	Midland General 503	179029	12350
November	444 SNU	Midland General 504*	179030	12351
		*Last seen in USA in June 2001		
November	445 SNU	Midland General 505*	179031	12352
		*Last seen in USA in June 2008		

Month/Year New	Registration	Company & Original Fleet No.	Chassis No.	Body No.
1962				
February	53 JAL	Mansfield District 537	179032	12340
February	54 JAL	Mansfield District 538	179033	12341
1961				
November	5106 HN	United Automobile BL106	179034	12365
November	866 VFM	Crosville DFB56	179035	12305
November	150 ACY	United Welsh 356	179036	12388
November	151 ACY	United Welsh 357	179037	12389
November	152 ACY	United Welsh 358	179038	12390
November	153 ACY	United Welsh 359	179039	12391
November	804 MHW	Bristol Omnibus G6039	179040	12302
November	805 MHW	Bristol Omnibus G6040*	179041	12608
		*Last seen in USA in March 2008		
1962				
January	875 VFM	Crosville DFG65*	179042	12312
		*Last seen in Liverpool in 2010		
January	876 VFM	Crosville DFG66	179043	12313
January	877 VFM	Crosville DFG67	179044	12314
February	878 VFM	Crosville DFG68	179045	12315
February	446 SNU	Midland General 506	179046	12353
February	447 SNU	Midland General 507	179047	12354
February	448 SNU	Midland General 508	179048	12355
March	DGM 430	Central SMT B130	179049	13519
March	DGM 431	Central SMT B131	179050	13520
March	55 JAL	Mansfield District 539	179051	12342
March	56 JAL	Mansfield District 540	179052	12343
March	57 JAL	Mansfield District 541	179053	12344
April	879 VFM	Crosville DFG69	179054	12316
March	DGM 432	Central SMT B132	179055	13521
March	DGM 433	Central SMT B133	179056	13522
March	DGM 434	Central SMT B134	179057	13523
March	DGM 435	Central SMT B135	179058	13524
April	880 VFM	Crosville DFG70	179059	12317
April	881 VFM	Crosville DFG71	179060	12318
April	882 VFM	Crosville DFG72	179061	12319
May	883 VFM	Crosville DFG73	179062	12320
March	DGM 436	Central SMT B136	179063	13525
March	DGM 437	Central SMT B137	179064	13526
March	DGM 438	Central SMT B138	179065	13527
March	DGM 439	Central SMT B139	179066	13528
May	884 VFM	Crosville DFG74	179067	12321
March	DGM 440	Central SMT B140	179068	13529
March	DGM 444	Central SMT B144	179069	13534

Month/Year New	Registration	Company & Original Fleet No.	Chassis No.	Body No.
1962 continued				
March	DGM 441	Central SMT B141	179070	13530
March	DGM 442	Central SMT B142	179071	13531
March	DGM 443	Central SMT B143	179072	13532
April	DGM 445	Central SMT B145	179073	13533
April	DGM 446	Central SMT B146	179074	13535
March	WNJ 36	Brighton Hove & District 36	179075	12272
March	WNJ 37	Brighton Hove & District 37	179076	12273
April	WNJ 38	Brighton Hove & District 38	179077	12274
April	WNJ 39	Brighton Hove & District 39	179078	12275
April	WNJ 40	Brighton Hove & District 40	179079	12276
May	867 VFM	Crosville DFB57	179080	12322
May	868 VFM	Crosville DFB58	179081	12323
Sanction 197				
June	58 JAL	Mansfield District 542	197001	12345
June	59 JAL	Mansfield District 543* *Last seen in USA in October 2008	197002	12346
June	885 VFM	Crosville DFG75	197003	12324
June	886 VFM	Crosville DFG76	197004	12325
April	DGM 447	Central SMT B147	197005	13536
April	DGM 448	Central SMT B148	197006	13537
April	DGM 449	Central SMT B149	197007	13538
April	DGM 450	Central SMT B150	197008	13539
April	DGM 451	Central SMT B151	197009	13540
April	DGM 452	Central SMT B152	197010	13541
April	DGM 453	Central SMT B153	197011	13542
April	DGM 454	Central SMT B154	197012	13543
April	DGM 455	Central SMT B155	197013	13544
June	887 VFM	Crosville DFG77	197014	12326
June	888 VFM	Crosville DFG78	197015	12327
June	889 VFM	Crosville DFG79	197016	12328
April	DGM 456	Central SMT B156	197017	13545
April	DGM 457	Central SMT B157	197018	13546
April	DGM 458	Central SMT B158	197019	13547
April	DGM 459	Central SMT B159	197020	13548
June	60 JAL	Mansfield District 544* *Last seen in USA in September 2009	197021	12347
June	449 SNU	Midland General 509* *Last seen in USA in October 2008	197022	12356
June	450 SNU	Midland General 510* *Last seen in the USA in July 2001	197023	12357
June	890 VFM	Crosville DFG80	197024	12329
June	891 VFM	Crosville DFG81	197025	12330

Month/Year New	Registration	Company & Original Fleet No.	Chassis No.	Body No.
Sanction 197 continued				
June	892 VFM	Crosville DFG82*	197026	12331
		*Last seen in Spain in September 1995		
June	893 VFM	Crosville DFG83	197027	12332
November	258 DCY	United Welsh 360	197028	13024
November	259 DCY	United Welsh 361	197029	13025
November	260 DCY	United Welsh 362	197030	13026
November	261 DCY	United Welsh 363	197031	13027
November	262 DCY	United Welsh 364	197032	13028
November	263 DCY	United Welsh 365	197033	13029
November	264 DCY	United Welsh 366	197034	13030
November	265 DCY	United Welsh 367	197035	13031
November	266 DCY	United Welsh 368	197036	13032
September	8109 HN	Durham District DBL9	197037	13041
September	8110 HN	Durham District DBL10	197038	13042
September	8111 HN	Durham District DBL11	197039	13043
October	8112 HN	Durham District DBL12	197040	13044
October	8113 HN	Durham District DBL13	197041	13045
November	267 DCY	United Welsh 369	197042	13033
November	268 DCY	United Welsh 370	197043	13034
November	269 DCY	United Welsh 371	197044	13035
November	270 DCY	United Welsh 372	197045	13036
November	271 DCY	United Welsh 373	197046	13037
November	272 DCY	United Welsh 374	197047	13038
November	273 DCY	United Welsh 375	197048	13039
November	274 DCY	United Welsh 376	197049	13040
1963				
Sanction 215				
September	FGM 160	Central SMT B160	215001	14322
September	FGM 161	Central SMT B161	215002	14323
September	FGM 162	Central SMT B162	215003	14324
September	FGM 163	Central SMT B163	215004	14325
September	FGM 164	Central SMT B164	215005	14326
September	FGM 165	Central SMT B165	215006	14327
September	FGM 166	Central SMT B166	215007	14328
September	FGM 167	Central SMT B167	215008	14329
September	FGM 168	Central SMT B168	215009	14330
September	FGM 169	Central SMT B169	215010	14331
September	FGM 170	Central SMT B170	215011	14332

COMPANY TOTALS

Bath Electric Tramways Ltd	1	Gardner engine
Bath Tramways Motor Co Ltd	2	Gardner engines
Brighton Hove & District	15	Bristol engines
Bristol Joint Services	13	Bristol engines
Bristol Omnibus Co Ltd	12	Gardner engines
Central SMT	48	Gardner engines
Cheltenham District Traction	4	Gardner engines
Crosville Motor Services Ltd	30	Gardner engines (25); Bristol engines (5)
Cumberland Motor Services	5	Bristol engines
Durham District	5	Bristol engines
Gloucester Joint Services	6	Gardner engines
Mansfield District	10	Gardner engines
Midland General	10	Gardner engines
United Automobile	28	Bristol engines
United Welsh	28	Gardner engines
West Yorkshire	1	Bristol engine
TOTALS:	**218**	**72 Bristol engines; 146 Gardner engines**

This list is the recorded number of new Bristol FSFs received by these companies.